Reports of the Research Committee of the Society of
Antiquaries of London, No. 66

THE ARCHAEOLOGY OF GREEK AND
ROMAN SLAVERY

F. Hugh Thompson's interest in slavery was first inspired by his excavation of the Iron Age hill-fort at Bigberry near Canterbury in 1978-80, where iron neck-chains and fetters had been discovered in the nineteenth century. Later he participated in international expeditions to the slave-worked Roman quarries in Egypt's eastern desert. A study tour in search of slavery evidence took him all over Europe and the Mediterranean and ultimately led him to write this book. He died in 1995, aged 72.

Kenneth Painter was formerly Deputy Keeper of Prehistoric and Romano-British Antiquities and then of Greek and Roman Antiquities at the British Museum. He has also been Secretary, Director and a Vice-President of the Society of Antiquaries of London.

Ralph Jackson is Curator of the Romano-British collections at the British Museum, which he joined in 1977. His publications include *Doctors and Diseases in the Roman Empire* (1988), *Camerton: The Late Iron Age and Early Roman Metalwork* (1990) and, with T.W. Potter, *Excavations at Stonea, Cambridgeshire, 1980-5* (1996).

The Archaeology of Greek and Roman Slavery

F. Hugh Thompson

Duckworth

in association with
The Society of Antiquaries of London

First published in 2003 by
Gerald Duckworth & Co. Ltd.
61 Frith Street, London WID 3JL
Tel: 020 7434 4242
Fax: 020 7434 4420
inquiries@duckworth-publishers.co.uk
www.ducknet.co.uk
in association with
The Society of Antiquaries of London
Burlington House
Piccadilly
London W1J 0BE
www.sal.org.uk

This book has been published with the generous assistance of
the Gerda Henkel Foundation, Düsseldorf.

ISBN 0 7156 3195 0

A catalogue record for this book is available from
the British Library.

Edited for the Society of Antiquaries of London by Lynn Pitts.
Picture research by Kathy Lockley.

Typeset by Ray Davies
Printed in Great Britain by
Bookcraft (Bath) Ltd, Midsomer Norton, Avon

Contents

Contents

Contents

8. Flight and Revolt

Illustrations and Sources

Every effort has been made to contact the copyright holders of material used in this book; any omissions are inadvertent, and will be corrected in future editions if notification of the amended credit is sent to the publisher in writing.

Many illustrations are from unique archive sources. They have been reproduced as clearly as is possible within the constraints of the format of this book.

Foreword

Kenneth S. Painter

Frederick Hugh Thompson, MC, MA, FSA, former General Secretary of the Society of Antiquaries of London, died on 24 October 1995, aged 72. Among his papers was the text of this book, the product of his retirement, most of it completed during the years of his final illness.

Hugh Thompson was a man who gave his all to whatever he was involved in. This was true of the young man, as well as of his maturity. In August 1942 he joined the army and he was posted in September 1944 to the 51st Highland Division, serving through into 1945 with the Gordon Highlanders in France and in Holland. After the campaign, his colonel, recommending him for his Military Cross, described him as fearless in action and a brilliant leader of men in action. 'It became a legend in the Battalion,' he continued, 'that if Lt Thompson's platoon were ordered to carry out a fighting raid or take the toughest objectives in an attack then the job would be done. His platoon, inspired by such unparalleled leadership, would follow him anywhere.' This went on almost until the end of the War. The colonel again: 'Outside Delmanhorst on the 20th April 1945 during the trying thirty-six hours when the enemy fought continuously to reoccupy the Company position on an aerodrome, despite very heavy and accurate fire from mortars and S.P. guns, Lt Thompson went round his platoon continuously giving confidence to his men, completely disregarding his own personal safety. By his display of cool courage and fearlessness he was an inspiration to all around him.'

Frederick Hugh Thompson, the son of John Augustus Thompson, a lace-maker, and his wife Victoria, was born in Gunthorpe, Nottinghamshire, in 1923. He was educated at the village school in Lowdham and then at Nottingham Boys' School, and in 1941 he won an open exhibition in classics to Exeter College, Oxford. The War, however, interrupted his education, and it was not until 1945 that Thompson went up to Oxford, where he took the shortened degree course of two years, gaining a BA in Modern Greats (politics, philosophy and economics) in 1947. He went back to Nottingham and began work as a management trainee in a paint factory but left after ten days, having set fire to the laboratory! A new career, in insurance, followed, but he had had an interest in archaeology since schooldays, roused by an eccentric geography master, and this was revived by joining the Thoroton Society. He attended its lectures, including one given by the then Chief Inspector of Monuments, Brian O'Neal. This inspired him to write, asking if there was any hope of joining O'Neal's department. O'Neal responded, and in due course Thompson became an Assistant Inspector of Ancient Monuments, at Lambeth Bridge House, where he assisted Gerald Dunning, who was responsible for rescue archaeology. This was the key appointment in Thompson's career, because Dunning, a medievalist, trained at University College, London, as an anthropologist, laid the foundations of Thompson's archaeological training as they travelled the country together for the next two years. He never really enjoyed living in London, however, and he felt ready to conduct his own excavations, rather than arranging excavations for others to do, and so in 1951, succeeding Graham Webster, he became Keeper of the City and County Museum at Lincoln, where he stayed for five years. While he was there, he not only cared for and developed the museum but pursued the archaeology of the city as well, which in the ethos of the times meant the Roman rather than the medieval period, excavating the Roman aqueduct and public fountain, and investigating the Roman defences and the city gates right down to their earliest timber phase. The value and quality of this work, planned as research rather than rescue, was recognized when Tom Baker from Lincoln, Gilyard-Beer and Arnold Taylor from the Inspectorate of Ancient Monuments, and Ian Richmond, from the University of Newcastle, supported his candidature as a Fellow of the Society, a distinction which he received in 1956.

In 1955 Thompson became Curator of the Grosvenor Museum at Chester, again in succession to Graham Webster, who had moved on to the Extra-Mural Department at the University of Birmingham. The coincidence was not a matter of chance, but had much to do with each man's skill in and understanding of the similar problems of Roman military archaeology at the two places, although, of course, there were and are at the same time great differences. This was an exciting time to be in archaeology. Much of the work on sites in the historic cities was carried out, as it had been before the Second World War, by *ad hoc* excavation committees, but the time of their greatest flowering was the middle 1950s and the 1960s, to cope with the increasing need for rescue archaeology in face of the rising tide of development. Just as he had had the support of the Archaeological Research Committee at Lincoln, including Tom Baker and Ian Richmond, so he also had strong backing at Chester from the Archaeological Society, particularly its Chairman, Archdeacon Burne, and its Secretary, David Evans (senior). With their support, Thompson continued the excavation of the Roman granaries in Commonhall Street, which Dennis Petch had started, and undertook the Woolworth's site in Eastgate Street, Trinity Street and sites outside the city such as Vale Royal. Soon, however, he found himself undertaking the major excavation of his career, the Chester amphitheatre. This was to occupy him for ten years from 1960, continuously from 1965 to 1969. The excavation overlapped both with his move in 1962 to a post as Lecturer in Archaeology at the University of Manchester and also with his move to Burlington House at the beginning of 1967. When he began work at Chester, the only amphitheatre thoroughly excavated, and the only one fully published, was that attached to the legionary fortress at Caerleon, investigated in 1926 and 1927 by Mortimer Wheeler and his wife. Not only was the Chester amphitheatre a massive undertaking, which was to add a permanent and valued feature to modern Chester; but it attracted international attention for its contribution to Roman archaeology, not least because of the amphitheatre's first phase, which was proved by the skilful trowelling of David Morgan Evans and his brother Huw (as Thompson always meticulously and generously acknowledged) to have been a timber and turf structure, like the amphitheatre at Vindonissa in Switzerland.

Academic success and international renown came from that project, and this was when Thompson gained many friends and colleagues abroad, particularly in Germany, which led to his being elected a Corresponding Member of the German Archaeological Institute, a distinction of which he was particularly proud. However, it was not mere academic ability that led to that success. It was his ability to lead and inspire a team, and it is the picture of Thompson the man that breaks through. His archaeologists at Chester worked all the better and more effectively because of the annual Christmas play or pantomime, which is described by those who were there as 'a riot'.

By 1966 Thompson had acquired a distinguished record in archaeology, and he might have expected both that his future lay in the university world, at Manchester and elsewhere, and also that he would have a reasonable chance of being promoted to a chair. This time, however, his move to the most important post of his career was being planned for him. He was head-hunted from Manchester and on 1 January 1967 was appointed Assistant Secretary, or chief executive officer, of the Society of Antiquaries, the oldest and foremost archaeological society in the country, based in Burlington House in Piccadilly.

The twenty-one years that Thompson held the post of Assistant Secretary, later more properly entitled General Secretary, were a period of continuous growth, not only in the number of the Fellowship, which grew from 1,200 to 1,400, and then to 2,000, but in all spheres of the Society's activity, with all that implies in the management and deployment of the Society's resources. Yet at the same time his most important contribution to the Society was perhaps his work maintaining and indeed enhancing the editorial and publication standards of the great series of the *Antiquaries Journal*, *Archaeologia* and the Research Reports, and he was also the driving force of the newly instituted seminars, on subjects ranging from river gravels and coastal change to Victorian art and architecture, and of their prompt publication. Under Thompson's care, the Society's publications began their change from being largely the products of a Society of amateur gentlemen to being the research tools produced by a professional archaeological society of international standing, and the rows of volumes produced by Hugh or under his care will be perhaps his most lasting memorial.

Yet, while presiding over these and all the other regular activities at Burlington House, he coped with a major redecoration of the Society's rooms, the absorption of the rush of legacies, which through its research grants transformed the Society's role in archaeology, and the development of the role of Kelmscott Manor (the historic summer home of William Morris on the Thames near Faringdon, which the Society manages and opens to the public), and all that these things implied in a multiplication of Thompson's own tasks. While all this was going on, however, the Fellows found their rooms in Burlington House to be still a centre of calm research, where the General Secretary recognized everybody who came in and always found time to talk to them. This human touch was not reserved for the great senior figures. Indeed, more than one President found that on occasions they were dealing with a tough-minded champion of the Society's long-term interests and traditions, who would not necessarily humour their whims during their temporary occupation of office. The young and junior, however, were always helped and treated with kindness and friendship. Thompson's extraordinarily wide knowledge of the Fellows and their interests never flagged, and it was this that made his friendly welcome special to so many of the Fellows.

In addition to his duties at Burlington House Thompson maintained and developed his personal reputation as a scholar. He represented the Society abroad, notably with the Limes Kommission in Germany, and later, from 1987, on the Mons Claudianus project in Egypt. He maintained his interests at Lincoln and Chester, where he made the city take archaeology seriously, and he was President of the Royal Archaeological Institute from 1984 to 1987. He continued his research, directing valuable excavations of Iron Age hillforts in Kent and Surrey, and it was one of these, the excavation from 1978 to 1980 of the hillfort at Bigberry, near Canterbury, that led directly to his great study of the archaeology of ancient slavery, which was to occupy him almost until his death. After his retirement in July 1988 Thompson deepened this study, travelling all over Europe and the Mediterranean to see the evidence at first hand. Many people had worked on the documentary and epigraphical sources for ancient slavery, but nobody before had attempted a synthesis of the archaeological evidence. The result of this ground-breaking work is this book. It shows that Thompson has made a truly significant contribution to our understanding of the ancient world, that world of Greece and Rome, the study of which at school led to such a distinguished career in archaeology in spite of military attempts to distract him.

Preface

My interest in the archaeological aspects of slavery in the Classical world was inspired by excavation undertaken at the Iron Age hillfort of Bigberry, near Canterbury, in 1978-80 and its subsequent publication.[1] The discovery there in nineteenth-century gravel-digging of complete and fragmentary iron neck-chains and fetters had often been cited as material evidence for the slavery and slave-trading supposedly endemic in Celtic Britain, and these artefacts seemed to offer a useful point of departure for a more general study of aspects of the 'peculiar institution' in the ancient world. Initially, this took the form of a presidential address to the Royal Archaeological Institute in 1986, under the title 'Fetters and chains: the archaeology of slavery in antiquity'. One result of that was a detailed paper on Iron Age and Roman slave-shackles, based on museum visits in Britain and western Europe.[2] Much of the travel for this was funded by a generous grant from the Gerda Henkel Stiftung in Düsseldorf, while the cost of later research in libraries and elsewhere was met by the same foundation and by subsequent grants from the Society of Antiquaries, the Royal Archaeological Institute and the Marc Fitch Fund. To all these institutions and their governing bodies I offer my sincere thanks, and in particular to Fr Lisa Maskell and Dr Hans-Joachim Ulbrich of the Gerda Henkel Stiftung. Similarly, I am grateful to all those, at home and abroad, who have endured visits or letters from me and on the whole have responded in a courteous and helpful manner. It would be difficult, if not invidious, to single out individuals in these introductory words but I shall make acknowledgement in the text or references where my debt is particularly heavy.

I confess at once that I am an archaeologist rather than a trained historian and that I may be accused of presumption in attempting to break new ground in so well studied a subject as ancient slavery. Some would argue, in fact, that our knowledge of the history of slavery has increased vastly in the twentieth century and certainly perspectives have changed in the last 150 years. The monumental work of H. Wallon (1847; 1879), rooted in Christian piety and an abolitionist enthusiasm, might now seem superseded by W.L. Westermann's general survey (1955), based on a teamwork approach and a greater use of such disciplines as epigraphy. But the earlier work cannot be dismissed, while Westermann's book received critical reviews on publication.[3] Between these two extremes stands R.H.

Barrow's more restricted monograph on slavery in the Roman Empire (1928), conventional in its framework but still of value. Since the Second World War there has been a flood of books and papers, of which one of the most notable features has been a difference of ideological approach. Among these, one of the more constructive initiatives was the decision of the Mainz Akademie der Wissenschaften und der Literatur to sponsor the publication of a series on ancient slavery, first in the *Abhandlungen der Geistes- und Sozialwissenschaftlichen Klasse* from 1953 and then, from 1967, in its *Forschungen zur Antiken Sklaverei*, as well as translations into German of Russian works on ancient slavery, largely under the leadership of the late Joseph Vogt. Useful bibliographies appeared in this series[4] and earlier,[5] while a useful synthesis of ancient sources, appropriately classified, is available.[6] Works on the ideological, particularly Marxist, approaches to the study of ancient slavery have also been a feature of recent years.[7]

These are only a limited selection from the torrent of published material on ancient slavery now available and the student could be forgiven for a feeling of confusion. The sheer weight of these secondary studies is nowhere better illustrated than in the original Mainz bibliography, later substantially revised and reissued.[8] Dr Herrmann (now Herrmann-Otto) kindly provided me with additional references in 1989, bringing the total of published studies to *c.* 5,200 from the 1,700 or so listed in 1971. This splendid compendium is naturally classified under a number of main headings – sources, previous studies, revolts, economic, social, religious, legal, granting of freedom, etc. – with detailed subheadings, while a second part is devoted to a list of publication abbreviations and detailed indexes. It is instructive to note that Section IID – *Sklaven in archäologischen Zeugnissen* – contains a mere 63 references, with 20 cross-references to other parts of the bibliography, and Garlan, for instance, comments on the dearth of archaeological material for the Greek period.[9] Himmelmann (1971), also in the Mainz Academy series, arouses expectation but his study relies largely on iconographical sources, such as vase-painting and funerary reliefs.

So there is clearly room for a general survey of the archaeological evidence for ancient slavery; but this would be self-defeating if it attempted to cover every aspect of the use of slaves by the Greeks and Romans. Limits have been set in the following pages: an introductory section on the sources of slaves and on slave-trading is followed by chapters on archaeological evidence for slave-labour in agriculture, in mines and quarries, in corn- and weaving mills, and in water-lifting, with concluding chapters on means of restraint and on slave revolts. Material evidence for revolts is admittedly tenuous; but their geographical distribution and relationships are worthy of consideration. It is, of course, true that any discussion of slave-labour in semi-industrial enterprises runs the risk of diversion into a description of techniques, many of which have been the subject of previous monographs. But the use of slaves, particularly in penal policy, is so inextricably bound up with working practices that the latter demand description, at the risk of some repetition. Finally, epigraphy is largely omitted, since this form of evidence has been widely used by historians as a documentary source, but isolated inscriptions of particular relevance have been included, as too with sculptural iconography.

1

Sources of Slaves and the
Trade in Slaves

General introduction

In a terse, almost Tacitean, definition of the origin of slaves, Roman civil law stated: *Servi autem aut nascuntur aut fiunt* – 'slaves are either born or made'.[1] Though late in the history of the institution, this can hardly be bettered as a succinct statement of the sources of slaves for both Greece and Rome. The reason for the origin of slavery is scarcely in dispute: it was essentially the result of the application of force, by which one or more individuals were placed in a position of inferiority to others. This objective criterion avoids any tendentious suggestions of natural superiority or inferiority in the parties concerned and can be seen to correspond with the facts. Like other political and social institutions, which began as unconscious assumptions, slavery in Greece and Rome was regarded as part of a natural order, and it was only later, in response to attacks or criticism, that a theoretical basis evolved and took a legal form. As often, language and etymology provide clues: in Homer and Hesiod, conventionally dated to the eighth century BC, one word for 'slave' is *dmôs* or *dmôos*, from *dama[z]ô*, to conquer, hence to enslave. The Latin word *servus*, it was claimed by ancient writers, denoted one who after capture was not slain but preserved, *servatus*, as a captive. Doubts have been expressed about this etymology but the general principle of original enslavement by capture commands widespread acceptance.[2] Paradoxically, one may see some sort of moral progression in the enslavement of the vanquished by the victor. In human aggressive behaviour a problem arises if a defeated enemy is not killed at once. Captives might be slain subsequently in primitive societies and possibly eaten. Alternatively, they might be ransomed, especially if they stood high in the social order. There was also a difference in the treatment of the sexes and of the young, in that, while men might be killed in fighting or after capture, women and children might be taken into slavery. This difference in the treatment of the sexes, noted by Finley, was given a statistical basis by Lencman, who quotes eleven references to female slaves to one male in the *Iliad* and a ratio of 46:34 in the *Odyssey*; he suggests that with the change from war to peace the ratio altered, since piracy superseded fighting as a means of obtaining slaves.[3] Instances of these various practices are to be found in Homer, particularly in the *Iliad*. In the Olympian scene at the beginning of Book 4, Zeus intervenes in the quarrel between Athene and Hera on the one hand and Hephaistus on the other, and suggests to his wife that her anger against Priam and the Trojans might be appeased by cannibalism. In Book 9, the embassy to Achilles which seeks to regain his support for the Greeks is headed by Odysseus, who conveys the offer of gifts made by Agamemnon to appease Achilles, including seven women captured at Lesbos, the return of Briseis (Achilles' original prize), and the promise of twenty selected Trojan women if Troy should be captured. Achilles himself, at the beginning of Book 21, takes twelve young Trojans prisoner, to be sacrificed at the funeral of Patroclus, and then slays Lykaon; he had captured him before and sold him on Lemnos, presumably as a slave, and he had then been ransomed.

As agriculture developed from simple husbandry to the working of larger estates, and with the introduction of small-scale manufacture, the incentive for keeping males alive became stronger. Here we see the beginnings of a trade in slaves derived from various sources: the sale of prisoners of war or of those forcibly abducted by brigandage or piracy, the sale of foundling children or, more deliberately, by their poverty-stricken parents, self-sale by debtors, but above all the sale of children of existing slaves, the *vernae* who became under the Roman Empire the most prolific source of new slaves.[4]

This conventional view of the origins of slavery is contested by some: for instance, Finley argues that 'logically, the demand for slaves precedes the supply'.[5] The necessary economic conditions in his view are, first, an agrarian world with private ownership of land in which a permanent labour force is required outside the family; secondly, the presence of surplus commodity production and markets, since slaves are imported and must be paid for; and thirdly, the unavailability of an internal labour supply (for example, after Solon's reforms of the early sixth century BC which eliminated debt-bondage in Attica). So, the huge number of captives made by the Romans in the Italian and Punic Wars supplied a demand already there, rather than created it. Finley, then, sees the origin of slavery and of the slave-trade as a form of economic determinism, but not necessarily in Marxist terms.[6] His argument is brilliant and persuasive, though some would no doubt argue that cause and effect are not so separable as he suggests. His conclusion, though, that slavery was a psychological preference, arising inevitably from an unwillingness of free peasant citizens to become wage-labourers, is much easier to accept as the reason for the continuation of Fustel de Coulanges' 'primordial fact' of slavery.[7]

Garlan contrasts and compares the two forms of involuntary labour in Greece, 'chattel slavery', the conventional and absolute form, and 'communal servitude', for example debt-bondage or the Spartan helots, where the individual remains an integral part of the community.[8] He concludes that chattel slavery of the Classical Athenian type is the acceptable definition for Greek slavery and that, in Marxist terms, Greek slaves formed a social class within a slave society, but dismisses the further Leninist definition that such a deprived class is necessarily conscious of its exploited condition because Greek slaves were so fragmented, geographically, politically, socially and economically. Finally, Wiedemann refers to the structuralist concept of 'marginality' as a definition of the role of slaves in ancient society, with their ambivalent character of chattels in human form.[9] But all such reappraisals of slavery as an institution of the Greek and Roman world tell us less about the reality of slavery than about changing fashions in recent historiography. By contrast, archaeological evidence, however fragmentary, can claim a permanent objectivity.

The older standard works on ancient slavery concentrate on the sources of Greek and Roman slaves and only discuss in passing the trading mechanism by which they were brought to the market;[10] Finley, in fact, comments: 'No serious study of ... the slave-trade exists, to my knowledge.'[11] Sources can be discussed under two heads: methodologically, how men became slaves, and geographically, the areas from which they were derived. On method there is substantial agreement: for Greece, if we ignore communal slavery with its serf-like character, that is an indigenous population tied to the land, and concentrate on chattel slavery, the sources, in no special order, can be listed as: birth, sale or exposure of children, debt, war, piracy, and, allied to the last, brigandage and kidnapping;[12] for Rome the sources are broadly the same, with a stronger emphasis on prisoners of war during the late Republic and early Empire, and a greater recognition of extreme forms of slavery in penal policy, for example, *servitus poenae*.[13] At Rome the sources of slaves were codified: universal law (*ius gentium*) covered enslavement by war, whereas civil law (*ius civile*) was applicable to slavery through birth or exposure, and listed the crimes for which condemnation to slavery was appropriate.[14] For Greece, on the other hand, the main evidence is in literary references, though the Code of Gortyn contained provisions relating to the status and treatment of slaves in fifth-century BC Crete.[15]

If we consider the sources of slaves geographically, there are marked changes in the pattern during the millennium between Archaic Greece and the late Roman Empire, if only because of the shift of power westwards from Greece to Rome. But this was more by way of enlargement than replacement as Rome extended its power to Spain, Gaul and Britain, and, ironically, Greece was to become a source favoured by the Romans for the recruitment of slaves as teachers and administrators. In Classical Greece the ancient authors and epigraphical evidence indicate that, in Athens at least, the majority of slaves were derived from regions to the north and east – Thrace, the lower Danube, the coasts of the Black Sea, and Asia Minor. For Rome the military campaigns which extended its power provided slaves in vast quantities, if we are to believe ancient historians: from

North Africa, Sicily and Spain during and after the Punic Wars, from Gaul and Britain as a result of Caesar's campaigns, and intermittently thereafter from campaigns on the Rhine and Danube, and in Judaea and Parthia. From literature and epigraphy we can conclude that the well-established sources in the Black Sea area and Asia Minor continued to supply their quota, as well as Illyria and Transalpine Gaul, through the normal processes of trade supplemented by kidnapping and piracy.

This brief statement of geographical sources serves as a preliminary to the detailed description of the mechanism whereby slaves were obtained, transported and sold to their ultimate purchasers, together with a selection of the evidence, in short a discussion of slave-trading in the ancient world. Finley commented on the absence of any study of the slave-trade in antiquity, and this was evidently a topic which fascinated him.[16] He had written earlier about the trade in the Black Sea and Danube regions, and had used the well-known Amphipolis tombstone as the basis for a wide-ranging discussion of slave-making and slave-trading.[17] Unfortunately, this brilliant essay was originally intended for a wider audience, so lacks references and is not entirely free from error, for instance the confusion of Arlon in Belgium with Arles in Provence as the source of another tombstone with a possible slavery scene. Westermann includes details of sources and trade on a chronological basis without discussing them in a coherent manner.[18] Wiedemann has a selective but useful collection of textual references to sources of slaves in Greek and Roman times, but nothing specifically on trade.[19] Garlan is stronger on sources but has some useful comments on trade.[20] Harris has published a more detailed study of sources and trade of a limited period; he takes as his chronological limits 50 BC and AD 50 for sources, but runs on into the third century AD when citing instances of possible trade.[21] Finally, useful comments on the trade in slaves are to be found incidentally in Minns, Glotz, Toutain, Frank and Rostovtzeff.[22]

A discussion of where slaves originated and the channels by which they reached their eventual owners is essentially geographical, but the pattern of the trade varied over the centuries and was related to shifts of power in the ancient world. It is difficult to say anything useful about sources and trade in early Greece though Lencman, writing from a Marxist standpoint, gives an interesting comparison between slavery in the Mycenaean palace-economy from the evidence of the Linear B Pylos tablets and in the regal economy of the Homeric period from the eleventh to the mid-eighth century BC.[23] Generally, historians emphasize the casual and sporadic nature of slavery in the Homeric period, and the mild and patriarchal character of the institution. The source is recorded in the *Iliad* and *Odyssey*: the taking of prisoners, of whom the men are ransomed and the women and children consigned to slavery. The slight references to trade attribute this to the Phoenicians and the Taphians, and one of the best-known instances is the kidnapping of Odysseus' swineherd, Eumaeus; he was nobly born and seized as a child on the island of Syros, near Delos, through the treachery of his nurse.

It is argued that by 600 BC slavery existed in Greece on a large enough scale to warrant the view that it had changed its character to become chattel slavery. Slaves were now regarded as possessions, which could be freely bought and sold on the open market, though this is not to say that the earlier patriarchal system may not have persisted, particularly in rural areas. The change itself is neatly encapsulated in Aristotle's fourth-century definition of a slave as an 'animate piece of property' – *ktêma ti empsuchon.*[24] The reasons for the change may broadly be classed as social and economic. Westermann cites the establishment of colonies on the Mediterranean coastlines, and the willingness of indigenous peoples to provide the Greek colonists with the captives they had taken in intertribal warfare, as steps leading to expansion of the institution.[25] However, in the older colonies the economic basis was still primarily agricultural, and the great expansion of chattel slavery in both the mainland and colonies seems to have originated in the development of small-scale industrialization, supported by the introduction of coinage as a means of exchange. For Attica, one source of slaves was clearly from those citizens who had fallen into debt and by self-sale become the virtual property of their fellow citizens. However, in c. 594 BC Solon eliminated this practice, which was causing civil strife, by cancelling existing debts and mortgages and forbidding future borrowing on the security of the person or of the wife and children. The reform spread widely through the Greek world, and citizens were compelled to look elsewhere for a source of slaves.

For Attica at least, and Athens in particular, it seems broadly true that citizenship precluded slavery. This would explain the intense social and economic resentment felt by those enslaved for debt and the pressure that led to Solon's reforms. The other city-states of mainland Greece and the Mediterranean coast followed the same rule, with some exceptions such as Gortyn in southern Crete. The elimination of this source of supply meant that throughout the Classical period the emphasis was thrown upon force – war, piracy and kidnapping – as a means of satisfying the demand for slaves, and so in turn on the activities of slave-traders. The exposure of infants and their adoption as potential slaves seems not to have been an important source, while slavery by birth is difficult to quantify. Increased industrialization certainly seems to have led to a massive growth in slave numbers: statistics in ancient writers are unreliable but Thucydides' well-known statement that more than 20,000 slaves employed by the Athenians as skilled labourers – *cheirotechnai* – in the Laurion silver mines deserted after the Spartan occupation of Dekeleia in 413 BC gives an idea of numbers.[26] Attempts to satisfy demand by raiding and kidnapping ran up against severe legal penalties, including death, enacted by various city-states, such as Athens, Corinth and Teos.[27] Generalization for Greece as a whole is difficult, but in those city-states where agriculture remained predominantly the basis of economic life it is probable that serf-labour was preferred to chattel slavery.

In the period between Alexander and Augustus the main change was the switch of power from Hellenistic Greece to the Roman Republic and the effect which this had on the sources of and trade in slaves. It is argued that Alexander and his successors did not resort to the sale of prisoners on any large scale, and the implication must be that piracy and kidnapping met the demand.[28] However, by the end of the third century BC Hellenistic rulers seem to have reverted to the enslavement of prisoners of war, either for sale or for their own use.[29] To the west, in Sicily, the position was probably different. The rivalry between Phoenician and Greek colonists during the seventh and sixth centuries BC resulted in continuous warfare and the enslavement of prisoners, a process which reached its climax under the tyrant Dionysius I (430-367 BC). After his death, a period of instability saw the growth of Carthaginian power during the fourth century, leading under Hieron II of Syracuse to the clash with Rome which precipitated the First Punic War in 264 BC. The agricultural richness of Sicily and the growth of large estates there, as well as in the corn-growing belt of North Africa, meant an increasing use of prisoners of war as slave-labour by both sides. To the east, the gradually crumbling Hellenistic empires of Antigonids, Seleucids and Ptolemies and their endemic rivalries led to Roman intervention from the early second century BC, culminating in their subjection in the first century BC by Pompey, Caesar and Augustus. One of the most dramatic events of the period was the enslavement by the Romans in 167 BC of 150,000 inhabitants of Epirus in north-west Greece, though the reliability of the numbers cannot be taken for granted.

Equally large numbers of captives came on the slave-market during the Punic Wars of the third and second centuries BC, if ancient sources are to be believed. Although both Romans and Carthaginians took prisoners, it is argued that fewer were sold into slavery by the Carthaginians because they took fewer cities by siege.[30] The trend was evident over much of the Mediterranean, from Sardinia in the west to Greece in the east. Roman losses in manpower were made good by these captives and the change to large ranches and estates in Italy and Sicily was a complementary movement to meet the labour shortage, though the latent danger of slave revolts was an adverse factor. The focus of attention shifts during the first century BC with the campaigns of Marius against the Cimbri and Teutones and of Caesar in Gaul, when again large numbers of captives reached the slave-market. Even so, war was by no means sufficient to meet the huge demand, and the piracy and kidnapping endemic in the eastern Mediterranean continued on an increasing scale. As early as the fourth century Ephesus and Crete had served as slave-markets, followed by Rhodes in the late third and second centuries. By *c.* 200 BC Tyrrhenian, Aetolian and Cretan pirates felt the pressure of the Roman fleets appearing in the Aegean, and the southern coast of Asia Minor, specifically Cilicia and Pamphylia, with the mountainous hinterland of the Taurus, developed as a new centre of piratical activity. Ironically, Rome had returned the formerly independent island of Delos to Athenian control in 166 BC and given it the status of a free port, to offset the importance of Rhodes. Its central position in the southern Aegean made it a useful staging point for the Cilician pirates and their slave cargoes from the Levant, though Strabo's often quoted statement (14.5.2) of the transhipment of 10,000 slaves a day must be open to doubt. The first recorded attempt by the Romans to quell the pirates was in 102 BC, but success was not finally achieved until Pompey defeated them in a sea-battle in 67 BC and destroyed their stronghold of Coracesium, the modern Alanya, in Rough Cilicia. Delos had lost its commercial importance before this, after the Mithridatic general Archelaus sacked the port in 88 BC, followed by a further attack on the island in 69 BC by the pirates, who had allied themselves with Mithridates against Rome. Its place as a slave-market was taken by the port of Side in Pamphylia.

The elimination of piracy in the eastern Mediterranean may have been advantageous for legitimate seaborne trade but presumably created problems by reducing the supply of slaves from this source. But slave-traders were still active elsewhere and Strabo, for instance, mentions the Black Sea and its northern hinterland, and Illyria at the head of the Adriatic as areas where merchants could buy slaves.[31] War and the consequent enslavement of prisoners continued as a major source in the last years of the Republic and the first twenty years of Augustus' reign. In the first century AD the conquest of Britain and the capture of Jerusalem fed the constant demand but the Hadrianic policy of settled frontiers meant an inevitable scaling down. Frontier wars of the second and third centuries AD on the Rhine and Danube and in Asia Minor may have contributed their quota, but the ancient sources are unhelpful on this point.

Intertribal warfare on the borders of the Empire must have provided a steady if not vast supply for the slave-traders to lead back to Rome and its provinces, supported by a certain amount of selective kidnapping. But increasing emphasis must have been placed on such sources as the sale of children by poverty-stricken parents, the acquisition of foundlings to be reared as slaves, voluntary submission to slavery (for example, by self-sale for debt), and the novel concept of *servitus poenae*. Condemnation to slavery as the penalty for a crime provided useful recruits for such harsh forms of labour as quarrying and mining, and to serve as gladiators in the arena. Above all, demand must have been met by the children of existing slaves – *vernae* in Latin and *oikogeneis* in Greek – and Barrow regarded this as the most important source.[32] However, these local forms of slavery have little relevance to an inquiry into the external sources of and the trade in slaves.

As regards the mechanics of the transport of slaves and their actual sale, not much evidence is available. There is little mention of them in

Fig. 1. Detail of chaingang from Amphipolis relief

Fig. 2. Chaingang demonstrating use of neck-chains

Greek ship cargoes and in periods of war it seems likely that captors quickly disposed of their prisoners to attendant slave-dealers, who may then have moved them by land, chained and in columns, to the final slave-market. The Amphipolis tombstone, though late, vividly illustrates the process (figs 1-2). Westermann suggests that the final sales took place in the agora of the Greek city-states, perhaps in some well-defined area; they probably occurred at regular intervals and would have been preceded by announcements by public heralds, in order to regulate the trade, the collection of any sale tax, and the hearing of disputes over earlier owner-ship.[33] But actual archaeological evidence of such markets is difficult to find, though it has been suggested that the Agora of the Italians at Delos may have served as the slave-market there. There were, no doubt, irregu-lar and spasmodic sales in smaller centres, whenever supply and demand reached some sort of balance.

The poverty of the evidence for slave-trading reflects the distaste felt by the Greeks and, to a lesser extent, the Romans for the traffic in human beings. Aristophanes and Herodotus record their contempt for slave-mer-chants in Thessaly and Chios, but by the Roman period there was a greater willingness to admit involvement.[34] The mechanics of the trade seem to have been broadly the same as for the Greeks. The Roman army took its captives and sold them 'under the crown' (*sub corona*) or 'under the spear' (*sub hasta*) – indications of their status as booty – to the hovering dealers (fig. 3). Transport to the market followed, and for Rome itself the forum near the temple of Castor was a known location. Auction seems to have been a regular practice and details of conditions of sale survive: the whitening with chalk of the feet of newly imported slaves to distinguish them from those of local origin, the hanging of placards around the neck listing medical history and record of conduct, etc.

The detailed evidence

In his monograph on Greek and Roman slavery, Westermann (1955) adopted a chronological approach, and within the successive periods dealt with the various aspects of the institution in a broadly systematic manner. The use of archaeological evidence necessarily adopts the same method, and in this detailed discussion of the evidence for sources and trade a similar sequence is followed, with the evidence for the various periods subdivided by ancient authors on the one hand and archaeology on the other; the latter is heavily weighted by epigraphy and the evidence from archaeology in the narrower sense is fairly slight.

c. 800-500 BC

The earliest literary evidence for the existence of slaves in Greece, and the sources from which they were drawn, occurs in Homer. The well-known

Fig. 3. Two slaves in neck-chains on relief from Mainz

problem immediately arises, whether he was really describing social conditions in Late Bronze Age Greece of the thirteenth century BC or attributing conditions of his own era, the eighth century BC, to that earlier period.[35] For safety, it seems best to take *c.* 800 BC as a starting point, and to suggest that the fairly static system of that date may have survived intact from much earlier. From Homer to the Persian Wars contemporary evidence for slavery is slight. Hesiod, perhaps a little later than Homer, suggests, in *Works and Days* (*passim*), the use of slaves on a modest scale in Boeotian agriculture, indicating that the limited type of domestic slavery described by Homer continued in the eighth and seventh centuries BC; this may have been true for much of Greece except where serf-labour was used, as in Sparta or Thessaly. But meanwhile major economic changes were underway, coinciding with the beginnings of chattel slavery on a larger scale: these were the expansion of Greek colonies to the west, east and north along the Mediterranean and Black Sea coasts, coupled with the beginnings of small-scale industry and the introduction of coinage to facilitate the corresponding growth of trade.[36] The limited evidence suggests that Chios, with its key position on the littoral of Asia Minor, played a leading part in these developments. Two references to enslavement by capture in Italy are also included.

Sources of slaves

1. Achilles states that he sold Trojan prisoners as slaves (*Iliad* 21.102).

2. Hector fears that his wife Andromache will become a Greek on his death (*Iliad* 6.455).

3. Phoenix tells the story of Meleager whose wife, Cleopatra, roused him to fight by her description of the enslavement of women and children after the capture of a town (*Iliad* 9.594).

4. As he slays Patroclus, Hector taunts him for his hope of sacking Troy and carrying away captive the Trojan women (*Iliad* 16.830).

5. Odysseus weeps like a woman being led away into captivity after her husband has been killed (*Odyssey* 8.527).

6. Chryseis, the daughter of the Trojan Chryses, had been captured in an attack on the Trojan town of Chryse in the Troad and allocated to Agamemnon; he only agrees to return her to her father if he can take in exchange Achilles' prize, Briseis, who was captured in the attack on Lyrnessos, also in the Troad (*Iliad* 1.182ff.; 2.685).

7. The Egyptians attacked Odysseus' crew and sent their prisoners inland to work as slaves (*Odyssey* 14.274).

8. Early in the sixth century BC Cleisthenes, tyrant of Sicyon on the Gulf of Corinth, besieged and captured the neighbouring town of Pellana (Pellene) and enslaved its inhabitants – the first recorded instance of wholesale enslavement (*P.Oxy.* x (1914), 103, no. 1241, col. 3, 11. 2ff.).

9. Early in the sixth century BC the Spartans attacked Tegea but were defeated and forced to work in the Tegean fields, wearing the chains which they had brought with them to enslave the Tegeans. The chains were later hung in the temple of Athena Alea at Tegea (Herod. 1.66; Paus. 8.45.3).

10. Solon recorded that many free-born poor Athenians had gone as fettered slaves to foreign lands,[37] a reference to self-sale through debt, cancelled by his legislation of the early sixth century (Plut., *Sol.* 13ff.) which enabled him to bring them back to Athens.[38]

11. The Thracians were said to sell their children as slaves (Herod. 5.6), as were the Phrygians (Philostratus, *Apollonius* 8.7.12).

12. Early in the sixth century BC the Etruscan king of Rome, Tarquinius Priscus, captured Apiolanum, Corniculum and Suessa Pometia, and enslaved the women and children (Dion. Hal. 3.49.3; 3.50.6; 4.1.4).

13. In 502 BC the Aurunci of Pometia surrendered to Spurius Cassius, who treated them as prisoners and sold most of them into slavery (Livy 2.17.5f.).

14. The Samians, who founded Kydonia in Crete in 524 BC, were attacked and enslaved by the Aeginetans with Cretan support (Herod. 3.59).

The trade in slaves

15. Odysseus describes how he was taken from Egypt by a Phoenician merchant and sent to Libya to be sold as a slave (*Odyssey* 14.287-98).

16. Eumaeus describes how he was kidnapped as a child from his home on the island of Syros by Phoenician merchants who sold him on Ithaca (*Odyssey* 15.403-84).

17. Mesaulius, Eumaeus' servant, was bought as a slave from Taphian merchants (*Odyssey* 14.452).

18. Eumaeus' nurse was a Phoenician woman from Sidon; she was captured by Taphian pirates who sold her on Syros to Eumaeus' father (*Odyssey* 15.425-9).

19. Penelope reminds the suitor Antinous that his father had joined the Taphian pirates to harass the Thesprotians of north-west Greece (*Odyssey* 16.425ff.).

20. Apollo asks Cretan sailors voyaging from Knossos to Pylos whether they are genuine merchants or pirates threatening men in foreign lands, viz. to kidnap them and sell them as slaves (*Homeric Hymn to Apollo* 452-5). This interrogatory formula appears twice in the *Odyssey*, first addressed by Nestor, king of Pylos, to Telemachus and his crew (3.71-4), and secondly by Polyphemus to Odysseus and his crew (9.252-5), reflecting the deep-seated fear of pirates masquerading as merchants.

21. Melanthius threatens to sell Eumaeus as a slave after shipping him from Ithaca (*Odyssey* 17.250); similarly, the suitors threaten to ship Odysseus and Theoclymenus to Sicily to be sold (*Odyssey* 20.383).

22. A biblical reference of the early sixth century BC mentions Greeks involved in the slave-trade at Tyre: 'Javan [Ionia] ... dealt with you, offering slaves and vessels of bronze as your imports' (Ezekiel 27.13).

23. Archilochus of Paros, writing in the eighth or seventh century BC, refers to the danger that storm-tossed sailors would be seized by the 'top-knotted' (*akrokomoi*) Thracians and sold as slaves.[39]

24. Hipponax of Ephesus, writing in the sixth century BC, refers to the barbarians (*soloikoi*) who kidnap Phrygians and sell them as slaves to work in the mills of Miletus.[40]

25. The famous sixth-century courtesan, Rhodopis, was a Thracian slave transported to Naucratis in Egypt by Xanthus of Samos, presumably a slave-trader (Herod. 2.134-5).

26. After his defeat at Salamis in 480 BC Xerxes sent his sons to Ephesus, where

their guardian Hermotimus was kidnapped and sold by the dealer Panionius (Herod. 8.103-5).

27. From as early as the Persian Wars Scythian archers, bought as slaves, were employed as police at Athens, suggesting a sixth-century trade in slaves from that area.[41]

28. At Gortyn in Crete serfs and chattel-slaves are recorded in the Law Code of the middle of the fifth century BC or earlier, implying that both existed by, say, 500 BC when Gortyn first began to use coinage; the trade in slaves also existed at that time and was subject to official control, on the evidence of Col. VII, 11.10-15, dealing with responsibility for damages caused by slaves bought in the market place.[42]

c. 500-300 BC

These two centuries cover a period of vastly increased contact between the Greeks and other peoples of the Mediterranean world, partly commercial and partly military, and also the emergence of Rome as a Mediterranean power. The first half century saw the outbreak of hostilities with Persia, leading eventually to the independence of the Asiatic Greeks; in the final third of the fifth century the Peloponnesian War, though primarily a struggle among Greeks, had repercussions farther afield, as in the disastrous Athenian expedition to Sicily of 415-413 BC; finally, in the last third of the fourth century, the rise of Macedon and Alexander's campaigns took Greek power far into Asia. Apart from the demand for chattel-slaves occasioned by changes in production and the introduction of coinage, the taking of captives in war must have had marked effects on slave numbers, sources and trade. Aristotle and Plato provide the theoretical basis for the practice of treating captives as the property of the conqueror, modified to some extent by the feeling (at least before the bitterness engendered by the Peloponnesian War) that the enslavement of fellow Greeks was to be condemned, whereas a captive barbarian was by definition a slave. Ducrey (1968) and Volkmann (1961) have published general studies of prisoners of war in ancient society, differing in their approach but overlapping to some extent. Ducrey discusses the taking of prisoners both in war and as a result of the capture of cities; he quotes 120 cases of combat of which 28 led to the enslavement of the defeated, and 100 cases of captured cities of which 34 led to the enslavement of all or part of the population,[43] and concludes his study with the conquest of Greece in the second century BC. Volkmann, on the other hand, confines his study to the enslavement of all or part of the inhabitants of captured cities from Hellenistic times to the end of the Roman Empire and consequently takes in a much larger area of the ancient world. Taken together, they provide a large corpus of ancient references for the supply of slaves from military operations and these are briefly synthesized below in chronological order, excluding, however, references which imply enslavement rather than unequivocally mention it and instances where the booty includes existing slaves. Sections on other

13

sources follow, especially piracy, where the evidence is conveniently brought together in two other monographs by Ormerod (1924) and Ziebarth (1929), again complementary rather than repetitive. But war as a source of slaves takes precedence, both in this period and later: Finley claimed that between 600 BC and AD 400 the Greeks and Romans disposed of several million men, women and children by capture on to the slave-market.[44] Certainly, the wealth of references in this and the succeeding section as compared with their paucity for the earlier period would support this view; some reasons may suggest themselves – a rising Mediterranean population, land hunger, endemic warfare.

Sources of slaves

1. Warfare

29. Early fifth century: the consul Opiter Verginius Tricostus sold the greater part of the inhabitants of Cameria in Latium as slaves (Dion. 5.49.5).

30. Early fifth century: Coriolanus, after the capture of Pedum, Bola and other towns, divided the male captives as slaves among his soldiers (Dion. 7.17.6-18; Plut., *Cor.* 28.5).

31. 483 BC: Gelon captured Hyblaean Megara and sold the inhabitants out of Sicily (Herod. 6.17).

32. 480 BC: before the battle of Himera in Sicily, the Sicilian Greek cavalry attacked the Carthaginian raiders and each trooper took captive as many as he could, presumably to sell as slaves (Diod. 11.21.2); after the defeat of Hamilcar's forces Gelon divided the captives among the allied Sicilian cities where they were chained and set to labour on public works (Diod. 11.25.1-2).

33. 476 BC: Cimon attacked and defeated the Persians in Eion in Thrace and shortly afterwards seized the island of Skyros, off Euboea; in both places he enslaved the inhabitants (Diod. 11.60.1-2; Plut., *Cim.* 8.3-5; Thuc. 1.98.1-2).

34. 468 BC: the Argives captured Mycenae and sold the inhabitants into slavery (Diod. 11.65.4-5).

35. 468/467 BC: the Athenians under Cimon defeated the Persians on the river Eurymedon in Pisidia and took 20,000 captives who were sold into slavery (Diod. 11.62.1; Plut., *Cim.* 12.13); Lauffer has suggested that many of these were assigned to the silver mines in the Laurion peninsula of Attica.[45]

36. 468 BC: the Romans captured a small coastal town near Antium in Latium and all the free men were given as slaves to the army (Dion. 9.56.5).

37. 459 BC: the Aequi, in their war against Rome, captured the towns of Tusculum and Ortona and enslaved the women and children (Dion. 10.20.3; 10.26.3; Livy 3.23.1 f.).

38. 457 BC: Cincinnatus enslaved the inhabitants of Corbio (Dion. 10.24.7).

39. 447 BC: the Athenians captured Chaeroneia in Boeotia and sold the inhabitants into slavery (Thuc. 1.113.1).

40. 431 BC: after their surrender to Postumius Tubertus, the Volsci were sold as slaves, apart from the senators (Livy 4.29.4).

41. 425 BC: following the capture of Fidenae, the inhabitants were sold into slavery, after an allocation by lot to the army (Livy 4.34.4).

42. 423 BC: the Athenians captured Skioni in Chalcidice, slew the men and enslaved the women and children (Thuc. 5.32.1).

14

43. 422 BC: the Athenians captured Torone in Chalcidice and enslaved 700 women and children (Thuc. 5.3.4).

44. 421 BC: the Samnites destroyed Cumae and sold the Greek survivors into slavery (Diod. 12.76.5; Dion. 15.6.4).

45. 416 BC: the Athenians captured Melos, massacred the men and enslaved the women and children (Thuc. 5.116.4).

46. 415 BC: during the Athenian expedition to Sicily Nicias captured Hyccara and sold the inhabitants at Catana; some were used as oarsmen in the Athenian fleet (Thuc. 6.62; 7.13.3), while one young girl was sold in the Peloponnese, where she became the famous courtesan, Lais (Plut., *Nic.* 15.4; *Athen.* 13.588c).

47. 413 BC: the defeat of the Athenian forces in Sicily under Nicias and Demosthenes led to the capture and enslavement of some 7,000 men (Thuc. 7.80-7; Diod. 13.19-33; Plut., *Nic.* 27-9).

48. 412 BC: the Peloponnesian fleet captured Iasos in Caria and sold the inhabitants to the Persian satrap, Tissaphernes; the Athenian garrison of Methymna on Lesbos experienced the same fate (Thuc. 8.28.4).

49. 404 BC: Lysander captured Iasos again, killed 800 men of military age, and sold the women and children (Diod. 13.104.7).

50. 403 BC: Dionysius of Syracuse captured Catana and Naxos and sold the inhabitants into slavery (Diod. 14.15.2-4).

51. 401 BC: the 10,000 Greek mercenaries who served Cyrus under Xenophon took slaves to some extent before the battle of Cunaxa, for example, in Lycaonia and Cilicia; during the subsequent march supply problems prevented the accumulation of captives, apart from some women and children. Once they had arrived on the Black Sea coast, they again took prisoners among the local peasantry to sell as slaves in the Greek cities of Asia Minor (Xen., *Anab. passim*).[46]

52. 398 BC: Dionysius captured Motya and sold the inhabitants (Diod. 14.53.2).

53. 396 BC: the Spartan king Agesilaus found Greeks working as slaves in the gold mines at Lampsacus in the Troad (Polyaenus, *Strateg.* 2.1.26).[47]

54. 396 BC: Furius Camillus destroyed Veii and sold the male inhabitants (Diod. 14.93.2; Livy 5.22.1 – *sub corona vendidit*).

55. 390 BC: the Spartans captured and sold the men, women and slaves who had taken refuge in Perachora (Xen., *Hell.* 4.5.5-6 and 8).

56. 387 BC: Dionysius captured Rhegium and took 6,000 prisoners; those who were not ransomed were sold as slaves at Syracuse (Diod. 14.111).

57. 364 BC: the Thebans finally seized Orchomenus in Boeotia, killed the men and sold the women and children into slavery (Diod.15.79.6; cf. Dem., *C. Lept.* (20), 109; *Megal.* (16), 4; Pausanias 9.15.3 places the date earlier).

58. 356 BC: Philip II captured Poteidaia in Chalcidice, released the Athenian garrison but sold the inhabitants into slavery (Diod. 16.8.5).

59. 356 BC: Philomelos, leader of the Phokaians in the Third Sacred War, seized Delphi and planned to kill the men, enslave the women and children, and destroy the town, but was restrained by the Spartan king, Archidamus (Paus. 3.10.4).

60. 353 BC: Onomarchos, successor to Philomelos, captured Thronion on the north side of the Gulf of Corinth and sold the inhabitants into slavery (Diod.16.33.3).

61. 353 BC: Philip II captured Coronea and Orchomenus, now rebuilt (see 57), and reduced the inhabitants to slavery (Dem., *De falsa leg.* (19), 112).

62. 352 BC: the Athenian general Chares had the young men of Sestos in the Thracian Chersonese put to death and sold the remaining inhabitants into slavery (Diod. 16.34.3).

63. 349 BC: Philip captured Stagira in Chalcidice (birthplace of Aristotle) and enslaved the inhabitants (Plut., *Alex.* 7.3).

64. 348 BC: Philip captured Olynthus in Chalcidice and enslaved the inhabitants (Diod. 16.53.2-3; Polyb. 9.28.2-3).

65. 346 BC: the Romans attacked the Volsci besieging Satricum and sold into slavery 4,000 captives after they had been led in triumph at Rome; alternatively, the slaves taken with other booty were sold (Livy 7.27.7f.).

66. 341 BC: the Corinthian general, Timoleon, defeated the Carthaginian forces in Sicily at the battle of the river Crimisos; according to Plutarch (Tim. 29.2) 5,000 prisoners became public property, while his troops seized others, presumably to sell as slaves. Diodorus simply remarks that 15,000 prisoners were taken (16.80.5).

67. 335 BC: Parmenion destroyed Gryneion, south of Pergamum, and sold the inhabitants into slavery (Diod. 17.7.9).

68. *c.* 334 BC: after the battle on the river Granicus near the Hellespont, Alexander sent the captured Greek mercenaries in the Persian army to do forced labour in Macedonia, possibly in the gold mines of Philippi (Arrian, *Anab.* 1.16.6; Diod. 16.8.6-7).[48] It is argued that Alexander did not make a practice of selling prisoners into slavery, but preferred to use them as bargaining counters in imposing terms of surrender.[49] The following episodes (69-74) are recorded for his campaigns.

69. 332 BC: a large number of prisoners were sold after the capture of Tyre – 30,000 (Arrian, *Anab.* 2.24.5) or 13,000 (Diod. 17.46.4).

70. 332 BC: the women and children were sold after the capture of Gaza (Arrian, *Anab.* 2.27).

71. 331 BC: women were enslaved at Persepolis (Diod. 17.70.6).

72. 330 BC: at Areia, the prisoners were given the choice of death or slavery (Arrian, *Anab.* 3.25.7).

73. 329 BC: Craterus captured five towns in Bactria and enslaved the inhabitants (Arrian, *Anab.* 4.2-3).

74. 326/325 BC: in India settlements of the Agalasseis near the river Hydraotes, in the kingdom of Sambos, in Musikanos, and of the Mallians were enslaved (Diod. 17.96.3, 102.6; Arrian, *Anab.* 6.7.3, 17.1).

75. 322 BC: Perdiccas destroyed Laranda in Pisidia and enslaved the inhabitants (Diod. 18.22.2).

76. 312 BC: Ptolemy I took Marion on Cyprus and moved the enslaved inhabitants to Paphos (Diod. 19.79.4); in Cilicia he sold the captured inhabitants of Mallos as slaves (Diod. 19.79.6); after his victory at Gaza, he sent 8,000 of Demetrius' troops to Egypt (Diod. 19.85.3-4; Plut., *Dem.* 5.3).

77. 311 BC: C. Junius Brutus seized Samnite Cluviae, slaughtered the men of military age and sold the women and children as slaves (Diod. 20.26.3f.).

78. 307 BC: after the defeat of Agathocles' army in Libya, the Greek leaders were crucified, and the others were fettered and put to work on the land (Diod. 20.69.5).

79. 306 BC: the inhabitants of Sora and Calatia, allies of Rome, were enslaved in the second Samnite War (Diod. 20.80.lf.).

80. 303 BC: the Spartan Cleonymus helped the Lucanians against the Tarentines and enslaved the inhabitants of an unnamed city of the Metaponti (Diod. 20.104.3-4).

81. 302-301 BC: Ptolemy I again invaded Palestine and took Jewish prisoners to work as slaves in Egypt, though another tradition asserts that they went voluntarily (Jos., *C. Apion.* 186-9, 209-12; *Ant. Jud.* 12.1-9; App., *Syr.* (11), 50).

16

2. Piracy and brigandage

The endemic but casual piracy of the period before the Persian Wars was
certainly a source, if only on a small scale, of slaves. But it is probable that
this was a development of trading activity and that its practitioners were
more interested in material than human booty; where prisoners were
taken, their captors preferred to make a quick profit by ransoming them.
On the other hand, the expansion of Persian influence under Darius and
the raiding activities of Polycrates of Samos before 500 BC marked the
growth of piracy as a semi-official aspect of naval warfare in the Persian
Wars and the Peloponnesian War of the fifth century BC, and in the
smaller-scale warfare of the fourth century. The activity of privateers on
the sea was matched by brigandage on land, where the employment of
mercenaries by feuding city-states led to lawlessness and the enslavement
of groups and individuals. Between the wars, from 480 to 431 BC, it is
generally accepted that conventional piracy was restrained in the Aegean
by the supremacy of the Athenian fleet and normal trade consequently
encouraged. Towards the end of the fourth century there is evidence that
piracy had also developed in the Adriatic, where the Tyrrhenians were
active. Two complementary studies again provide a detailed picture of this
source of slaves: Ormerod (1924) deals with the whole of the Mediterranean from the Homeric period to the Roman Empire and confines himself
to piracy; Ziebarth (1929) confines himself to the east Mediterranean,
devotes much of his book to Greek trading activity in general and concludes with Pompey's elimination of the Cilician pirates in 67 BC. Ducrey
also has a useful chapter: 'Pirates et corsaires'.[50] However, Finley felt that
piracy was rather exaggerated as a source of slaves and that land warfare
was by far the greater factor.[51]

82. Early fifth century BC: the exiled Aeginetans, based on Sounion, raided
Aegina and took prisoners (Herod. 6.90).
83. 470 BC: the Dolopes of Skyros had enslaved some Thessalian merchants and
Cimon in turn attacked and enslaved them (Plut., *Cim.* 8.3-5).
84. 410 BC: the decline of Athenian naval power saw an increase in piracy and
the enslavement of those travelling by sea (Andocides 1.138).
85. 395 BC: the Spartan king Agesilaus, based at Ephesus, gave orders that the
barbarians captured by his pirate allies should be sold as slaves (Xen., *Hell.*
3.4.19).
86. 369 or 365 BC: Nicostratus, while in pursuit of three fugitive slaves, was
himself captured by a pirate ship from Aegina and sold on the island. He was
ransomed, as was Plato in *c.* 387 after similar capture and imprisonment on the
island (Dem., *C. Nicostr.* (53), 6).[52]
87. 361 BC: Alexander of Pherae attacked the Cyclades and made numerous
slaves in the cities which he captured (Diod. 15.95.l; Dem., *C. Polycl.* (1), 4).
88. 340 BC: Philip II complained to the Athenians that their commander Callias

17

was treating all ships sailing to Macedonia as enemy vessels and selling their crews (Dem., *Phil.* (12), 5).

89. 345 or 336/335 BC: Cleomis of Methymna freed or ransomed Athenian prisoners captured by pirates.[53]

3. Other evidence for the sources of slaves

There is a little evidence for this period, mainly of an onomastic nature, which throws light on the geographical origins of Greek slaves. It varies, ranging from the uncertain witness of literary references to the reliable indications of epigraphy, but throws some light on trade routes.

90. 477-378 BC: as noted earlier, the police force at Athens was composed of Scythian archers; these were slaves owned by the state, originally numbering 300 but later rising to 1,000.[54]

91. The Laurion silver mines, worked from the fifth century, employed a huge workforce of slaves, possibly 30,000 at its maximum. They were largely non-Greek from countries to the north and east of the Aegean, especially mining areas such as Thrace and Paphlagonia. The evidence for origin comes from tombstones and the estimate of numbers is based on the recorded flight of more than 20,000 slaves to the Spartans after the siege of Dekeleia in 413 BC.[55]

92. 415 BC: the trial which followed the mutilation of the Hermae in Athens led to a public auction of the slaves confiscated from the accused. From the fragmentary lists that survive, the nationality of 33 slaves can be determined: 12 Thracian, 7 Carian, and the remainder from Cappadocia, Colchis, Scythia, Phrygia, Lydia, Syria, Illyria, Macedonia, and the Peloponnese. Even from such a small sample, it is clear that the lands bordering the Aegean and the Black Sea were the main area for the supply of slaves.[56]

93. Literary references also indicate, by the use of stock names for slaves, that Thrace and Asia Minor were thought of as main sources of supply: Thratta (the feminine form of a word meaning 'Thracian'), Davos (identified later by Strabo as a characteristic Dacian name, but more likely Thracian or Danubian), and Tibeios (a Paphlagonian – Aristophanes, *Acharn.* 271-5; *Peace* 1138; *Wasps* 826-8; Plato, *Laches* 187B). Other areas were Phrygia, Lydia and Caria (Eur., *Orestes* 507-8; *Alcestis* 675-6; Ar., *Birds*; *Knights* 44).

94. Vase-paintings from sixth- and fifth-century Athens, signed 'Kolchian' or 'the Scythian', were presumably the work of slaves.[57]

95. 414 BC: Cephisodorus, a wealthy metic of the Piraeus, owned 16 slaves: 5 Thracians, 3 Carians, 2 Syrians, 2 Illyrians, with 1 each from Colchis, Scythia, Lydia and Malta.[58]

The trade in slaves

For this period there is little in the way of specific evidence and we are driven to infer certain trade routes on the basis of the sources of slaves and their ultimate destinations. The means by which the vast numbers of captives taken in military operations and the much smaller numbers taken by piracy or kidnapping were eventually brought to market must surely have been the slave-traders following the army or themselves engaged in piracy and brigandage. The very lack of references must reflect the distaste felt by the Greeks for the slave-trade and its practitioners. Almost certainly, traders operating behind the armies were already in the district, particularly in non-Greek areas, engaged in the purchase of adults and children for export to recognized slave-markets.[59] The markets themselves are better attested and regular sales in the agora of the city-state were customary, since the legal and financial regulation of the trade could be more easily observed.[60] Less regular sales were apparently held in smaller centres and there seem to have been intermittent markets at fairs and in garrison towns.[61] Some of the references given below will have already appeared in the section on sources.

96. Panionius of Chios is recorded as a slave-trader in the early fifth century BC, specializing in the sale of eunuchs at Sardis and Ephesus. One of his victims, Hermotimus from Pedasa near Halicarnassus, ended up in the service of Xerxes; after his defeat at Salamis in 480, Xerxes used Hermotimus to escort his children to safety at Ephesus (where in fact he took his revenge on Panionius). Herodotus stigmatized the trade in castrated slaves as 'wicked practices' (*erga anosiotata*), reflecting the Greek distaste for the trade which provided them with slaves (Herod. 8.104f.).

97. Slaves are said to be kidnapped in Thessaly and brought by merchants to Athens (Ar., *Wealth* 519-21).

98. 395 BC: the Spartan Agesilaus ordered prisoners seized by his pirate allies to be sold at Ephesus after proclamation (Xen., *Hell.* 3.4.19).

99. 387 BC: the captives taken by Dionysius at Rhegium were sold as slaves at Syracuse (Diod. 14.111).

100. 320/319 BC: Eurylochus of Cydonia ransomed Athenian prisoners in Crete, destined for the slave-market (*IG* II², 399, 10f.).[62]

101. 307 BC: Agathocles of Syracuse attacked Segesta, which had sided with Carthage, and destroyed the city; he sold the women and children to the Bruttii of modern Calabria (Diod. 20.71.5) and may also have enslaved some of the males (Diod. 21.16.2).

The appearance of slaves in Classical Greece

A description of the sources of slaves and the means by which they were traded is an essential background to the archaeological study of the institution, but still provides little information about the individuals involved. Attempts have been made to invoke the evidence of ancient art as an aspect of archaeology in order to illustrate the reality of the phenomenon, notably by Garlan.[63] He notes that towards 500 BC some effort is made to distinguish master from slave in vase-painting, a trend which becomes more marked in the fifth century, when the figure of the barbarian acquires certain clear characteristics: the standard dress becomes a rough woollen tunic, belted at the waist and reaching to the knee, sometimes supplemented by a goatskin or short jacket, with a dog-skin cap and laced boots or sandals; the hair is cut short, 'pudding-basin' fashion, and a pointed beard is occasionally depicted; the features are coarse and some-times negroid; and the slave is often shown as a squatting figure of small stature. But it should be noted that these elements can also be charac-teristic of free men of the artisan class or humble status.[64]

c. 300 BC to Augustus

This period is both prolific in references and perhaps the most interesting for the study of sources of slaves and the slave-trade, in that the centre of power moves westward as the influence of Rome steadily grows. During the third century continuous warfare in Greece again provided a steady flow of prisoners to meet the demand for slaves: in the East the struggles of the Diadochi resulted in the formation of the Antigonid, Seleucid and Ptolemaic dynasties, and towards the end of the century the Attalid dynasty of Pergamum. From *c.* 200 BC Rome began to intervene and by 146 BC was in control of the Greek mainland; in the first century BC the whole of the Greek East came under Roman rule with the campaigns of Pompey, Caesar and Augustus. Meanwhile in the central and western Mediterra-nean the previously peaceful co-relationship of Rome and Carthage col-lapsed and the three Punic Wars between 264 and 146 BC led to military action in Sicily, Africa, Spain, Corsica and Sardinia, and Italy itself, again with profound effects on the supply of slaves. The prolonged campaigns in Spain and the conquest of Gaul led to vast numbers of prisoners, until the consolidation of the Empire by Augustus brought the process to a halt.

Sources of slaves

1. Warfare

102. 298-290 BC: the third and final Samnite War led to the capture of a number of towns, whose inhabitants were taken prisoner. The instances noted in Livy are listed by Volkmann, who comments that sale into slavery is not always expressly stated.[65] But it is noteworthy that the large sum of two and a half million asses from the sale of prisoners was paid into the treasury at Rome after the triumph of Papirius in 293 BC (Livy 10.46.5). The actual instances are as follows:

297 BC: 2,900 prisoners at Cimetra (10.15.6).

296 BC: 2,100 prisoners at Murgantia (10.17.4ff.) and 6,000 at Romulea (10.17.8).

295 BC: 1,740 Perusini sold for 310 asses (10.31.3).

294 BC: 4,700 prisoners at Milionia (10.34.3ff.).

293 BC: 4,270 prisoners at Amiternum and a smaller number at Duronia (10.39.4), 2,000 prisoners from Rusellae (10.37.3), at least 5,000 from Velia, Palumbinum and Herculaneum (10.45.9f.), and nearly 3,000 from Saepinum (10.45.12ff.).

103. 283 BC: the defeat of the Gallic Senones by Dolabella is variously described by Roman historians, but Appian (*Kelt.* 11; *Sam.* 6) expressly states that the able-bodied men were slaughtered, and the women and children sold into slavery.

1. Sources of Slaves and the Trade in Slaves

104. 264-241 BC: the First Punic War produced a number of instances of the sale of prisoners after the capture of towns, mainly in Sicily:

261 BC: the fate of Agrigentum is described in different terms but it seems likely that all the inhabitants, more than 25,000, were sold (Polyb. 1.19.15; Diod. 23.9.1; Oros. 4.7.6; Zon. 8.10).

258 BC: the inhabitants of Mazara (Diod. 23.9.4), Mytistraton (Polyb. 1.24.11; Diod. 23.9.4; Zon. 8.11) and Kamarina (Polyb. 1.24.12; Diod. 23.9.4; Zon. 8.12) were sold.

256 BC: the campaign of Regulus in Africa led to the transport to Italy of Carthaginian captives, variously estimated at 27,000 (Oros. 4.8.9) and 200,000 (*De. vir. ill.* 40).

254 BC: the inhabitants of Panormus were ransomed (14,000) or sold into slavery (13,000) – accounts vary (Polyb. 1.38; Zon. 8.14; Diod. 23.18.5).

241 BC: Carthaginian soldiers captured in Sicily were sold at Lilybaeum (Polyb. 1.41.8).

105. 243 BC: Aratus seized Corinth and sold 400 captured Syrians, of uncertain status (Plut., *Arat.* 31.2).

106. 241 BC: the Aetolians attacked Pellene in Achaea and marked out the captured women as booty by placing helmets on their heads, but they were foiled by the arrival of Aratus (Plut., *Arat.* 31.2).

107. 241 BC: after the revolt of the Falisci at Falerii, the Romans seized their slaves as booty (Zon. 8.18).

108. 240 BC: the Aetolians enslaved more than 50,000 *perioikoi* in Laconia (Polyb. 4.34.9).

109. 231 BC: the conquest of Corsica and Sardinia led to the enslavement of many of the native inhabitants, but the Romans found the Corsicans unsuitable as slaves because of their savagery (Zon. 8.19; Strabo 5.224).

110. 223 BC: after the capture of Mantinea in Arcadia by the Achaeans under Aratus, the men were led off in chains or sold as slaves, as were the women and children (Plut., *Arat.* 45.4; Polyb. 2.54.11, 62.11f.).

111. 220 BC: the men of Lyttos in Crete left their city undefended when they went to war and it was destroyed by the inhabitants of Knossos who took the women and children to their own city, presumably as slaves (Polyb. 4.53.3-54).

112. 220 BC: the Aetolians attacked Cynaetha in Arcadia, enslaved the inhabitants (Polyb. 4.17-18) and seized their slaves as booty (4.29.6).

113. 219 BC: Philip V defeated the Elean troops on the Apelauron pass and sold 1,200 captives in the slave-market at Corinth (Polyb. 4.69; sales in *IG* V, ii, 351).

114. 219 BC: Philip captured 5,000 men at Thalamai and took them to Olympia, presumably for sale (Polyb. 4.75.7).

115. 219 BC: Antiochus III captured Seleucia and sold the slaves (Polyb. 5.60f.).

116. 218-201 BC: the Second Punic War produced a number of instances of enslavement, mostly in Spain, but also in Italy:

218 BC: Saguntum was captured by Hannibal, giving rise to the war; the inhabitants were enslaved (Livy 21.12.5).

214 BC: the Romans refounded Saguntum and resettled the original inhabitants; they destroyed the city of the Turdetani whom they sold into slavery (Zon. 9.3; Livy 38.39.18; 24.42.11).

214 BC: Q. Fabius Maximus invaded Samnium, captured nine towns and captured or killed 25,000 men (Livy 24.20.3ff.); he took 7,000 prisoners at Atrinum (24.47.14).

211 BC: Capua was punished by the sale of a number of Campanians (Livy 26.16.7, 24.3).

210 BC: after the capture of Agrigentum, Laevinus sold the inhabitants (Livy 26.40.13).

209 BC: at Tarentum 30,000 men (or slaves) were sold (Livy 27.16.17; Oros. 4.18; Eutrop. 3.16.2; Plut., *Fab.* 22.6); at Manduria 3,000 captives came on the slave-market (Livy 27.15.4).

209 BC: starting with the capture of Carthago Nova, Scipio seized control of some eighty towns; the captured native Spaniards were released but the Africans were sold into slavery (Livy 27.19.2; Oros. 4.18.7).

204 BC: Scipio took prisoner 8,000 inhabitants, free and slave, of a rich town in Africa (Livy 29.29.2; Zon. 19.12); he and Masinissa freed the many Roman prisoners captured in Spain, Sicily and Italy and compelled them to labour in chains on the land (App., *Pun.* 15).

203 BC: Scipio attacked town after town, enslaving the inhabitants, after the Carthaginians broke the truce (Polyb. 15.4).

203 BC: Hannibal's retreat from Italy was accompanied by the capture and enslavement of the inhabitants of Italian towns, despite his orders to the contrary (App., *Hann.* 58-9; Diod. 27.9; Livy 30.20.5).

117. 217 BC: Philip V captured Phthiotic Thebes and sold the inhabitants as slaves (Polyb. 5.100.8).

118. 210 BC: in the first Macedonian War against Philip, the Romans under Laevinus captured Antikyra, gave the town to their allies, the Aetolians, but took away the inhabitants (Polyb. 9.39.2; Livy 26.26.3).

119. 210 BC: Galba took Dyme and enslaved the inhabitants, who were later ransomed by Philip (Paus. 7.17.3; Livy 32.22.10).

120. 208 BC: Galba captured Oreas and the inhabitants were sold as slaves (Livy 28.5.18-6.7, 7.7f.; Dio Cass. 17.57-8; Zon. 9.11.4).

121. 208 BC: Philip seized Pyrgos and took 4,000 captives (Livy 27.32.7-9).

122. 207 BC: Thrasykrates accused the Aetolians of enslaving Greeks (Polyb. 11.5.1; App., *Mac.* 3.3).

123. 202 BC: Philip captured Kios and sold its citizens (Polyb. 15.21.3).

124. 200 BC: Thasos was captured by Philip and the inhabitants sold as slaves (Polyb. 15.24.1; Livy 31.31.4).

125. 200 BC: L. Apustius captured Antipatreia and the women and children were given to the soldiers as booty (Livy 31.27.3).

126. 200 BC: Sulpicius captured Pelion, sold the captured slaves but freed the inhabitants (Livy 31.40.4).

127. 200 BC: the Aetolians captured Cercinium and treated the free-born and slaves as booty (Livy 31.41.3).

128. 200 BC: the enslaved Jews in Jerusalem were freed by Antiochus III (Jos., *Ant.* 12.138).

129. 199 BC: Oreos was captured; the town went to Attalus and the inhabitants to the Romans as booty (Livy 31.46.16).

130. 198 BC: the Romans seized the slaves of the inhabitants of Elateia; these were restored in 191/190 through the intervention of Stymphalos (Livy 32.24.6; Paus. 10.34.4).

131. 199/198 BC: Lysimacheia was captured by the Thracians and the inhabitants taken into slavery; they were ransomed by Antiochus III in 196 when the town was rebuilt (Livy 33.38.12; App., *Syr.* 1; Polyb. 18.3.11, 4.5f., 51.7; Diod. 28.12).

1. Sources of Slaves and the Trade in Slaves

132. 197 BC: after the battle of Cynoscephalae, Flaminius sold some of the 5,000 prisoners and distributed the rest to the soldiers (Livy 33.10.7, 11.2).

133. 195 BC: Flaminius freed many Italian slaves at Corinth, who had been captured and sold in the Punic War (Livy 34.52.4ff.).

134. 195 BC: Cato captured Bergium and sold the inhabitants (Livy 34.21.5f., 16.10).

135. 190s BC: Cato threatened to enslave the inhabitants of all the fortified towns north of the Ebro if they did not dismantle their defences (Polyb. 19.1; Livy 34.17.11; App., *Hisp.* 41; Zon. 9.17.6).

136. 189 BC: Same on Kephallenia was captured by the Romans and the inhabitants sold (Livy 38.28.8, 29.11).

137. 189 BC: the Romans ordered the slaves in Laconia to be handed over to the Achaeans for sale (Livy 38.34.2).

138. 189 BC: Paullus conquered 250 strongholds in Hispania Ulterior and took over 20,000 prisoners, whose fate is uncertain (Livy 37.46.7f., 47.6; Plut., *Aem.* 4.2f.).

139. 189/188 BC: Vulso attacked the Galatians and drove them to the Olympus area; 10,000 were killed and 30,000 taken captive and sold (Livy 38.45).

140. 184 BC: Varro sold the prisoners captured at Corbio (Livy 39.42.1).

141. 182/181 BC: Flaccus gave booty to his soldiers after the capture of Urbiena (Livy 40.16.8f.).

142. 179 BC: after the death of Philip V, the Thracian chief of the Sapaei attacked Abrupolis and took away many prisoners, free and slave (Livy 42.41.11).

143. 177 BC: Pulcher sold 5,632 survivors from his capture of Lesactium, Mutila and Faveria in Istria (Livy 41.11.8).

144. 177 BC: Gracchus killed or captured 80,000 men during his campaign in Sardinia (Livy 41.28.8; Zon. 8.20); the number coming on to the slave-market was so great that it gave rise to the saying *Sardes venales: alius alio nequior* – 'Sardinian (slaves) for sale, one more worthless than the other' (Aur. Vict. 57; Festus 428).

145. 171 BC: during the third Macedonian War, the inhabitants of Mylae in Thessaly were enslaved by Perseus (Livy 42.54.6); Haliartos was captured by Lucretius, the old and young were massacred and 2,500 men were sold as slaves (Livy 42.62.10; Strabo 9.2.30; Paus. 9.32.5, 10.35.2).

146. 170 BC: Perseus captured Uscana in Illyria and sold the men at Stuberra (Livy 43.10.1; Oros. 4.20.38); he then took Oaeneum, killed the men, and eventually sold the women and children, again at Stuberra (Livy 43.19.12, 20.3; Polyb. 38.17.8); at Thisbe the Romans seized the inhabitants' slaves, while possibly at Larissa Cremaste, and certainly at Koroneia and Abdera, the inhabitants were sold into slavery, to be freed later by decree of the Roman Senate (Thisbe: Livy 42.62.12; Lerisa Cremaste: Zon. 9.22.6; Livy, *Epit.* 43; Koroneia and Abdera: Livy, *Epit.* 42.4.11).

147. 168 BC: the women and children in Jerusalem were sold as slaves after the capture of the city by Antiochus IV (I. Macc. 1.32; Jos., *Ant.* 12.251).

148. 167 BC: after the defeat of the Macedonians at Pydna in 168, the Romans captured 70 places in the territory of the Molossians and Atintanians in Epirus and sold 150,000 men into slavery (Livy 45.34; Polyb. 30.16; Strabo 7.322).

149. 155 BC: Nasica captured Delminium and sold the prisoners (Zon. 9.25; Strabo 7.5.5).

150. 154 BC: the Romans helped Massilia when it was attacked by the Oxybieres, captured Aigitna and sold the inhabitants (Polyb. 33.10.3).

151. 151 BC: Galba attacked the Lusitani in Spain, slaughtered some and sold the others to the Gauls (Livy, *Per.* 49; App., *Hisp.* 60).

152. 149-146 BC: the Third Punic War was confined to Africa: at the capture of Tezaga 7,000 Africans were taken prisoner (Oros. 4.22.8); the fall of Carthage itself in 146 BC is described by a number of writers and the number of survivors sold into slavery varies accordingly, but Appian gives it as 50,000 (Zon. 9.30; Oros. 4.23.7; Cic., *Tusc.* 3.22.53; App., *Pun.* 130).

153. 146 BC: the Achaean War culminated in the destruction of Corinth and the enslavement of much of the population by the Romans; the event was noted by many writers, but enslavement by only a few, 12,000 being the only figure quoted (Paus. 7.16.8; Plut., *Quaest. conviv.* 9.1.6; Justin. 34.2f.; Zon. 9.31.8).

154. 144 BC: the Thracian chief Diegylis destroyed Lysimacheia and probably enslaved the inhabitants (Diod. 33.14.2).

155. 141 BC: Servilianus captured a number of towns in Spain and sold off 9,500 prisoners (App., *Hisp.* 68).

156. 133 BC: Scipio captured Numantia and sold nearly all the inhabitants (App., *Hisp.* 98).

157. 133 BC: Titus Didius sold all the citizens of Kolenda in Spain (App., *Hisp.* 99).

158. 129 BC: Himeros, governor of the Parthian king Phraates II, sold a large number of Babylonians to the Medes (Diod. 34.21).

159. 123 BC: in his campaign against the Ligures, Vocontii and Saluvii in Gaul, C. Sextius Calvinus sold as slaves the inhabitants of a wealthy Celtic town (Diod. 34.23).

160. 109 BC: Metellus captured Vaga in Africa and probably sold off the inhabitants (Sall., *Jug.* 69.3).

161. 107 BC: Marius captured Capsa and sold the inhabitants (Sall., *Jug.* 91.6).

162. 103 BC: in the Ptolemaic Wars in Judaea, Ptolemy IX captured Asocheito and sold off 10,000 men (Jos., *Ant.* 13.337).

163. 102/101 BC: Marius' victories at Aquae Sextiae and Vercellae yielded 150,000 captives (Livy, *Epit.* 18).

164. 98 BC: Sertorius captured a Spanish town near Castulo and sold the citizens (Plut., *Sert.* 3.5).

165. 89 BC: in the Social War Pompey sold off the slaves of the inhabitants of Asculum (Livy, *Per.* 76; Flor. 2.6.14; Oros. 5.18.26).

166. 88 BC: in the Mithridatic Wars Fimbria allowed his troops to plunder and enslave the citizens of the Roman allies (Diod. 38.8.l); the citizens of Nicomedia were enslaved (Diod. 38.8.2f.).

167. 86 BC: the inhabitants of the island of Chios were unable to pay a fine to Mithridates and were removed to the Black Sea coast (to be sold as slaves?); they were returned after the peace of Dardanus in 84 BC through the help of Heracleia (Nicholas of Damascus, Jacoby *FGH* 90, F95; Poseidonius, *FGH* 87, F3; App., *Mithr.* 47; Memnon, *FGH* 434, Fl, 23).

168. 86 BC: Sulla sold the Athenians' slaves after the capture of Athens (Livy, *Per.* 81; App., *Mithr.* 38).

169. 85/84 BC: Sulla sold off the inhabitants of many towns of Asia Minor (App., *Mithr.* 61).

170. 76 BC: Sertorius captured Lauro in Spain and possibly sold the citizens (Oros. 5.23.7).

171. 70 BC: Heracleia in Pontus was sacked by Cotta and the inhabitants enslaved.[66]

172. 63 BC: after Pompey had captured Jerusalem many Jewish prisoners were

1. Sources of Slaves and the Trade in Slaves

Fig. 4. Captive on relief from Neumagen

taken to Italy and sold as slaves, but were soon freed (Philon, *Legatio ad Gaium* 23).

173. 58-51 BC: Caesar's conquest of Gaul resulted according to Appian (*Kelt.* 1) in the capture of one million men:
57 BC: he sold off 53,000 of the Atuatuci (*BG* 2.33.6f.).
56 BC: he sold off the captured Veneti (*BG* 3.16.4).
52 BC: the Carnuti at Cenabum were probably sold (*BG* 7.11.8f.).
52 BC: after the capture of Alesia one prisoner was given to each man in the army as booty (*BG* 7.89.5); on the basis of an army with ten legions plus auxiliary troops, Volkmann suggests that 40,000 were enslaved,[67] and many soldiers retained their slaves on the evidence of Caesar's order of 48 BC to the army to leave their slaves and baggage behind on their departure from Brundisium to Greece (*BC* 3.6).

174. 52/51 BC: in the Parthian campaign, Cassius took 30,000 Jews prisoner at Tarichaea in Galilee and sold them (Jos., *Ant.* 14.120; *BJ* 1.180).

175. 51 BC: in Cilicia Cicero handed over the inhabitants of Pindemissum to the slave-dealers (Cic., *Att.* 5.20.5; *Fam.* 15.4.10).

176. 48 BC: Caesar's campaign in Thessaly seems to have used enslavement as a psychological weapon; at Gomphoi it is not clear that the inhabitants were sold but prisoners from there were paraded at Metropolis (Caes., *BC* 3.80; Dio Cass. 41.51), while at Megara the inhabitants were sold off cheaply to their relatives, in order to make a return to free status easier (Dio Cass. 42.14.3).

177. 45 BC: in his campaign against the Pompeian forces in Spain Caesar may have enslaved the inhabitants of Corduba and Hispalis (Dio Cass. 43.39.2).

25

178. 43 BC: in Judaea Cassius sold off the inhabitants of Gophna, Emmaus, Lydda and Thamna for 700 talents (Jos., *Ant.* 14.275; *BJ* 1.222).

179. 42 BC: Cassius demanded 1,500 talents from Tarsus and the city authorities sold off the inhabitants to raise the money (App., *BC* 4.64).

180. 42 BC: Brutus used enslavement as a threat in Lycia, where he used the few prisoners taken at Xanthus to persuade the inhabitants of Patara to surrender (Plut., *Brut.* 30, 31; App., *BC* 4.80; Dio Cass. 47.34.1f.).

181. 35-33 BC: in his Illyrian war Octavian slew the men of military age on the island of Melite near Corcyra in the Adriatic and sold the rest of the inhabitants (App., *Illyr.* 16); in 34 BC Helvius slew the chief men of the Poseni in Illyria and sold the rest (App., *Illyr.* 21).

182. 25 BC: in the war against the Salassi of north Italy 44,000 men were sold at Eporedia, with the condition that none should be released before twenty years had elapsed (Dio Cass. 53.25.4; Strabo 4.205; Suet., *Aug.* 21.2).

2. Piracy and brigandage

The three centuries before the establishment of the Roman Empire and the pacification of the Mediterranean saw a high level of piratical activity. This was not simply a reaction to an increased demand for slaves in Greece and Rome, but more a reflection of the troubled times after the collapse of Alexander's empire, so that there was only occasionally a dominant power capable of policing the seas. Endemic strife led to the presence of disaffected and homeless groups of men ready to prey on defenceless cities, seizing goods and human beings, the latter to be ransomed or sold in the slave-markets which became an established part of life in the eastern Mediterranean. Pirate communities became larger and better organized, so that they could from time to time offer their services as mercenaries to warring rivals (best illustrated by the alliance of the Cilician pirates with Mithridates VI in his three wars against Rome in the first century BC) until their destruction by Pompey in 67 BC. As with the previous period, the studies of Ormerod (1924) and Ziebarth (1929) provide the essential background, with references to the slave-making activities of the pirates. Brigandage, which may be defined as land-based piracy, sometimes involving the capture and sale of prisoners, was a smaller activity; a few references are collected by Ducrey.[68]

The third century saw the rise in succession of Tyrrhenian pirates on the west coast of Italy, Aetolian pirates based on the north coast of the Gulf of Corinth, and finally of Cretan pirates, though their activities overlapped to some extent. The Tyrrhenians were in fact equated by Strabo (5.2.2) with pirates, but much of their activity can be explained as the natural resistance of the Etruscans to Greek colonization. Their elimination, or at least their diversion to the western Mediterranean or the Aegean, was the result of a growing Roman naval presence from c. 300 BC. The Aetolian League benefited from the clash between Macedonia and Egypt around the middle of the third century; Polybius is a hostile witness but the League's control of Delphi and, further afield, of Delos is evidence for its military power which took the form of piratical operations, countered by the police activities of Rhodes. Aetolian depredations tailed off towards the end of the century, and Cretan piracy, always a feature of that island, increased. The Cretans in fact acted as mercenaries during the Social War of 220-217 BC, first for Rhodes but then for the Macedonians led by Philip V. The intervention of Rome in the eastern Mediterranean curbed Macedonian power and the Macedonian Wars tilted the balance towards Rhodes again, so that once more piracy was quelled. But Rome, offended by the equivocal attitude of Rhodes in the third Macedonian War, established Delos as a free port in 167 BC, Rhodes declined, piracy flourished, and Delos assumed its role as the great slave-market of antiquity.

Rome again, by default, instigated the final and greatest outburst of piracy, based on the rocky coastline of Rough Cilicia, where the Taurus range drops abruptly into the sea, and westwards into Pamphylia. During the first half of the third century BC the area was controlled by the Seleucid dynasty of Syria, in the second half by the Ptolemies of Egypt; Syria resumed control from 197 BC onwards, but Rome defeated Antiochus III at the battle of Magnesia in 190 BC and the peace terms limited Syrian control of the seas off Lycia. Rome failed to impose its own authority – in any case, it had a direct interest in the supply of slaves through Delos – and it was from this moment that Cilician piracy really flourished. With its base at Coracesium, the modern Alanya, its activities were first centred on the sea routes of the Levant, but gradually extended along the whole coastline of Asia Minor; Side developed as a slave-market second only to Delos. Even today, almost submerged in the rash of hotels and villas along the Turkish coast, Alanya's Gibraltar-like conformation gives eloquent testimony to the impregnable nature of the pirates' stronghold.

Rome was eventually forced to take action against the pirates, not least because of their support for Mithridates VI in his three wars against the Romans between 88 and 68 BC;[69] Pompey defeated the pirates off Coracesium in 67 BC and on land the earlier campaigns in Lycia and Pamphylia led in turn to the control of the northern slopes of the Taurus range in Cilicia. This virtually marked the end of piracy in the eastern Mediterranean, though pirate mercenaries from the area seem to have been involved in the war between Octavian and Sextus, in which the latter was finally defeated in 36 BC. Elsewhere in the Mediterranean piracy was a threat on a lesser scale as the provisions of the Lex Gabinia of 67 BC and the general course of Pompey's naval campaign make clear. The east coast of the Adriatic remained a problem and both Caesar and Octavian were compelled to act against the long-established Illyrian pirates; the area was clear by the time of the battle of Actium (31 BC). The founding by Octavian of the fleet, with its main bases at Ravenna and Misenum, was a final step in ensuring safe travel in the Mediterranean.

Beyond the limits of the Classical world piracy was prevalent along the Black Sea coasts. Strabo (11.495-6) gives a fascinating description of the tribes inhabiting the harbourless and mountainous east coast at the foot of the Caucasus mountains. Using light portable craft (*kamarai*), they raided their neighbours by land and sea, and carried off prisoners for sale in the cities of the Cimmerian Bosporus. Ziebarth ascribes their activity to the period *c.* 300 BC,[70] and Strabo (11.2.3) names Tanais, the modern Rostov-on-Don, as a principal emporium, founded by Greeks from Panticapaeum on the Bosporus *c.* 500 BC. The attempt by Emmelos to crush these pirates (309-304 BC) was foiled by his early death.[71]

The threat of piracy to those travelling by sea has already been illustrated by the capture and ransom of Plato in *c.* 387 BC; the episode finds a counterpart in the capture and ransom of the young Caesar in 75 BC. These historical events provide the evidence for widespread kidnapping, which in turn became the stuff of New Comedy, as depicted in the works of Menander, Terence and Plautus, which in turn were taken over for rhetorical themes and romances.[72]

183. *c.* 300 BC: the inhabitants of the east coast of the Black Sea indulged in the kidnapping of their neighbours whom they sold as slaves (Strabo 11.495-6).

184. *c.* 260 BC: prisoners from the island of Thera are recorded as settled at Allaria in Crete, where they had captured slaves; the Therans were to be released but to give up the slaves, of whom some were Greek and 45 were non-Greek (*IG* XII, iii, 328).

185. Early third century BC;[73] second half of third century:[74] Aetolian pirates raided Aegiale on the island of Amorgos and kidnapped 30 women, slave and free (*IG* XII, vii, 386).

186. Third century BC: Aetolian pirates seized 280 men from Aulon on the island of Naxos who were later ransomed (*IG* XII, v, 36).

187. 252 BC: prisoners taken by (?) Aetolians on Salamis were ransomed (*IG* II², 1225).

188. 230-220 BC: three women and their children from Theangela in Caria were seized by pirates and offered for sale at the slave-market in Delos, where they were freed by the intervention of Semos the Delian (*IG* XI, iv, 1054).

189. *c.* 230 BC: Illyrian pirates attacked Elis and Messenia (Polyb. 2.5); they ransomed the freemen they had captured at Phoenice in Epirus, but took away the slaves (Polyb. 2.6.5-6); Italian merchants were also seized, which led to the first Illyrian War (Polyb. 2.8.1-2); men and women were seized by trickery from Mothone (Paus. 4.35.7).

190. 217 BC: the Illyrian Scerdilaidas stationed himself, with Macedonian ships seized from Philip V, off Cape Malea and from there attacked shipping and seized merchants (Polyb. 5.101.1-2, 108.1-2).

191. 217/216 BC: the Aetolian chief Bucris descended on Attica and seized Athenian citizens, who were carried off to Crete but later ransomed (*IG* II², 844).

192. *c.* 200 BC: the Cretans owned many Roman slaves captured by Carthage in the Second Punic War (218-201 BC) and sold in Greece; Rome sent a mission to secure their freedom but only Gortyn agreed, releasing 4,000 (Livy 37.60.3-5).

193. Second century BC: the people of Samothrace were captured and later ransomed (*IG* XII, viii, 159).

194. 155/154 BC: a Cretan fleet attacked the island of Siphnos and enslaved the inhabitants (Diod. 31.45).

195. *c.* 100 BC: pirates, possibly Cilician, attacked a shrine of Artemis near Ephesus and took a number of prisoners, free and slave; the citizens of Astypalaia on Kos came to their rescue (*IG* XII, iii, 17).

196. 75 BC: the young Caesar was captured by pirates, probably Cilician, and ransomed (Plut., *Jul.* 1-2; *Crass.* 7; Suet., *Jul.* 4; Velleius 2.41.3).

197. 72 BC: Antonius made an abortive attack on Crete, which was accused of providing pirate mercenaries for Mithridates; the fetters which Antonius had loaded on his ships were used by the Cretans to bind their Roman captives (Flor. 3.7).

198. 69 BC: the pirate Athenodorus attacked Delos and took a number of prisoners.[75]

199. 67 BC: Pompey defeated the Cilician pirates; the prisoners were ransomed or set to work in chains (App., *Mithr.* 96), while others were settled in colonies.

3. Other evidence for the sources of slaves

The onomastic evidence for the origins of slaves, both ethnically and geographically, is of increasing importance for this period, as also for the Roman Empire, and has been discussed by a number of scholars on the basis of slave names recorded in inscriptions and literature. The difficulties are considerable, since the purchaser might simply coin a name for his new slave, particularly if he came from an area where the language presented difficulties. The maximum reliability is obtained from those names that are accompanied by a precise ethnic description, though obviously this seriously diminishes the number of instances.

For Greece the manumission records from Delphi provide valuable evidence for one particular place between *c.* 200 and 50 BC.[76] These inscriptions appertain to a limited category of slaves freed at the shrine of Apollo as trust sales to the god, and are discussed, with tables, by Westermann.[77] He shows a proper scepticism about any attempt to extrapolate the position at Delphi to a wider area of central Greece, both as regards total numbers of slaves and changes during the period in question. What is clear from his table 1 is that there was a marked reversal at Delphi from a preponderance of slaves brought in from outside in the early years to a majority born there (*oikogeneis*) later on. Table 2 analyses chronologically and geographically the areas from which slaves were drawn: at first, Greece and the Balkans provide a large number, with Asia Minor and the Levant second, but by the second half of the second century BC the role of Greece has declined (coinciding, no doubt, with the growing influence of Rome), while the East provided as many as before; for the final period, of course, foreign-born slaves are a negligible proportion. The few Italian slaves in the early period only emphasize the marginal role played by the West, and their disappearance and that of foreign-born slaves generally is ascribed by Westermann to the dominant position achieved by Rome after 146 BC. However, it should be noted that Finley commented that Westermann was using less than half the texts available, and that his regional groupings of foreign-born slaves were not entirely satisfactory.[78] He himself notes that one-fifth of the Delphi slaves came from the areas round the Black Sea, including the northern coast of Asia Minor, and cites the evidence of slave-burials from Hellenistic Rhodes where perhaps one-third are derived from the same region.[79] Westermann[80] had earlier suggested that Rhodes had received a high proportion from Asia Minor generally, using Rostovtzeff's conclusions.[81]

For Italy, two pioneering studies of the onomastic evidence were made by Bang.[82] The names recorded in epigraphy and literature for the Republic indicate that generally slaves came from areas outside Roman rule and that, by contrast with Greece, up to one-third were derived from countries to the north and west from the late third century BC onwards.

A compact source of evidence for late Republican Italy is provided by the lists of *magistri* and *magistrae* from Minturnae, on the river Liris between Latium and Campania.[83] They date from the period 100-50 BC, and a final total of 170 names, representing 312 individual slaves, is drawn from the annual lists of twelve persons serving the minor cults of Ceres, Venus, Mercury, Spes, etc. Of these a mere one per cent are of Celtic origin, conflicting with Bang's one-third just quoted, and the historical evidence of Marius' victories at Aquae Sextiae in 102 BC and Vercellae in 101 BC, which produced 150,000 captives. In his discussion Johnson explains the difficulty by arguing that the Celtic element among the slaves at Minturnae had no great interest in the cults and that the lists need represent no more than, say, one-tenth of all the slaves at Minturnae:[84] the apparent eastern predominance, which Westermann unfortunately accepted at face value, is possibly quite misleading.[85] This underlines the problem of generalizing from particular instances such as Delphi and Minturnae.

Finally, literary evidence provides frequent examples of the kidnapping and sale of children, and the sale of those captured by pirates and not subsequently ransomed; the themes of Greek New Comedy employed by Menander were taken over by Plautus and Terence in the third and second centuries BC.[86]

The trade in slaves

The immediate sale of captives into slavery on the conclusion of a battle or a campaign is again attested, as in the preceding period. In 221 BC the Aetolians established a market at Clarion in the territory of Megalopolis in Arcadia, though they took much of their booty on board with them when they left the Peloponnese (Polyb. 4.6.3, 9.10, 10.4). Similarly, Philip V, when he was campaigning in the Peloponnese, had the habit of picking a large open space for such sales, at no great distance from the scene of his victory. In Elis, for example, and particularly after his capture of Thalamai he chose the nearby city of Heraia for the sale (Polyb. 4.73.5, 75.2, 77.5), and again later (Polyb. 4.80.16). Next, Dyme and Tegea were used (Polyb.

4.86.4; 5.24.10), and finally, Leucade, where he used his ships to carry the booty, perhaps because demand in the Peloponnese had decreased. The slave-dealers attracted by such sales are attested by two biblical references: the Seleucid expedition into Judaea of 165 BC drew merchants, ready with cash, to buy the captured Jews (I Macc. 3.41; II Macc. 8.9-10). Otherwise, references to dealers are sparse, no doubt reflecting the continuing hostility to such entrepreneurs and to the enslavement of fellow citizens. Barbarians were also active on the fringes of the Classical world, like the Celtic Boii who sold slaves into Italy in 230 BC (Zon. 8.19).

As in the immediately preceding period, what may be called established trade in slaves took place at different levels, from the local fair at the bottom of the scale to the great commercial centres. Of the latter the best attested centre is, of course, Delos, handed over in 166 BC by the Romans to the Athenians, who turned it into a free port in order to damage Rhodian trade. Thus it became the great slave-market of the Aegean, used extensively by the Cilician pirates (Strabo 14.5.2). This much quoted passage from Strabo refers, perhaps rhetorically, to tens of thousands of slaves passing through in one day, and emphasizes the importance of Roman demand, stimulated by the destruction of Carthage in the West and Corinth in the East in 146 BC. The Cilician and Pamphylian pirates also used the Pamphylian port of Side for the trade (Strabo 14.3.2). References exist for other centres: Tanais on the Don (Strabo 11.2.3); Byzantium (Polyb. 4.38.4); Ephesus (Varro, *LL* 8.21); Rome (Livy 26.16.6; Plautus, *Curc.* 481); and Aquileia (Strabo 5.1.8); while Athens, Chios, Corinth, Aegina, Rhodes and cities of the Phoenician coast such as Tyre must also have been much used.[87]

References to intermittent trade, associated with festivals at religious sanctuaries, come from Actium, where games associated with the cult of Apollo were held biennially,[88] and Baitokaike in Syria, a twice-monthly market at the temple of Zeus (*OGIS* 262, ll. 26-7), both of the Hellenistic period. At the major centres sales were conducted in the agora or forum, preceded by notice of the sale by the public herald and subject to a sales tax levied by the city authority; they were probably at a fixed time and point. At Athens it has been suggested that they were held every month at the new moon, and there are references to a particular point in the agora.[89] At Delos, with its enormous trade, an attractive suggestion has been made that the so-called 'Agora of the Italians' may have served as such a market (fig. 5), a claim denied and supported in later papers.[90] This apparently Franco-Italian contest has been re-opened by Le Roy, who concludes: 'L'identification de l'Agora des Italiens avec un marché aux esclaves n'a plus de valeur', and argues that it had a more general commercial function in which slaves no doubt played some, but by no means an exclusive, part.[91] He sees the courtyard, with its restricted access and lack of shops around its periphery, as a sort of fairground with visiting merchants camped round its edges. In a postscript Le Roy dismisses a suggestion by Rauh that

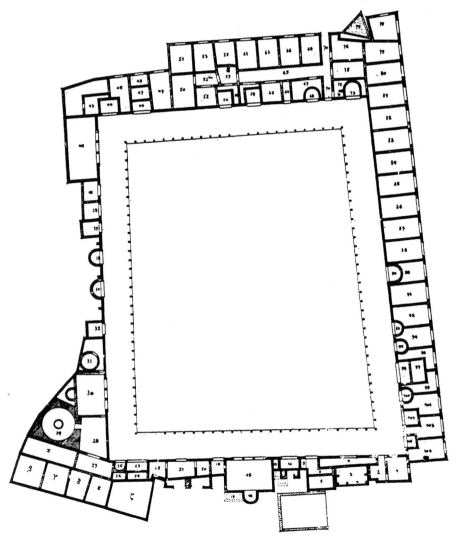

Fig. 5. Plan of the Agora of the Italians, Delos

it served as a sports centre.[92] Clearly, absolute proof is lacking but Cocco and Coarelli make a good case: the very large size of the structure, the utilitarian aspect of the courtyard, the presence of only two very narrow entrances, and of baths, latrines and wells may be said to argue for transitory use by very large numbers during the period after the slave revolt of 130 BC.

Coarelli continues with a useful if speculative discussion of the Greek and Roman slave-market (*statarion* and *venalicium* respectively) and suggests that there is epigraphical evidence for the Greek word at Thyateira, Magnesia-on-Maeander, Ephesus and Akmonia, all in Asia Minor and of the late first century BC to the early first century AD.[93] At Magnesia, the building at the south-west angle of the agora (fig. 6), with a date of *c.* 100 BC, identified as a *prytaneion* bears, he claims, resemblances to the Agora of the Italians at Delos, while at Ephesus an inscription with the Latinized form, *statarium*, of the Greek word suggests that the large porticoed piazza south-west of the commercial agora and associated temple of Serapis may perhaps be identified as the slave-market (fig. 7); its date is AD 42-3, so strictly it belongs to the next period. Finally, two fragmentary inscriptions of Republican date from Puteoli may indicate the presence of a *venalicium* in the town. There is other evidence, direct and indirect, for the slave-trade at Puteoli in the late Republican period,[94] and it is interesting to note that it bore the title of 'Little Delos' – *Delus minor* – at the end of the second century BC.[95]

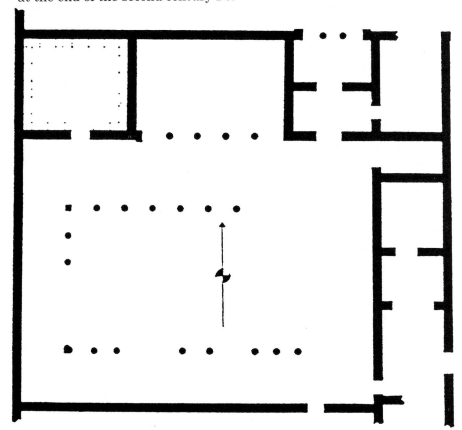

Fig. 6. Plan of the *prytaneion* at Magnesia-on-Maeander

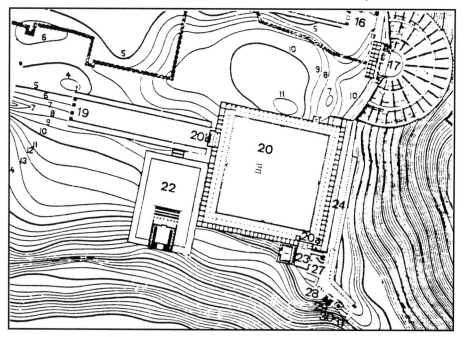

Fig. 7. Plan showing piazza and Temple of Serapis at Ephesus

The Roman Empire

The pacification of the Mediterranean by Augustus meant that warfare was, for a time at least, no longer to play such a dominant part in the supply of slaves. The demand remained constant, however, and may actually have increased as the imperial household and wealthy citizens enlarged their domestic staff, let alone the demand from the public sector. So, it was necessary to resort to the supply from the children of existing slaves (*vernae*), the exposure of infants or the sale of children through poverty, self-sale for debt, penal condemnation to slavery (*servitus poenae*), and, always an important element, from the activities of slave-traders in border areas. The change was by no means sudden: after Actium, Augustus waged campaigns in north Italy, Spain, Pannonia, Gaul and Galilaea, and his successors were intermittently engaged in the acquisition of new provinces such as Britain and Dacia, frontier warfare, or the suppression of risings such as the two Jewish revolts, which must all have supplied their quota. Only with the Hadrianic policy of static frontiers and the relative peace of the Antonines can there have been an almost complete cessation of warfare as a source of slaves. However, from the late third century down to the sixth there are numerous instances of the taking of prisoners by both sides during the incursions into the Empire from the north, by waves of invasions of Franks, Saxons, Goths, Huns and Vandals.

Sources of slaves

1. Warfare

200. 27-25 BC: the campaigns of Augustus in Spain led to a number of cases of enslavement of the hill tribes in the north (Flor. 2.33.52).

201. 24 BC: in his campaign against the Ethiopians, who had attacked and enslaved the inhabitants of towns in Upper Egypt, Petronius defeated and enslaved them; he sold some of the prisoners at Alexandria and allocated 1,000 to Augustus (Strabo 17.820).

202. 22 BC: the Astures and Cantabri revolted, and were captured and enslaved (Dio Cass. 54.5.1f.); in 19 BC they killed their masters and rebelled, but were defeated and, presumably, returned to slavery (Dio Cass. 54.11.2ff.).

203. 20 BC: Augustus enslaved the inhabitants of Cyzicus because they had killed Roman citizens there (Dio Cass. 54.7.6).

204. 12 BC: Tiberius campaigned against the Scordisci in Pannonia and sold most of the young men (Dio Cass. 54.31.3).

205. 11 BC: the conquest by Drusus of the German tribes of the Cherusci, Suebi and Sicambri is said to have led to enslavement (Flor. 2.30.25), but Volkmann interprets this as a rhetorical response to the earlier success of the tribes against the Romans.[96]

206. 11 BC: the Thracian Bessii were enslaved (Dio Cass. 34.7).

207. 6-4 BC: during the campaign of Varus in Galilaea the city of Sephoris was captured and the inhabitants enslaved (Jos., *BJ* 2.68; *Ant.* 17.288).

208. The two great Jewish revolts of AD 66-70 and AD 132-5 produced many instances of enslavement:

AD 67: 2,130 women and children at Jaffa (Jos., *BJ* 3.304-5); 1,200 women and children at Jotapata (*BJ* 3.337); at Tarichaea 6,000 captives were sent to work on the Corinth Canal and 30,400 were sold (*BJ* 3.532ff.); 2,200 prisoners were taken at Jordan (*BJ* 4.436); 1,000 prisoners were taken at Idumaea (*BJ* 4.447); the women and children were enslaved at Gerasa (*BJ* 4.488).

AD 68: the women and children were enslaved at Bethel and Ephraim (*BJ* 4.551-2) and Machairous (*BJ* 7.208).

AD 70: the capture of Jerusalem produced 97,000 captives; those over the age of 17 were sent in chains to the Egyptian mines and quarries or to the amphitheatre (*BJ* 6.416ff.).

AD 115: the Jewish revolt in Cyrenaica may have led to enslavement, but this is not specifically stated (Dio Cass. 68.32.1; SHA, *Hadr.* 5.8; Euseb., *Hist. Eccl.* 4.2).

AD 132-5: after the suppression of the second revolt, a vast quantity of prisoners were sold at the Terebinth market at Hebron; any not sold were taken to Gaza for a further sale or for shipment to Egypt (Dio Cass. 59.14.l; Jerome, *ad Jerem.* 31.15).

209. AD 172: in their negotiations with Marcus Aurelius, the Germanic Quadi were only willing to return those Roman prisoners who were not suitable for sale or work (Dio Cass. 71.13.2).

210. AD 174: the Jazyges returned 100,000 captive Romans (Dio Cass. 71.16.2).

211. In the Parthian Wars of the second half of the second century a number of cities were captured, but the only specific mention of enslavement was after the

capture of Ctesiphon by Septimius Severus in AD 197 when the women and children were enslaved (Dio Cass. 75.12.1ff.).

212. AD 233: in his Persian campaign Severus Alexander took prisoners but these were ransomed (SHA, *Sev.* 55.3).

213. AD 250: after the capture of Thracian Philippopolis by the Goths, Trebonianus Gallus handed over the inhabitants to the enemy (Amm. Marc. 31.5.17; Zos. 1.24.2).

214. AD 264: Tarraco was plundered by the Franks (Eutrop. 9.8.2; Aurel., *Vict.* 33).

215. AD 310: in his campaign against the Bructeri Constantine consigned his captives to slavery or to the arena (*Panegyr. Lat.* 7.12).

216. AD 350-5: the invasion of Gaul by the Franks, Alamanni and Saxons led to the enslavement of large numbers of the inhabitants (Zos. 3.1.1; Liban., *Orat.* 12.44.48; 18.34) who were however released after Julian's victory at Strasbourg in 357 (Zos. 3.4.4; Amm. Marc. 17.10.8).

217. AD 368: the Alamanni under Rando captured Mainz and carried off a large number of the citizens (Amm. Marc. 27.10.1-2).

218. AD 372-3: the usurper Firmus plundered Caesarea (Jol) in North Africa (Oros. 7.33.5; Symm., *Ep.* 1.64).

219. AD 376: the Goths under Fritigern again attacked Philippopolis and enslaved the inhabitants (Amm. Marc. 31.6.7).

220. AD 395-6: Alaric and the Goths captured all the towns of Greece except Athens and Thebes and enslaved the women and children (Zos. 5.5.5-8; Procop., *B. Goth.* 3.38).

221. AD 405: Stilicho defeated the Goths under Radagais at Faesulae, near Florence, enrolled 12,000 of noble birth in his army and sold the rest (Oros. 7.37.16f.).

222. AD 424: Cartagena and Hispalis were seized by the Vandals and the inhabitants probably enslaved (Hyd. *c.* 86).

223. AD 439: Geiseric and the Vandals captured Carthage and enslaved many of the inhabitants (Victor Vit., *Hist. Persecut. Afric.* 1.12).

224. AD 452: Attila captured Aquileia and killed or enslaved the inhabitants (Paulus Diac., *Hist. Rom.* 14.9; Marcell., *Comes* 84; Procop., *BV* 3.40.30f.).

225. AD 455: the Vandals under Geiseric captured Rome and took many captives back to their base at Carthage (Procop., *BV* 1.5.4); once in Africa, the Vandals and Moors divided them, separating husbands from wives and children from parents (Victor Vit. 1.25).

226. AD 456: Theodoric and the Goths captured Bracara in Galicia and took the inhabitants captive (Hyd. *c.* 174 in Mommsen 1892-8, ii, 29).

227. AD 467: Geiseric and the Vandals attacked Zakynthos and took 500 prisoners (Procop., *BV* 1.22).

228. AD 470: the inhabitants of Javols in Aquitania were taken prisoner and put in chains (Auson., *Ep.* 5.13).

229. AD 476: the Vandals were clearly in possession of slaves on the evidence of the negotiations between the emperor Zeno and Geiseric (Malchus Philadelph. fr. 3).

230. AD 507: the Burgundians overran Brionde in the Auvergne, killed the men and took the rest prisoner (Gregory of Tours, *Miracles of St Julian*, c. 7).

231. AD 533: after Belisarius reconquered Africa at the battle of Trikamaron, much of the Vandal army was taken captive and the women and children enslaved (Procop., *BV* 2.14.7f.).

1. Sources of Slaves and the Trade in Slaves

232. AD 536: Belisarius captured Naples and his men took the women and children captive, but they were later released on the orders of Belisarius (Procop., *BG* 1.10).

233. AD 538: the Goths, with help from the Burgundians, captured Milan, slaughtered the men and enslaved 30,000 women (Procop., *BG* 2.7, 2.21).

234. *c.* AD 538: two generals of Belisarius captured strongholds in the Cottian Alps and enslaved the inhabitants (Procop., *BG* 6.28.33).

235. AD 538: the Huns attacked Illyria and took the women and children prisoner, whereupon the Illyrian troops in the Roman army deserted and returned to their own country (Procop., *BG* 7.11.15).

236. AD 540: the Persians captured Dura on the Euphrates and enslaved the inhabitants, but later 12,000 men were ransomed (Procop., *BP* 2.5.8f.).

237. AD 543-4: Sergius and Pudentius defeated the Moors near Leptis Magna and enslaved their women and children (Procop., *BV* 4.21.14); at the same time the Moorish chief Iabdas enslaved many Libyans (Procop., *BV* 4.13.1).

238. AD 543: the Antae attacked Thrace and enslaved Romans living there (Procop., *BG* 7.14.11).

239. AD 550: the Sclaveni crossed the Ister and captured Topeiros on the Via Egnatia, killed 15,000 men and took the women and children prisoner (Procop., *BG* 7.38.18).

2. Piracy and brigandage

Ziebarth concludes his study of piracy and maritime trade in ancient Greece with Pompey's defeat of the Cilician pirates in 67 BC.[97] Ormerod takes a wider geographical view, but even his final chapter on the Empire deals quite briefly with the last spasms of piracy.[98] As noted earlier, the introduction of the standing fleet after Actium gradually led to the virtual elimination of this threat to travel and trade in the Mediterranean.[99] Not until the confusion of the third century was the Roman command of the sea threatened; the decline and fragmentation of the navy was accompanied by the incursions of Scythians and Goths into the Black Sea and eventually the Aegean, using tactics learnt from the piratical tribes of the Black Sea coasts.[100] Not until Diocletian obtained power in AD 284 was Roman control of the sea re-established, to be continued into the fourth century with very different naval forces from those established by Augustus.[101] Under the Empire land travel was also more secure and consequently piracy and brigandage as a large-scale source of slaves may be discounted for much of the Imperial period, except in outlying areas such as the Red and Black Seas.[102]

3. Other evidence for sources of slaves

As in the previous period, nomenclature has been invoked as an indication of the origins of slaves, subject to the caveat entered by Varro (*LL* 8.21): 'If three men each bought a slave in Ephesus, one might take his name from that of the seller Artemidorus and call him Artemas; another from the

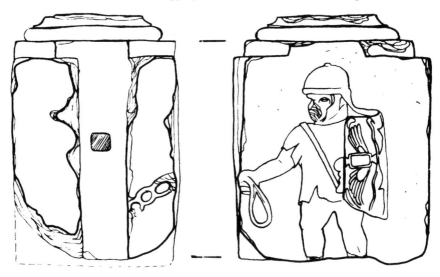

Fig. 8. Roman soldier holding chain on column base from Mainz

region in which he made the purchase, hence Ion from Ionia; the third names his Ephesius from Ephesus'. But for Rome in the imperial period it seems fair to conclude that Greek and Latin names for slaves and freedmen give a broad indication of eastern or western origin, subject to the proviso that Greek names may apply to a large area extending north to the lower Danube and the shores of the Black Sea and east to the remoter parts of Asia Minor.[103]

Bang studied the onomastic evidence for changes in sources between the Republic and the Empire.[104] He claimed that in the earlier period the bulk of slaves were drawn from outside the limits of Roman rule, and particularly from the East, whereas under the Empire the greater part came necessarily from within the frontiers. In fact, he argued that many came from Italy itself, but this conclusion was attacked by Barrow on the grounds that Italian-born freedmen would, out of pride, have requested an epigraphical memorial of their origins, whereas the vast numbers from the traditional areas of the East and the recently conquered provinces of the West, condemned to menial work, would have left no such record, apart from a passing mention in literary sources.[105] Bang's largely epigraphical sources were supplemented by more general references in Gordon's useful general study which leads, however, to the stereotyped conclusion about the extraordinarily mixed character of the population of the Empire and the extent to which this influenced the second-generation *vernae*.[106] Tenney Frank's study of a large number of inscriptions from Rome and Italy led him to suggest that nine-tenths of the population of Rome under the early Empire were of foreign descent, and that this was to some extent true of the rest of Italy, though Barrow expressed doubt about the latter conclusion.[107] Westermann broadly accepted these earlier views, but offered a somewhat paradoxical conclusion that 'the great majority of the slaves who appear in any province of the Empire were native to that locality'; clearly he is referring to *vernae* since he speaks of 'uncertainty as to the original home of the parents of these slaves'.[108]

Literature and art offer general support for these conclusions without affording any good evidence. Thus Seneca (*Ep. Mor.* 80.9) can speak of Scythian or Sarmatian slaves, Martial (*Ep.* 7.80) of a slave from the Danube area, Juvenal (*Sat.* 9.42) can ask for a couple of strong Moesian porters to carry him to the circus, and Cicero (*ad Att.* 4.16.13) can lament the lack of artistic talent in slaves from Britain. Sculpture gives graphic representations of chained captives, presumably destined for slavery, as on the column base from the headquarters of the legionary fortress at Mainz (fig. 8) or the grave-relief from Nickenich near Bonn (fig. 9).[109]

More relevant, especially as regards date, are the sculptured representations of captive barbarians, again intended for slavery, which appear on the great commemorative monuments at Rome. Thus, Trajan's Column, which depicts the events of the Dacian Wars of AD 101-2 and 105-6, bears graphic illustrations of bound prisoners and of a prison camp.[110] The Aurelian Column records the wars waged by Marcus Aurelius, on the Danube again, against the Marcomanni and their allies in AD 172-5 and has graphic depictions of the execution of tribal chieftains, contrasting with their captive womenfolk; finally, the Arch of Septimius Severus carries detailed views of chained Parthians in the emperor's campaigns of AD 197-9 (fig. 10).[111] The contemporary views complement the recorded instances of the capture and enslavement of Rome's enemies.

The trade in slaves

Finley's comment: 'No serious study of ... the slave-trade exists, to my knowledge' was partly met by Harris.[112] This sketch, rather than a study in detail, was part of a symposium on trade in the Roman Empire held at the American Academy at Rome in 1978: the first half dwells speculatively on sources and numbers but the second part provides a useful summary of the then state of knowledge, however imperfect, for the period 50 BC to AD 150.

As in the previous period, the sale of slaves covers a wide commercial spectrum, from the individual purchases in towns and villages to the mass transactions in the agora or forum of certain recognized trading centres. Between these extremes were the more haphazard sales, as at games and fairs, or, in a period of warfare, at the successful conclusion of a campaign. For the last, the sales occurred at some designated centre where the slave-traders following in the wake of the army could quickly congregate. But, in a discussion of the slave-trade in general, it is the major centres

Fig. 9. Roman soldier controlling two captives with neck-chains on relief from Nickenich

Fig. 10. Chained Parthian with Roman soldier on the Arch of Septimius Severus, Rome

with a permanent mechanism for slave-sales that require first consideration; there will necessarily be some repetition of references from the previous period.

Asia Minor and the Black Sea area, including the lands bordering the Danube, continued to provide vast numbers of slaves both for the eastern provinces and Italy; to a lesser degree they also appeared in the western provinces, possibly as the result of successive sales at different centres. Delos suffered a sharp setback after it was sacked by the pirates allied to Mithridates in 88 and 69 BC; in any event, the suppression of the Cilician pirates by Pompey in 67 BC robbed it of much of its importance as a main centre for the slave-trade in the East, though it still retained some commercial importance. The major towns of the coast and interior of Asia Minor presumably continued to serve as trading centres, probably on an increased scale: Byzantium, Pergamum, Thyateira, Ephesus, Magnesia-on-Maeander (where a *statarion* was in existence in the first century BC), Miletus, Acmonia (where again a first-century *statarion* is attested), Sardis, Xanthus, Myra and Side.[113] For the Levant the evidence is less secure, though Syria was a great source of slaves;[114] Harris suggests Tarsus, and lists with negative evidence Tyre, Sidon, Antioch, Aradus, Tripolis and Berytus;[115] he also postulates a regular trading centre at Gaza, where the Jewish prisoners were sold after the fall of Jerusalem and the rebellion of AD 132-5. The role of major temple sites is attested by the inscription from Baitokaike in Syria, where the great temple of Zeus Baitokaikeus was associated with a regular slave-market.[116] The Aegean islands probably continued to serve the seaborne trade: Mytilene on Lesbos – Martial (7.80.9) speaks of a Mytilenian slave-dealer, *Mytilenaeus Mango* – Chios, Samos (*Aesopica* 41, 84), and Rhodes.[117]

At the north end of the Aegean, Amphipolis, conveniently placed near the mouth of the Strymon, evidently served as a major slave-market for Thrace and the Danubian provinces. The well-known and evocative Greek tombstone found there in 1939 has attracted an abundant literature: it commemorates a freedman, Aulus Capreilius Timotheus, described as *sômatenporos* (correctly *sômatemporos*), a slave-dealer, in the inscription below the upper register, a characteristic funeral banquet scene.[118] The lower register depicts a line of eight male slaves in belted tunics, chained by the neck, accompanied by two unchained women and two children, and led by a man wearing a hooded cloak (*paenula*), possibly the slave-dealer himself. The central register adds yet another dimension, two pairs of men, each carrying a bronze cauldron, led by a fifth man with an amphora on his shoulder and a second in his left hand, reflecting the outward trade of luxury goods, such as bronze vessels and wine, so keenly sought by barbarian and particularly Celtic peoples. Harris notes that the dead man was the only Greek (if such he was) to confess his trade of *sômatemporos* on a tombstone, so going against the normal prejudice against the trade.[119]

Fig. 11. Wall-painting from House of Julia Felix, Pompeii

It is, of course, fairly late in date (first century BC to first century AD) by
which time this feeling may have abated.

In the West, Italy's main market continued to be in the Forum at Rome,
ad Castoris, with Aquileia in the north; elsewhere Capua (*CIL* X, 8222),
Brundisium (Suet., *De gramm.* 25), Puteoli, and possibly Pompeii traded
in slaves.[120] The evidence for a market at Pompeii depends on a wall-
painting from the House of Julia Felix (II.4.3) where a woman presents a
young girl before two men seated on a bench in the forum (fig. 11).[121] Harris
follows Étienne in accepting this as the sale of a slave, but the evidence
cannot be accepted as unequivocal.[122] The wall-painting has most recently
been described in neutral terms as 'the presentation of a young girl before
seated magistrates'.[123] Ostia would almost certainly have functioned as a
major slave-market in view of its close links with Rome as a trade centre,
but precise evidence is so far lacking and Meiggs does not discuss the
possibility.[124] The great Piazzale delle Corporazioni would be an obvious
candidate and it is interesting to note that Lapalus compared the Agora of
the Italians at Delos to it in certain respects before the later suggestion
that the latter may have been a slave-market.[125] The so far unlocated
Forum Vinarium at Ostia would be another possible candidate.

Harris also collected such evidence as survives for actual slave-merchants,
but this is only useful where it adds substance to the evidence for markets,
just discussed, or provides details of the methods of sale, as in the Capua

Fig. 12. Tombstone from Capua with relief showing slave-sale

tombstone already mentioned (fig. 12), where there is a relief of an actual slave-sale.[126]

Actual procedure in the slave-market was discussed by Wallon and more recently by Westermann and is briefly presented here in order to complete this section.[127] Within the agora or forum the merchants (Greek, *andropodokapêloi*; Latin, *mangones*) exhibited their slaves in the designated area (fig. 13); these merchants should no doubt be distinguished from the slave-traders already discussed, who served as wholesalers, purchasing slaves in quantity in other areas, transporting them by sea or road to the final market, and particularly in the case of seaborne cargoes making themselves responsible for port formalities, including import tax. The slaves were exposed naked on a wooden platform (*pratêrion*, *catasta*), in the open or in a pen if they were of high value, where their physical appearance could be assessed. The curious practice of chalking the feet of imported slaves was observed in the West, and Wallon suggests that prisoners of war wore a chaplet (*corona*), though this may have been confined to sales in the rear of the army (*sub corona vendere*).[128] A placard might be placed round the neck of the slave, with his name, age and origin, which would then be publicly called out at the moment of sale. The merchant, either at his own initiative or at the request of a prospective purchaser, might put the slave through his paces to demonstrate his liveliness and agility. It was, in fact, a requirement of Roman law, under

Fig. 13. Bronze plaque recording a '*mango*' (slave-merchant) from Switzerland

the *edicta* of the curule aediles, that the placard should state any physical or character defects, and the vendor was required to disclose any legal liability against the slave, all designed to protect the purchaser, as in the case of sales in early Greece.[129]

The Republican tax of five per cent on manumission was continued under the Empire and in AD 7 Augustus introduced a sales tax of two per cent, levied on purchasers who were Roman citizens. This was raised to four per cent by Nero, who tried to compel the vendors to pay it, but without success. This was, of course, quite distinct from any import or export tariff levied at harbours. The details of sales were embodied in contracts, of which a number survive in the Egyptian papyri or on wax tablets, such as those from Puteoli or Dacia.[130] These state name or ethnic origin, as required by law, physical condition and price; the contract would be officially registered and provide the basis for the sales tax.

Slaves in Greek Agriculture

Introduction

There is scarcely any need to stress the importance of agriculture in the pre-Classical Greek world and Republican Italy. The development of human society into the Neolithic period was based on an irreversible shift to settled communities, which had developed crop-growing and stock-breeding. In the succeeding Bronze and Iron Ages technological innovation coupled with wealth derived from agricultural surpluses fostered trade and its counterpart, war. A free peasantry provided a massive resource of strong and hardy fighters, inured to physical hardship, who were led by an aristocratic minority. The complete conquest of an indigenous population could result in the development of communal slavery in the form of serfs attached to the land, while the taking and sparing of captives led to the growth of chattel-slaves who could be treated as property to be bought or sold without restriction. In the latter case the captors might return to their farms or holdings and resume cultivation with the help of slaves allocated to them as the prizes of war. Those with a moralizing instinct argued that this inevitably caused the decay of the old rustic values and eventually a flight from the land to the comfortable life of the cities, a theme more in vogue among Roman writers than Greek.

Nevertheless, agriculture in one form or another continued to underpin Greek and Roman society, with slave-labour as an important element, though not necessarily on its own. But any attempt to tease out the archaeological element of slavery in Greek and Roman agriculture encounters the same problem as in other aspects of ancient society, the difficulty of detecting anything specifically servile as opposed to free in rural life.

So the survey of agriculture in this and the next two chapters will be largely confined to a description of possible slave-quarters in Greek and Roman settlements and farms. It will not concern itself with serfs or communal slaves, such as the Spartan helots, living side by side with their overlords, since they were attached to the land rather than to the master and, to the writer's knowledge, there exists no study of, for example, Greek rural settlement which can be specifically attributed to such a class of farm labour. Literature and epigraphy will not be used except as background since this evidence has already been widely quarried by other writers.

Geometric to Archaic periods

The ancient Greek sources for agricultural practice in general and, more specifically, for the role of different forms of labour are slight in comparison with the later Roman authorities.[1] For Homeric and pre-Classical Greece we turn naturally to the *Odyssey* with its numerous scattered references and to Hesiod's *Works and Days,* with its famous description of a year in the life of a farm; for Classical Greece, Xenophon's *Oeconomicus,* with a central date of *c.* 400 BC, provides the main source.

From such works we can obtain a picture of a complex but carefully regulated agricultural system, with its roots going well back into the Mycenaean Bronze Age. As yet it is probably true that insufficient work has been carried out in Greek environmental archaeology to provide the corresponding material evidence as at Western European sites of the same period. The picture which we may infer shows the traditional division into stock-breeding and agriculture, including vine- and olive-growing, with a host of ancillary activities such as bee-keeping, the rearing of poultry, fruit- and vegetable-growing and so on.[2] What prevents a generalized view of Greek agriculture in the lands west, north and east of the Aegean is the extreme fragmentation of the component states due to geographical and pedological factors.[3] Of this the most striking example is Attica itself, where the dearth of good cultivable land prevented crop-growing on any large scale; instead, there was a concentration on a pastoral economy, centred on sheep and goats, and the olives for which Attica was famous. But corn was necessary for the staple diet of bread, a need accentuated by the growth of towns. The island of Aegina, the city of Corinth, and above all Athens, were compelled to import vast quantities of grain, not from adjacent corn-growing areas (with the exception of Euboea) but from farther afield – Macedon, the Thracian Chersonese, the coastal plains of the Black Sea, the Near East, Cyprus and Phoenicia, and ultimately from Egypt and Libya, with Rhodes acting as an international market. Later, when Macedon took control of the Aegean and cut off Athens from Pontus and Asia, there was a switch to trade with the West; Thucydides (3.86) records that Sicilian corn was coming to the Peloponnese as early as 427 BC. On the other hand, there were areas of the mainland of Greece where river valleys and plains, allied with favourable soils, made crop-growing a practicable proposition: such were Boeotia, Locris, Phocis, the area between Corinth and Sicyon, Phlius, Argolis, the Eurotas and Messenian plains, Elis and Thessaly. The last was especially important because of the extent of its plains, particularly along the Peneios where there is evidence of the growth of large estates and a baronial class. Elsewhere in the Greek world, for instance in the colonized coastal areas of the Pontus and the Aegean coast of Asia Minor, crop-growing was self-evidently a major agricultural activity in view of the corn trade with Athens referred to above.

Alongside this very generalized description of Greek agricultural practice must be placed what is known of the various forms of rural settlement. In the Bronze Age the mainland was dominated by the Mycenaean citadel with the characteristic *megaron* house, the rectangular porch and hall structure developed to palatial status at Mycenae itself; in Asia Minor, at least in the Troad, the same house plan can be observed at Troy II and VI. In Minoan Crete the complexity of the royal palaces disguises the presence of this basic type, but in the east wing at Knossos it can be detected in the residential area (the King's Megaron and Queen's Megaron). The problem is whether such a widespread but simple plan[4] provides a stereotype for Greek rural settlement and, if so, whether there was any provision for slave-quarters, since this institution is thought to have been a feature of Mycenaean civilization. On balance, this seems unlikely and slaves were either housed separately in simple huts or patriarchally treated as members of the owner's family.

In any event, the breaking of Mycenaean power by the Dorian invasions and the interruption of the Greek Dark Age of the eleventh to ninth centuries BC meant a loss of continuity, presumably, in rural settlement, with dispossession of the different classes of landowner. Those who did not flee, either to other areas of the mainland or further afield as colonists, became serfs of their conquerors, like the helots of Sparta or the *clarotes* of Crete. If not specifically named, they were later termed *douloi* or 'slaves' by the Greeks, but they were evidently the property of the state and regarded as serfs attached to the land rather than as the personal property of landowners. In any case, as already stated, they do not form part of this inquiry.

In the eighth and seventh centuries BC our knowledge of slave conditions in the countryside is entirely literary. From Homer, and mostly from the *Odyssey*, we derive a generalized picture of agricultural life, based on a stratified class structure of king, nobles, freemen and slaves, which probably reflects life in the Greek Iron Age, unlike the warfare of the *Iliad* with its mixture of Bronze and Iron Age features. Heitland (1921) still provides a useful summary of pre-Classical Greek agriculture from the literary standpoint, principally the Homeric poems and Hesiod. More broadly, Hasebroek (1931) provides a detailed analysis of the changing class structure of the early Greek world and its relationship to a continuing agricultural economy. By dealing successively with the areas of Boeotia, Attica and Sparta, he brings out differences in their social make-up, but emphasizes the importance of land, flocks and herds to the ruling class as a basis for power. Hesiod's Boeotia of, say, 700 BC seems a relatively simple society: a ruling class of rich landowners to whom the struggling small farmers stand in a close dependent relationship; the latter are helped as necessary by propertyless *thetes*, free men working as paid labour (as in Homer). Side by side with the *thetes* are slaves, again as in Homer, but identified as male fieldworkers rather than female domestics.[5] It seems a static society, with seasonal markets for the disposal of a sporadic surplus, rather than permanent outlets for which farmers would produce and which would provide an incentive for social and economic change. The final interesting element in the structure is the group, distinct from the *thetes*, of itinerant individuals (Hasebroek's *vagabundierendes Proletariat*), a nucleus of craftsmen who were joined by those marginalized by society for one reason or another;[6] Hesiod's father, driven by poverty from his native Cyme, can be cited as a small landowner forced to join this group.

The position in Attica appears to have been broadly similar. Most land, and certainly the best, was in the hands of a small ruling class, the *eupatridae* and their successors. The large second group, the *demos* of small farmers and peasants, went under various names, reflecting the social and economic changes which occurred before the reforms of Solon at the beginning of the sixth century BC: many peasants fell heavily into debt and eventually became virtual serfs, the so-called *hektemoroi* (Aristotle, *Ath. Pol.* 2.2). Lower still were the paid labourers (*thetes*) and craftsmen forming a rootless but free group without property. Slaves seem to have formed a relatively negligible proportion, working in ones or twos with farmers, as in Hesiod's Boeotia.[7]

Sparta shows the same concentration of economic power in the hands of a small nobility, but at first without the individual ownership evident in, say, Attica.[8] Within that small élite the emphasis was on social equality, as shown by the later title of *homoioi*. But economic equality did not long survive any original land allotments by the state (*klaroi*), and there was a steady growth of private property, held by a class of farmers below the nobility. These formed the *demos*, supplemented by a landless proletariat and craftsmen coming from outside. What distinguishes Sparta from Attica and Boeotia is the presence of the *helotes*, the original population subdued by the Dorian invaders and reduced to the level of serfs, living in settlements attached to the land, which they farmed for the nobles and farmers living in Sparta itself. They constituted a potential source of danger to landowners and naturally gave rise to the *krypteia*, the secret police composed of young Spartans, which was introduced in the sixth or fifth century BC to watch and control the helots. The position was further complicated by the presence of the *perioikoi*, a class known from other city-states of Greece but best attested in Sparta. Like the helots they were descended from the original population but had retained their independence, although thrust out to the fringes of Spartan territory. However, they were landowners, living in their own settlements and enjoying citizenship, though at a lower level than Spartans proper. As regards the presence of slaves, there were no doubt some in Sparta, but it seems likely that the substantial class of helots meant that there was little need for them. Sparta always remained an agricultural city-state with only the seasonal markets for an occasional surplus that such an economy demanded. Without permanent markets there could scarcely have been the buying and selling of slaves necessary to maintain a substantial body of chattel-slaves. The wives and children of helots would have served in the homes of Spartan nobles and farmers, which again removed the need for chattel-slaves (such helot servants were in fact called *oiketai* or *douloi*).

The archaeological evidence for the presence of chattel-slaves in Greek agriculture of the eighth and seventh centuries BC is, unfortunately, so slight as to be almost negligible. The excavation of individual farmsteads and the functional interpretation of their layout belong to the Classical and Hellenistic periods, while the pre-Classical origins of Greek city-states have been little studied. If we can regard quasi-urban sites based on farming of surrounding land as candidates for analysis in the hope of detecting a slave presence, then two recently excavated settlements deserve notice. The first, Zagora, lies on the Cycladic island of Andros, which itself is not far removed from the mainland of Attica. The excavation reports[9] and guide to the Archaeological Museum of Andros[10] show that the site belongs to the Middle / Late Geometric period, with a *floruit* of 750-700 BC and an abandonment *c.* 700, that is at the end of the Geometric period. Surrounded by a fortification wall terminating on a sea cliff, it can technically be classed as a *polis*; the houses so far explored (Areas D, E, F, H, J) began as simple one-roomed, flat-roofed rectangular structures, occasionally with a porch opening to the south, though abutting one another to form building blocks. By Late Geometric I and II houses of paired rooms, one behind the other, had developed. A change was also seen to more complex houses composed of several rooms grouped round a courtyard in the period shortly before the abandonment of the settlement. Described as a 'town' (Zagora II), the site must have represented the concentration of a basically agricultural population for purposes of defence. Internally, the original one-roomed houses display an unsurprising simplicity, sometimes with only a hearth and stone benches along one or two walls to suggest sleeping arrangements. Occasionally there are benches along three walls as emplacements for pithoi to indicate storerooms. No social interpretation is attempted, though it could be argued that the final, more complex, arrangement might suggest the growth of extended families. Where slaves might fit into such arrangements is impossible to say, but there is no indication of any separate cubicular plan and one may assume that, if present, they lived together with their owners in a shared patriarchal fashion.[11]

The second site is Emporio on the island of Chios in the eastern Sporades; it forms a useful contrast to Zagora in its closeness to the coast of Asia Minor. The Archaic Greek site (occupation in the area was long, extending from the prehistoric period to late Roman times) was excavated during 1953-5.[12] The settlement, described as a 'town',[13] took shape *c.* 700

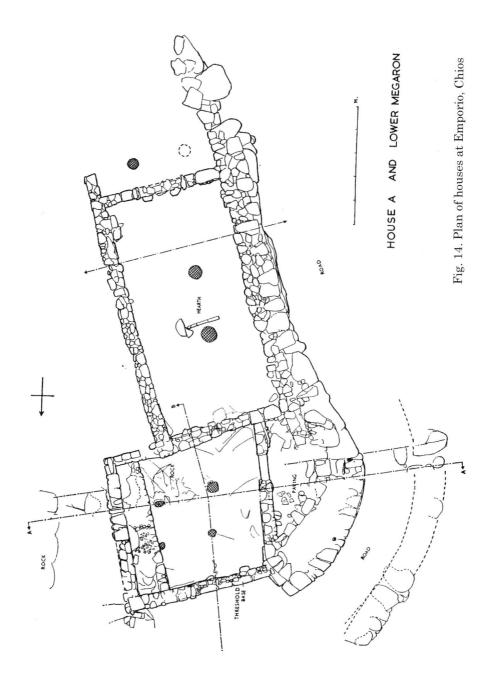

HOUSE A AND LOWER MEGARON

Fig. 14. Plan of houses at Emporio, Chios

BC and was abandoned by 600 BC, so forms a useful chronological sequel to Zagora. Emporio itself lies on the east side of the southern tip of Chios around a small protected harbour and the Archaic site flanks the west side of the hill Prophetes Elias to the north, crowned by the protective acropolis. In an area of about 4 ha (10 acres) some 50 houses were identified, totalling over half, and in fact perhaps most, of the buildings, representing no more than 500 inhabitants. 'Town', then, may be a slight misnomer, and in social and economic terms we may be considering a concentrated agricultural settlement, an early example of a local *polis,* looking for its defence to the acropolis above, where stood the 'palace' of the local chief, side by side with a temple dedicated to Athena, which continued in use, with reconstruction, into the Hellenistic period. The agricultural economy, if the traces of terrace cultivation around the settlement are contemporary, may have been based on the vine, and possibly the gum mastic bush and the olive, while grain may have been largely imported, as in Attica.[14]

The stone-built houses fall into two classes: the *megaron* house with south-facing porch supported on two columns and with a central doorway leading into the single main room, and the bench-house with no porch but a door facing north or south and leading into a roughly square room with one to four irregularly set roof supports (fig. 14). Both types are thought to have had a flat roof or one with a slight one-way pitch. The eponymous bench-houses contained a stone bench in some cases, built against the upper rear wall, and were not only poorer dwellings than the *megara* but may also have been later. Like Zagora, Emporio shows no specific slave-quarters, but is it possible to see in the bench-houses the additional quarters which the acquisition of chattel-slaves might demand? It is worth recalling that Chios seems to have led the way in the introduction of chattel-slaves; a population of, say, 100,000 citizens in the whole of Chios *c.* 500 BC would need to have been served by a considerable body of slaves.[15]

The Classical period

If there is negligible archaeological evidence for the existence of slaves in Greek agriculture of the eighth and seventh centuries BC, what can be said for the long period from the end of Archaic times down to the rise of Alexander, centring on the power curve of Athens in the fifth century BC? Within the period of, say, 600 to 350 BC culminating in the rise of Macedonian power under Philip II, certain events and changes can be isolated in the development of slavery in general, which have already been touched upon in the discussion of origins and sources. The single event of note is the remission of debt-slavery at Athens by Solon in 594 BC (*seisachtheia*) through which the enslavement of Greeks by fellow Greeks virtually disappeared, except in the extreme stress of war. To this can be added economic and social change on which there is a general consensus among twentieth-century writers: the slow introduction of an exchangeable silver currency as a basis for trade from the seventh century BC, in which Solon again played an important part in Attica; the development of handicrafts and small-scale industrialization in Athens and elsewhere (again, the offer of citizenship to immigrant craftsmen by Solon needs to be noted); and, as a framework for economic change, the expansion of trade within the Aegean and Black Sea as Greek colonies developed and sought luxury goods in exchange for agricultural produce.[16] But none of these changes should be regarded as swift or decisive; colonies were of political as much as economic importance, trade remained for a long time on a barter rather than a monetary basis, and craftsmen were marginal members of society for whom the Greek citizenship entertained a degree of contempt. For Athens, however, it is possible to cite the exploitation of the Laurion silver mines initiated by Pisistratus in the mid-sixth century and reaching a climax in the fifth century, which enabled her to rival the earlier coinages of Aegina, Corinth and Chalcis and laid the foundation of the Athenian empire. The role of slaves in mining and the archaeological evidence for their presence belong to a later chapter.

Agriculture remained the basic economic activity in Greece throughout the fifth and fourth centuries BC and was a respectable occupation as opposed to the contempt felt for handicrafts as 'banausic'.[17] The inability of Attica to produce an adequate supply of grain from its own territory was met by huge imports, calculated as four-fifths of its requirements for a population, slave and free, of *c*. 300,000-400,000.[18] The sources to north, south and west are discussed in detail elsewhere;[19] but the dangers in this departure from self-sufficiency (*autarkeia*) were amply demonstrated during the Peloponnesian War. Nevertheless, agriculture was the most important activity in Attica during this period, characterized by the extension of farming up hillslopes in times of prosperity, regression during war and expansion again in the fourth century.[20] A study of agriculture and slavery in Classical Athens takes agriculture as the basic activity in Athens and Greece at large and argues that the small landowner employed at least one slave (*oiketes*), especially in a period of population growth and pressure on the food supply.[21]

The rich landowner no doubt lived in Athens, and the usual view is that even for the small farmer the isolated farmstead was the exception. We may suppose that there was no distinct dividing line between townsman and countryman and that cultivators lived in country towns and villages and even in the suburbs of Athens.[22] On the assumption, then, that even the small farmer may have owned one or two slaves, it proves necessary to look for slave accommodation in Classical Greece in reports of the excavation of urban sites, supplemented by the meagre evidence from isolated farmsteads. Hopper presents the alternative views on the use of slaves in agriculture;[23] Heitland discusses the fifth- and fourth-century literary evidence and suggests that agricultural slavery was common-

2. Slaves in Greek Agriculture

place;[24] Jones, on the other hand, suggests that in Attica 'slaves were in fact probably little employed on the land'.[25]

Standard works on Greek architecture are primarily concerned with the great secular and religious public buildings and the discussion of houses occupies a minor place.[26] Following Zagora and Emporio, the most completely excavated site is that of Olynthus in Chalcidice, explored between 1928 and 1938 and shown to be laid out, at least for the northern area, on a regular Hippodamian grid plan.[27] Occupied in the main from c. 432 to 348 BC, it is thought to have had a population of c. 12,000-15,000 at the time of its destruction by the Macedonian army in 348 BC. There is no discussion in the reports of the economic basis for a city with a population of this size, apart from the presence of shops combined with some of the houses. We must suppose that large numbers were engaged in agriculture, with farmers and slaves travelling to and from their fields in the morning and evening. No doubt fishing and trade played some part, but cultivation was surely the main activity. The standard house on the North Hill was called the *pastas* type because of its south-facing open courtyard, flanked on the north by a portico, which could in fact be continued round some or all of the courtyard to form a peristyle. The house centred on the *andron* (*oecus*), a room devoted to eating and entertainment, sometimes combined with an anteroom to form the so-called *andronitis* (men's quarters).

At this point one enters the difficult area in which one tries to reconcile literary and archaeological evidence. In his well-known description of the Greek house, Vitruvius (6.7.1) makes no physical distinction between what are called the *prostas* and *pastas* porticoes to the courtyard round which rooms are grouped. He then discusses the so-called *andronitis* or elaborate men's quarters surrounding the greater courtyard of the house, of which the *andron* or dining-cum-entertainment-room, provided with couches, was the central feature. A lesser courtyard formed the centre of the *gynaikonitis* with the surrounding rooms allocated to the women of the household, isolated from contact with male visitors in an oriental fashion. It is a useful distinction but the late date of the description makes it difficult to apply to the Classical Greek house of the fifth and fourth centuries, which was simpler in character. A contemporary description of the *gynaikonitis* is the passage, also frequently quoted, from Xenophon (*Oecon.* 9.5) in which he emphasizes its separation from the men's quarters by a strongly bolted door, though the main reason given for this is the need to prevent physical contact between men and women slaves and the resultant casual breeding. This point is mentioned without comment by writers on Greek architecture,[28] but it would seem to follow that the slaves of each sex were housed along with their master or mistress in separate quarters.[29] It seems probable that Wycherley is correct in thinking that the term *gynaikonitis* at this period had no precise architectural significance and could vary from a single room to a set of rooms, possibly related to a courtyard or frequently on an upper floor or in a 'tower'.[30] Support for this idea of the variable location of female quarters can be found in a passage from Lysias (*Or.* 1.9): his defence of the Athenian Euphiletus for the murder of Eratosthenes, whom he had caught in the act of adultery with his wife, incorporated a statement by Euphiletus that his wife slept on the first floor until she had a baby, when he changed rooms with her in order to avoid the danger to the child caused by the wife's climbing up and down the staircase. The problem with the upper floor of the Greek house of the Classical period is that there is no evidence of layout once it is accepted that a staircase indicates the presence of such an upper level. The normal structural technique in the Greek house of this period seems to have been the use of mud-brick on dwarf stone walls (*socles*), and at Olynthus it was thought that an upper floor consequently followed the ground floor plan in general, possibly with the insertion of additional partitions of a flimsy nature.[31]

It has already been noted that Greek agriculture was largely based on a workforce concentrated in the town (*polis*) or village (*kome*) from which the workers commuted to and from the fields and that the isolated farmstead was the exception. But farms did exist and two studies address themselves to their presence and planning, though from different standpoints.[32] Jones, broadly accepting the concentration of farm owners and workers in *polis* or *kome*, deals first with the architectural evidence from house sites in Athens and Piraeus and secondly with the largely fragmentary traces of houses in villages or in isolation, from Eleusis in the north to Sounion in the south. His discussion of house plans at Thorikos, where the excavation of the mining settlement was the starting point for his study, is best reserved for the later chapter on the presence of slaves in mines and quarries. Athens, given the irregularity of its terrain, presents a variety of plans in the fifth and fourth centuries BC, but fairly common features are a courtyard and an *andron*, the latter identified by size, more sophisticated flooring and grooves denoting the position of couches. Elsewhere in Attica, houses in villages or in isolation seem to have adopted a rectangular plan with rooms approached from a yard or court, usually with a portico; it seems likely that an upper floor was sometimes present. The isolated farmstead is best represented by the excavation of the house at Vari, south of Athens (fig. 15).[33] One noteworthy feature was a square tower-like structure (*pyrgos*) at the south-west corner. This links it with an investigation of farmstead sites in southern Attica, where towers, circular and rectangular, were a frequent feature.[34] Young argued that the essential features of a Greek country estate were *pyrgos*, *aule* and *oikia* – tower, court and house – with the tower serving as a barn for the storage of oil and wine on the ground floor and grain above; women could work on the ground floor and in emergency the building could serve as a place of refuge (fig. 16).[35] In an appendix he lists 80 published examples of towers,[36] scattered throughout the Greek mainland and islands, and elsewhere

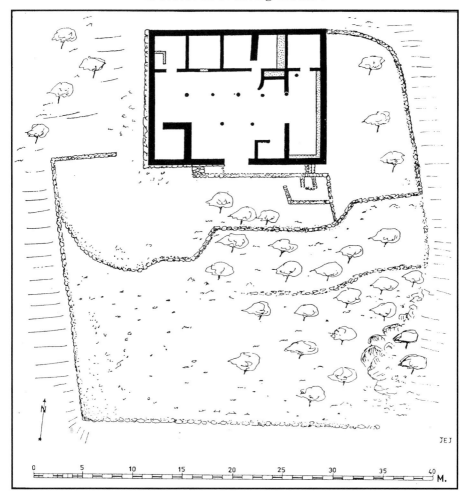

Fig. 15. Plan of house at Vari, Attica

speaks of 'hundreds'.[37] It is clear that they were a frequent feature of the isolated farmhouse.

This tower element features strongly in Pečírka (1973), whose study ranges more widely in space and time. By excluding the *polis* and *kome* from consideration (although he emphasizes their function as centres for an essentially agricultural population) he is able to concentrate on the presence of homestead farms in the *chora* or territory surrounding a *polis*, arguing that these were not 'a common phenomenon in classical Greece'[38] but at the same time suggesting that various factors favoured their growth in the transition from Classical to Hellenistic times. Side by side with the republished plans from Young, he offers for comparison a number of

57

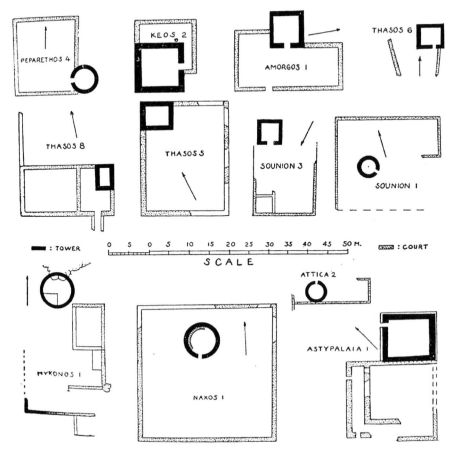

Fig. 16. Twelve tower-houses

farmsteads with towers excavated in the Crimean Chersonese.[39] He argues that towers were a common feature of Mediterranean and Near Eastern farms, particularly in Hellenistic and Roman times, and discusses their function as agricultural buildings.[40] Following Hasebroek (1922), he quotes the passage from pseudo-Demosthenes (47.56), where a *pyrgos* on the plaintiff's farm served as accommodation for female slaves; the women closed the door leading into the tower so that the accused could not seize them and the farm equipment. Thus we may make a claim for slave-quarters in towers on Greek farms, where these occurred, although the precise date of the Crimean examples remains uncertain, some claiming a Classical date, others a Hellenistic to early Roman.[41] Pečírka himself favours a starting date in the second half of the fourth century, with a further expansion towards 300 BC.[42] The whole system might coincide with the expansion of the *polis* of Chersonesos in the latter part of the fourth century.

There is probably still much to learn about the archaeological background to Greek agriculture, not least because of the concentration on the excavation of major monuments in the Classical period. It may be that there were more individual farms than is supposed, a point made by Bradford (1956) in his discussion of field-systems revealed by air photography on Mount Hymettos. Extensive field survey, on the lines of that being carried out in many areas, such as Boeotia, the *chora* of Megalopolis in Arcadia, the Argolid, and elsewhere, will increase the number of farms of the Classical period.[43] The number of sites doubles between the fifth and early third century BC providing a 'classic market-oriented central-place distribution'. The larger towns such as Hermion and Halieis, with their own coinage, are to be classed as *poleis*; these and larger villages had satellite villages and hamlets, while a large number of sites can be identified as farmsteads, many with characteristic towers; other areas of Greece will increase the number of farms of the Classical period.[44] But ultimately excavation of selected sites will be required to reveal plans and, it may be hoped, offer an identification of different elements of the plan, particularly slave-quarters. A more conventional approach is demonstrated by intensive fieldwork on the high plateau of Mount Aipos, north-west of Chios and so within the *chora* of the ancient city.[45] An apparently infertile landscape can be shown to have supported a range of habitations from shepherds' huts to self-sufficient farmsteads, roughly dated on the evidence of surface finds to the late Classical, Hellenistic and Roman periods. We may have here evidence for expansion of agricultural activity to marginal lands after, say, 400 BC. It is possible that the huts represent the quarters of unfree shepherds but it would be difficult to determine, even with excavation, the status of the more elaborate farms. However, they may represent the living-quarters and farm-buildings of a workforce of agricultural slaves, controlled by an overseer (*epitropos*), himself a slave,[46] working for an owner living in Chios itself.

The Hellenistic period

The period between the death of Alexander in 323 BC and the annexation of Macedonia, until then the dominant power in Greece, by Rome in 146 BC, saw great political and social changes in the eastern Mediterranean, but of economic conditions, particularly agriculture, much less is known. The spread of Greek culture to Asia Minor and beyond, and to Egypt, meant that the city-states of Corinth and Athens faced intense competition from the growing power of Rhodes, later to be supplanted by Delos and Alexandria. But this rivalry was in the fields of trade and industry, and there can be little doubt that agriculture continued in its traditional areas, though possibly with some changes of organization.

The conflict between Alexander's officers which led to the foundation of the Antigonid, Seleucid and Ptolemaic dynasties, and the formation of the Achaean and Aetolian Leagues in Greece itself, meant that, on the one hand, many farmers chose to leave the land in order to seek their fortune as soldiers, while, on the other, the constant sectional wars of the third century led to an increased demand for food to supply the warring troops. Heitland quotes a number of references from Polybius about the extent to which the campaigns of Philip V towards the end of the third century were conditioned by the necessity to secure an adequate supply of corn for his troops.[47] His conclusion is that unsettled conditions and political measures favouring the rich caused small farming to decline, with a consequent move to large crop-growing estates in favoured areas, owned by wealthy absentee landlords living in the cities.[48] The exception was Macedonia where the absence of towns and the presence of a hardy peasantry ensured a reliable source of troops to maintain domination over much of Greece. The nature of the labour supply for such large estates is uncertain, but the slight literary references, including the Latin versions of Greek New Comedy by Plautus and Terence, would suggest a staff of slaves under a bailiff (*vilicus*), responsible to a town-dwelling owner.[49] The evidence from epigraphy is slight: at Delphi the manumission inscriptions for the first half of the second century BC give information about numbers and to some extent origins of slaves, but for outright grants of freedom there is only rarely any mention of occupation. For paramone manumissions (those in which the new freedman contracts to work for his former owner for a period of years), on the other hand, there are indications of occupation which suggest that the former slaves were mostly engaged in household work, as personal attendants, or as handicraft workers.[50] Epitaphs of former slaves from Rhodes for the same period also suggest that they were employed in small-scale industry.[51] The likely inference is that agricultural slavery was largely permanent and that opportunities of obtaining freedom by self-purchase were relatively limited.

Any attempt to identify specifically servile quarters in Hellenistic houses meets the same difficulties as in the preceding Classical period: first, it is likely that many landowners continued to live in towns, accentuated by the likely trend towards larger estates and, secondly, there is the problem of the identification of rooms, particularly where an upper room can only be inferred and no plan survives. There is the possibility that an isolated farmhouse on a large estate may have been occupied by a gang of slaves working under a bailiff, also a slave, but the archaeological evidence for this is lacking.

The best-known urban site is the Ionian city of Priene, built from *c.* 350 BC onwards on the Hippodamian grid system within an irregular defensive wall. Substantial areas of housing in the western part of the site were excavated by the Germans in 1895-8.[52] A constant feature of the substantially built stone houses, probably with mud-brick upper floors, was an

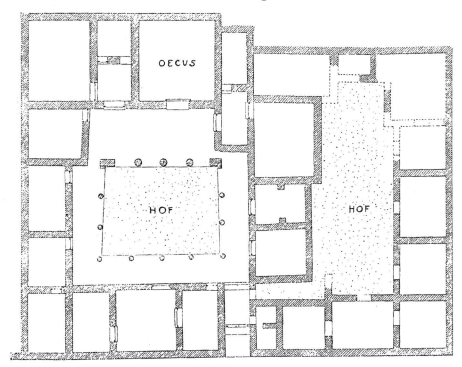

Fig. 17. Plan of House XXXIII at Priene

oecus, approached through a two-columned *prostas*. The similarity to the *megaron* plan has been commented on in a number of general architectural works,[53] but this may not be very significant. Among the many published house plans,[54] one often quoted is House XXXIII west of the theatre.[55] In its final form, probably in the second century BC, it was the largest so far known in the city (fig. 17): it was composed of 26 rooms, divided into women's quarters of 16 rooms grouped round a peristyle courtyard to the west, and men's quarters of 10 rooms round a smaller courtyard to the east (the two areas had formerly been separate houses divided by a street). The two sets of apartments were quite distinct, with separate means of access, and can be credibly identified as a *gynaikonitis* and *andronitis* respectively. The physical separation of male and female slaves referred to earlier could easily have been achieved on this ground floor or, quite possibly, on an upper floor about which we know nothing.

The Cycladic island of Delos, with its long history first as a great religious centre based on the shrine of Apollo, then as the political centre of the Delian confederacies and finally in its role as a great commercial centre rivalling Rhodes, offers an interesting comparison with Priene. Most relevant perhaps are the inscriptions recording leases of the estates of the temple of Apollo on Delos itself and the adjoining islands of Rheneia and Mykonos.[56] Of the 26 estates on the three islands little is known archaeologically, but the inscriptions provide useful details of rooms and buildings, especially in the leases of 250 BC. Kent concludes that the lessees were mostly from the upper moneyed class of Delian society, 'gentlemen farmers' who leased the estates as investments.[57] He further argues that the estates were 'largely, if not wholly, worked by slave labour'. From this it follows, according to Pečírka, that the lessees did not live on the farms and that the living-quarters listed in the inventories were for the farmworkers, presumably slaves working under overseers.[58] The actual agricultural operations were stock-breeding, the growing of grain, and the cultivation of grapes and figs.[59] Kent's discussion of buildings and rooms assumes considerable importance if the occupants were slaves.[60] The word *huperôidion* is peculiar to the Delian inventories and is a diminutive of *huperôion*, 'upper storey'; these, he suggests, were women's sleeping-quarters. The word *andrônion*, a diminutive of *andrôn*, thus denotes men's sleeping-quarters, presumably on the ground floor, while *thalamos*, 'bedroom', was intended to serve married couples. *Oikia* and *oikêma*, 'house', appear rarely, but *kleision* seems to be the common word for 'farmhouse' in the sense of dining-quarters and so on. Pečírka expresses doubt about this interpretation of *kleision* and refers to Robinson's list of Greek words concerned with the house, where it is translated as 'outhouse' or 'shed'.[61] Two estates had a tower (*purgos* and *purgion*) and Kent identified one on the estate of Charoneia on Rheneia.[62] It would be highly desirable to investigate archaeologically one or more of the estates listed by Kent in order to arrive at a more precise identification of the quarters listed in the inventories.

Delos itself ranks with Olynthus and Priene as one of the most extensively excavated sites of the Greek world, as a result of the efforts of the French School since 1873. The buildings reflect the changing character of the island's occupation, from its importance as a religious sanctuary from the seventh century BC to its commercial prosperity as a free port in the second and first centuries BC. It is its later history that is of interest from the point of view of slave accommodation, though the link with agriculture may be tenuous. It seems likely that some of the estates on the island were covered by houses and shops during the colonial period, that is from 166 BC,[63] so the evidence for slave-quarters may lie at a lower level. On the other hand, among the earliest houses, those in the Theatre Quarter which in their original form date from the third century, there may have been some of those of the absentee landlords who owned the estates on Delos, Rheneia and Mykonos. This area is irregular in its planning, whereas houses in the Lake Quarter demonstrate a grid plan of streets and building blocks.[64] In their final form, in the second and first centuries BC, the Delian houses achieved a high degree of luxury and architectural complexity.

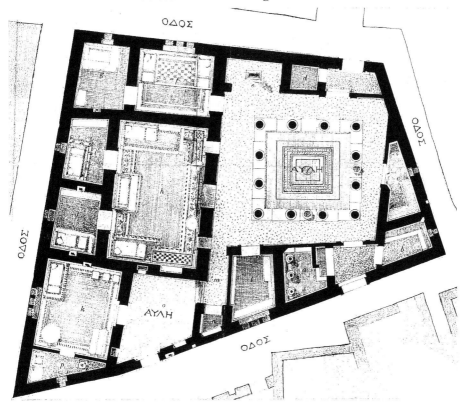

Fig. 18. Plan of La Maison du Lac, Delos

It is rarely that slave-quarters are specifically identified by the excava-tors of Greek houses, but this purpose has been claimed for rooms in five houses at Delos: La Maison du Dionysos, where Room d is claimed as a *cella familiarica* and Prolongation n of the north portico as sleeping-quar-ters; La Maison du Lac, where Rooms c and d are identified as slave-quarters (fig. 18)[65] – on a wall of Room c is a graffito by a slave from Antioch-on-Maeander who expresses his longing for the figs and abundant water of his birthplace;[66] La Maison de l'Inopos, where the small rooms on the south side are claimed as *cellae* (fig. 19);[67] La Maison de l'Inopos again, where the two extensions to the north portico are described as slaves' sleeping-quarters;[68] and La Maison du Trident, where Rooms e, f, g, 1 and m are classed as *cellae*, on the basis of their small size and plain decoration or lack of it.[69] It seems more than likely that in their final form these were houses of wealthy cosmopolitan merchants of Delos in the second and first centuries BC, who did not live in close proximity to their compatriots but were scattered throughout the urban area.[70] Some houses had one or more upper stories, and possibly slave-quarters for women were at a higher

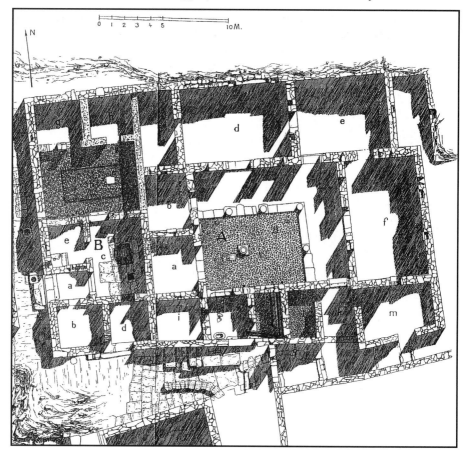

Fig. 19. Plan of La Maison de l'Inopos, Delos

level. At all events, these Delian houses may be comparable to the elaborate houses of farmers, whether in the city or the country, as regards slave accommodation.

Conclusion

The archaeological evidence for the presence of slaves in Greek agriculture can only be described as slight, for the two reasons that have emerged in the preceding pages. First, there is the problem of the identification of farmhouses and estates, complicated by the tendency of owners and workers to live in nucleated settlements such as towns and villages. Secondly, even where farms or urban houses have been excavated it is rarely that the excavators have attempted to allocate individual rooms to slaves. So there has developed a tendency, which will be apparent through-out this work, to discuss in general terms the differing economic activities, and in particular the structural evidence for these, in which slaves were involved. Thus, in farming there has been an inevitable concentration on different house types, *megaron, pastas, prostas* and peristyle (with its Rhodian variant). In all these there is evidence for planning around an open space, a yard or court, so that the house presents a generally inturned aspect, with outer walls which can even be blank.

A few valuable conclusions have emerged. There is the function of the rectangular or circular tower, which appears on the Greek mainland, in the islands and as far north as the Crimean peninsula; it seems likely that such structures could have served the dual purpose of farming activities and accommodation for (?female) slaves. There is the intriguing possibility that the Delian estates were worked partly or wholly by slave-labour, so that the identification of living-quarters in an excavated farmhouse would logically demonstrate the nature of slave-quarters. And, again on Delos, there is the excavator's suggested allocation of certain rooms to slaves in late Hellenistic town houses, which could point to the nature of their accommodation in agricultural premises.

3

Slaves in Roman Agriculture:
the Republic

The background

To talk about 'Roman' agriculture encounters a number of objections, but some can be met if we take the view that the term is in part temporal and in part topographical. There has already been some anticipation of this section, for instance in the description of the houses at Delos, which in their final appearance belonged to the second to first centuries BC when the island, nominally ruled by Athens, was in fact a dependency of Rome. Conversely, areas of the Italian peninsula, including Sicily and certain points on the coast of the western Mediterranean, had early experienced the effects of Greek colonization, itself primarily agrarian in its early stages, and something must be said of this. But the main thrust of this chapter will be a description of agriculture in the Italian peninsula, in the provinces acquired in the latter part of the Republic and finally in the expansion under the Empire, and of what can be detected archaeologically of the role of slaves in this fundamental aspect of the ancient economy.

Sicily and southern Italy felt the impact of Greek colonization before 700 BC and a brief description is needed of the natural environment which faced the early settlers. The social and political development of the Greek city-states was fostered by the division of the Greek mainland into narrow valleys separated by difficult mountain barriers; an increasing population and land hunger within these relatively isolated communities required an outlet which could best be satisfied by the establishment of colonies in other Mediterranean lands. The earliest settlers came from eastern Greece in the second half of the eighth century BC and, following the early trading routes to such points on the west coast of Italy as Ischia and Cumae, they found their natural landfall was around the instep and toe of Italy and on Sicily. Here they found comparable climatic conditions and soils, particularly on the coastal plains, rather more fertile than in their homeland. Thus was formed Magna Graecia, originally southern Italy but extended by Strabo (6.1.2) to include Sicily. Sicily, although fairly moun-tainous, lent itself to the cultivation of cereals in the interior, so much so that it was the legendary birthplace of wheat.[1] Athens, and later Rome, imported a great deal of corn from the island. The coastal strips and the bigger plains, such as those inland from Catania, carried the vine and the olive. Cattle and sheep could also be pastured on upland areas and altogether the colonists found favourable conditions. The instep and toe of Italy, the modern Basilicata and Calabria, offered the same contrast of river valleys and coastal strips and plains on the one hand, and upland pastures on the other. The fifth-century coins of most states of Magna Graecia display at some time a grain or ear of wheat.[2] Forests were still widespread and resulted in a better rainfall as well as providing ample supplies of timber.[3]

The later colonization of the seventh and sixth centuries BC moved into western Sicily and up the west coast of Italy, as well as to the coasts of southern France, Spain, North Africa, the north coast of the Aegean, and so through the Hellespont and Bosphorus to the coasts of the Black Sea. Within Italy the spinal chain of the Apennines is the main mountain barrier to communication across the peninsula, but on the east and west the sea and coastal plains offered complementary routes for north-south traffic. Variable soil types caused differences in fertility, but by and large crop- and fruit-growing were fostered by a favourable climate, while stock-raising may have been adapted to summer drought conditions in coastal areas by a transhumance policy of moving cattle and sheep to upland pastures. This was a recognized practice in settled periods within historic times, but may have already been used in prehistory and into Republican times, if only on a small scale.[4]

Early Greek agriculture in Italy

If we are to believe Homer, Sicily was already involved in the slave-trade before the arrival of Greek colonists. The indigenous inhabitants, the Sicans in the west of the island and the Sikels in the east, appear in the role of slaves or slave-traders (*Odyssey* 20.383; 24.366, 389). The colonists in turn reduced these inhabitants to serfdom in certain cases and there can be no doubt that from Archaic times onwards individual Greek land-owners and farmers were buying and employing chattel-slaves for agricultural work. The problem lies in determining, first, the extent to which the colonists practised agriculture in the same way as in their Greek home-land and, secondly, how far it is possible to identify structural evidence for slave-quarters in buildings of the period. We are concerned essentially with those colonies in Sicily and Magna Graecia which were primarily agricultural and were composed of a *polis*, an urban centre, and a *chora*, its surrounding agricultural territory, such as Gela in Sicily and Locri and Metapontum in southern Italy; in contrast are those colonies which because of their location depended on trade for their existence.[5] Air photography, by the British and German air forces during the Second World War and later by the Italians, has helped to clarify the relationship between *polis* and *chora* in the first group; for instance, it would appear that at Metapontum the grid plan of the urban settlement was extended into the countryside on the north,[6] a hypothesis later tested by actual excavation.[7] Adamesteanu had already proposed a similar grid of land allotment in the hinterland of Gela in Sicily and had located seventh-century farms of a first phase of settlement, with others belonging to a second phase of expansion lasting throughout the sixth century. He postulated a similar expansion by stages of Metapontine territory to the west of the city, where air photography had indicated some 39 land-divisions and about 100 farms, the latter mostly placed on the boundaries. Many had been destroyed by deep ploughing, but of the eight excavated there were in most cases indications of an Archaic phase (first half of the sixth century BC). These early farms were of one or two rooms only, as at Gela, but gradual enlargement led by the fourth century to a central peristyle with smaller rooms on the sides for animals. The owners he would identify as inhabitants of Metapontum, normally leading a country life with a workforce partly of Greek slaves from conquered Siris and partly of indigenous serfs. If Adamesteanu's conclusions are correct, the colonial farms of Magna Graecia and Sicily housed slave-labourers but so far there has been no suggestion about the location of their quarters. It may be that, as in the Greek homeland, the landowners lived in the city and the workers on the farm under the control of a bailiff; Adamesteanu's suggested parallel with the onset of the Peloponnesian War, when Athenian citizens came in from the countryside (Thuc. 2.14) may be anachronistic.

Certainly, there seems to be general agreement that in the Greek colonies of Sicily and Magna Graecia *polis* and *chora* were closely linked and the orthogonal grid plan of both, as demonstrated by air photography, suggests a simultaneous overall allocation of plots (*kleroi*) at the moment of foundation.[8] This was based on an arrangement *per strigas*, parallel main axes (*cardines*) which were then subdivided into rectangular plots by side streets in the city and lanes in the surrounding countryside (the subdivision would obviously be much closer in the urban area than in the country). Much discussion has centred on the origins of such systematic urban planning, so long before that of fifth-century Hippodamus of Miletus and, curiously, without prototypes in the Greek motherland.[9] It would be wrong to generalize excessively on urban planning and house types until large-scale excavation has been carried out in a larger number of colonial cities. Some are overlaid by modern Sicilian and south Italian towns and the best that can be hoped for is reports of isolated rescue excavations with occasional syntheses.[10]

Two cities in Sicily have, however, been subjected to large-scale excavation: Megara Hyblaea on the east coast, with a foundation of *c.* 750 BC and a destruction by Gelon in 483 BC, followed by a virtual gap until its re-foundation by Timoleon *c.* 340 BC; and Himera on the north coast, founded in 648 BC and destroyed by the Carthaginians in 409 BC. At Megara Hyblaea French excavations have distinguished three phases between the foundation and destruction of 483 BC.[11] From the beginning there was a close correspondence between the city plan and the layout in the *chora*; the urban street plan, although not a precise rectilinear grid, followed a system of parallel streets with a subdivision into building blocks (*insulae*), more reminiscent of a rural than an urban layout. The earliest one-roomed houses were 4-5 m square, representing the allocation to the first colonists; they might have children, but no dependants or slaves. During the seventh century the accommodation was increased to make a two- or three-roomed house, opening on to a courtyard, normally on the south. During the sixth century there seems to have been a decline, and the high point was probably *c.* 600 BC, with enslavement of the indigenous inhabitants (*Kyllirioi*) to form a workforce of serfs and a division of the population into wealthy landowners and a servile *demos*.[12] To return to the underlying theme of this study, it is difficult to identify slave-quarters within such simple urban houses, and one is tempted to suggest that the workforce was housed outside the defences in the farm buildings of the *chora*, as at Metapontum, but the evidence for this hypothesis is still lacking.

At Himera, excavations by Palermo University extended from 1963 to 1973.[13] The residential area saw considerable changes during its 250 years of occupation but three phases were detected. Traces of early houses were found of a period extending from the last quarter of the seventh century to 490-480 BC; although later alterations made it impossible to distinguish a well-defined house type, there was evidently, as in other colonies, a close correlation between the urban and the agrarian plan.[14] In the second phase, from 490 to 480 BC, a systematic grid plan appears, with 16 x 16 m house blocks, in which the larger rooms face on to the main street and the smaller on to the narrower side streets; it was difficult to define the internal courtyard which must have been an essential part. The final phase, down to the destruction of 409 BC, saw a change of two kinds: some houses grew and extended over the side streets (*ambitus*), while others simply saw a subdivision of the original plan into an increased number of smaller rooms. In date the Himera houses would correspond to Olynthus, but there was no trace of the *pastas* feature characteristic of Olynthus, nor of the general planning evident there. Upper storeys were virtually absent at Himera and it was difficult to identify the function of the rooms, to define service-quarters, or, by extension, rooms allocated to slaves. Quite possibly the latter were housed in farms in the *chora* as was suggested for Megara Hyblaea. In any event, the housing represents the fairly modest level of domestic life known from elsewhere in Sicily, or further afield in Attica and Athens.

Sicily and Magna Graecia, including North Africa, up to the Roman conquest

After the initial period of Greek colonization of southern Italy and Sicily in the eighth and seventh centuries BC there was clearly a period of prosperity and consolidation in the sixth century. The simple evidence of temple foundations is supported by the introduction of coinage in the second half of the century, and we may suppose that agricultural output was the main key to the undoubted wealth of the Greek cities. The grain surplus was exported to markets in Italy and Greece, and in particular to Rome from *c.* 500 BC. This trade, balanced by the import of luxury goods, encouraged the growth of a merchant class and of shops in the colonial cities.

During the fifth century the tumultuous history of Sicily, and to a lesser extent Magna Graecia, saw the growth of some colonial cities, notably Syracuse, and the corresponding decline of others. The succession of tyrants, from Hippocrates and Gelon to Theron and Hieron, brought the Greek culture of Sicily to a zenith in the first half of the century; in the second half external politics played their part, culminating in the disastrous failure of the Athenian expedition against Syracuse in 413 BC and the Carthaginian capture of many of the important cities in the last decade. The success of Dionysius of Syracuse in reversing Carthaginian expansion by a combination of military and diplomatic skill was followed after his death in 367 BC by a succession of petty tyrants preoccupied with the threat of Carthage, until Sicily became a province after the end of the First Punic War in 241 BC, and the surrender of Syracuse in 211. The cultural mixing associated with the military and political events of the first half of the fifth century evidently had a powerful effect on town planning, as we have seen already in the case of Himera, as well as on growth and development in individual houses.

The usual major assumption must be made in the difficult process of identification of quarters for servile farmworkers in the cities of Sicily and Magna Graecia, namely that many of these labourers lived within the city walls and 'commuted' to the fields. This is the sole justification for discussing town plans and the layout of individual houses, but we have already seen that farms existed in the *chorai*, possibly intended to house slaves under the control of an overseer, while the owner lived in the city and made periodic visits. There is the further possibility that *kleroi* near the city were worked from the city, and those at a distance by labour living on the spot. At all events, urban houses and farms both require consideration, even if no clear results are apparent.

Two major studies of the Greek house in Sicily are partly overlapping and partly complementary: de Miro discusses house plans in the three cities of Gela, Agrigentum and Heraclea Minoa, lying in the centre of the south coast of Sicily, and in four inland sites to the north, Sabucina, Monte Saraceno, Vassallaggi and Morgantina, marking the penetration of Greek culture into the interior of the island.[15] The chronological limits of his inquiry are stated to be from the sixth to the third century BC, though some of the Heraclea Minoa and Morgantina houses extend down to the second and first centuries BC. It is a useful factual study, though not made easy to use by the failure to relate detailed to general plans and by the omission

71

of north points. The second study by Martin and Vallet covers 20 sites throughout Sicily and the entire period of Greek settlement from the initial period of colonization of the eighth and seventh centuries (Megara Hyblaea and Syracuse) to the Hellenized town of Morgantina with houses of the third century BC.[16] The authors conclude with an examination of the influence of Greek architectural traditions on other indigenous settlements and on Carthaginian sites in the west of the island. They emphasize the simplicity of the houses of the eighth to sixth centuries BC, with their limited development from a single room to two or three opening on to a courtyard; despite the regularity of the overall urban plan, extended into the *chora*, there is nothing to suggest any real change in the status of the inhabitants. With the fifth century there are the first indications of the development of a small aristocracy in the form of the occasional peristyle house, but otherwise the adoption of Hippodamian town plans, for example at Naxos and Himera, only defines residential blocks with rather more spacious accommodation. In the fourth and third centuries there are more examples of wealthy houses, with rooms opening on to a central peristyle courtyard, and even the more functional houses of re-founded sites (for example, Kamarina) present a courtyard, sometimes with service rooms. The authors emphasize the difficulty of formulating a continuous evolutionary sequence for the Greek house in Sicily, and certainly no great attempt seems to have been made to identify the function of rooms and so of potential slave-quarters. But, in contrast to de Miro, they devote space to the farms excavated by Adamesteanu and Orlandini in the hinterland of Gela, which provide evidence for the fourth-century agricultural expansion of the colony and offer a useful link with similar farms in the *chora* of Metapontum in Magna Graecia.

Both studies devote space to the inland site of Serra Orlando, identified as the ancient Morgantina and excavated over a number of years by Princeton and Illinois Universities.[17] The site was the centre of a rich grain-producing area and prospered in the third century BC, as shown by a number of rich houses, for example the House of the Official (fig. 20). This house is a good example of the developed Greek type with two peristyle courtyards and a division into separate more formal quarters for the men and a *gynaikonitis* with smaller rooms for the women. An upper storey could presumably have held separate slave-quarters. To the farmhouses in the territory of Gela and Metapontum should be added those at Jurato and Capodicasa in the *chora* of Kamarina: both date from the fifth century and exhibit a similar plan in which rooms are ranged round three sides of a courtyard.[18] There is some attempt to identify working areas but no mention of slave-quarters.

It would be wrong to conclude this section without a brief mention of agriculture and slavery in North Africa and specifically Carthage and its territory, in view of its rivalry with the Greek colonists in Sicily and ultimately with Rome in the Punic Wars. The well-known passage of

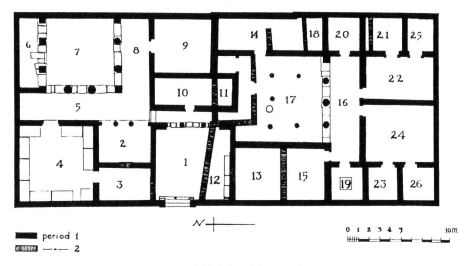

period 1
—·— 2

Fig. 20. Plan of the House of the Official at Morgantina

Diodorus Siculus (20.8.3-4) describes how Agathocles, tyrant of Syracuse, landed in Carthaginian territory in 310 BC and found that the area was covered with prosperous farms belonging to the nobility, with vineyards, olive groves, orchards and fields full of sheep, cattle and horses. Half a century later the Romans found similar conditions (Polyb. 1.29.7) and after their defeat in the Punic Wars the Carthaginians concentrated on agriculture in their own North African territory.[19] Their skill is confirmed by the survival of passages from the works of the Carthaginian writer Mago in later Latin writers such as Varro and Columella,[20] and by early material embedded in the Byzantine treatise *Geoponia*.[21] The social structure of Carthage, in the period when it contended with the Greek colonies in Sicily, that is down to the mid-third century BC, was of a ruling nobility and a popular majority, superimposed on the indigenous Berbers. The Phoenician peoples of the Levant and later of North Africa had a strong mercantile tradition[22] and trade and industry, such as the production of the famous purple dye (*purpura*), must have been the basis of a number of coastal settlements, for example Kerkonane on Cape Bon.[23] But agriculture was clearly the essential feature of life in the coastal strip and it is argued that the ruling families owned farms which were to be the pattern for Roman farming of the later Republic, with intensive vine- and olive-growing as the main activity.[24] Gsell suggests that the lower classes cultivated smallholdings for the supply of fruit and vegetables, while the indigenous inhabitants grew corn and reared flocks.[25]

There is no doubt that slaves were employed in Carthaginian agriculture. Diodorus (20.13.2, 69.5) refers to the preparation of chains for the prisoners they expected to capture at the time of Agathocles' landing, and to the employment of Greek prisoners in chains to work on the land they had devastated. Otherwise, the direct evidence is fairly limited.[26] Most of the literary references relate to the later period of the Punic and Jugurthine Wars,[27] but it is clear that agricultural slavery was of long standing. Unfortunately, excavation of the numerous coastal and inland sites in the province of Africa, as in the other Roman provinces to east and west, has rarely produced plans of houses of the pre-Roman period from which it might be possible to infer slave-quarters.

Italy to the time of Augustus

The Etruscans

Away from the Hellenized areas of Sicily and southern Italy the Italian peninsula was inhabited by tribes of differing origins, whose unification under Rome was a long and fluctuating business.[28] Of these peoples the Etruscans, whatever their origins, exhibited a high degree of cultural achievement but were basically agriculturalists, like the other tribes of Italy. It is held that the Etruscans possessed large farms, worked by peasants who were either free or serfs, but that they had domestic slaves.[29] Much of the discussion of Etruscan houses has centred on the possible derivation of the Roman *atrium* house from the Etruscan farm and its translation to an urban setting.[30] The slight literary evidence is outweighed by the results of excavation at such urban sites as Marzabotto and the agricultural centre of San Giovenale. Marzabotto, founded shortly before 500 BC, already shows the grid plan evident at an early date for the Greek colonies of Magna Graecia and Sicily, and it is clear that the fifth-century, so-called, 'Hippodamian' plan was only the formal recognition of a well-established principle.

Within the *insulae* formed by the streets the typical house plan displays, normally, an arrangement of rooms round a central courtyard, often approached by a narrow corridor from a narrow front.[31] Mansuelli regarded Houses 2 and 6 of *Insula* 1 in Region IV, dated to around 450 BC, as prototypes of the *atrium* house, with axial *fauces*, *tablinum* and *alae*, and so reinstated the theory first advanced by the nineteenth-century excavator of the site, Brizio, but controverted by Grenier and others during the first half of the present century.[32] This is a point of considerable architectural interest, but the preoccupation with internal planning overshadows any possible identification of slave-quarters. The literary evidence for the possession of slaves by wealthier Etruscans matches well with the spaciousness of the Marzabotto houses (fig. 21) and there is the telling reference from Diodorus (5.40.1), who claimed that the Etruscans invented the *atrium* in order to separate masters from slaves. It is possible that slaves were housed in an upper storey above the proto-*tablinum*; the Marzabotto houses were probably timber-framed on stone foundations and

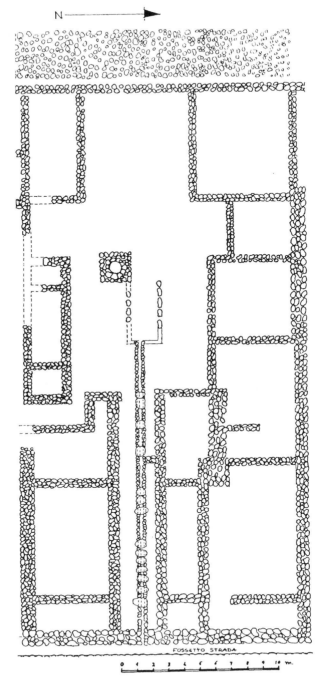

Fig. 21. Plan of House
2 at Marzabotto

it would have been relatively easy to carry the building higher at selected points. Even the simpler rectangular houses opening directly on to the street, which served as shops (*tabernae*), workshops, or merely as living-quarters for the poor, are thought to have had garrets above.[33] These various houses at Marzabotto, and the simpler *megaron*-type house as at Vetulonia and Veii, find their counterparts in rock-cut tombs and cinerary urns, and this range of types is thought to reflect the social division of Etruscan society, with proto-*atrium* houses of the nobility and modest rectangular dwellings of the common people at the two extremes. It seems highly probable that such an urban site as Marzabotto was the home of a large agricultural population working in the surrounding countryside.[34]

Marzabotto is so frequently cited as one of the best-known Etruscan sites, both for its overall urban plan and for the individual houses, that it is easy to forget that it belongs, with Felsina and Spina, to a later phase of Etruscan expansion into northern Italy.[35] A similar expansion southwards led to rivalry with the Greeks of Sicily and Magna Graecia, and expansion into Campania, until they were driven back to the Etruscan heartland in the early years of the fifth century, as they were from the north a century or so later.[36] In Etruria itself most of the evidence from the numerous city sites is in the form of a general plan of the defences and of cemeteries.[37] However, at San Giovenale, between Lakes Vico and Bracciano, the Swedish excavations have revealed houses of an Etruscan settlement of *c*. 600 BC, the successor of Bronze and Iron Age occupation. The houses themselves are built in rows but have a comparatively simple rectangular plan of two rooms, one behind the other, giving on to the alleys between the rows. There is little here to denote the presence of slaves, and possibly a patriarchal system obtained in this essentially agricultural settlement.[38] Eventually, the settlement seems to have dispersed and the population in later centuries lived and worked in *villae rusticae* under the late Republic, scattered over the countryside, as at the nearby site of Villa Sambuco where slave-quarters have been tentatively identified.

Italy to 200 BC

By 201 BC Rome was established as the controlling power in Italy, through her successive victories over Etruscans, Samnites and the Greek colonies in the south, and the expulsion of the Carthaginian armies. This was the period of the early Republic chosen by Wallon (1879) and Heitland (1921) for their discussion of slaves in general and slaves in agriculture respectively. It was also a period when the farmer-soldier epitomized the old Roman virtues of hard work allied with patriotism as portrayed by later writers in the persons of Cincinnatus in the fifth century and Curius and Fabricius in the third.[39] The spread of Roman power was strengthened in the fourth and third centuries by the foundation of *coloniae* with Latin or, more rarely, Roman status, the underlying purpose of which was both to satisfy the land hunger of the poor in the founding cities and to provide a reservoir of military manpower. Agriculture was, then, a constant element in Italian society, varying no doubt according to geographical and cultural differences, but probably incorporating a substantial slave element supplemented by continuous military conquest. The new *coloniae* adopted a grid pattern on the *decumanus / cardo* principle for their cities and centuriation for the surrounding *territorium*, on the lines of the Greek colonies and Etruscan cities, and probably the inhabitants, free or slave, went daily to and from the fields.

The literary evidence for slaves in agriculture in the early to middle Republic is slight; only Dionysius says that Cincinnatus worked his tiny farm with a few slaves. Heitland argues that slavery was widespread in Roman farming but was essentially of a domestic nature.[40] His most telling quotation is of the passage from Livy (28.11.9), which describes the appeal in 206 BC by the Latin colonies of Placentia and Cremona after Hannibal's retreat from Italy for assistance from Rome to resettle the land; one of the difficulties noted by the Senate was the shortage of slaves (*inopia servitiorum*) which Heitland accepts as referring to small farms as much as to large estates. Nor is the archaeological evidence yet available in any quantity. The most recent work of a comprehensive nature, by White (1970), is almost entirely concerned with the late Republic and the Empire and scarcely deals with historical development; his second chapter, however, is a useful regional survey of differences throughout Italy as a whole. Similarly, the more narrowly structured study of Spurr (1986) confines itself to the three centuries from *c.* 200 BC to *c.* AD 100, so only becomes relevant later; it also has the curious defect that it fails to discuss the size of estates, the character of farms and the function of farm buildings except in passing references. Altogether, the fourth and third centuries remain an archaeological enigma for farms and the housing of slaves, though there is clearly no lack of sites. The survey of the *ager Capenas* speaks of the dispersal of the earlier Etruscan *pagus* sites to scattered farmsteads under the Republic, and this in an area not especially favourable to settlement.[41] This view is confirmed by Potter's later study of 1979 covering a wider area, which subsumes in a general way earlier work (the Sutri survey, *ager Capenas*, *ager Veientanus*, *ager Erextanus*, *via Gabina*, the Cassia / Clodia survey, and so on), though there are some variations, for example the *ager Faliscus*.[42] The growth of rural settlement was even more marked in the late Republic.[43] Archaeological survey of defined areas of Italy, as opposed to detailed excavation of particular sites, has been a feature of recent work, much of it centred on the British School at Rome; in addition to the areas already cited, there have been studies of the *ager Cosanus* in Etruria, the Biferno valley of Molise in Samnite territory, the San Vincenzo survey, also in Molise, the San Giovanni survey of central Lucania, the Metaponto / Croton survey in Magna Graecia, the Venosa / Gravina survey on the Apulia / Lucania border and others.[44] The key areas of the *ager Falernus* and *ager Campanus* are touched on by Frederiksen in a posthumous study;[45] but this unfortunately provides little detail of the early Republican agricultural settlement of a very important area of Italy. In general, archaeological survey provides an immensely useful indication of the extent of settlement in different areas but only a coarse approach to chronology, for which detailed excavation of selected sites is required and is of course taking place. Only then will it be possible to present plans of farms, to identify rooms and their function, and possibly to reach conclusions on slave-quarters.

From 200 BC to Augustus

The last two centuries of the Republic were a period of unrest in Italy matched by Rome's expansion elsewhere; it was also accompanied by major changes in agriculture in the Italian peninsula and in the institution of slavery itself. All these phenomena were inter-related, and can be briefly recapitulated.

The withdrawal of Hannibal from Italy and his defeat at Zama in 202 BC marked the end of the Second Punic War and the Carthaginian threat to Rome. The Third Punic War (149-146 BC) formalized the outcome and turned Africa into a province. In the first century BC, the Social War of 91 to 88 was followed by continuous civil strife and power struggles until the foundation of the Empire ('the restoration of the Republic') by Augustus in 27 BC. In the East the four Macedonian Wars led to the sack of Corinth in 148 when Macedonia became a Roman province; the kingdom of Pergamum was bequeathed to Rome by Attalus III in 133 BC and became the province of Asia; while the Syrian Wars of the second century and the Mithridatic Wars of the first reached a climax in 63 BC with Pompey's reorganization of the East. In the West the Romans had conquered Cisalpine Gaul by 191, Gallia Narbonensis became a province in 121, the capture of Numantia in 133 BC marked the end of resistance in Spain, while Caesar's campaigns in Gaul and raids on Britain in the 50s saw the extension of Rome's power to the north.

Continuous warfare was a drain on the Roman army and so on the peasantry of the countryside. The creation of a professional army by Marius before 100 BC was a realistic recognition of this brutal fact. Many farmers failed to return to the land, through death or disinclination, and rural depopulation led to the formation of large estates by wealthy landowners. These were the so-called *latifundia* – though the term itself does not appear until the first century AD[46] – estates employing a big labour force to grow crops in large quantities, or run ranch-like areas for the pasturage of large flocks of sheep or herds of cattle. The model for these may well have been the Greek farms of Magna Graecia and Sicily, themselves influenced by the Carthaginian plantations of North Africa.[47] Certainly the process began before 200 BC and in Italy was a consequence of Rome's struggles with the Etruscans and the Samnites, leading to its control of Italy south of the Po. The acquisition of land through warfare brought about the formation of the *ager publicus*, public land allocated to colonies of Roman citizens and, on a larger scale, to Latin colonies. No citizen might occupy more than 500 *iugera* (*c.* 300 acres), but huge additions to the *ager publicus* after 200 BC led to wholesale evasion of the Licinian-Sextian laws by big landowners. The Gracchan reforms of 133 aimed at confiscation of excess holdings and their redistribution to the poor as smallholdings, but clearly the *latifundia* persisted. However, they were by no means a universal phenomenon and in many areas small farms coexisted with big estates, for example in Sicily and in southern Etruria.[48]

There is general agreement that slavery provided the labour necessary for *latifundia*, especially of the crop-growing variety (wheat, vines and olives).[49] The warfare of Republican Italy yielded not only land but captives who, if not ransomed, were given as booty to the victorious armies. Slave-dealers, following in the wake of the troops, were quick to snap up able-bodied men at bargain prices, or whole families after the capture of cities, and sell them later in the forum at a good profit.[50] The primacy of Sicily in the development of *latifundia* and the use of slave-labour is attested by the slave revolts of 135-132 BC and 104-101 BC, a direct expression of growing resentment about working conditions;[51] they were followed by outbreaks in Italy and Greece, culminating in the great revolt led by Spartacus which began in Capua in 73 BC and was, no doubt, primarily an agrarian outbreak.

Any discussion of the archaeological evidence for slaves in Italian agriculture in the last two centuries of the Republic must start from the literary sources, which now become of considerable importance. The three writers of most value are Cato, Varro and Columella, but the last falls in the next chapter where his work will be discussed in more detail. Marcus Porcius Cato (234-149 BC) wrote his *De agri cultura* not long before his death and it is chiefly concerned with the cultivation of the vine and olive as a commercial enterprise. Marcus Terentius Varro (116-27 BC) published his *De re rustica* in 37 BC, also towards the end of his life. Like Cato, he regards vine- and olive-growing for profit as the basis of Italian agriculture, but ranges more widely into arable farming, stock-breeding, and the rearing of specialist requirements such as poultry. Views on their reliability have varied: Gummerus concluded that Varro should be used with caution, being a theorist rather than a practical farmer like Cato.[52] Heitland, on the other hand, regarded him as much in advance of Cato, a view followed by White and Spurr.[53]

As regards slaves, both writers regard these as the chief form of labour, with the use of additional paid labour at particular times or paid craftsmen for particular operations. Cato takes as his first standard an olive yard of 240 *iugera* (*c.* 160 acres) for which he lays down a labour force of 13, presumably all slaves: a steward or overseer (*vilicus*) and housekeeper (*vilica*), with 5 labourers, 3 ox-drivers, 1 mule-driver, 1 swineherd, and 1 shepherd – the last because 100 sheep are pastured on a farm of this size (*De agri cultura* 10). For his second standard, a vineyard of 100 *iugera*, he lays down a labour force of 16: a *vilicus* and *vilica* as before, 10 labourers, 1 ox-driver, 1 mule-driver, 1 willow-worker (*salictarius* – for the withies used in tying the vines) and 1 swineherd (*De agri cultura* 11). It is usually accepted that Cato envisaged that *vilicus* and *vilica* should be man and wife, though this is not explicit (*De agri cultura* 143).

Such numbers cannot be regarded as excessive and should perhaps be thought of as minima, though the farm areas in each case are not large. Finally, Cato makes a clear reference to chained slaves (*compediti*) working on vines, who are to receive additional rations of bread and wine at certain seasons (*De agri cultura* 56-7). His references to slave accommodation are slight: *cellae familiae* (*De agri cultura* 14.2) – cubicles for slaves – in the building of a new farmstead, and the instruction that of the three men required for the wine-pressing room, the two free men should have a bed there while the third, a slave, should sleep with the other slaves (13.1). He shows a ruthless attitude in his recommendation to sell off old or sickly slaves (*De agri cultura* 2) and this strictly commercial attitude is confirmed by Plutarch's comments that Cato dealt in slaves and encouraged them to breed in order to produce *vernae* (*Cato mai.* 21). Varro does not specify any particular size of farm for vine- or olive-growing; his rather banal division of farm stock into *vocale*, *semivocale* and *mutum* introduces a discussion of the relative merits of slaves and freemen and of the choice and treatment of slaves (*De re rustica* 1.17). In the next chapter he repeats Cato's recommendations on the numbers for olive plantations of 240 *iugera* and vineyards of 100, for some reason omitting the *salictarius* in the latter (*De re rustica* 1.18) and has useful suggestions on variations in numbers according to the size and location of the farm. He has very little to say about quarters: he suggests a ?rest-room for the slaves as a whole, with a specific recommendation that the *cella* for the overseer (*vilicus*) should be by the entrance, for security; he does not mention chaining. Generally, his broader approach, in contrast to that of Cato, is in Book 2 on stock-breeding, where he discusses transhumance for sheep between Apulia and Samnium (*De re rustica* 2.1.16-17; 2.2.9-11), and ranching (*saltus*) as a method of pasturage (*De re rustica* 3.1.7-8). Slaves appear again here in connection with the desirable qualities for those employed as herdsmen: strength, agility and capacity for self-defence against robbers and wild animals (*De re rustica* 2.10); these *pastores* may be accompanied by women slaves to act as helpers. It seems highly unlikely that we shall ever obtain any archaeological evidence for the temporary huts they presumably occupied in upland areas, following the rhythm of transhumance; ethno-archaeological parallels seem the likeliest source.[54]

It is generally accepted that, in addition to these large ranches (*saltus*), the late Republic saw the formation of large crop-growing estates, even if it is true that the term *latifundia* is not known before the first century AD. The best-known reference to rural depopulation and, by implication, the formation of large farms worked by slave-labour comes from Plutarch's life of Ti. Gracchus, where his brother Gaius is recorded to have noted the strong impression which this made on Tiberius as he passed through Tuscany on his way to Spain. This is regarded as one of the motives impelling Tiberius to introduce an agrarian law in the hope of resettling the peasantry on the land, and in turn of improving military recruitment.[55] So, although the word *latifundia* does not appear in literature until the Empire the fact that Pliny could say 'latifundia perdidere Italiam' (*HN* 18.35) must surely imply that such estates had existed long enough for their evil effects to become apparent. We need not think of vast prairies with extensive cultivation of cereals, as in the American Mid-West or, nearer home, East Anglia in the post-Second World War years, but rather of consolidation of a number of small farms into single ownership; the farms may have remained independent entities and been worked by slave-labour under bailiffs for an absentee owner.

The archaeological evidence for slave-quarters in Italian farms of the last two centuries of the Republic can be found partly in older general studies, subject to later critical assessment, and partly in recent excavation reports.

Naturally, both sources are concerned with overall planning and the only attempt known to the writer to study slave-quarters in farms is that by Rossiter.[56] In his introduction the author parts company with Rostovtzeff's long-standing classification of the Campanian *villae rusticae* of the Pompeii area, following instead a structural classification like that proposed by Crova.[57] Nevertheless, these sites provide an indispensable starting point because of their number, the evidence for their manner of operation and above all the evidence for the presence of slaves from structural detail and from finds. The main problem is date, which hinges on the four styles of Pompeian wall-painting. By definition slave *cellae* are undecorated and their date must depend on that assigned to the part of the villa to which they belong; with that proviso in mind the salient facts bear repetition.

Twelve were excavated over two centuries ago in the area of Castellammare di Stabia,[58] and the remainder, to a total of 43, just before and just after 1900, to the north in the valley of the Sarno, around Pompeii, and on the lower slopes of Vesuvius. The sites of the second group were mostly published individually in *Notizie degli Scavi*, and the first general study of 36 sites was in Rostovtzeff's *Social and Economic History of the Roman Empire*, increased to the total of 43 in the second edition.[59] By 1985 the total number of villas of all kinds between Vesuvius and Castellammare di Stabia and outside the walled towns had risen to over a hundred, varying from great coastal villas on the outskirts of Stabiae, known since the eighteenth century, and newly discovered examples such as Oplontis

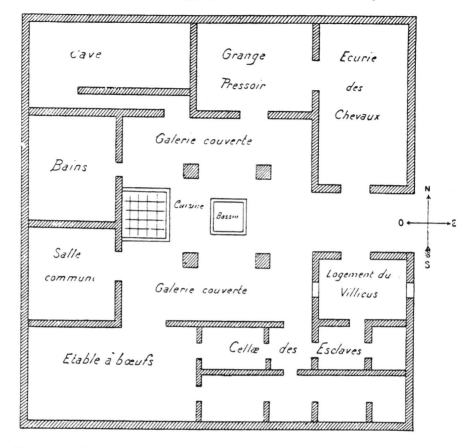

Fig. 22. A *villa rustica* after Vitruvius

('Villa of Poppaea') at Torre Annunziata to *villae rusticae* extending from the Pompeii foothills in the north to the Gragnano and Varano hills in the south.[60] Discoveries continue[61] and the total will no doubt increase. But Kockel does not discuss slave-quarters as a specific element, except in the case of the *villa rustica* at Santa Maria la Carità; he differs from de Caro in dating the stucco reliefs to just before AD 79 rather than as Neronian.[62] The classification proposed by Rostovtzeff and followed, with reservations, by others,[63] was in fact social and economic rather than architectural. His three types were: first, a combined summer residence and working farm (*villa rustica*) visited occasionally by the owner, a town resident, and run by a manager (*vilicus*), slave or free, and slave-labour; second, a working farm occupied probably full time by a well-to-do farmer; and third, an agricultural 'factory' producing wine and olive-oil and run by slave-labour like the first type. Given the circumstances of excavation, the dating of the individual villas is not easy[64] but a range from shortly before 100 BC to the time of Augustus seems likely for their construction, with later alterations in some cases and, of course, their demise in AD 79. Rossiter's alternative classification is based mainly on size and layout and he ranges widely over Italy and includes examples from post-Second World War excavation.[65] Unfortunately, in his discussion of small farms and combined farm and house he labours a suggestion of Greek influence in overall planning, ignoring the possibility of the derivation of the Roman *atrium* house from an Etruscan prototype, as instanced at Marzabotto. Graham has pointed out the 'superficial similarity' between the Olynthus *pastas* and the *alae* of the *atrium* which he described as a 'freak rapprochement'; whether or not both derived from an original *megaron* prototype is arguable, and the truth may lie in the tendency of Mediterranean houses to emphasize an internal courtyard, around which individual rooms were grouped.[66]

The archaeological approach to slave-quarters is two-fold; the word *cella* used by Cato and Varro implies a small cubicle and, if such appear as a row of identical rooms in the plan of a farm, there is a strong presumption that they constitute a slave-dormitory (*cellae familiae*), particularly if the floors are unpaved and the walls unrendered or, if plastered, without decoration; if, in addition, there is evidence in the way of fetters from these or adjacent rooms, the hypothesis becomes more compelling. A single *cella*, to one side of the main entrance, might be a room allotted to a *vilicus*, as recommended by Varro, but there is less certainty in the absence of other evidence.

In fact, no distinction need be drawn between slave-quarters in *villae rusticae* and those in the great *domus* of, for instance, the wealthy senatorial families in Rome in the late Republic, except so far as the latter contained a large number of *cellae* arranged in a more symmetrical plan. A good example of the latter has emerged from the excavation in the 1980s of the northern slope of the Palatine, with its group of great houses extending from the late Republican period to the fire of AD 64. Thus the house of M. Aemilius Scaurus, praetor in 56 BC, shows a semi-subterranean floor beneath the vast *atrium* on the piano nobile, with a uniform arrangement of plainly plastered *cellae* in a square plan; each *cella* was about 3 m (10 ft) square, with a base for a single bed set against one wall, and the whole group was associated with a shrine and the principal bath suite.[67] The total accommodation was sufficient for a staff of *c.* 50 slaves, that is, the normal complement of 25-30 with an addition for entertainment and security reasons.[68]

Villa 31 at Boscotrecase, excavated in 1903-5, meets these requirements (fig. 23).[69] It was apparently built early in the first century BC and in a compound east of the residential wing was a series of nine identical small rooms, each 2.8 x 1.9 m (9 x 6 ft), with earth floors and plain plastered walls. Della Corte stated that a further nine similar rooms existed above,

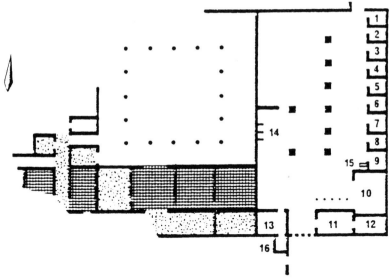

Fig. 23. Plan of Villa 31 at Boscotrecase

reached by a wooden ladder, to give a total of eighteen. Each ground-floor room had a single window, a niche for a lamp and a simple hearth near the entrance. He compared these *cellae* to those in the gladiators' amphitheatre (*ludus gladiatorius*) at Pompeii, and the other comparison is with the *contubernia* of barrack-buildings in legionary fortresses. If the total of eighteen rooms is right, then there must have been at least that many slaves, and conceivably double that number, since the size of each *cella* seems fairly generous for single occupancy;[70] the individual rooms (*papiliones*) in legionary barracks held eight men each with four times the area (4.6 m square).[71] One possible objection to their identification as slave-quarters is the discovery of jewellery etc. in the fill of the rooms,[72] but there seems to be no reason why slaves could not have owned such objects as their *peculium*. It is interesting to note that a set of iron stocks, with ten rectangular apertures to hold one or both ankles of imprisoned slaves, was found in a larger room east of the main entrance, identified as a combined *cella ostiaria* and *ergastulum* by Della Corte.[73]

The second example is Villa 34 at Gragnano (fig. 24); here a main courtyard was flanked on the south side by two smaller courtyards.[74] The west side of the main courtyard held five identical rooms with a staircase leading presumably to five similar rooms above, which have been identified as slave *cellae*. The south-east courtyard was surrounded by at least nine similar rooms, but the report does not indicate that there was an upper floor. The walls were plain and again the discovery of similar iron stocks with fourteen apertures in the south-west courtyard, where one room may have served as an *ergastulum*, helps to confirm the slave-quar-

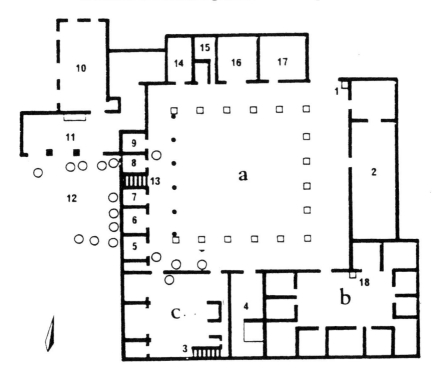

Fig. 24. Plan of Villa 34 at Gragnano

ter hypothesis. The villa itself was cited by Rostovtzeff as an example of his third type, an agricultural factory worked by slave-labour, but possibly a residential portion existed there, which was not revealed by excavation.[75] With rooms somewhat larger than those at the Boscotrecase Villa 31 – 3 x 2 m (10 x 6.5 ft) – a minimum of nineteen slaves,[76] and possibly twice that number, can be envisaged. The date is uncertain but the similarities between Villas 34 and 31 suggest that Villa 34 may have been built in the first century BC, as a production centre for oil, wine, bread and cheese.[77]

The third example is Villa 29 at Boscoreale (fig. 25), excavated in 1906, where from the plan it appears that part of the building was entered, not from the courtyard but from outside, where a staircase led up to slave dormitories.[78] It was built early in the first century BC and remained unaltered until *c.* AD 50. Slave-quarters are also claimed for Villas 2 and 5 at Castellammare di Stabia and Villa 27 at Boscoreale (fig. 26).[79] No. 27 belongs to the first century BC and it is suggested that Rooms 1-3, with a latrine (4), grouped round Courtyard B should be identified as *cellae* for slaves.[80] Four other villas in the area belong to the first century AD.

The identification of more examples of slave-quarters in Italian farms of the Republican period must largely depend on their excavators' reports.

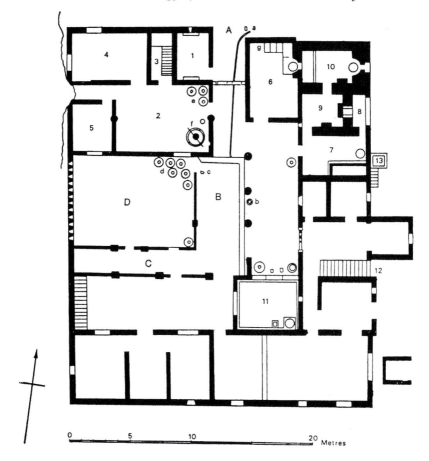

Fig. 25. Plan of Villa 29 at Boscoreale

Some no doubt have been alive to the possibility and have referred to it in their texts, but others have not; in all cases plans need to be examined, especially of areas containing the working part (*villa rustica*) of a farm, in the hope of locating replicated *cellae* (single small rooms are scarcely susceptible to identification in the absence of other evidence), while supporting evidence, fetters, graffiti and so on, can be very valuable. Unfortunately, apart from the examples just mentioned, Italy does not seem to produce fetters on the same scale as, say, Gaul.

A farm no doubt typical of many in Etruria is the Villa Sambuco (fig. 27), close to the Etruscan town site of San Giovenale. Thought to have been built *c.* 100 BC, it is claimed by the excavator to represent a *villa rustica* worked by slaves under a *vilicus*.[81] It is argued that it is typical of many such farms in Etruria which acted as the working units of large holdings

86

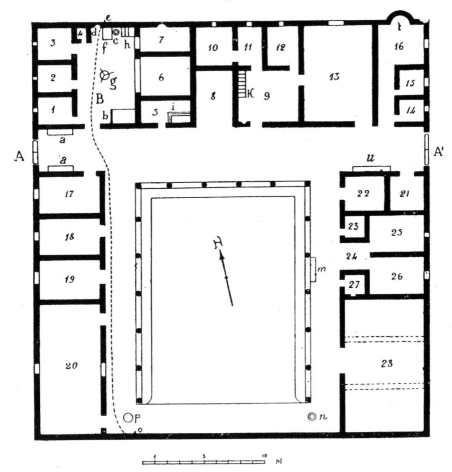

Fig. 26. Plan of Villa 27 at Boscoreale

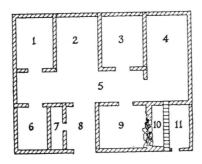

Fig. 27. Plan of Villa Sambuco

87

owned by a few families; if so, this may be all we can reasonably expect in the way of archaeological evidence for *latifundia* in Italy. On the plan it is suggested that Room 9 on the south side, suitably partitioned, may have served as slave-quarters; it stood by the entrance and, on the other side, Room 7 may have functioned as the *cella ostiaria* for a porter (*ianitor*) or bailiff (*vilicus*).[82] Vines, olives and cereal crops were evidently cultivated. The identification of slave-quarters here must be rather tenuous.

South of Rome, in the *ager Falernus*, two nearby villas of Republican date have recently been excavated near Francolise. The first, a *villa rustica* at Posto, was compared by the excavator to the Sambuco farm but no attempt was made to identify slave-quarters.[83] At the second, San Rocco, a *villa rustica* was added in the second period *c.* 50 BC (fig. 28). This consisted of a double courtyard forming an H-shaped series of rooms linked by what the excavators called 'Commons', a communal mess-room used by the *familia* of slaves sleeping in dormitories round Courtyard 2.[84] Both villas could fall into the category of small farms worked by an owner with a few slaves, or a bailiff working similarly for an absentee owner. The suggested 'Commons' might well equate with the rest-room recommended

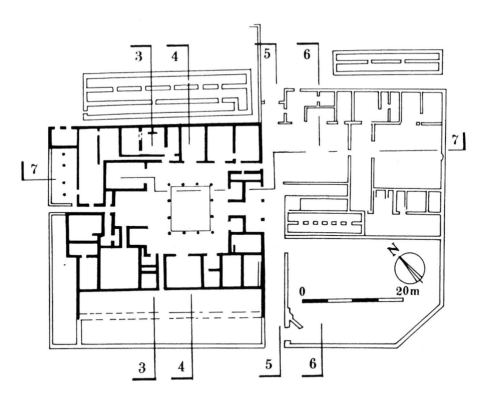

Fig. 28. Plan of Period II villa at San Rocco

by Varro for slaves. Whether the two villas fell under one ownership or simply functioned at different economic levels is difficult to determine.

To the east of Rome, in Latium, excavation at a villa site on the Via Gabina led the excavators to speculate on the presence of slave-quarters in the Republican phase of its occupation. The U-plan farmhouse (curiously reminiscent of the supposed Etrurian prototype of the *atrium* house) received a range of rooms on its west side *c.* 200 BC of which some 'were probably sleeping rooms for slaves'.[85] North of Rome the sheer intensity of villa sites in southern Etruria in the early Imperial period must indicate a late Republican phenomenon, in which evidence for slave-quarters will no doubt emerge from more detailed research and excavation.[86]

Finally, east of Rome again, in the vicinity of Horace's Sabine farm near Vicovaro, a small *villa rustica* at Prato la Corte was excavated in 1913 and described with other sites of the area (fig. 29).[87] In addition to the granary which was a distinctive feature of the *villa rustica*, Lugli described Rooms L, M and N as 'abitazione del personale addette all'azienda';[88] L and M measured 2.95 x 3.20 m and N 2.95 x 5.20 m, and, if they are to be identified as *cellae*,[89] could have accommodated ten to twenty slaves.[90] It might well have been one of the outlying farms to be inferred from the passage in Horace's *Epistles* (1.14) as forming part of his estate.[91]

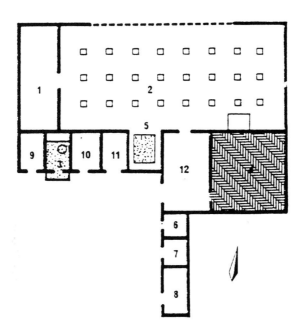

Fig. 29. Plan of *villa rustica* at Prato la Corte, Vicovaro

Slaves in Roman Agriculture: the Empire

Italy under the Empire

A chronological division at the time of Augustus presents some difficulties in a study of slave-quarters on Italian farms, since villas frequently continue from Republican into Imperial times. But the literary background offers a new perspective; some villas clearly develop into large slave-run establishments in the first century AD, and comparisons with sites in some of the western provinces are much easier under the Empire. There is also the growth of the tenant (*colonus*), especially in imperial domains (*praedia Caesaris*), and all that the development of this method of working the land implies.

The evidence from literature now becomes of considerable importance. There is some useful comment on farm buildings in Vitruvius (*De arch.* 6.6) and scattered references to agricultural practice in various writers.[1] But the most detailed information on all aspects of Roman farming in the first century AD is to be found in the twelve books of Columella's *De re rustica*. The greatest of the three agronomists, he displays an overall grasp of the theory and practice of contemporary agriculture, together with knowledge of literature of the period. He has, of course, received a large amount of study and analysis: Gummerus comments that his work has an encyclopaedic character; Heitland sees him as a conservative who laments the passing of the small independent landowner but combines his regrets with shrewd advice on the management of large estates, for example by tenants (*coloni*) of local origin; White discusses the work under this head and from the structural aspect in his section on farm buildings; and Spurr cites him frequently as a comparison in his ethnoarchaeological approach to Roman arable farming through present Italian practice.[2]

From the point of view of this study, the vital sections appear in Book 1. Columella's description of the model villa (*De re rustica* 1.16) has the familiar division into the residential section (*pars urbana*), the farmhouse proper (*pars rustica*) and storehouses (*pars fructuaria*). The *villa rustica* exists on its own, of course, when there is no resident owner and the use of this term has been anticipated already. In 1.6.3 Columella gives the desirable qualities for the kitchen in the farmhouse, and we learn that it should be regarded as a rest-room for the slaves, a use reminiscent of Varro

(1.13.1-2). Immediately afterwards appears the important division between unchained (*soluti*) and chained slaves (*servi vincti*), with the recommendation that the former should be housed in cubicles (*cellae*), sited to receive the midday sun in spring and autumn, and the latter in a communal workhouse (*ergastulum*). This last building is to be of a semi-basement type (*subterraneum*) but reasonably healthy (*quam saluberrimum*), suggesting that it should be dry; it should be lit by narrow windows placed high above the ground to prevent escape.

Quarters for the slave overseer (*vilicus*) are to be by the farm entrance, also as recommended by Varro (1.13.1-2), and there is also mention of quarters for a free-born steward (*procurator*), set above the entrance to observe general comings and goings and the *vilicus* himself. Quarters for oxherds and shepherds are to be placed near the flocks and herds, yet grouped together for convenience of supervision by the *vilicus*.

In 1.7 he discusses tenancies, with an initial repetition of the distinction between chained and unchained slaves, after which 1.8 deals with selection and treatment of slave-labour. In 1.8.16-17 we learn that chained slaves are confined to the *ergastulum* as a punishment, and in 1.9.4 that fettered slaves are commonly used in vineyards because of their strength and lively intelligence – an interesting comment on the nature of the rebellious slave. The chapter (and the book) concludes with a recommendation that slaves should work in squads (*classes*) of not more than ten men, a convenient size for supervision and control by their leader (*monitor*). Columella invokes the old term *decuria* for such a squad, a point of some importance in the arrangement of quarters for a large body of slaves in quasi-military fashion. Some repetition of recommendations on the treatment of slaves appears in the first chapter of Book 11, where Columella goes into some detail on the duties of the *vilicus*. 11.1.22 mentions the *ergastuli,* those condemned to the lock-up, and the need for them to be carefully fettered. There is further discussion (11.7) on means of restraint, the chaining and fettering of slaves and how this could be modified to enable them to work in the fields. For the moment, it is clear enough that fettering as a means of punishment was commonplace, even if the use of such prisoners in chaingangs on the land was evidently not to Columella's liking; he is critical (1.3.12) of owners of vast estates who let the land go to waste or work them with chaingangs composed of debtors. It is difficult to say how widespread was the use of the *ergastulum*, and no doubt much depended on the landowner's temperament. A frequently cited passage from the younger Pliny (*Epist.* 3.19), writing in the time of Trajan, mentions that neither he nor his neighbours use chained slaves on their estates in Gallia Cisalpina (*nam nec ipse usquam vinctos habeo nec ibi quisquam*). But one cannot say whether this was local practice or a change in attitude with the passage of time.

For the archaeological evidence we turn naturally in the first place to the same group of Campanian villas already discussed in the section on

92

the late Republic. The distinction is somewhat artificial, since the whole group persisted until the eruption of AD 79, and the evidence for precise dating is based on decorative detail, for example wall-painting, rather than stratigraphy. In spite of the early date of their investigation, the twelve villas in the vicinity of Castellammare di Stabia can now be mentioned in the context of slave-quarters.[3] Carrington dismissed Nos 6, 9 and 12 from his general study on the grounds that they provided too little information;[4] Day cited Nos 2 and 5 as having slave-quarters, relying on nineteenth-century reports of the original excavations in the eighteenth century.[5] Villa 2 is said to have had two very simple rooms (11 and 12) which could possibly be termed *ergastula*, while Villa 5 had five small rooms (2, 3, 4, 8 and 9) which appeared to be *cellae* (fig. 30).[6] The great villa in the Varano area known today as Villa del Pastore was partly explored in the eighteenth century and recently in the 1960s, though the modern excavations have been back-filled (fig. 31); among the interesting finds was the eponymous statue of a shepherd.[7] An approximately east-west range consisted of a row of fifteen small rooms with an equivalent number on an upper floor, each approximately 4 m (13 ft) wide by 5 m (16 ft) deep.[8] At first sight there is an impression of a row of slave-quarters serving a great villa, and Ruggiero's description of the range and the finds from the rooms led him to the view that these were certainly bedrooms (*cubicula*) or more properly *cellae*, but his conclusion was that the range was best explained as an inn (*hospitium*) or more probably a hospital (*valetudinarium*).[9] Fortunately, not all the evidence of villas in the Stabiae area is contained in these early and unsatisfactory reports. A further site 4 km south of Pompeii was investigated in 1958 and published recently.[10] The plan shows a series of 'celle rustiche', Rooms A, 1-3, 6 and 9, each 3.3 x 2.4 m (11 x 8 ft), except Room 9, 3.3 m (11 ft) square. The date is most likely first century AD, since the adjacent bath-house had stucco of Neronian date or possibly a little later.[11]

Of more recent investigations the Boscoreale villa (Rostovtzeff No. 13), excavated between 1876 and 1896, and famous for the discovery of the silver treasure now in the Louvre, shows a combination of *villa urbana* and *rustica*, with four slave *cellae* in the latter.[12] There were probably four similar rooms on an upper storey reached by a wooden staircase; the internal measurements were 3 x 2.5 m (10 x 8 ft) and correspond well with those already cited. Although the villa was probably constructed at the beginning of the first century BC, Carrington suggests that construction was later, and White assigns it to the first century AD.[13] There was certainly activity in the later period, which suggests that the slave-quarters should be referred to that time.[14]

In contrast, Villa 26, also at Boscoreale, seems to have been a simple *villa rustica* worked by a *vilicus* and slaves (fig. 32);[15] excavated in 1904, it was described as 'rustica e disadorna' and Rossiter suggests that the eastern range of four small *cellae*, each 3 x 3.5 m (10 x 11.5 ft), may well

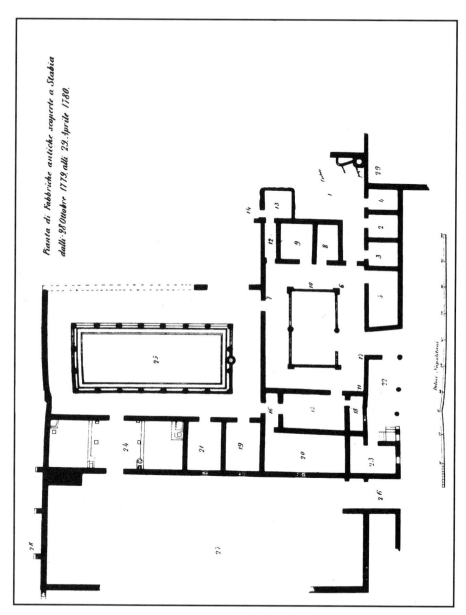

Pianta di Fabbriche antiche scoperte a Stabia dalli 28 Ottobr 1779. alli 29. Aprile 1780.

Fig. 30. Plan of Villa 5 at Stabiae

94

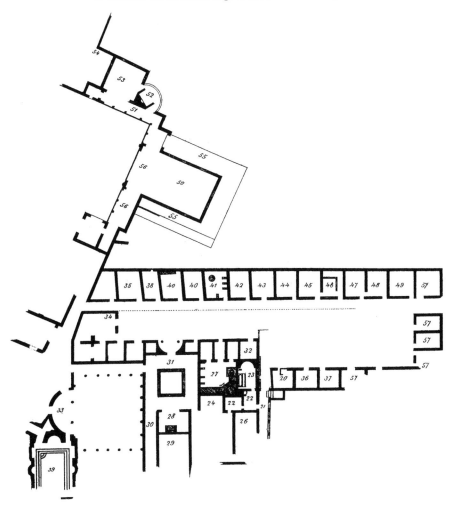

Fig. 31. Plan of Villa del Pastore, Varano

have been slave-quarters, though they are described in the original report
as a series of storerooms ('ripostigli'), with the exception of 4, a mess-room
for the slaves.[16] In the absence of decorative detail there must be uncertainty about date (Rossiter suggests the first century AD), so the villa is
again included here.

The well-known Villa dei Misteri at Pompeii (Rostovtzeff No. 24) is of
interest because of its suburban position and also because of additions and
conversions in the first century AD which changed the character of the
earlier luxurious villa.[17] Excavated mainly between the First and Second
World Wars, it received a new wing on its north-east side with rooms

95

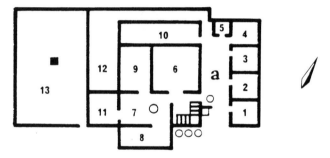

Fig. 32. Plan of Villa 26 at Boscoreale

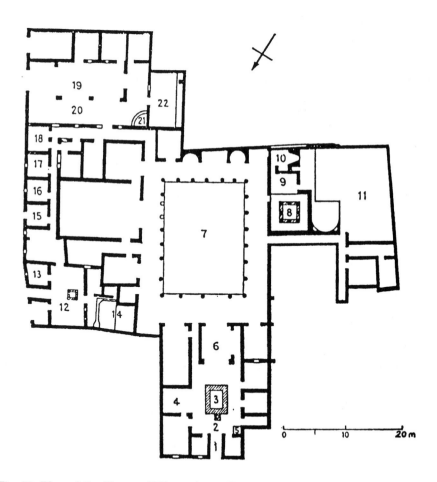

Fig. 33. Plan of the House of Menander at Pompeii

96

devoted to agricultural purposes, while a former dining-room was turned into a wine-press. An approximately triangular area in the new wing is identified as slave-quarters, although there are no uniform *cellae*. At this point, reference can also be made to the House of Menander, set in the heart of Pompeii, where again agricultural additions were made in the first century AD to the original town-house which originates in the third century BC, in this case a complete *villa rustica* on the north-east side (fig. 33).[18] Four slave *cellae* (or storerooms), each measuring 3 x 3 m (10 x 10 ft), lay on the north-east side of the courtyard (Rooms 35-38), with others on an upper floor, sufficient to house twenty slaves. There was also a small latrine (39) and a room (40) for a ?*monitor*.

The importance of these two Pompeii examples is the emphasis they throw on the close inter-relationship between town and country in the early Empire, a feature we have already encountered in both Greece and the Greek colonies of Sicily and Magna Graecia. This point had already been made by Day in 1932, following Rostovtzeff, who referred to the graffito on the wall-plaster of a room in a *taberna vasaria* (pottery shop) in Reg. III, Ins. IV, an *index nundinarius* enumerating agricultural fairs (*nundinae*) at Pompeii, Nuceria, Atella, Nola, Cumae, Puteoli and even at Capua and Rome.[19]

Thus, in the vicinity of Rome, Widrig's Site 11 continued into the Empire and in Phase 2A became a standard *atrium* house; a staircase in the south-west corner clearly served an upper storey and Widrig poses the question: 'Could the western upper rooms have been the quarters for the slaves moved from below?'[20] The more residential nature of the villa in the early Imperial period evidently did not change its essentially agricultural function, though the buildings for this may have been placed in a new compound.

North of Rome and in symbiotic relationship with the shrine-town of Lucus Feroniae was the large Villa of the Volusii, excavated in the 1960s.[21] First built towards the end of the Republic, it was substantially enlarged in the first century AD by its owners, the senatorial family of the Volusii. On the west side of the residential villa a large open court was added, flanked by a colonnade and ranges of rooms (fig. 34). Rossiter has suggested that many of the uniform small rooms in these ranges may have been the *cellae* of the villa's slave-workers though this is not entirely accepted, as Manacorda argues that the complex may have been a granary with only slight accommodation.[22]

Approximately 140 km north of Rome the excavation in 1976-81 of the villa of Settefinestre has yielded valuable evidence for the working of a villa by slave-labour from the first century BC through to *c*. AD 200;[23] it is dealt with here as a whole. Like villas already cited, this example was closely related to an urban centre, in this case the coastal town of Cosa, founded in the territory of the Etruscan city of Vulci as a Latin colony in 273 BC. In its early history the territory of the colony (*ager Cosanus*) was

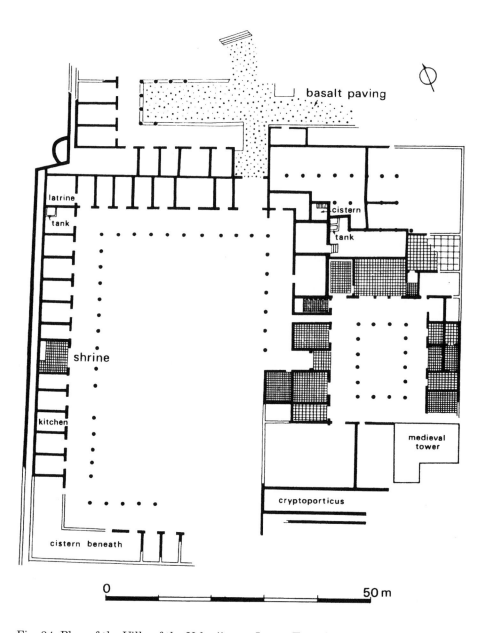

Fig. 34. Plan of the Villa of the Volusii near Lucus Feroniae

rapidly parcelled out by centuriation into smallholdings for the new colonists of possibly eight *iugera*, sufficient for a family of three to four people. Towards the end of the second century BC, and during the first, there was a move, as elsewhere, to larger farming units, villas with a scatter of small farms, possibly in dependence. Thus, in the Valle d'Oro east and south of Cosa 35 villas can be recognized, possibly with an average size of 500 *iugera* (125 ha) and related to the earlier boundaries (*limites*) of centuriation. In the Imperial period there was some abandonment (10 of the 35 in the Valle d'Oro during the second century, and a similar tendency in the whole *ager Cosanus*), for reasons which are not entirely clear.[24]

The villa itself stood on a small hill (Poggio Settefinestre) above the coastal plain, 4 km from Cosa to the west. The excavation disclosed two main periods of occupation: primary construction in the period Caesar / Octavian and an occupation until *c.* AD 100; secondary construction and occupation until the late Antonine period. Final occupation and collapse followed in the Severan period. For much of Period I ownership was vested in one of the leading families of Cosa, the Sestii, but by Period II the villa had evidently become part of the imperial domains under a procurator. Throughout, it was planned as Varro's *villa perfecta* (3.1.10), composed of a *pars urbana* and a *pars rustica*; these were less rigidly differentiated in the first period than in the second, but throughout the villa front faced north-west down the hillslope to the sea. The report offers a thoroughgoing interpretation of individual areas and rooms, for which the evidence is more convincing in some cases (for example wine-presses, olive-mill and press) than in others.

From the point of view of this study interest centres on the supposed slave-quarters, which in both periods are clearly separated from the main villa complex (fig. 35). In Period I they lay south-east and in Period II were moved to the south, in both cases grouped around a courtyard.[25] In Period I the *cellae* formed a double row of small rooms on the south-west side of the courtyard, ten being 3 m square and two 3 x 4 m with unplastered walls and earth (possibly planked) floors.[26] A quasi-military disposition is suggested, say a century (*centuria*) of 80 men, or more probably a half-century of 40, of whom four would be *monitores*, each in charge of nine slaves and given the right to have a *conserva* (female slave) in his room. Two hypothetical arrangements for their accommodation are shown.[27] In Period II the slaves were moved to *cellae* grouped round three sides of the new courtyard to the south, placed between the old courtyard and a newly built pigsty (*suile*). The former slave-quarters were converted, it is suggested, half to apartments for the overseer (*vilicus*), formerly housed in the main body of the villa, and half to quarters for the *monitores*.[28] In the new quarters the *cellae* were single rows of rooms, 17 in the first phase and 19 in the second; the dimensions were roughly the same as before (3 x 3.5 m), the walls were unplastered, and the floors, on the evidence of nails, probably boarded.[29] It is argued that there was a social change to a family

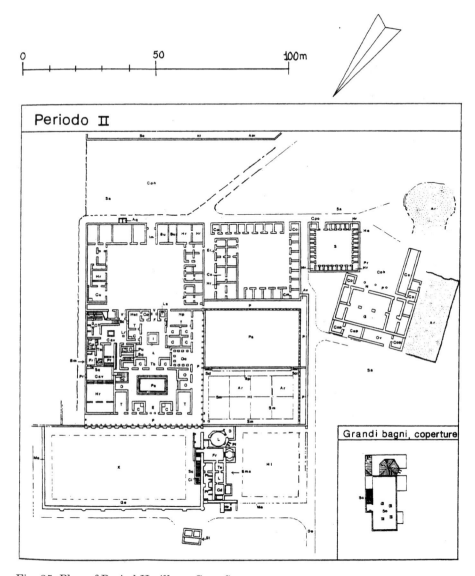

Fig. 35. Plan of Period II villa at Settefinestre

unit, and the 17 *cellae* of the first phase housed a male and female slave, with an average of two children, to give a total of 68; with those quartered here and elsewhere a rough total of a hundred is suggested for the entire slave-force.

The suggestion of military influence in Period I is further developed in the detailed discussion of individual areas: possible urban prototypes are discarded in favour of the plan of legionary fortress barracks.[30] The presence in legionary *contubernia* of space for weapons (*arma*) in front of each barrack-room (*papilio*) may strengthen the case for treating the two larger rooms in the Settefinestre *cellae* as storerooms or workrooms. Finally, in the new courtyard of Period II there was a range of rooms on the north-east side: one interpretation of their function proposes that one room served as an *ergastulum*, not of the accepted subterranean kind for chained slaves (*compediti*) but rather as punishment cells.

In general, Settefinestre provides valuable evidence for the Republican / Imperial overlap, in spite of the strong elements of conjecture. It also provides a pointer towards the total number of slaves employed in the *ager Cosanus*. It has been suggested by Dyson that upwards of 3,000 families were settled outside Cosa in the third and second centuries BC. He shows on his distribution map five villas of the Settefinestre type (Class A), for which 500 slaves would be required after AD 100;[31] his twelve Class B villas had fallen to eight in the early Empire, and could well have employed 50 each, a total of 400. The smaller Class C villas, 20 in the early Empire, might well have employed 10 each, to give a further 200. The smallest Class D sites can be excluded, but a number in excess of 1,000 could be argued for the whole *ager Cosanus*.

The American excavations at Cosa itself have shed little light on slave-quarters in the houses built there after its establishment as a Roman colony in 273 BC. One house, built *c.* 40-20 BC and occupied into the Flavian period, was a double-*atrium* structure succeeding a pair of Republican houses and the division is regarded not as the consequence of its predecessors but as a division between family and service areas, as at Pompeii. But if slaves were present, they may have been for household purposes only.[32]

In northern Italy, that is in the Po plain and Gallia Cisalpina, the evidence for slave-quarters in Roman farm buildings is still largely lacking. The larger villa certainly exists, but much of the settlement of the late Republic and early Empire is related to the foundation of colonies along the line of the Via Aemilia and the centuriation of the land still so evident from the air in the flat lands of the Po valley. Conditions were evidently not so favourable for the formation of large estates as they were further south, and probably a great deal of farming was carried on from the towns themselves in the way already referred to. So it may be necessary to look at urban house plans in the colonies themselves for the elusive *cellae*. Both aspects of agricultural life in North Italy, from the villa and from the town, have been studied in two papers.[33] The same dichotomy exists, of course, as round the Bay of Naples, presenting the same problem of the definition of the term *villa*: on the one hand, we have the luxurious residential establishment such as the villa of Catullus on Sirmione or the maritime villas on the Adriatic coast around Pola and Trieste, which compare with Hadrian's villa at Tivoli or the coastal villa of Oplontis, near Pompeii; on the other are more workaday establishments combining residential and agricultural sections of the same type as those round Pompeii. There can be no doubt that the palace-like villa must have had a substantial workforce of slaves, and probably their quarters can be identified and shown to be similar to those on big farms. But in the context of agriculture it is the second type which concerns us.

Of these, the best-known example is the villa at Russi, *c.* 14 km west of Ravenna. Despite the problem of excavating a site deeply buried in flood silt, the overall plan is now emerging. Founded in the Augustan period, it passed through various developments and enlargements until it was abandoned in late antiquity. Though large, there was no rigid separation of residential and working quarters but in time evidence for slave-quarters will no doubt emerge.[34] It seems more than likely that, as in the case of Settefinestre, there was a process of merging of the original land allocations in the colonies of North Italy in the late Republic and early Empire to produce a number of larger estates centred on villas such as Russi in which a slave labour force, and consequently accommodation, must have been prominent.

Later developments in Italian agriculture can only be discussed summarily. We have on the one hand some decline in the use of slaves, partly because of diminished supply and partly through a change in attitude. At the same time, and possibly connected, there is the increase in the number of *coloni*, 'tenants' as opposed to the earlier use of the word simply to indicate a cultivator, side by side first with *latifundia* and then imperial and municipal estates. Finally, in the fourth century, tenants were legally tied to the land and those who had worked the land as free men, sometimes employing slaves, had themselves become quasi-servile in the role of serfs.[35] It seems probable that from the late third century there was agricultural prosperity associated with a limited class of large landowners. We return in fact to southern Italy, and in particular to Sicily, where a limited number of great villas may be the evidence for such a change. It is by no means certain that Piazza Armerina, built in the fourth century, was purely residential, set as it is in good farming country; further buildings remain to be discovered beyond the limits of excavation and these may include agricultural buildings, and consequently slave-quarters.[36] Other late Roman villas in Sicily and Magna Graecia may fall into a similar category and ultimately produce evidence for their agricultural and social context.

The provinces

Any attempt to make a general survey of the role of slaves in the agriculture of the Roman provinces and, more narrowly, the evidence for their presence is confronted with a mass of literature in the form of reports on individual sites and their excavation. Such an effort would, in fact, be self-defeating, largely because the reports themselves do not address the problem, and it would be difficult to isolate slave-quarters in individual plans except in rare cases. So, it is necessary to return to older general syntheses which give a useful background picture.[37] But for greater detail one needs to turn to studies of particular building types, and particularly the villa, such as that by Percival, who not only sketches the historical and agricultural developments in the Empire but devotes a long chapter to regional types and distribution, with maps and lists for Gaul and Britain and a critical apparatus of notes and sources.[38] Individual provinces have been studied, for example Britain, Pannonia and Spain, and these and the more general studies provide some kind of starting point.[39] The order adopted below is that in which the provinces were acquired and follows the example of Percival;[40] the emphasis is on Africa, Britain, Gaul and Spain – the agricultural provinces of the Empire.[41]

Spain

With the end of the Second Punic War in 201 BC Rome was able to consolidate its position in Spain after the defeat of the Carthaginians at Ilipa in 206 BC. But the establishment of the two provinces of Hispania Citerior and Ulterior in the east and west respectively in 197 BC did not lead to settled conditions, although Rome gained much in the way of grain and metals. It was the prospect of riches, especially from mining, that attracted Italian immigrants after 150 BC (Diod. 5.36.3), but agriculture was also a powerful attraction.[42] A final pacification was not achieved until the reign of Augustus, when Ulterior was divided into Baetica and Lusitania, while Citerior was ultimately to become Tarraconensis. The slower pace of conquest in the north-west was to be reflected in urbanization under the Empire and the associated agricultural development marked by the founding of villas. These were features of Baetica in the west and the coastal strip in the east, where fertile plains and river valleys were extremely productive. In these areas, then, we find the introduction of capitalistic husbandry which changed the peasant economy to one based on large estates, which gradually substituted the vine and olive for cereal crops, so much so that Domitian was eventually compelled to impose restrictions on the planting of vines.[43] During the first and second centuries AD native Spaniards and immigrant Italians prospered from these agricultural changes, and the cities of Baetica and Tarraconensis flourished, whereas the north-west never developed to the same extent. Side by side with the rich owners and their lands were the huge imperial estates acquired by confiscation and leased to larger (*conductores*) and smaller tenants (*coloni*). Such was the overall pattern to which the distribution of villas in imperial Spain was related: thus they occur on the coastal plains and on good arable land below 500 m in the valleys of the Ebro in the north-east, the Guadalquivir in the south and the Tagus in the west.[44] Although Spain was an exporter of corn to Italy, its wine and oil seem always to have been more important and its olive-oil in particular was of better quality (and cheaper) than its Italian counterpart.[45] The changes in agricultural production in Spain have been summarized chronologically by Menéndez Pidal.[46]

The use of slaves in Spanish agriculture is beyond doubt though the archaeological evidence for their presence in the countryside is less clear. Even before the arrival of the Romans, Polybius and Livy comment on the taking of prisoners by the Carthaginians for slaves, and the process continued in the last two centuries BC. Many of these must have gone to the mines, for example the 40,000 sent to the silver mines of Cartagena, but the growth of colonization in the first century BC meant that land-owners were eager to use them on the land, a process which continued in the first two centuries AD, particularly with the development of absentee landlords running large estates through *vilici*.[47] A recent study asserts: 'Luxurious villas staffed by large numbers of slaves, as in central Italy, are largely absent in the Spanish provinces of the late Republic and early Empire.'[48] But this is surely an overstatement and a confusion of the purely residential type of Italian villa, as at Oplontis or Tivoli, with large agricultural establishments such as the Campanian villas around Pom-peii. It is certainly true that great self-sufficient villas were a feature of northern and central Spain from the fourth century, after the crisis brought on by the third-century barbarian invasions and the decay of the towns, but this should not be allowed to obscure the presence of large villas with a substantial slave labour force in predominantly agricultural areas in the earlier period.

The problem of a satisfactory definition of the word *villa* has preoccu-pied writers from antiquity onwards and no time will be spent on it in this study which is content to use the term for a Roman or Romanized farm, that is, a building or group of buildings with an agricultural function and accommodation for owners and / or workforce; Columella's distinction between *villa urbana* and *villa rustica* has, of course, already been fre-quently used to define the owner's quarters as opposed to those of the workers. This question of definition figures early in a recent study of Spanish villas which provides the basic information on structural details.[49] A historical study of the growth of villas in the peninsula is accompanied by distribution maps for the different periods.[50] Of these the map covering the period AD 280-400 is particularly pertinent, showing the relatively even distribution of the great country estates as compared with the southern and eastern concentrations of the earlier periods. As regards typology, Gorges distinguishes (1) a linear plan, (2) a rectangular plan with peristyle and (3) the 'villa aulique', a monumental type of the later period. His types 1 and 2 are not mutually exclusive in Spain, or farther afield, but only to the extent that the peristyle plan is essentially Mediterranean, and so finds its limit in southern Gaul.

Gorges' discussion of the *villa rustica* in the Iberian peninsula and, in particular, the recognition of slave-quarters at certain villas promises to be helpful.[51] But in fact, apart from stressing the need for clearer identification of slave-quarters in order to arrive at a quantitative assessment of the labour force, he merely cites the villa of Foz de Lumbier in Navarre.[52] First built in the second century AD, it was destroyed by barbarian raids *c.* AD 270, and then rebuilt on a larger scale in the fourth century, with extensive additions later in the same century. In the fourth-century rebuild the slaves' rooms are identified as those east of the central peristyle,[53] with plain pebble-concrete floors and two wash-basins, one for men and one for women. Even more interesting is the slightly later extension to the south-east, a courtyard 85 m long and 27.5 m wide, flanked on the long sides by 44 more or less identical small rooms.[54] Doubt has been expressed whether these are quarters for slaves or serfs and the suggestion has been made that they were quarters for a peasant-militia.[55]

Other possible examples are at the villa of Santervas del Burgo, Soria, where it is suggested that Rooms VII and VIII next to the owner's quarters may have been for slaves;[56] and the villa at Falces, Navarre, where the fourth-century rebuild shows a series of four identical rooms with simple paved floors, adjacent to a wine-press.[57]

In a sense, it is not possible to distinguish the Roman villas of modern Portugal from those of modern Spain, but some useful material has recently become available for Portugal.[58] Little is as yet known of villas generally in Portugal except for those in the south and in the coastal strip. *Latifundia* are well represented in the form of great villas in Alentejo and Algarve, such as São Cucufate, Torre de Palma and Milren. Alentejo particularly, with its undulating plains south of the Tagus, was well suited to large-scale agriculture and the vine and the olive were preferred crops.

As regards slave-quarters, these have been suggested for Milren on the south-east side of the peristyle, and for Torre de Palma surrounding the trapezoidal patio to the west; a fourth-century date is probable for both.[59] They are both peristyle villas, whereas São Cucufate is classed as a villa with loggia; vaulted rooms in the central part may have been servants' quarters, but there is in addition a *pars rustica* with the residence of a *vilicus* and slave-quarters adjoining a wine-press.[60] But the author emphasizes the lack of knowledge about small farms in the rest of Portugal and comments that slave-quarters are almost entirely unknown.[61]

If the published evidence for slave-quarters in the villas of Spain and Portugal is so far slight, there has on the other hand been some attempt to suggest the presence of *ergastula*. Gorges discusses the feature: he discounts its existence at the Liedena villa, as suggested by some, and refers to the hypothesis that one existed at the Portuguese villa of Monte de Meio, Beja.[62] Here were combined a *villa urbana* and *villa rustica*, a wine-press and bath-building, all probably of the late fourth century. The building conjecturally identified as an *ergastulum* had thick walls and a heavy door set on iron hinges. Another may have existed at the Portuguese villa of Alcontin, Faro; the chronology is uncertain, though the site has produced early material and may have been a cloth-making centre; the supposed *ergastulum* is again a thick-walled building, without windows.[63] A third example has been claimed at yet another Portuguese villa, Quinta de Rebeira, Braganca, also of the late third or fourth century AD, but with occupation of the late Republic; a building set apart is claimed as a possible *ergastulum*.[64] But the one fairly certain example is at the villa of Els Munts, Altafulla, 12 km north-east of Tarragona.[65] The main period was between AD 100 and 250; the villa was sacked and burned soon after 268, and then rebuilt in the fourth century. The *ergastulum* was a narrow semi-subterranean structure with walls of triple thickness for over half its length. In it were found iron fetters, presumably for slaves, some with traces of bones, thought to have been the remains of *vincti* at the time of the raid of AD 268.[66]

In comparison with Sicily and Magna Graecia little can be said of the Greek colonies of the east coast of Spain, such as Rhode, Emporion, Hemeroskopeion and Mamake, except that their basis was evidently trade rather than agriculture. As a result they attracted Carthaginian hostility, though the losses sustained in the sixth century were offset by the foundation of new sites and the resumption of trade by Emporion and Hemeroskopeion. The Roman *coloniae*, founded for motives of military control as well as of urbanization, were linked with agricultural exploitation of the surrounding countryside: as in the earlier Greek colonies, the internal layout of the new towns was carried into the country by a process of centuriation, of which evidence has been recovered in a number of cases.[67] But much work remains to be done on the identification of the farmsteads built by the colonists in their land allotments, and consequently on the slave-quarters for the labour force which must surely have been used.

North Africa

The provinces acquired by Rome along the coast of North Africa from the Red Sea in the east to the Atlantic in the west showed some similarities with Spain, but also some significant differences. The events leading to their formation can be stated quite briefly. The destruction of Carthage in 146 BC was followed by the formation of Africa Proconsularis, a fairly small province centred on the city, which was then extended south to cover most of modern Tunisia and east along the coast into modern Libya, where it met the province of Cyrenaica, formed in 74 BC. To the west, into modern Algeria, the Numidian territories were annexed to Africa by Caesar after the battle of Thapsus in 46 BC and eventually established as a separate province of Numidia; while farther west still, into modern Morocco, the Moorish territory of Mauretania was established as the two provinces of Mauretania Caesariensis in the east and Mauretania Tingitana in the west before AD 44, in the reign of Claudius. The original Carthaginian territory was, of course, the most productive agriculturally, irrigated by the Medjerda and its tributaries, and farming was the mainstay of the economy before the arrival of the Romans. The new territory was declared *ager publicus* and, despite the failure of Gaius Gracchus to promote settlement there, there was evidently a considerable movement of Roman and Italian merchants on to the land in the first century BC,[68] followed by the foundation of colonies under Caesar and Augustus. The same process seems to have taken place in the other provinces in the first and second centuries AD. There was an inevitable tendency towards the formation of large estates and *latifundia*, with owners living in the coastal cities, though their position was not without risk as is shown by the well-known confiscation of the estates of six great landlords by Nero, by which half of the province of Africa became an imperial domain (Pliny, *NH* 18.6.35). But, so far as it is possible to generalize, there was evidently still a large body of independent and indigenous farmers, of peasant or higher status, cultivating their small plots side by side with tenants and hired workmen on the great estates.[69]

For North Africa as a whole, the narrow coastal belt offered a favourable environment for agriculture so long as the rains were adequate; in the province of Africa itself, the river Medjerda (ancient Bagradas) and its valley offered an extremely favourable microclimate, with a relatively high annual rainfall which has continued to modern times, sufficient to enable the climate to be described as Mediterranean.[70] Cereal crops were the mainstay of this Numidian territory, but the Carthaginian nobility are held to have favoured the olive and the vine. This was changed by Roman colonization; the emphasis switched back to cereals, so that Africa, with Egypt, became the granary of Rome. Encouragement was given to the bringing back into cultivation of waste lands by the Lex Manciana, probably in the Flavian period, while Domitian's edict against vine-growing tended to work in favour of grain. But it is probable that there was always a temptation to pursue the profitable vine and olive, even though African wine and oil were cheap and of inferior quality. Away from the coast, where the mean annual rainfall was low, it was only possible to cultivate the olive and then only by careful conservation of water for irrigation.[71] But, although there was specialization in some areas, the impression of North African agriculture is one of fertility and variety, as is attested by the mosaics of rural scenes from the villas.[72]

It was long held that there was a tradition of gang-slavery in North Africa, originating in a plantation system developed by the Carthaginians, but this has now been discounted.[73] With the Roman conquest and the influx of colonists, it seems likely that agricultural slavery may have been relatively widespread in the late Republic, supplied from the large number of captives after the end of the Third Punic War. But then, it is argued, there was a progressive decline in the role of slaves under the Empire, accentuated by Nero's seizure of *latifundia*, compensated by the increased presence of *coloni* on imperial estates, free-born farmers who met their obligation to their landlords by payments in kind or by labour service (*operae*). But these *coloni* were far removed from the serf-like peasants of the late Empire and could themselves employ slaves. There is certainly literary and iconographical evidence for the use of slaves in North Africa under the Empire: Apuleius (*Apologia* 93) asserts that a farm owned by his wife, Pudentilla, had 400 slaves in its workforce; elsewhere (*Apologia* 47) he refers to the keeping of chained slaves (*vincti*) in a lock-up (*ergastulum*). His trial, at which the *Apologia* was his defence, took place in Tripolitania in AD 158. Negro slaves are depicted on North African mosaics.[74] But by and large, it seems likely that slaves did not play such an important part in the agriculture of North Africa as they did in that of Italy.[75] Duncan-Jones comments on the lack of archaeological evidence but suggests that small landowners had one or two slaves each.[76]

Any attempt to identify slave-quarters in North Africa comes up against the problem of the variety of domestic architecture in the agricultural life of the various provinces. At one extreme are the *villae* of the *coloni*, set on huge imperial or private estates, or on marginal lands away from the better-irrigated coast; at the other are lavish coastal villas occupied by an owner who preferred this type of residence to urban life; and somewhere in between are houses in the various cities and towns, which in some cases had owners directly involved in agriculture. The farms of *coloni* were evidently classed as *villae*, self-sufficient installations producing a variety of crops, from the evidence of epigraphy (for example, the frequently studied inscriptions from the Bagradas valley south-west of Carthage), literature (for example, Caesar's description of farms he saw in his African campaign of 46 BC (*Bell. Afr.* 67.2)), and archaeological evidence from the *fundus Aufidianus*, north of the Bagradas valley estate.[77]

Unfortunately, the coastal villas have not been studied in detail from the economic point of view, there having been a concentration on art historical aspects, e.g. mosaics. *Villae* of *coloni* have been considered extensively, for example in Mauretania Caesariensis, where the territory surrounding Caesarea (Cherchel) has been surveyed by Leveau. He notes the presence of larger villas, a few with an identifiable *pars urbana* on the coast or main road to Tipasa, involved in the production of oil and wine, with smaller farms in the hinterland.[78] Farther west, in Mauretania Tingitana, a villa such as Jorf el Hamra, which seemed to concentrate on olive-growing, displays a courtyard surrounded by various rooms of which some might possibly be slave-quarters of the first to third century AD.[79] At the other extreme are the olive farms of Tripolitania, probably established to exploit marginal land from the late first century AD onwards. A good example is Henseir Sidi Hamdan, with its courtyard flanked on two sides by olive-presses and with stores or labourers' (?slaves') quarters opening directly on to the yard.[80]

Villas related to towns or the town-houses of landowners are perhaps the most likely source of evidence for slave-quarters. Urban growth in the new provinces had certain marked phases: the original towns of the Carthaginian period persisting into the late Republic, colonies founded by Caesar and Augustus, and the final outburst of town building, again an aspect of colonization from the Flavians onwards.[81] It seems certain that the territory of the newly founded colonies underwent centuriation to allocate plots to its new inhabitants.[82] Those cultivating land near the town would no doubt work their fields from there, sending out their slave labour force or hired men each day, while those with land further out would presumably have their labourers quartered there, managed for day-to-day purposes by a *vilicus*. Within towns there is as yet no body of evidence which would permit generalization, and each needs to be considered in the light of particular excavations. For instance at Caesarea, Leveau comments on the difficulty of identifying slave-quarters there as opposed to Djemila and Timgad.[83] At Uthina on the other hand, in Africa Proconsularis, we have an essentially agricultural colony dating from the time of Caesar, which possessed fairly lavish houses with mosaics; a notable example is the so called 'House of the Laberii' (fig. 36), a peristyle villa in which Rooms 13, 14, 15 and 16 'semblent avoir été réservées au portier et aux esclaves', presumably household rather than agricultural slaves.[84] Tripolitania seems to have been the exception, with coastal villas east and west of Leptis Magna, such as Zliten, 35 km to the east; the excavation before and after the First World War was notable chiefly for the rich floor and wall mosaics, with their pictorial representations of agricultural life and buildings; the plans suggest that much has still to be learned of the overall complex.[85] The villa had a long life from the Flavian period on, and it seems likely that it was the centre of a large and self-sufficient agricultural estate with an owner permanently in residence. Where the slaves used for labour were housed must remain a matter for speculation.

Villas of this size were a late feature elsewhere, not appearing until the fourth century,[86] as for instance in Mauretania, for example the great stables at Val d'Or and the oil farm at Kharba.[87] But these can only have been the rural centres of wealthy landowners, living on a self-sufficient basis in a semi-feudal style and working their vast estates with, possibly, a mixed force of *coloni* and slaves who could also be used for defensive purposes. They were matched by the flight of smaller farmers to the towns, presumably for security, and the appearance of agricultural features, for example olive-presses, in the former town houses, as at Utica.[88]

In the earlier centuries of the Empire a large proportion of the essentially agricultural population of Roman North Africa was concentrated in the numerous flourishing cities of the different provinces, going to and from the fields on a daily basis, as in Greece and Italy; the peasantry of imperial and private *latifundia* lived locally in the *fundus*.[89] So, it is to town-houses that one naturally turns for evidence of slave-quarters, except

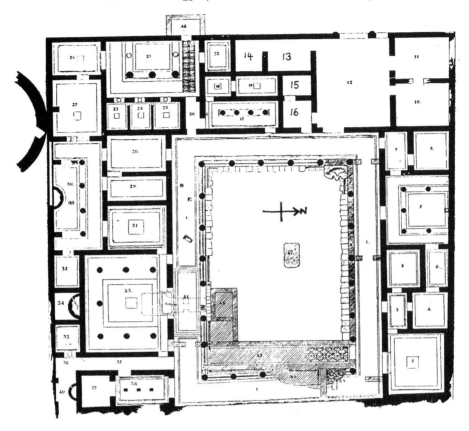

Fig. 36. Plan of the 'House of the Laberii' at Uthina

that excavation has largely concentrated on the richer examples with quarters for domestic servants, and the humbler quarters of slave field-workers are virtually unknown.[90] Excavation reports for the major urban sites have little to reveal. In Mauretania Tingitana a number of town-houses are known from Volubilis: in the so-called 'Palace of Gordian', of the first to third centuries AD, it is suggested that the servants' quarters were on the first floor, but in any case these were probably for the house staff.[91] The third-century houses in the north-east quarter are of greater interest: of the 26 houses investigated, 10 were engaged in oil-pressing and 7 in corn-grinding and baking, a direct link with surrounding agriculture. The report suggests moderately prosperous owners using a *'familia* nom-breuse'.[92] In Mauretania Caesariensis the position at Caesarea has already been discussed. A little further east, the Villa des Fresques is described as having 'Des locaux secondaires à usage de celliers ou … d'habitation pour la domesticité'.[93] In Numidia the *colonia* built in AD 100

110

for veterans of the Third Legion at Timgad has been extensively excavated and the rectilinear plan shows much of the interior to have been occupied by *insulae* of houses; fairly soon expansion led to extra-mural house building on a much less regular pattern, and the city clearly prospered,[94] but the only suggestion of slave-quarters is at the large House of Sertius, where a staircase is thought to have led to an upper floor with *coenacula* of servants.[95] Coastal villas are known at Hippo Regius, also in Numidia, in 'Le quartier du "Front de Mer" ', peristyle houses at Utica, near Carthage, in Africa Proconsularis with a history extending from late Republican times until late in the imperial period,[96] at Carthage, where the results of recent excavations await publication in some cases, inland at Thugga, and at Thysdrus (El Djem). The House of the Laberii at Uthina has already been discussed, as has centuriation round Hadrumetum (Sousse), to which may be added La Maison des Masques in the town. Farther east, a few houses have been excavated at Leptis Magna in Tripolitania and fewer still at Cyrene in Cyrenaica. Ward-Perkins would separate Cyrenaica from the rest of Roman North Africa on the grounds of Greek influence;[97] but the peristyle house is ubiquitous along the North African littoral. Other towns of the provinces have been investigated, but on the whole, with the exception of Timgad and Volubilis, the evidence for town-houses is patchy and consequently slave-quarters have not been identified. In principle the town of Bulla Regia, set in the fertile Bagradas valley and with colonial status from the time of Hadrian, might seem to offer potential for research into slave-quarters for those commuting to the fields on a daily basis, but the third- to fourth-century houses excavated there have not been discussed from this point of view; interest has rather concentrated on the subterranean living-apartments for the owners, instituted for climatic reasons.[98] A conclusion reached by the excavator of houses at Djemila (Cuicul) could well apply to the North African cities as a whole: 'Les pièces de service sont rares et difficiles de distinguer des autres salles, comme toujours dans la maison africaine.'[99]

Gaul

A fundamental question arises immediately in the study of slaves in agriculture in Roman Gaul, even before the customary discussion of the environmental and geographical factors which determined the different farming methods in its component provinces: to what extent did slaves figure in the workforce? Views on this point have changed over the years and are best expressed in a striking volte-face by that authoritative writer on ancient slavery, Moses Finley. Originally he argued that slavery was more common in Gaul (and also in Spain and North Africa) than many writers would admit, claiming that this was the only way to explain the large farm building complexes of imperial Gaul.[100] In the second edition he retains the note but adds a later rider: '... large sectors (in both time and

111

place) of the Graeco-Roman world never employed productive slave labour on any significant scale ... I now also believe that in North Africa certainly, and in Spain and Gaul probably, local varieties of dependent labour survived the Roman conquest as they had done in the East.'[101] His references indicate that this change of view was the consequence of published work rather than his own independent research, but as always his brilliant and magisterial style tends to induce acceptance.

Recent general works on Roman Gaul or its component provinces also tend to minimize the role of slaves in the rural economy. Drinkwater, excluding Narbonensis because of its similarity to Italy and Spain, and dealing with Gallia Comata between 58 BC (Caesar's conquest) and AD 260 (the Gallic Empire) argues that: 'It is generally agreed that the landlords of both periods [sc. late Iron Age Gaul and fourth- and fifth-century Roman Gaul] exploited the labour of a, at least nominally, free population, not that of slaves.'[102] He accepts the view that continuity can 'reasonably' be claimed during the intervening centuries, when the countryside was, on the evidence of numerous villas, being heavily farmed. Like Finley, he relies on recently published work as his authority.[103] In the most recent general study King develops the 'social' explanation of the great double courtyard villa of northern Gaul, with the patron in the main building and clients (that is dependent workers) in the small buildings of the outer courtyard; he claims that epigraphy and literature give little support for the idea of large slave numbers in the Gaulish and German countryside, but concedes that, from epigraphic evidence, rural slaves were more numerous in Narbonensis, with its similarity to Italy.[104] He cites MacMullen and his review of the literary and epigraphic evidence for agricultural slavery in the provinces and his conclusion that this can never have been more than a 'few per cent' under the Empire, as opposed to a figure of up to 25 per cent of the urban population, but not the reply by Samson, who makes the point that the dearth of epigraphy for rural slaves does not necessarily mean that there were very few slaves but simply that they were rarely able to afford grave inscriptions.[105] Samson laments the lack of archaeological study of possible slave-quarters in villas but adds the welcome comment that 'chains ... are not unknown archaeologically'.[106] He further suggests that *servi* and *coloni* together formed the workforce for the great villas of the Somme; certainly, the distinction between the two groups may have become blurred in late Roman times, when slavery was not an important feature anyway, but it might be argued that they were quite distinct groups in the first two centuries AD.[107]

To one not involved in the interchange of views on the social composition of rural life in Gaul and Britain there is an overall impression of speculation, not obviously supported by decisive historical or archaeological evidence. As often in unresolved questions there is a tendency for writers to follow the current trend, in the case of Gaul to substitute serf-like *coloni* for slaves as the labour force throughout the Roman period (the hypothesis that the villa plan expresses the structure of the occupying family seems even more speculative). Certainly, the earlier view that the number of slaves on Gaulish farms was very large[108] should perhaps be largely discounted, but it may not be wrong to suggest that slaves formed an important element. Wightman proposed a range of large, medium and small villas, the last inhabited by owner-occupiers or bailiffs, or even a good class of tenant, perhaps the *coloni* of the inscriptions.[109] But she pointed out that the position was more complex than this at the lower end of the social scale, with 'villages', for example, in the Vosges, and on balance she favoured the survival of the Iron Age class of agrarian serfs into the villa system, speculating that the inhabitants of *villae rusticae* or hamlets were such serfs, labelled *coloni* on inscriptions. Samson makes the point that the two inscriptions from Gaul naming *coloni* are as slight in number as those for slaves so that, using the MacMullen argument, one might make the equally valid proposition that *coloni* were a negligible factor in the agrarian workforce.[110]

The problem is considered from the reverse direction by Belova who considers agriculture in Roman Gaul from the premise that slavery was an essential element of the social framework.[111] The Marxist methodology is conventional enough, but the use of excavation evidence and such finds as fetters is interesting. The conclusion is that there was a mixed pattern of labour: slaves, *coloni* (related to clients) and probably hired labour when necessary, and that a serf-like colonate was a feature of the third and fourth centuries.[112] This would agree with the older view of a development of *coloni* as serfs rather than tenants after the barbarian invasions and crises of the second half of the third century.[113]

A final remark: the long tradition of slave-trading in Celtic Gaul expressed in Strabo's equation of a slave for an amphora of wine (5.26.3) and Caesar's vast haul of prisoners during his Gallic wars must surely have offered a familiar background to the use of slaves by a Romanized Gaulish aristocracy? But more of this below.

This is perhaps the moment to consider, if only briefly, the development of the rural labour force other than slaves. The most accessible discussion remains that of Heitland and his index of Latin words provides a useful list of the changing definitions of the word *colonus*.[114] At the risk of over-simplification, we begin with the colloquial use of the word as a 'cultivator', and the legal definition of the veteran or citizen with freehold possession of land allotted by the *colonia*. Possibly simultaneously, we find the use of the word to denote a tenant farmer, free in status but bound by the terms of his lease to render produce or labour (*operae*) to his landlord. It is suggested that the tenant farmer was the result of a growing shortage of slaves and that steadily both small freeholders and these tenant farmers declined in economic status to become a peasant class, bound to the land that they worked. This ultimate definition of *coloni* had developed by the third century AD, and Constantine's law of AD 332, forbidding the migration of *coloni* from the land that they worked, was probably an attempt to give legal authority to a *de facto* practice. It is this provision which, it is claimed, marked the introduction of a serf class; at all events slaves appear to have been a diminishing element. Mention should also be made of the *inquilini*, the barbarians settled within the borders of the Empire during the third century, chiefly in the northern provinces. Legally, they seem to have ranked below free-born *coloni* but above slaves.

'The Gaulish provinces are the villa provinces *par excellence* ...',[115] so it is not surprising that Percival's study of the Roman villa devotes more space to Gaul than to any other area of the Empire. However, slaves do not figure in the section on Gaul, nor do they appear in his discussion of villa society and tenure patterns, where the role of the colonate and the emergence of a 'seigneurial' class are emphasized. It may be that *coloni*, in the sense of free but landless peasants (proto-serfs), provided the labour force rather than slaves, but inferences from villa sizes, plans and distribution must remain speculative.

Taking the Gaulish provinces individually, we begin naturally with the earliest, Narbonensis, annexed as a province towards 100 BC and already subject to Mediterranean culture through Greek colonization. Rivet's study is a detailed source book but does not provide any synthesis of rural life nor, more specifically, any discussion of the role of slaves. Ferdière and King both accept that the evidence for rural slaves is strongest in Narbonensis.[116]

The great villa of Chiragan, on the Garonne south of Toulouse, has for long typified the high degree of Romanization achieved in Narbonensis.[117] Explored as early as the seventeenth century, it was definitively excavated by Joulin in 1895-9. Possibly the centre of the great estate of a wealthy local family, the Aconii,[118] the first of its four main periods of occupation was probably Augustan, when a peristyle villa with baths was built overlooking the Garonne. In a vast courtyard to the east lay three lines of farm buildings, of which the second consisted of simple rectangular, timber-framed huts, of varying dimensions and sometimes with a veranda. These Joulin suggested were the individual family huts of the farm-workers, 'esclaves ou colons', totalling 100 individuals.[119] They continued in use throughout the second (Trajanic) and third (late second-century) periods, and in the third period further workers' accommodation and a residence for a *vilicus* were built in the third line, with potential room for 60 individuals. Two buildings of the second period, LV and LVIII, to the east of the second line, were conjecturally identified by Joulin as poultry houses, while Grenier made the further suggestion of pigsties.[120] At all events, they have the barrack-like plan reminiscent of slave-quarters in Italian villas. This third period of the villa's life may have endured until the second half of the third century. Even if the barbarian invasions may have had little physical impact on the area, a fourth and final period of the late third and fourth centuries saw structural changes before destruction

by the Vandals *c.* AD 400, with humble living-quarters placed in what had
once been the more luxurious areas of the villa.[121] Now we may suppose
that the estate was being worked by serf *coloni*. Joulin discussed other
villas and settlements of the area and speculated on their relationship
with the great villa. He has been followed in this by later writers, but the
evidence can only be inferential and in any case cannot afford any direct
help for this particular inquiry.[122]

The villa of Montmaurin, 30 km to the west, is strictly in Aquitania, but
can be discussed here in view of similarities in plan and chronology (fig.
37). Set on the left bank of the Save, a tributary of the Garonne, it was first
excavated in 1879-82 and more methodically in 1947-60.[123] It began life in

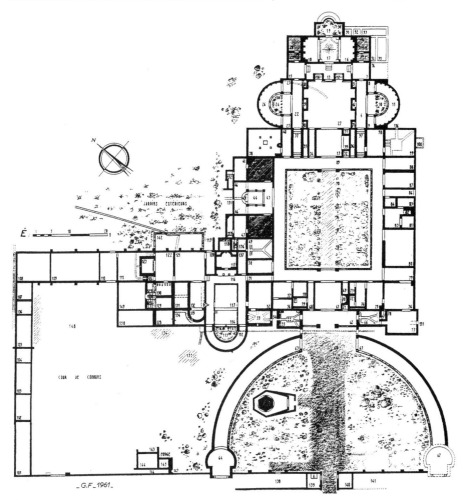

Fig. 37. Plan of the villa at Montmaurin

the middle of the first century AD as a winged peristyle villa with farm buildings extending over a large area to the west. These were more irregularly disposed than at Chiragan and were partly destroyed by a great flood *c.* AD 200, together with the south-east wing of the villa. They were mostly identified as farm buildings, though some (for example Building IV) had living-quarters; but the main labour force was thought to have been housed in rooms in the wing running west from the main building. After the great flood a policy of dispersal seems to have been adopted, with dependent farms placed under the control of leaseholders, and the earlier workforce, 'esclaves et ouvriers agricoles', being replaced by *coloni*.

Some changes occurred in the main building during the third century, but the main development was *c.* AD 350 when it was converted to a luxurious residence, still on a peristyle plan but approached by a great hemicycle court and with the addition of a *nymphaeum* to the rear. The former rooms of the farm labourers of the original *villa rustica* in the north-west wing were apparently retained for the domestic servants of the remodelled villa. This final occupation was short lived; gradual abandonment, punctuated by fires, led to final destruction *c.* AD 400. There is a discussion of the possible extent of the estate, which suggests, on place-name evidence, that the owner's name was Nepos or Nepotius.[124]

The other three provinces of imperial Gaul, Aquitania, Lugdunensis and Belgica, show considerable regional differences, but are distinct from Narbonensis with its Mediterranean geography and climate. They can then be discussed together as one agricultural area, defined by types and distribution of villa, a method adopted by Percival.[125] After Narbonensis, his survey follows a generally clockwise route through Aquitania into Lugdunensis via Armorica, then into Belgica and the great corn-growing areas of the north, south into the Saône and Rhône valleys, and east to the borders of Lower and Upper Germany and Raetia. This useful survey, stronger on distribution[126] than typology, is supported by numerous references to villa excavations, though these are frequently only a brief mention in Circonscription reports in *Gallia* with incomplete plans. Grenier's earlier essay still provides an essential typological background,[127] though overtaken by recent work in the valley of the Somme. He also discusses size and tenure of estates, supported by a number of case studies.[128] In historical terms, Grenier sees the first great period of agricultural expansion and prosperity as occupying the period from the first to the mid-third century AD, when military anarchy and the invasions of AD 253 and 276 led to the almost total destruction and abandonment of villas. He adopts an agnostic attitude over generalization about the size and tenure of these earlier estates (*fundi*), but notes the profound change of the fourth century, when the isolated *villae rusticae* of tenant farmers were abandoned for closer-knit village settlements, inhabited by property-less *coloni*, bound to the land, even to the extent of chaining, by Constantine's law of AD 332. This was the traditional view of the workforce in the Gaulish countryside, in which *coloni*, tenant farmers in the Upper Empire, changed to serfs in the Lower Empire and largely replaced the slaves of the earlier period, with the addition of barbarian settlers (*inquilini*). It is a different view from the hypothesis of a continuous social relationship between great owners and a serf-like class of clients, proposed, or discussed with reservations, in recent years.[129] But, as all recognize, the solution can scarcely be sought in conventional archaeological methods.

Side by side with overall assessments of rural settlement in Gallia Comata are the studies of smaller areas. Grenier's study of the Metz area is of interest in that he refers to slave-labour, with an ideal plan of a *villa rustica* as described by Varro and plans of slave-quarters in the villas at Sorbey, Rouhling and St Ulrich.[130] At the other extreme, Wightman's views have already been discussed and are summarized in her last book: 'Plentiful labour, some of it tied and only just above slave status, renders it unlikely that slaves formed a major part of the work force', in the period before the third-century crisis.[131] In her discussion of villa plans in Gallia Belgica, she takes the view that much of this labour, whatever its status, was housed in buildings in the farmyard;[132] the hypothesis for the later Empire is of the formation of large estates centred on seigneurial villas, with *coloni* (and some slaves?) dispersed to hamlets.[133]

In his section on the distribution of villas in Gaul Grenier made one statement, which now demands revision: 'On n'en connait qu'un petit nombre dans le nord de la France, en Picardie et en Artois ....'[134] The results of aerial photography carried out from 1960 by Agache over the fertile arable of the Somme basin have demonstrated an astonishing density of occupation of all periods, above all of Gallo-Roman villas. Originally thought unlikely to respond to air reconnaissance, the heavy loam of Picardy, or *limon*, revealed virtually complete plans, particularly where deep ploughing brought to the surface the debris of chalk wall foundations.[135] Dealing mainly with the Gallo-Roman period, Agache discusses rural settlement and proposes a detailed villa typology, that is of the residential portion of the numerous large working farms of the area.[136] Small villas are relatively rare and the ubiquitous complex, sometimes very large, is a rectangular or trapezoidal arrangement of two axial courtyards, the first with the owner's house constituting the *villa urbana* and the second, beyond a dividing wall, the *villa rustica* in which rectangular farm buildings are arranged axially along the two side walls and occasionally along the end wall or in the courtyard space. Also aligned along the main axis, but sited in either courtyard, is another house attributed to the *vilicus* or farm manager. Agache expresses caution about the precise function of the buildings in the outer farmyard, which might be described as barns and sheds for the most part. This is, of course, a consequence of the recording and planning of structures from the air or ground, where these are not followed by detailed excavation. The same can be said of the attempt of Agache to relate his findings to the works of the

117

agronomists, Cato, Varro, Columella and Palladius, and his discussion of the economy of the Picardy villas.[137] While it may be acceptable to see these great villas and associated lands as veritable *latifundia*, indicating a deliberate policy of land improvement with high-farming techniques (the spreading of clay or chalk dug from the *mardelles*), it would be straining the evidence to argue for a bilateral and complementary policy of corn-growing and sheep farming. The villas were no doubt more than self-sufficient units, certainly as regards their corn production, but to suggest a semi-industrial function as well, particularly in the making of wool cloth, can be no more than speculation.

What seems beyond doubt is the necessity for a large workforce, fluctu-ating according to the season. Agache leaves the question of its status open, expressing a traditional view on slave-labour but quoting a view that it was largely a free peasantry.[138] He does, however, add a pertinent comment: '... la découverte d'entraves de fer est loin d'être rare dans les villas gallo-romaines du nord de la Gaule', when speaking of the treatment of the lowest grade of slave. As far as their quarters are concerned, these were, no doubt, in the buildings of the outer farmyard, but again only excavation would determine which ones. Finally, these great villas belong, Agache argues, to the Upper Empire before the general collapse of the second half of the third century, with the possibility of some decline even before that. Their successors, eventually to become the villages of France, may lie over such of these villas as survived, or over clusters of minor rural buildings (*vici*), or over sanctuaries; these possibilities (and there may be others) are not easily detectable by air photography, and proof will require excavation.

One early excavation whose results have been used by Agache as an aid in the interpretation of the farm buildings and general character of his Picardy villas is that of the Anthée villa, near Namur in Belgium, investi-gated by del Marmol between 1863 and 1872 (fig. 38). Frequently cited (and re-assessed) since del Marmol's orignal excavation reports, the later summary by Grenier brings out the close resemblance to the Picardy

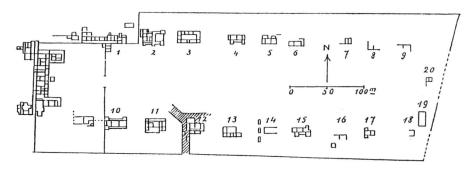

Fig. 38. Plan of the villa at Anthée

sites.[139] In particular, the two parallel ranges of farm buildings in the vast farmyard to the east of the main house and its court were fully excavated and revealed much of their function; of these, Building 3 in the north range, with its central large room surrounded by ranges of small rooms on all four sides, may possibly be regarded as a candidate for the living-quarters of the workforce, whatever its status. The site had a long history, from the mid-first century AD to its destruction in AD 275, followed by renewed occupation until the end of the fourth century, and the variety of processes carried out in various of the farm buildings is cited by Agache as support for his theory of a mixed agricultural and industrial basis for the Picardy villas. Excavation elsewhere, for example Hosté and Haccourt in Belgium, and Athies, Warfusée-sud and Estrées-sur-Noye in Picardy, has concerned itself with the main house and farm buildings largely await investigation.[140] Wightman cites Köln-Müngersdorf as the only example where there has been '… any really systematic attempt to establish function', but makes the general observation '… that the housing of people was one of the functions of the farmyard'.[141] It may be that further regional studies, especially those based on the results of air photography, will eventually reveal a satisfactory typology of villas in the provinces of Gaul. For example, in Berry it is interesting to observe that the great villa of the Picardy area appears there in the departments of Cher and Indre to the west where, for instance, the Villa du Champ des Pois has a vast farmyard 600 m long by 150-200 m wide.[142] Ranges of widely separated farm buildings placed axially along both sides of the yard suggest cereal production, but some of the buildings must have been intended for the accommodation of labour. It is likely that most interest will concentrate on villa (that is, main residence) plans and will attempt to define, for instance, the distribution boundary between peristyle and courtyard in great houses, but one may hope that some thought will be given to the overall plan and the identification of labour-quarters.

The passing reference by Agache to the discovery of iron fetters in Gallo-Roman villas in the north of Gaul does not stand alone. As noted above, Belova refers to the discovery of fetters at the Guiry-Gadancourt villa (actually at the nearby villa of Rhus) and the supposed neck-collar and chain from the Sorbey villa noted by Grenier.[143] Wightman makes an unreferenced mention of 'fetters found in one smallish Somme villa',[144] and, as noted earlier, Samson comments that 'chains … are not unknown archaeologically' in Gaul.[145] But in no case has there been any attempt to quantify, classify and study the overall distribution of such material and its possible significance in the Gallo-Roman countryside. However, an important regional study of fetters in Burgundy and the Lyonnais usefully spans the junction of Gallia Lugdunensis and Belgica and provides an indispensable starting point.[146] There is a brief study of such finds from Normandy but it is unfortunately undifferentiated chronologically.[147] For the rest, the combing of excavation reports and museum collections provides the essential data and the overall results are presented in Chapter 7 on means of restraint, and in greater detail in a study by the author.[148] Caution is required in any attempt to draw meaningful conclusions from a study of the distribution of fetters. There is first the doubt about a Roman date with some types, then the over-emphasis resulting from research and publication in a number of areas, and finally the significance of river finds. But one conclusion seems inescapable: the concentration of finds between the Seine and the Meuse / Maas, the very area where air photography has revealed such striking evidence for large agricultural establishments. Between the Meuse and Rhine enough have been recorded to reinforce this conclusion and to link with the *limes* area, though here a military presence may argue for a different usage, as in the case of manacle distribution, presumably for the shackling of captives. However, many of the fetter types found in the rural areas seem to be generally late in date, so the question of whether they were intended for slaves or *coloni* must remain unresolved.

One final point requires discussion, namely the extent to which Gallo-Roman towns had recognizable areas of agricultural land attached to them which was subjected to division into holdings by centuriation and then cultivated, directly or vicariously, by owners living in the town. And, if so, was there a labour force, servile or free, commuting daily to the fields, as in Greek agriculture or in other Roman provinces? These are questions to which no ready answers can be given, though the recognition of possible labourers' quarters in town or country may act as a pointer.

Greek colonization, predominantly of Massilia (Marseilles) as early as 600 BC, was essentially for trade along the Mediterranean coast; some territory was no doubt acquired to provide a local food resource but no evidence for allotment has yet been recognized except at Agatha (Agde).[149] The planting of Roman *coloniae* in Narbonensis, with Roman or Latin rights, begins with Narbo (Narbonne) in 118 BC and ultimately totalled eighteen, of which there is evidence for centuriation at eight.[150] In Gallia Comata the three early *coloniae* of Lyons, Nyons and Augst were eventually joined by Cologne, Xanten, Avenches and probably Trier.[151] Possible centuriation has been detected around some *coloniae* and also around some of the *civitas* capitals,[152] the towns fostered by the Roman administration to form the centres of the old tribal areas. Again, air photography has added this sort of information to give us a very different picture from Grenier's statement: '... on n'a jamais reconnu jusqu'ici, autour des anciennes colonies romaines, la moindre trace d'une telle division du sol.' There is, of course, some epigraphic evidence for land allotment around Orange (*Arausio*) in the form of fragments of marble tablets identified as land registers of the first and second centuries AD.

In most cases, the ancient towns are covered by their medieval and modern successors and only occasionally, for example at Avenches where the Roman town is still open for excavation, has it been possible to record house plans. At other smaller towns such as Glanum (Saint-Rémy-de-Provence) with its Hellenistic peristyle houses and Alesia (Alise-Sainte-Reine), residential areas have been uncovered, but any attempt to define slave-quarters, whether of domestic servants or field workers, remains for the future.

Britain

In many ways there were distinct similarities between Gallia Belgica and the so-called 'lowland zone' of Roman Britain, and this is true of the agriculture. Curiously, in spite of the interval between Caesar's conquest of Gaul and Claudius' conquest of Britain, the advent of large and palatial villas seems to have taken place in both around the middle of the first century AD. The conventional view was that the south-east was the more Romanized portion of the province, marked by a heavy concentration of villas, while the uplands of the north and west remained largely under military control.[153] The effective contrast between these two zones was, of course, the presence of *civitas* capitals in the lowland zone and of legionary fortresses and auxiliary forts in the highland zone, though there was naturally a blurring of the line where the two met. It would be going too far to argue that corn-growing was a lowland zone preoccupation and stock-breeding in the highland zone, though there is an element of truth in this, if only for environmental reasons.[154] But the villa farm was by no means the stereotype in the lowland zone and its absence from such areas as Salisbury Plain, Cranborne Chase and the Fens may indicate imperial estates (or *latifundia* of private individuals?), farmed by tenants (*coloni*) living in small farmsteads or villages.[155]

However, the villa in the sense of the Romanized farm with residential portion and farm buildings is where the search for slave-quarters should begin. As with Gaul, there has been a tendency to extrapolate the pattern of tenure in Britain from pre- and post-Roman conditions, and to argue for a serf-like labour force of *coloni* rather than of slaves,[156] but this is speculation without unequivocal archaeological, specifically epigraphical, evidence. There *were* slaves in pre-Roman Britain, if only prisoners as objects of trade: the frequently quoted passage from Strabo (4.5.1-2) lists them among the exports, and finds of neck-chains and fetters in Iron Age contexts add to the evidence. But their presence in villas has scarcely been touched on, and the discussion of the 600 or so villa sites in Britain has largely centred on the typology of the residential portion;[157] only recently has there been an attempt to treat the villa and its excavation as an economic whole, as at Stanwick, Northants.[158] Even so, the identification of particular buildings or rooms remains an elusive and largely untouched problem. Apart from the villa plan, there has also been in recent years a preoccupation with social and tenurial patterns in the rural life of Roman Britain, based on the speculative application of the medieval laws on landholding to the Roman period.[159] This approach, analogous to the suggestion of Celtic continuity in Roman Gaul as regards the status of the labour force, emphasizes the importance of Celtic institutions, and specifically kinship, in Roman Britain, but is scarcely susceptible to archaeological proof.

Were slaves, then, used in Romano-British agriculture? The taking of prisoners in tribal warfare and their sale clearly happened in Celtic Britain and we may suppose that the tribal aristocracies could have owned slaves, both as personal servants and as labourers on their estates. From this it would follow that the Romanized landowners continued the practice, but the evidence is sparse. General studies of the period tend to repeat the same limited facts: the slave-chain from pre-Roman levels at the Park Street villa near St Albans as evidence for slave-owning before Romanization, the 97 baby-burials at the Hambleden villa and the conversion of the Llantwit Major villa to bailiff occupation.[160] Frere takes the commonsense view that large villas would have demanded a large staff of slaves, both for the household and for agricultural work, and these must be the sites where a study of farm buildings might conceivably point to slave-quarters.[161]

A recent survey of slavery in the western provinces in the first three centuries of the Empire largely ignores Britain.[162] If one adopts the largely epigraphical approach of the contributors, it speedily becomes apparent that inscriptions on stone in Britain rarely mention slaves (*servi*). There are in fact only two, from Old Carlisle and Halton Castle, both military in origin; the Halton Castle inscription is of incidental interest in that it is a tombstone set up to the unknown dead slave by a guild of fellow-slaves (*collegium conservorum*), which indicates the prevalence of this class on Hadrian's Wall.[163] Freedmen are more numerous; if one excludes two *aliena*, there are in fact 30 references, usually on tombstones, to a *libertus* or variant.[164] But these too are largely military in origin, and even those from the civil zone, for example at Bath, are mainly former slaves of military personnel. So agriculture is almost entirely absent as a context, the one notable exception being the re-used building dedication from the Combe Down, Bath, villa or possibly a mine- or quarry-centre.[165] Its reference to the rebuilding in the early third century AD of a ruined *principia* has been interpreted as an allusion to the chief building of an imperial estate, run by a former imperial slave as agent (*adiutor*) for provincial procurators.

Frere suggests a considerable variety of ownership and tenancy in Roman Britain, and accepts the presence of *coloni*, for instance in the Winchester area with its mix of villas and native settlements, as Rivet has also argued for the villas in the Sussex plain, with dependent farms on the Downs behind.[166] Again, Frere notes the absence of villas around the *coloniae* of Colchester, Gloucester and Lincoln, where centuriation gave an allocation of plots for cultivation by owners living in the towns; the same absence is pointed out for Canterbury, Silchester, London and Caistor-by-Norwich, even if actual centuriation may not have been present.[167]

Villa plans in Roman Britain find many parallels in Gaul, particularly in the corridor / winged-corridor type *vis-à-vis* the 'galerie-façade' type, but by and large the great axial double-courtyard villas of Picardy do not appear in Britain. On the other hand, the so called 'courtyard villa' is a British feature, composed of one, sometimes two, large open courtyards with buildings on all four sides, possibly the result of continuous development. It is to these we must mainly look for attached farm buildings and labourers' quarters.

The other approach, as in Gaul, is to study the types and distribution of fetters. Again, the study of excavation reports and, more frequently, the presence of examples in museum collections, even if the context is uncertain, can yield useful results. They are discussed here in general terms, mainly their distribution, and a detailed analysis of types is given below in Chapter 7 on means of restraint. The thick scatter between the Seine and the Maas in Gallia Belgica is mirrored across the Channel in East Anglia, where similar agricultural prosperity based on corn-growing may have prevailed in the Roman period, if the wealth of the pre-Roman Iceni and Trinovantes is a reliable guide.[168]

The Germanies, Raetia and the limes

The eastern boundary of Gallia Belgica lay along the Rhine after Caesar's conquests, but the presence of military garrisons had a strong influence on the pattern and nature of rural life and, presumably, on the role of slaves. The attempt by Augustus to advance the frontier to the Elbe and to create the new province of Germania was to end in failure, and it was not until the Flavian period that the provinces of Lower and Upper Germany were created on the eastern flank of Belgica, as well as the fortified *limes* bounding the re-entrant angle between the sources of the Rhine and Danube. The *limes* joined the Danube farther down the river, and the artificial barrier and the river together formed the northern border of Raetia, which can be conveniently considered here. If rural life was influenced by the presence of Roman garrisons and their needs, so too the threat of barbarian invasions prevented the adoption of the luxury villa and associated working farms which appear away from the frontier in the Trier region. Even if the theory of general destruction in AD 275-6 may have been over-stressed, it still seems probable that rural settlement in the fourth century had changed from that of the period before the invasions.[169]

To the west of the Rhine, the villa of Mayen near Coblenz, excavated in the 1920s, is frequently cited as the exemplar of a common Rhineland type.[170] Beginning life as a simple rectangular structure in the pre-Roman period, it was enlarged in the first century AD by the addition of a corridor and projecting rooms at each end, and subsequently by the addition of a small bath-suite and further alterations; outbuildings were also present. A constant feature was the central hall with hearth, unlike the corridor villa of Britain, and some writers have developed the comparison with the medieval hall, and suggested that the plan denotes a kinship group, in which the farm was worked under a patron / client system.[171] This theory obviously has a bearing on the presence of slaves as opposed to a serf-like workforce, but cannot be more than speculation.

Rather more elaborate was the villa of Köln-Müngersdorf, a few kilometres west of Cologne (fig. 39); the whole complex was uncovered in a rescue excavation in 1926 and provides an excellent overall picture of a villa and its outbuildings between AD 50 and the end of the fourth century.[172] The owner's villa itself underwent six periods of alteration, but for much of its life was of the *galérie-façade* type with projecting rooms at the angles (*Porticusvilla mit Eckrisaliten*). To the sides and rear and within an enclosing wall were eleven outbuildings, placed rather unsystematically but functionally identified. Of these, Building I, a large but simple rectangular structure with a veranda facing towards the villa and a large central hearth, was identified as living-quarters for the farmworkers, whatever their status may have been; the building remained unaltered throughout the villa's history. Another interesting feature of Köln-Müngersdorf was a cremation cemetery outside the enclosure wall to the east; 55 burials were found in close proximity and six more away from the main concentration. Most were laid directly in the earth without a cremation urn and the sparse finds indicated that the majority were of the Flavian period to the end of the second century, though a few were as early as *c.* AD 50, the date of the first stone villa. The excavators concluded that these were the burials of the farmworkers and servants, while those of the owners were some distance away in a *columbarium*. Later inhumations of the farmworkers were not found, though, paradoxically, fourth-century sarcophagus burials of the owners were found north of the villa.

Farther south, in the fertile lands east of the Rhine protected by the artificial barrier of the *limes* (the modern Baden-Württemberg), villas were scattered thickly, though there are exceptions, for example in the fertile areas of Alsace, where it has been argued that imperial estates led to their exclusion.[173] But these villas of Upper Germany and Raetia must have looked for their markets to the legionary fortresses on the rivers and the auxiliary forts on the *limes* itself, and the abandonment of the latter *c.* AD 260 meant that the villas themselves largely lost their *raison d'être*. Very characteristic is the villa of Burgweinting, near Regensburg, where a hall-type villa stood inside an enclosure wall with ten dependent buildings, of which two were identified as living-quarters. The occupation was from the time of Vespasian to the first half of the third century.[174]

Farther back from the frontier areas and behind the headwaters of the Rhine there was evidently a feeling of greater security which led to the

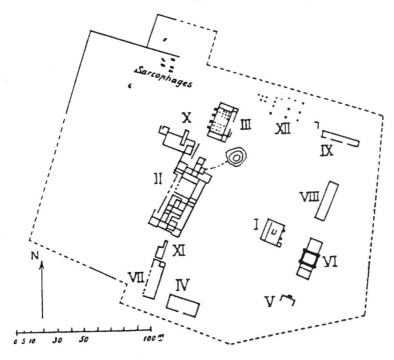

Fig. 39. Plan of villa at Köln-Müngersdorf

building of larger and more luxurious villas in what is now modern
Switzerland, spanning the area between Gallia Belgica and Raetia.[175] Two
such are the villas at Oberentfelden, with its axial arrangement of villa at
the head and a long courtyard, with outbuildings (including workers'
quarters) along the side walls, and Winkel (Seeb), partially known but
apparently a similar axial arrangement in a double courtyard.[176] The
authors accept that the numerous servants' quarters were occupied by
slaves or serfs, but do not argue for one or the other. But the main
distribution is of the simpler *villa rustica*, where it is correspondingly more
difficult to identify workers' quarters.

The attempt to use the presence of fetters as a means of identification
of slave-quarters in the farms of the Germanies and Raetia does not meet
with any success. Fetters are almost entirely found in the legionary
fortresses and auxiliary forts on the Rhine, Danube and *limes*, and are
frequently of what may be regarded as a military pattern, the Künzing
type; they are consequently best regarded as evidence of an aspect of army
policy, the capture of prisoners and their sale as slaves (with the caveat
that they may also be an indication of penal policy in military establishments).

Dalmatia and the Danube provinces: Noricum, Pannonia and Moesia

These provinces are conveniently dealt with together, since events on the Danube frontier which affected rural settlement were broadly similar; Thrace is excluded as it has already been touched on in the section on the Greek East in the Roman period, while Dalmatia is included because of its close relationship with Pannonia.

As a province, Noricum can be defined easily as an area contained between the Danube to the north and the Alps to the south, and extending across Austria from the river Inn in the west nearly to Vienna in the east. The valleys of the foothills of the Alps and the rich lands bordering the Danube offered attractive prospects for agriculture. Rostovtzeff emphasized Noricum's close unity with Italy and suggested that the wealthy Romanized inhabitants of the larger towns, the earlier tribal aristocracy, owned the best lands.[177] Certainly, the villas known in the province show a tendency to cluster around the large towns, themselves of pre-Roman origin, such as Virunum in the south and Iuvavum in the north.[178] In fact, the northern villas seem to begin earlier, in the first century AD, while in the rest of the province others were being built by the end of that century or early in the second.[179] The Marcomannic Wars of the 160s and 170s caused some devastation, but rural occupation continued well into the fourth century apart from some destruction in the north-west of the province in the warfare of the later third century.[180] As in Gallia Belgica, villas were of the luxurious type comprising a *pars urbana* for the owner and *pars rustica* for workers and farm buildings, or of the simple *villa rustica* variety.[181] However, scrutiny of the reports on the various villas listed by Alföldy does not throw any light on the specific question of slave-quarters, which must remain a matter of inference.[182]

Slavery seems to have been an important element in the social structure of pre-Roman Noricum, itself largely Celtic.[183] We may suppose that tribal warfare, the taking of prisoners and their sale into slavery, may have been endemic, as in other Celtic areas before Romanization. Equally, we may suppose that trade in slaves and metals was an important element in the pre-Roman Norican economy. The strong links between Aquileia on the Adriatic and Noricum emphasize the main route for this trade with the Italian market, in which the hilltop *oppidum* of Magdalensberg, north of Klagenfurt, played an important part in pre-Roman and Roman times. The discovery of the elements of at least three slave-fetters from the site provides some archaeological evidence for this trade, and one can also cite the Celtic *oppidum* of Sanzeno, near Trento, where trade across the Brenner to Raetia and Noricum seems, again on the evidence of fetters and chains, to have included a large slave element.[184] Otherwise, the evidence for slavery in Roman Noricum, especially in agriculture, seems largely epigraphic.[185] One interesting difference between urban and rural slavery, at least on the not entirely reliable evidence of nomenclature, is that owners in towns, some of them foreign merchants, were obtaining their slaves from Italy and other provinces, presumably at established slave-markets, while in the country landowners were employing slaves of Norican origin.[186] Alföldy argues that in agriculture the native *peregrini* were using slaves and free-born labourers side by side and that an almost patriarchal relationship existed between owners, themselves non-citizens, and their slaves. His interesting correlation of inscriptions of *liberti* and slaves with farming establishments before and after AD 180-200 demonstrates graphically the degree to which slavery was an important element in Norican agriculture;[187] but the closeness of the relationship between master and man makes it correspondingly more difficult to detect slave-quarters in the farms of the province.

East of Noricum lay the vast territory originally known as Illyricum, bordering the Adriatic on the west and extending northwards through the flatter lands of modern Hungary, watered by the rivers Sava and Drava, as far as the Danube. Its conquest was a protracted business, from the Illyrican wars of the third century BC until the final expansion to the Danube by 11 BC. After the great revolt of AD 6-9 the northern area was formed into the province of Pannonia, while the rump of Illyricum became the province of Dalmatia later in the century. The peculiar geography of Dalmatia, virtually the modern former Yugoslavia, meant that much of its settlement was confined on the one hand to valleys leading inland from the Adriatic coast and on the other to small areas of favourable land in river valleys in the formidable barrier of the Dinaric Alps.[188] The latter areas are typified by relatively simple villa plans, but slave-owning is suggested.[189] In the coastal areas the villas could be larger and more luxurious, as at Dracevica, reflecting the taste of Italian immigrants, but others were quite simple; again the quality of the internal decoration no doubt reflected Italian taste.[190] Otherwise, Wilkes suggests that much rural settlement was in the form of land allotments, either to veterans on the *prata legionis* of former legionary fortresses or to immigrants in the *territorium* of newly established *coloniae*; he does not attach great importance to the use of slaves in agriculture and there is insufficient evidence for the presence of slave-quarters in the Dalmatian villas.

To the north, the geography of Pannonia was very different: two great rivers, the Drava and the Sava, flowed east to join the Danube through an area of plains and low hills, while two great lakes, Balaton and the Neusiedler See, were an attractive focus for rural settlement. In her comprehensive study of villa distribution in Pannonia Thomas emphasizes the concentration of villas round these two lakes, especially the northern slopes of Lake Balaton, with smaller groups between the upper reaches of the rivers Sava and Drava, along the Danube and around Pécs (*Sopianae*); she suggests early settlement in the Drava-Sava enclave from the first century AD, because of close commercial ties between Italy and southern Pannonia which led to rapid Romanization.[191] In this she is followed by Percival, but evidence from the excavated sites is meagre and the cited example of Smarje is thought to have begun in the second century AD.[192] In fact, Mócsy takes a contrary view: he suggests that early villas built by north Italian settlers and Romanized native chieftains (for example of the Boii) lay in the Neusiedler See and Balaton areas and pre-dated those of the Drava valley, citing the great Parndorf villa.[193] Whatever the final verdict, it appears that the great Balaton villas, such as Keszthely-Fenék-puszta and Nemesvamos-Balacapuszta, did not assume their final arrangement, with numerous outbuildings, until the late Roman period.[194] Possibly some of the farm buildings may have served as slave-quarters, or alternatively have housed serfs (*coloni*), but the status of the rural work-force remains doubtful. There is also the likelihood that veterans settled on the *prata legionis* of fortresses at Vindobona, Carnuntum, Brigetio, Aquincum, Singidunum and Viminacium and inhabitants of *coloniae* farming allotments on their *territorium* may have employed slaves.[195] It is interesting to note the epigraphic evidence for slaves on a *latifundium* in the *territorium* of Ulpianum in the southern part of Upper Moesia.[196]

In greater detail, Thomas suggests the possibility of an *ergastulum* at the Balaton villa of Örvényes in its second-century phase, but gives no evidence; at Winden am See, on the Neusiedler See, the simple *villa rustica* of centre-corridor type is interpreted in its fourth-century phase, not as the main building of the estate, but as a building devoted to agricultural work and occupied by slaves or freedmen.[197] Generally, she follows the conventional view of the change of status for the agricultural slave, from a chattel to be bought or sold at the owner's whim, to a worker tied to a particular estate, with a convergence in the late Roman period towards the status of *coloni* and *inquilini*, nominally free labourers who were in fact also tied to their estates, the beginnings of feudalism.[198]

Percival argues that villa development in central Pannonia, for example round Lake Balaton, was closely linked with the acquisition and loss of Dacia, a period of roughly a century and a half.[199] But the geography of the area suggests that it was Upper Moesia which was closely related to the buffer zone of Dacia and, to a lesser extent, Lower Moesia. Mócsy points out the lack of early villas on the northern and eastern fringes of Pannonia, and the same probably held for Upper Moesia.[200] In the later period villas of the lavish Pannonian type, such as Parndorf, seem to be lacking, although palaces as the centre of imperial estates, set within massive defensive walls, such as Gamzigrad, do appear.[201] The comparison is with the great villa of Fenékpuszta with its irregular scatter of buildings enclosed by the fourth century in massive rectangular defences and classed by Mócsy as the centre of a *latifundium*.[202] The problem of quarters for workers in such huge establishments and their status, whether slave or serf-like *coloni*, is still to be addressed.

4. Slaves in Roman Agriculture: the Empire

The short-lived province of Dacia was the scene of intense Romanization, marked by the foundation of *coloniae*. Agriculture was prominent and the occasional *villa rustica* is known, but it seems likely that exploitation of the land depended largely on the allotment of plots in the *territorium* of the new urban foundations. Slaves were no doubt there, but information about their quarters remains to be found. To the Roman conquerors mineral resources were probably of greater importance. In Lower Moesia and Thrace Greek influence is felt, related to the rich and powerful cities of the west coast of the Black Sea. The Thracians were so influenced by Greek culture that Romanization was little evident and villages rather than villas were the norm, and the newly planted towns, Greek rather than Roman, affected rural life very little.[203] Villas do appear, ranging from the simple type, as at Prisovo near Turnovo, where the residential and working-quarters are ranged round a central courtyard, to the elaborate site of Chatalka (fig. 40), with its *pars urbana* and *pars rustica*, the latter with workers' quarters.[204] Within the *pars urbana* the peristyle courtyard, reflecting Mediterranean influence, reappears, as at Armira.[205] Poulter

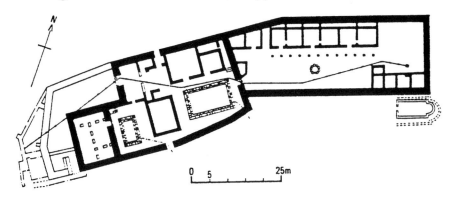

Fig. 40a. The *pars urbana* of the *villa rustica* at Chatalka

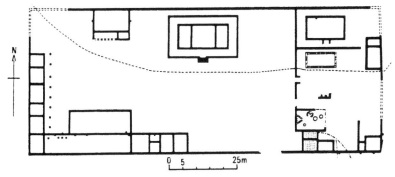

Fig. 40b. *Villa rustica* at Chatalka: complex with pottery workshop

makes the point that no villa has so far been found to be earlier than Trajanic and emphasizes the role of the military in their creation.[206] He also points out the contrast between elaborate villas, with a peristyle courtyard, and simpler villas, which may be some indication of outside influence as opposed to an indigenous tradition. There is little specific information on slave-quarters, except at the Montana 2 villa, where a large room adjacent to the main residential building is interpreted as such accommodation.[207]

Slavery in Quarries and Mines

The presence of slaves in Greek and Roman quarries and mines ought, in principle, to offer an interesting counterpart to their use in agriculture. The process of winning stone and ores from the ground was an arduous business in ancient times and one in which the use of slave labour on a fairly large scale might seem to be peculiarly applicable. It would be wrong, however, to suppose that forced labour of this kind would be suitable for the skilled work involved in both activities. In quarrying, the selection of stone for building and of marble for sculpture and the technique of detaching suitable blocks from the parent beds were eminently the province of skilled quarrymen; on the other hand, the movement of stone and marble from the quarries to an eventual destination was appropriate for relatively unskilled labour. In mining, however, the hard labour of extracting ore, especially in the unpleasant conditions of underground shafts and galleries, seems to have been undertaken by slaves, whereas its subsequent smelting and refining were both more skilled and less labour-intensive and consequently were carried out by specialist workmen, possibly of free status. The direct evidence for the use of slaves is, as often, literary and epigraphical; the latter is invoked here where it contributes knowledge about the spheres in which slaves were employed or where associated iconography tells us something about conditions of work, while literary references are quoted for background purposes. Specific archaeological evidence is limited to such areas as accommodation for slave-workers, their tools and clothing, or the rare occurrence of shackles. A generalized description of the quarrying and mining processes will be given as essential background but it is hoped to avoid the danger of excessive detail.

Quarries

The Greek world

The survival of major structures such as temples, theatres and city walls from Classical and Hellenistic times perhaps over-emphasizes the importance of building stone in Greece. Much domestic building, and even public buildings and city walls, consisted of mud-brick walls on dwarf walls of rubble, with tiled roofs supported on timber props. Admittedly, the geology of the predominantly mountainous landscape of Greece, largely sedimentary limestones, might suggest that stone was a favoured building material, but much of it was not entirely suitable; softer limestones might be fossiliferous and easily weathered, while the harder varieties might have a tendency to shatter. Older metamorphic rocks, crystalline gneiss, granite, or marble, were more durable but correspondingly less easy to quarry, and only marble was eagerly sought and worked for its appearance and suitability for, say, temples and their ornamental sculpture and the statuary within. In general, the consensus view is that Greek quarries were essentially local and based on their proximity to the buildings they served; transport was clearly the limiting factor.[1]

Attica provides a useful illustration of the sources from which the centre at Athens drew its supplies of building stone and marble.[2] The city stood on and was surrounded by limestone hills, some of a hard variety, as the Acropolis itself. The more easily worked varieties are often classified under the general term of *poros*, which covers a wide variety of limestones but does not have a precise petrological significance. Much of this was obtained from Piraeus, but some Athenian architects preferred a brown variety from quarries on the island of Aegina. For foundation work, pebbly conglomerates were frequently used, especially in Hellenistic buildings. Marble, itself a form of limestone, ranked highest among all building materials for its beauty, durability and the way in which it lent itself to fine sculptural detail, though it was necessary to pay a price in the skill and effort it required in comparison with softer and coarser stones. In the sixth century it was used on a modest scale for sculpture and architectural detail; the finest marbles were imported from the Cycladic islands of Paros and Naxos for the standing male figures known as *kouroi*, but already there was some exploitation of local sources on the hills of Hymettos and Pentelikon. For the great building programme of the fifth century, especially on the Acropolis, Pentelikon was the main source, but by the end of the century and throughout Hellenistic and Roman times Hymettian marble was increasingly favoured. The cost of moving building stone, however, was so high, even for relatively short distances, that other areas of Attica relied on local sources. The temple of Poseidon at Sounion, for example, was built of marble from quarries a short distance to the north at Agrileza.[3]

The same was true for other areas of Greece, except where there was a demand for a small supply of finer stone for decorative purposes, for example capitals. Thus, the drums forming the columns of the vast temple of Zeus at Olympia, now collapsed, were quarried from a local shelly limestone. At Bassae, the position of the temple high in the mountains determined the use of the local limestone, in spite of its sombre colouring. Special factors could, of course, operate: at Delphi, again in a difficult position high above the Corinthian Gulf, the local limestone was unsuitable for major religious or public buildings, but the sanctuary had large financial resources. So it was able to import stone and marble from some distance, as it did in the fourth century when it used limestone from Corinth. The building accounts, however, indicate that transport costs far outweighed the cost of the stone itself.[4] Much interest has centred on the exploitation and movement of marble for sculpture and inscriptions but, important though this was, it was of minor significance in the context of quarrying in Greece in general.

The same use of local materials was true for other areas of Greek influence and colonization, for example Magna Graecia and Sicily, and the Aegean coast of Asia Minor. Thus at Syracuse in Sicily, the Doric temple of Athena, which was later incorporated in the present cathedral, is largely of local limestone. Even more clearly, in the later extension of the city on the mainland, buildings such as the Greek theatre are built on and of the limestone of the hill on which they stand, while ancient quarries, such as the 'Ear of Dionysios', immediately adjoin the site. At Agrigento, the temple of Concord has columns of local tufa limestone, but this did not lend itself to a good finish and the columns were rendered with stucco, as were those of the temple of Zeus at Corinth. The Carian city of Aphrodisias in Asia Minor derived its handsome marbles for building and statuary from quarries on the lower slopes of Baba Dag, 2 km to the east. The city reached its apogee in Roman times, but the quarries seem to have been in use in the late Hellenistic period, for example for the temple of Aphrodite. Vitruvius (10.2.15) records that the accidental discovery of a good local quarry led to its use for temple building at Ephesus. Again, there are exceptions to the general proposition that Greek builders relied on local sources for their stone, but explanations can usually be found, for example a coastal position, for such variations.[5]

In his detailed study of the relationship between *astu* and *chora* in the Greek city-state, Osborne devotes a whole chapter to the exploitation of Athenian stone resources.[6] He argues, from epigraphic sources and from the close proximity of most quarries to the buildings for which they were intended to provide stone, that the raw material itself was not regarded as a precious resource. The costs involved were determined by labour factors and problems of transport; building accounts, for example for the Parthenon, record payments for quarrying or to quarrymen, rather than for cut blocks. He contends that quarrying in Classical Attica was not a regularly organized industry but fluctuated in response to building programmes and concludes, on the evidence of the quarrying of Pentelic marble from Pendele, that the number of quarrymen was quite small and that for the Parthenon projects in the fifth century, and for building at Eleusis in the fourth, recruitment for the labour required for quarrying and transport of stone was on an *ad hoc* and relatively short-term basis. In this he differs from those who claim that skill and specialization predominated and that stone was brought from some distance.[7]

Osborne develops his thesis by claiming that labour was largely locally recruited, and suggests that where there was a permanent need for workmen, as at Pendele, these were recruited from *metics* rather than *poletai*.[8] His argument would thus equate quarrying with agriculture, suggesting that those engaged in both activities would largely be drawn from nucleated settlements, possibly corresponding to the *deme*, and travel daily to and from the scene of work, as described above in Chapter 2 in the discussion of agriculture. If so, this clearly has an important bearing on the use of slaves in quarrying, and their identification through archaeological evidence from actual quarries may prove elusive. On the question of transport, which together with labour determined the cost of stone (itself having no intrinsic value in a country like Greece where it was freely available on a local basis), Burford argues that this was effected by yoked oxen with a minimal use of human labour. The question of whether the labour was slave or free thus becomes largely irrelevant.[9] In fact, she suggests that oxcarts were hired on an *ad hoc* basis from local farmers.[10] So, labour at the quarry face remains the one demand for manpower; Dworakowska suggests slaves as the source, while Osborne argues for a mixed force of slaves and *metics* only for those quarries which served a wider market on an erratic and small scale.[11]

As noted earlier, war and the taking of prisoners were the chief source of slaves in the ancient world and the Carthaginian invasion of Sicily in the early fifth century BC, coinciding with Xerxes' attack on Greece, is recorded to have given rise to the use of prisoners of war in quarries. In 480 BC, Gelon, tyrant of Syracuse, defeated the forces of Hamilcar at Himera and divided the captives among his Sicilian allies; those allocated to Akragas are said to have been chained and used to quarry stone for the grandiose programme of temple building initiated by the Akragantini (Diod. 11.29). Some have gone further and claimed that the temple of Olympian Zeus at Agrigento (Akragas) described by Diodorus (13.82-4) had representations of Carthaginian prisoners in the *telamones* supporting the architrave between the engaged Doric columns of the solid outer wall.[12] One of these huge figures, nearly 8 m high, survives in the museum at Agrigento with reconstructions in model form. Even if, as has been argued, the temple was begun before 480, this need not vitiate the argument, since it was evidently unfinished at the time of the Carthaginian destruction of Akragas in 406 BC. The suggestion is attractive, but may fall on the evidence of the use of *telamones* elsewhere as supporting figures in later architecture.[13]

Sicily, again, provides a second illustration of the imprisonment of prisoners in quarries, possibly as labour, this time on the occasion of the disastrous Athenian expedition to the island in 415-413 BC. Their final defeat in the naval battle of Syracuse in 413 led, according to the ancient historians (Thuc. 7.80-7; Diod. 13.19-33; Plut. *Nicias* 27-9), to the capture and enslavement of some 7,000 men, who were imprisoned in the quarries still visible at Syracuse, north of the major buildings of Neapolis. Conceivably the residue of those not ransomed or sent into slavery elsewhere in Sicily may have worked in the quarries themselves.

Inscriptions throw slight but uncertain light on the employment of slaves in Greek quarries, and there seems to be no archaeological evidence, for example of the provision of accommodation specifically for slaves. The emphasis on the use of local sources suggests that in Attica for instance the *demotai* controlling the quarry may have used *metics* and slaves on a short-term basis, who travelled to and from the site daily; a few of the *demotai* with special skills may have provided the necessary supervision. Osborne argues that a quarry in constant use, for example Pendele, may have induced some settlement, citing the case of the *metic* Manes from the Eleusis accounts; slaves may well have been present too.[14] The building accounts indicate that quarrying of the stone, its transport and its final use were envisaged as one unified project. The Erechtheum accounts of 409-408 and 405-404 BC list citizens, *metics* and slaves, all receiving equal pay for similar work, with little to argue that slaves were controlled by the free, while at Eleusis free and slave workmen cannot be distinguished.[15] The Erechtheum evidence suggests that slaves formed a significant proportion of masons and carpenters, though the Peloponnesian War may have been a contributory cause; they lived in various Athenian *demes*, perhaps separately from their masters, but archaeological identification has not been achieved. The same conclusions might hold for slave quarry-workers.[16] Osborne, on the other hand, argues that while stone was free and payment was for its quarrying by *lithotomoi*, as at the Parthenon, the listing of men who are presumably slaves means that a contractor was present.[17] But this does not affect the conclusion that in Attica, and probably in the rest of mainland Greece and the islands, the archaeological evidence for the presence of slaves in quarries is not as yet apparent. This rather negative conclusion can be set against an earlier, more positive, view: 'Die Steinbrecher waren nur selten freie Griechen, meist Sklaven manchmal auch Kriegsgefangene, nur ganz selten aber Straflinge.'[18]

The same conclusion would apply to the colonies of Asia Minor, Magna Graecia and Sicily, where the use of local sources for building stone has already been emphasized. In the Hellenistic cities which sprang up in the time of Alexander and after the partition of his empire, we may suppose that the same proposition applied, though endemic warfare may have had an effect on labour supply through the channelling of prisoners to quarries. Egypt was always a special case. The long tradition of quarrying along the length of the Nile was influenced by the autocratic rule of the Pharaohs, who commissioned the building of pyramids and temples. But the popular concept of mass employment of slaves, best typified in such extravagant paintings as Poynter's *Israel in Egypt* of 1867,[19] did not correspond to the reality of 'liturgy', the use of the free-born in forced labour, disagreeable as this no doubt was. The same practice may have persisted under the equally autocratic Ptolemies and some argue that forced labour rather than slaves

135

was used in Egyptian quarries;[20] others would prefer a system in which contractors provided labourers to work side by side with prisoners under military guard.[21] In any case no archaeological evidence is available to provide clarification.

The Roman world

The local origin for the supply of building stone in the Greek cities of Sicily has already been touched on, and the same can be said for the cities of Magna Graecia like Metapontum, or for Paestum in Lucania. Equally, the indigenous settlements of the Etruscans, like Marzabotto, made use of local materials, in this case river cobbles for foundations, on which were erected one-storey houses of timber framing with mud-brick infill, while the early streets of Pompeii were paved with the local basaltic lava. Brick remained a popular building material, improved in strength by firing as opposed to sun-drying, and led to the construction of the high tenements eventually to be seen in Rome and Ostia. By the late Republic concrete was extensively used, faced with small stone blocks which gradually became more regular until it became the famous herring-bone style (*opus reticulatum*) of the Empire. For Rome, there was much use of the local limestone tufa and travertine from Tivoli, though the faces of buildings were frequently stuccoed.

It can be argued then that Italy of the late Republic was largely dependent on local sources for its building materials, natural or man-made. However, from the second century BC onwards, increasing contact with Hellenistic Greece and Asia Minor led to the adoption of Hellenistic influence on native Italian styles, what Vitruvius labelled *consuetudo italica* (5.11.1).[22] The ubiquitous use of marble in Greek architecture could not fail to impress the Roman troops and their commanders, but the problem of transport was clearly a drawback until the opening of the famous quarries at Luna (the later Carrara), the Ligurian *colonia*, in Augustan times. This prized white marble was used on a large scale in Rome and elsewhere, and the problem of transport was eased by the neighbourhood of the quarries to the harbour at Luna, and the possibility of shipping the stone, for instance, up the Tiber to Rome. So Augustus could claim, in the words of Suetonius (*Augustus* 28.3), that he 'found Rome a city of brick and left it a city of marble'; while Pliny (*NH* 36.7) speaks of mountain ranges being transported to and fro (*huc illuc portantur iuga*) in ships built specially for marble (*navesque marmorum causa fiunt*). Much of the imported marble, especially with a distinctive coloration, was imported for use as a decorative material for floors, wall panels, columns etc., and the sources are well known from macroscopic or more precise scientific techniques. Marbles of different colours – green (*verde antico*), yellow (*giallo antico*), green-blue (*cipollino*), red breccia and others – came from North Africa, the Greek mainland and islands, and Asia

136

Minor, and in the course of time monolithic granite columns and decorative porphyry were imported in ready-made form from Egypt and elsewhere.[23] Most of the sources were under direct imperial control and it has been suggested that the quarrying and supply of many of these marbles and other foreign stones were virtually industrialized.[24] Rome, for instance, stockpiled marble at a specific yard, the so called Marmorata, on the banks of the Tiber.[25] The industrialization of stone-quarrying is a tempting theme, with all its implications of a permanent labour force, perhaps with a substantial slave element, but can be exaggerated; some differentiation needs to be made between the marble trade, which provided a decorative material, and the provision of large-scale architectural features such as columns, where there must have been direct communication between quarry and building site.

In contrast to this long-range movement of quarry products, much of the stone used in the Roman provinces continued to be of local origin.[26] In such cases it seems likely that ownership may have been vested in a municipality or even a private individual, as opposed to imperial or state ownership of the major quarries. There is no doubt that the army was involved directly in quarrying, and that legions and auxiliary units undertook the cutting of stone for the defences and internal buildings of their fortresses and forts, in continuation of the original practice of preparing earth and timber for construction in the earlier phases of conquest and settlement. Two examples will suffice: the red sandstone used extensively in the legionary fortress of Deva (Chester) was mostly quarried on the spot, while lengths of Hadrian's Wall were built with stone derived from numerous individual quarries south of the Wall, identifiable by inscriptions.[27] The military clearly provided the skilled element in these operations but it is suggested that forced labour of local inhabitants may have been used for unskilled work and maintenance.[28] The extent to which slaves may have been used remains uncertain, but the distinction between them and forced labour gangs is perhaps academic.

The extent to which quarries in various provinces were under central control is a complex matter.[29] The categories of labour cannot be closely identified either but under the Empire slaves and prisoners of war were no doubt employed, as well as freedmen, soldiers, free labourers and serfs. As in mines, labour in quarries could rank as punishment and *servi poenae* and *condemnati ad metalla* (*damnati ad metallum*) evidently had slave status.[30] Unfortunately, there is great difficulty in demonstrating archaeologically the presence of slaves of any kind in the quarries themselves; epigraphically, there is evidence from the important quarries for the employment of imperial freedmen and slaves in administration and control and even, with the formula *ex ratione*, as lessees equivalent to private individuals,[31] and it would be tempting to argue that they had acquired practical experience as slaves at the quarry face, but this is unlikely as many had previously served as slaves in the imperial household.

The bigger Roman quarries were no doubt equipped with ranges of residential and administrative buildings, but in many cases these have been destroyed by later working. In Egypt, however, two quarry sites have remained virtually intact since Roman times, largely because of their inaccessibility in the Red Sea mountains of the Eastern Desert: Mons Claudianus which produced granite, and particularly huge monolithic columns for Rome itself, and 52 km (32 miles) to the north Mons Porphyrites, the eponymous source of the purple porphyry so highly prized throughout the Empire. Their remoteness presented substantial logistical problems, both in the housing and provisioning of the labour force and in the transport of their products from the hills, across the desert to the Nile at Caenepolis (the modern Qena) and so downstream to Alexandria for transhipment. A network of tracks, with substantial intermediate stations to supply water and fodder, provided the essential link between the quarries and the Nile,[32] as well as east to the Red Sea and the coast road (via Hadriana) and the port of Myos Hormos.

After the first recorded visits to the site in 1823 they were both visited and described on a number of occasions, culminating in their inclusion in the *Tabula Imperii Romani Coptos* sheet and in various publications.[33] The first detailed surveys and descriptions of the two sites were carried out by German teams, who proposed an interpretation of the internal buildings of the walled enclosures at both sites, with a tentative chronology.[34] Finally, between 1987 and 1993, there have been annual seasons of excavation at Mons Claudianus by an international team under the direction of Professor Jean Bingen, which have begun to define the fairly complex development of the site and the chronology of the surrounding granite quarries, with the startling discovery so far of some 10,000 *ostraca*, texts painted on potsherds, mostly in Greek with a few in Latin. Some are of a personal nature but the vast majority are requests of an official nature for supplies of food and water, labour, equipment and so on.[35] Work began in 1994 at Mons Porphyrites under the direction of Dr Valerie Maxfield and Professor David Peacock from the Mons Claudianus team.

The basic chronology of both quarry centres had formerly depended on epigraphy. Temple dedications to Sarapis at Mons Claudianus and to Sarapis and Isis at Mons Porphyrites indicate their building around AD 117-18, and the general administration of both sites by the procurator (*epitropos tôn metallôn*), M. Ulpius Chresimus, with the actual working of the quarries by the imperial slave Epaphroditus Sigerianus. Most of the datable examples of *ostraca* were Trajanic (AD 106-12) but later excavation within the walled settlement produced examples dated to the reign of Antoninus Pius, one of Commodus (AD 180/1), and finally one of Septimius Severus of AD 197. However, the mention of Claudianus granite and porphyry from Mons Porphyrites in Diocletian's price edict indicates that both quarries were still operative around AD 300, though the archaeological evidence for this remains to be found. The German investigators argued on stylistic and structural grounds, particularly for Mons Claudianus, that there was an earlier period of, say, the late first to early second century, followed by enlargement and refortification *c.* AD 300.[36] But excavation does not in fact support this simple interpretation. What can be seen today belongs to a final stage of occupation, possibly as late as the third to fourth century, but the remains, complicated by the persistent Egyptian propensity to pile rubbish on the roofs of buildings, overlie a sequence of earlier structures, in some cases demolished before the building of existing structures or in others running beneath them. The name Mons Claudianus may indicate a date in the middle of the first century AD for the first activity on one, or even both, sites. Archaeologically, the earliest find is a Neronian *ostracon* of AD 68, and the latest an *ostracon* and two coins dating to AD 282.[37]

The evidence from inscriptions and *ostraca* makes it clear that both quarries were under Roman military administration and that troops were present; on the other hand, the workforce was predominantly civilian, including wives and families. But in the vast number of texts there is no mention of slave-workers, and the conclusion must be, for the present at least, that the workers were free craftsmen working under military control. At both sites the internal buildings of the walled settlements are largely unmilitary in style, though the defences suggest army influence. In addition, the working population at Mons Claudianus seems to have lived inside the walls and travelled daily to the adjacent quarries, whereas at Mons Porphyrites the walled area seems to have served as an administrative and supply centre, with the workers living in village-like settlements at the quarries, which lay at a greater distance and height above the wadi floor (fig. 41). The German investigators emphasized the skilled nature of the work at both places and discussed the possibility of fluctuating workforces, with the greatest activity in the winter months, based on easier climatic conditions and a greater availability of local food and water (though Aelius Aristides, writing in the second century AD (*Or.* 36.67), hints at summer work when he speaks of being burned alive in a land which is 'sandy and thirsts'). Reinforcement of the workforce could be easily achieved from the population of the Nile valley. Despite the literary evidence for convicts at Mons Porphyrites (*damnati*) Röder discounted their use there for skilled work and equally at Mons Claudianus.[38] His view is followed in Klein's survey of research on the two quarries which discusses the nature of the workforce and argues that convict-slaves cannot have provided a skilled workforce but were probably used for such menial tasks as road building, clearance of overburden and removal of rubble.[39]

The suggestion of seasonal work, with a fluctuating labour force recruited in the towns and villages of the Nile valley, is interesting. Certainly, the majority of the personal names on the *ostraca* are of Greek origin, while the occurrence of *entolai* or instructions which include provi-

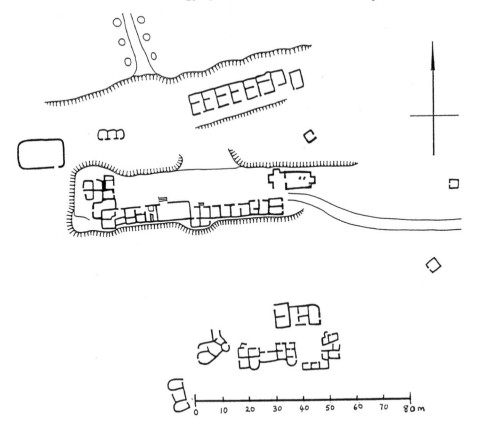

Fig. 41. Plan of south-west village at Mons Porphyrites

sions for the deduction of cash from workers' monthly payments for the care of a wife or mother left behind in the village suggests that money played only a small part in the economy of the site, a view supported by the sparsity of coins from the excavations. One might suppose that the workers built up a substantial nest-egg against their return home (as do, in fact, the local Egyptians employed as workers on the modern excavations, who have no opportunity to spend money at this remote site).

Farther west, in the province of Numidia, lay the famous quarries of Simithu or Simithus at the modern Chemtou in Tunisia, near the Algerian border. They produced the prized yellow marble, *giallo antico*, and were conveniently placed on the great east-west road from Carthage to Hippo through Bulla Regia. The quarries were under imperial control and were managed by imperial slaves or freedmen responsible to the *procurator metallorum* or *marmorum Numidicorum*, also a freedman. In the vicinity lay a large work camp for the final working of the marble and the housing

Fig. 42. The *fabrica* at Chemtou

141

of the quarrymen in barrack-like quarters, all within a strong defensive wall. Another notable feature was a workshop (*fabrica*) of *c.* AD 150-250 for the serial production of marble vessels and so on for export to all parts of the Empire (fig. 42).[40] Again, we can say nothing of the identity of the workmen, that is whether they were free craftsmen or slaves, paid in either case. But no doubt the army was in general control of the area, as the layout of the work camp shows.

Little can be said of the workers in the famous marble quarries of Asia Minor, at Proconnesus on the Sea of Marmara or Dokimeion in Phrygia. For Gaul, Bedon's study devotes a section to quarrymen and concludes that they were recruited among the lower classes – free, slave and military; it suggests that slaves were numerous but have left little trace archaeologically.[41] An altar from a marble workshop at Saint-Béat (Haute-Garonne) is dedicated by *Primu(s) Bedo(nis) ser(vus)*, a slave who was either named Primus or was the first slave of his owner Bedo.[42] The Rhineland quarries were evidently administered and worked by the Roman army.[43] They were extensively studied by Röder who argued that the local population could have supplied workers who eventually formed a skilled group, with a slave element.[44] He cites an instance of a skeleton found with leg-shackles at the Pellenz volcanic tuff (tufa) quarries south of Andernach, which he suggests might have been that of a slave trapped by an underground fall, though the discovery was not well documented.[45] A similar discovery is noted from Saint-Leu-d'Esserent, as well as houses found in the last century with iron rings for the fettering of convicts at night in quarries at Boulouris (Var), which sound reminiscent of *ergastula*.[46]

The literary evidence for the employment of slaves in Roman quarries has been frequently cited; the statement by Josephus (*BJ* 6.418) that, after the fall of Jerusalem in AD 70, a large number of Jews over the age of seventeen was sent to the 'works' in Egypt is usually understood to mean quarries and mines. An unequivocal view is that quarry-workers were largely slaves and freedmen, with the latter in a minority, and that slaves were used at Chemtou, Dokimeion, Pentelikon and Thasos, a practice harking back to the use of *servi publici* in the final years of the Republic, for instance at Luna, where the town owned the quarries.[47] Here, the inscription of AD 16-22 indicates that the slaves were organized in a college under a *magister* with four annually elected decurions and with *vilici* as overseers.[48] This is reminiscent of the lists of annually elected *magistri* and *magistrae* at Minturnae in charge of groups of slaves serving minor cults and thought to have originated as war captives in Marius' campaigns of *c.* 100 BC;[49] but at Luna the same names appear on other blocks of marble, which may indicate that they were lessees rather than slave workmen. A Christian text, the so-called *Passio Sanctorum Quattuor Coronatorum*,[50] has long been held to provide evidence for the employment of slaves in Roman quarries. The text mentions 622 *artifices metallici*, of whom four became martyrs at Rome. It has been argued that the *artifices metallici* were slaves working in Pannonian quarries in the final years of Diocletian's reign, and that the four martyrs were secret Christians, while professed Christians, converted by Cyril, Bishop of Alexandria, were working as convicts (*damnati ad metalla*) in harsher conditions nearby. The status of the latter seems beyond dispute but whether the *artifices* were slaves seems less certain; the text presents difficulties and the location of the quarries has been disputed.[51] In the narrative, Diocletian, while in Pannonia, requested the quarrymen to prepare architectural details and sculpture in porphyry, and earlier writers suggested a quarry near Sirmium in Pannonia, but the specific references to *metallum porphyreticum* and *mons porphyreticus* argue for the Egyptian quarry. Delbrueck argued for Mons Porphyrites while Simonyi preferred Pannonia and was followed by Mócsy, who also suggested an earlier date of AD 293, when the emperor made a journey along the *limes* in November, the month of the martyrdom.[52] Röder followed Delbrueck in preferring Mons Porphyrites and, in fact, in his description of the south-west village (Südwestdorf) at the site conjecturally identified the quarters of the *damnati*, with a church, barracks for their guards and a commandant's house, possibly occupied together in the fourth century and acting as the successor to the walled enclosure on the wadi floor.[53] As regards the location of the narrative at Mons Porphyrites, a point made by Delbrueck has not received sufficient emphasis: he calls attention to the words '... ad montem porphyreticum qui dicitur igneus', which must refer to Gebel Dokhan, the mountain west of the site, rising to a height of nearly 1,700 m (5,500 ft).[54] The Arabic can be translated as 'misty' or 'smoky' mountain, and the modern visitor is impressed by its cloud cap, a rare phenomenon in the otherwise cloudless atmosphere of the Red Sea mountains.

So, although there is no unequivocal evidence in the shape of archaeological material for the employment of chattel-slaves in Roman quarries, there is good literary evidence for the use of convicts, slave or free, condemned *in* or *ad metallum* or *metalla*, meaning mines or quarries. Criminals or Christians condemned to work in quarries lost their civil rights to become *servi poenae*, 'slaves of the penalty', and to that extent indistinguishable from chattel-slaves. Millar's study of this form of punishment assembles the geographical evidence, though accepting Pannonia as the location for the Diocletian episode.[55] Much of the literary evidence is of the third and fourth centuries and relates to the treatment of Christians, but it seems probable that imperial *metalla* were receiving *servi* of this kind at an earlier date, sometimes from a considerable distance.

Mines

The Greek world

Two passages from nearly contemporary Greek authors emphasize why slaves could be an important element in the operation of mines, as opposed to quarries, and the extent to which Athens, for instance, used them in the silver mines of the Laurion peninsula. In his *Ways and Means* (*Poroi*) the pragmatic Xenophon gave his final advice to his fellow-Athenians *c.* 355 BC on economic reforms designed to bring about recovery from the crippling effects of the Social War (4.1-12). He devotes himself specifically to the revitalization of the Laurion mines through the provision of slaves by the state to the mining managers. His argument is that there is no economic limit on the number of slaves which can be employed because of the insatiable demand for silver; certainly, his proposals may have influenced the politician Eubolus since the Laurion mines were in full operation again by the end of his administration in 339 BC. The second passage is earlier and comes from the seventh book of Thucydides' history of the Peloponnesian War (431-404 BC); in the later phases of the war, Sparta invaded Attica and in 413 BC seized and fortified the town of Dekeleia, 25 km (15 miles) north-east of Athens, which from then until the end of the war presented a constant threat to Athens and the mines of the Laurion peninsula (7.27). Worse still, a large number of slaves ('more than twenty thousand'), mostly mine-workers (*cheirotechnai*), had fled to the Spartans and whether or not this was an event of 413 BC or spread over a longer period it represented a crippling blow to Athens. The juxtaposition of these two passages emphasizes the slave basis of the workforce of the Attic mines, while Xenophon's analysis of the benefit to be obtained from increasing the number of slaves in the mines was applicable just as much in the fifth century as in the fourth. Certainly, the economic and political dominance of Athens after her victory over the Persians at Salamis in 480 BC depended largely on the increased exploitation of the Laurion mines and the extent to which her silver tetradrachms (*glaukes* – 'owls') dominated trade in the Aegean and beyond.

Only a brief description of the mines and metal-working sites of the Laurion peninsula is given here since, first, the area has been discussed in detail in a number of studies,[56] and, second, this study deals with the archaeological evidence for the presence of slaves and only presents detailed descriptions of areas and processes which offer this type of information.

Geographically, the mine area forms a peninsula of about 200 sq. km culminating in Cape Sounion and marked by Thorikos on the east and Anavyssos on the west; the overall length is *c.* 17 km (10 miles) and its width 10 km (6 miles) and a central ridge of hills, rarely exceeding 300 m

(1,000 ft), runs from north to south. The terrain is rocky, particularly along the coast, and cultivable plains of any size only occur at Anavyssos, Thorikos and Legraina, west of Sounion. The climate today is dry but temperate, with a strong wind off the sea in summer. The pine-clad landscape today is the result of recent planting and it is thought that, although it may have been wooded in its primitive state, there was considerable denudation in antiquity in order to supply the smelting furnaces. Geologically, the hills consist of superimposed schists and lime-stones, at the junctions of which the three so called 'contacts' had been deposited, particularly to the east – sulphides and oxides of zinc, iron and lead, with other minerals. Of these the most important was the lead ore, galena, because of its silver content which attracted attention through its appearance on the surface as veins of ore. Surface deposits were exploited first, as early as the third millennium, but as veins were followed beneath the ground, the second 'contact' was discovered and eventually, in the fifth century BC, the rich third 'contact'. The mining technique developed ac-cordingly, from simple horizontal passages running into hillsides until, in the final stages, there was a complex system of deep galleries reached from the surface by well-cut shafts as much as 100 m (330 ft) deep, while the galleries themselves ran for a distance of several hundred metres. Al-though the eventual yield from the lowest veins was much greater, the problems of extraction, ventilation and collapse were correspondingly more serious.

Once extracted, the ore was broken into lumps, pulverized into granules of less than 1 mm in hand-mills, and then separated into heavier and lighter fractions, denoting a greater or smaller quantity of metal-bearing ore, by throwing it into running water at the so called 'washing-tables'; the various grades of ore were heaped on the central rectangular area while the water circulated along a surrounding channel, to be re-used after the removal of sediment. After drying, the ores were smelted in furnaces to remove impurities and leave lead in a crude form; this was then re-smelted by so-called cupellation, which separated out the nearly pure silver from the resultant litharge or lead oxide which flowed out of the crucible (fig. 43). The silver was then re-melted in order to eliminate impurities, while the litharge itself was re-smelted to produce lead, a desirable metal for use in building construction, colouring matter, and medicine. Some of these processes could be harmful for the workers, for example the release of sulphur dioxide in the preliminary smelting.

The defeat of Athens in the Peloponnesian War meant that mining ceased in the peninsula by 400 BC; recovery was slow until the renewal of work c. 350 BC, which continued until the end of the century. A third period of less intensive activity followed from the end of the third century and through the second until the mines were finally abandoned by the Romans in the first century BC, when the Spanish mines came into full operation. Renewed exploitation of the Laurion mines and slag heaps at the end of

Fig. 43. Reconstruction of ore-processing

the nineteenth century led to increased archaeological interest, and since the Second World War excavation has shed a great deal of light on mining and smelting processes, notably the Belgian excavations at Thorikos since 1963 (fig. 44).

The complexity of the ancient cycle of operations, some hazardous and some unskilled, led to the employment of slaves on a large scale in many categories. The mines themselves were publicly owned and leased to individuals, as the inscriptions recording such leases found in the *agora* at Athens make clear. Individual lessees owned as many as 1,000 slaves, but doubtless there were many operating on a much smaller scale and even some working with their own hands; probably there were paid workmen of free status, working side by side with slaves, as in the quarries and on building sites, such as the Erechtheum. Lessees could buy slaves in the public markets at Athens and Sounion, and from the names surviving in literature and on tombstones and religious dedications it appears that many slaves originated in Thrace, Asia Minor, the Levant (including

Fig. 44. Reconstruction of tower-house and 'washing-tables' at Thorikos

Cyprus), or farther east.[57] The number of slaves employed annually in the productive periods of the fifth and fourth centuries BC has been much discussed. We need not regard Thucydides' figure of 20,000 slaves, many of them miners, who fled to the Spartans at Dekeleia in 413 BC as particularly accurate, but it does give an indication of the size of the servile workforce. Lauffer discusses the question in some detail and lists estimates proposed by various scholars of between 10,000 and 30,000 for the fifth century, 5,000 and 60,000 in the fourth century, and three of 1,000 in the second century.[58] A recent theoretical estimate of the number required for an annual production of twenty tonnes of silver during the fifth-century boom (the Penteconteteia of *c.* 480-430 BC) gives a figure of 11,000, that is, towards the lower end of earlier estimates, but this is based on an assumption that different slaves were required for each separate process.[59] Men could have been moved from one point to another, to make the true figure smaller. Lauffer makes some calculations for the fourth century on the basis of literary evidence and the lists of leases and presents them in graphic form to show a high point of *c.* 35,000 in 340 BC in the boom period under Eubolus and Lycurgus.[60]

Whatever the precise figures, it is clear that substantial numbers of slaves were employed in all phases of the industry during the fifth and

Fig. 45. Corinthian tablet depicting miners

fourth centuries, and it would be reasonable to suppose that there would be some material evidence for their presence. Lauffer deals briefly with the evidence for slave-quarters and cites the discovery at the end of the last century of a complex at Megala Peuka in the Legraina valley, 5 km (3 miles) north-west of Sounion.[61] This consisted of a row of hydraulic platforms for ore separation and cisterns, together with houses with plastered walls, separated by narrow alleys, some of them built against the wall enclosing the whole establishment. It seems likely that these were quarters for slaves working both on the ore separation platforms and other nearby establishments, and that they were concentrated inside the enclosure by the lessees to prevent flight and the theft of silver and lead and in general to economize on security arrangements. The slaves seem to have been a permanent workforce, accompanied by their families, to judge by the burials nearby. The building technique and the pottery suggest construction in the second half of the fourth century BC with occupation continuing until the Roman period; and it is likely that the working practices and living conditions remained unaltered with changes of lessee.

A more recent example of possible slave-quarters is in Insula 1 at Thorikos, excavated by the Belgian School in 1963-5.[62] This lies in the so-called industrial quarter of the town on the south-west slope of the hill called Velatouri, in 'laverie no. 1'. It stands within an enclosing wall at the junction of two streets called by the excavators 'rue de l'industrie' and 'rue Therippides'. An entrance to the west where these two streets meet at an acute angle leads into a courtyard, beyond which is a hydraulic ore platform flanked by a long room for ore crushing; but the chief interest lies in a group of small rectangular rooms with sides varying from 3 to 5 m (10 to 16 ft), interpreted as sleeping-quarters for the slave-workers, with adjacent washroom and mess-room. The complex would seem to have been in operation in the fifth and fourth centuries. No doubt more examples of slave-quarters await further excavation, but others must have been lost through modern mining operations.

Another example of ore separation platforms in association with living-quarters was excavated in 1977-8 in the adjacent Soureza valley.[63] It was designated the Asclipiacon complex by the excavators from an inscription 'Simos occupied Askalepikon', indicating a concession by Athens to a known figure of *c.* 350 BC in a region dedicated to Asklepios. Three of the five platforms excavated were thought to have been the property of Simos, and there was evidence for resumed activity in the fourth century AD. Various rooms were identified as bedrooms, washrooms, and rooms for technical purposes, for example ore grinding. It is suggested that free and slave-workers were working side by side, the former performing the more skilled operations and enjoying more comfortable conditions, for example an *andron* or dining-room, though the slave-workers had a tolerable existence. A mine gallery was located nearby, with a recess in the wall by the entrance, presumably for the overseer of the slaves mining the ore.

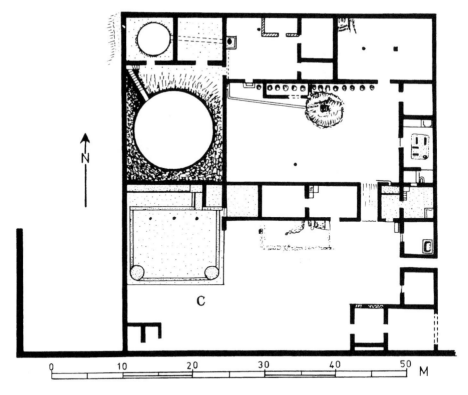

Fig. 46. Plan of Ergasterion C at Agrileza

Of similar date and general character is the group of three platforms with associated cisterns, workrooms, living-quarters and washrooms at the nearby site of Agrileza, excavated in 1977-83.[64] No specific identification is attempted but the rooms along the east side of the two courtyards of the building known as Ergasterion C present an appearance of mixed workrooms and sleeping-quarters (fig. 46).

It is interesting that the only structures in the Laurion area where slave-quarters can be hypothetically identified are in *ergasteria* with ore separation platforms, and this was presumably a process, like smelting, where a higher level of skill was required, with a small permanent staff, part slave, part free. Quarters for slaves involved in mining remain to be found; barrack-like accommodation at a site like Thorikos remains a possibility.

Small finds such as shackles are also useful archaeological evidence. As in the chapters on agriculture detailed treatment is reserved for Chapter 7 and all that need be said here is that there is a single instance of fetters from the Laurion mines. They were apparently found at Kamariza, 4 km

150

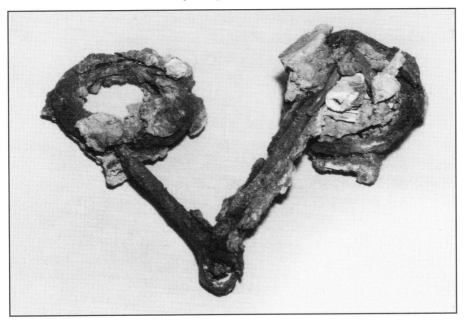

Fig. 47. Fetters with ankle bone still enclosed, from Kamariza

(2.5 miles) west of the Laurion settlement and consist of an iron ring still enclosing the ankle bone of, presumably, a slave who had met his death by accident (fig. 47). It was of the type known elsewhere in Greece composed of two circular shackles for the feet connected by straight bars to a central link from which ran a chain. The fragment has been preserved in the collections of the Bergakademie at Freiberg, near Dresden, since 1914.[65] It has been further discussed by Lauffer, who regards it as unusual for miners working in confined conditions to be fettered and suggests the wearer may have been chained for punishment, as various literary references, particularly those relating to prisoners, indicate.[66] He argues that such chaining belongs to late Hellenistic times, following the introduction of Roman capital and mining methods.

So far, the presence of slaves in the Laurion mines has been related to the ore separation platforms and the adjacent quarters. Furnaces have also been excavated and found to be arranged in rows, as at Megala Peuka, but not accompanied by workers' rooms.[67] It is likely that workmen, free or slave, did not sleep next to the smelting areas, probably because of the danger of the theft of the refined silver. On the other hand, the preliminary mining of the ore and its transport to the surface and so to the ore separation platforms have left archaeological indications of the presence of workers, slave and free. These can be briefly listed as mining tools for use at the ore face; the containers for moving the ore along the galleries to

151

Fig. 48. Pick found at Kamariza

the bottom of the shafts in the case of underground workings; and the means of lighting the galleries themselves. In a sense, the discussion of such material encroaches on mining techniques, but some of the objects are so closely linked to the individual workers that a brief discussion can be included here. The tools have already been previously described and the objects themselves survive in the Laurion Museum and the Freiberg Bergakademie.[68] In general, they resemble those used in stone-quarrying and appear to have been of high-quality iron; their simple but effective nature meant that they varied little over long periods. They can be classified as the hammer which, with the short iron spike (sometimes a longer crowbar), was used to break into the vein of ore; the pointed pick with a long or short handle (fig. 48), depending on the height of the gallery; and the shovel. From the working face the ore was loaded into leather bags with handles or straps and carried on the shoulders or back to the bottom of a shaft; this was work carried out by children where tunnels were low or narrow. From the shaft bottom the bags were hauled to the surface, by mechanical means in difficult cases, and the lumps of ore loaded into wagons for transport to the ore separation workshops for preliminary grinding in mills and then hydraulic sorting. Lighting in the galleries was effected by earthenware oil-lamps of the same design as the household lamp but deeper, so as to give a life of ten hours, the lamps themselves being placed in niches cut into the tunnel walls. Clothes worn by slaves in mines, particularly below ground, were of the simplest and, archaeologically, can only be determined from vase-painting, for example the well-known Penteskaphia tray. If not naked in the heat of the working face, they might wear a simple apron of leather or a shirt, as in a smithy or foundry, while the overseer would wear the *chiton*.[69]

Unfortunately, other areas of the Greek mainland and islands offer little in the way of archaeological evidence for the presence of slaves. The north Aegean island of Thasos was recorded by Herodotus (6.46-7) as a prolific source of gold in the sixth and fifth centuries BC and the mines themselves have been surveyed and recorded in recent years, while actual implements are preserved in the Freiberg Bergakademie (fig. 49).[70] But of mining establishments and workers' quarters, as in Laurion, the evidence is still

Fig. 49. Miners' tools from Thasos

lacking. On the mainland, in Macedonia and Thrace, gold, silver and base metals such as iron are recorded as having been mined in Chalcidice and the area eastwards to Kavala, but evidence for mines is difficult to assess. Slag heaps occur in the Athos peninsula as far south as Ierissos, and it is interesting to note that in the necropolis of ancient Akanthos at least eight burials of Hellenistic date are recorded as wearing leg-shackles; it is suggested that these were prisoners of war, Greek mercenaries captured by Alexander and sent to labour in Macedonia.[71] But the most important mines lay in the region centred on Mount Pangaion, between the valley of the river Strymon to the west and the Philippi plain to the east. As early as the sixth century BC silver was obtained here for the coins of Thasos and Pisistratus derived much of his personal wealth from the area after his expulsion from Athens, before he returned to Attica in 545 BC and possibly saw the potential of the Laurion peninsula.[72] The main centres for gold and silver, however, were Krenides, colonized from Thasos in the sixth century, and its harbour of Neapolis (Kavala). Thasos lost control, and by 350 BC Philip II of Macedon had seized Krenides, renaming it Philippi, and Neapolis as well as Amphipolis near the mouth of the Strymon. The vast amount of gold and silver which he obtained from the area was commented on by various ancient authors,[73] and is strikingly confirmed by the rich finds from the tomb of Philip II at Vergina now in the museum at Salonika. His son Alexander's conquests opened up the wealth of the Persian Empire but it is held that, while the mines of Asia Minor were no doubt worked by his successors, the Macedonian mines continued in full swing in order to cope with the growing needs of a widespread money economy.[74] Certainly the Laurion mines were in decline until there was a resumption of activity *c.* 150 BC through Rome's intervention in Macedonia. The problem with Macedonia and Thrace is the lack of good archaeological evidence for the precise location of Hellenistic mines. Casson listed the sites but was sceptical about Mount Pangaion itself, while Davies discusses the availability of placers on the edges of the Philippi plain as well as of ores from Pangaion.[75] Conophagos, during his spell as minister of Industry and Energy in the Greek government of 1974-7, instituted a study of Macedonian and Thracian gold resources in 1975.[76] The conclusions were that alluvial deposits were slight both today and in antiquity, but at the foot of Pangaion there was evidence for numerous narrow galleries for the mining of natural gold, the principal source in antiquity, while slag heaps indicated that gold was also derived from the arsenical ore known as 'mispickel'; this was smelted in conjunction with lead, and the resultant lead and gold ore was treated by cupellation to extract the gold. Silver was mainly obtained from the argentiferous lead ores of the Chalcidice, notably Olympias (modern Olimbiada), at the foot of the northern slopes of the Stratoniko hills. In Thrace itself there were small scale silver mines.

But in spite of this fairly conclusive geological evidence to support the statements of ancient writers, there is nothing to indicate so far that there were mining communities using slaves in large numbers to exploit these deposits, as in the Laurion.[77] So, for the moment, the archaeological evidence for slaves in this area must remain unproven. Nevertheless, there was a strong connection between this northern area and the Laurion, as the Pisistratus episode indicates. Slaves from the Thracian mines were recruited by Athenian mine-owners for work in the Laurion mines, on the evidence of literature and inscriptions, including the highly priced Sosias bought by Nikias as a supervisor around 420 BC (Xen., *Poroi* 4.14).[78] Similarly, gold and silver were mined in quantity on the Cycladic island of Siphnos (as well as iron on the neighbouring island of Seriphos) until the mines were inundated *c.* 500 BC, perhaps by a change of sea level. The presence of nearly 40 circular towers on Siphnos, regarded by some as watch-towers,[79] recalls such structures in the Laurion peninsula and the possibility of slave mine-workers. By Hellenistic times most mines of mainland Greece, apart from Macedonia and to a lesser extent the Laurion, were pretty well exhausted, though copper was perhaps now exploited in the Othrys range of Thessaly.[80] Farther east, Asia Minor was a great producer of silver in prehistoric times and continued into Classical antiquity, when it ranked next after Spain.[81] By Hellenistic times these resources were open to the Greek world, but of actual mines there is little to add to previous summaries, themselves largely based on references in ancient authors.[82] Cary argues that the silver deposits of Asia Minor were energetically worked after the Macedonian conquest but that this output was largely used to satisfy the needs of local currencies.[83] The most notable gold-producing centre was Lydian Sardis with its placer deposits in the sands of the river Pactolus. As capital of Lydia in 650-550 BC it achieved enormous prosperity through its ability to refine the gold and through its introduction of a bimetallic coinage. Workshops with cupellation and cementation furnaces have been identified in an industrial quarter in the Pactolus valley by the road leading to the temple of Artemis;[84] these were in operation in the first half of the sixth century BC, but no evidence was recovered for the status of the workers, though the Lydians certainly had slaves.[85] Gold probably continued to be recovered after the capture of the city by Alexander and in its subsequent Hellenistic occupation until it was bequeathed to Rome in 133 BC by the last Pergamene king, Attalus III. Rostovtzeff considered that slaves were employed by the Attalids on a large scale in agriculture and in the mines, and that the same held good in Asia Minor generally.[86]

In Egypt the use of criminals and prisoners in mines seems to have diminished under the Ptolemies, as in quarries. The Greek concept of free paid labour developed, but not the use of slaves. The lessees who now appeared on the scene made use of the liturgy principle by which the local population was compelled to contribute forced labour. The lot of such workmen, nominally free, must have been nearly as arduous as that of slaves.[87] It is doubtful if the Ptolemaic mines of the Eastern Desert were of great significance;[88] much more important were the Nubian gold mines (probably Wadi Alaki near the Sudan border) for which local labour was not readily available. The Ptolemies devoted much effort to their exploitation and criminals and prisoners were used under armed guard, in conditions graphically portrayed by the Greek writer, Agatharchides, in the second century BC, as preserved by Diodorus (3.12-14). The strongest were used at the mine-face, boys to move the ore along the galleries, and women and old men to grind the ore; the harshness of the conditions frequently led to death.

The Roman world

Towards the end of the third century BC Rome came into violent contact with rivals in the East and the West and her success in each case left her in possession of rich mining areas which, it might be claimed, largely formed the basis of her later empire. The background to her success is the relative scarcity of metal ores in Italy. Orth's statement: 'Die italische Halbinsel ist nicht mit metallischen Schatzen ausgestattet' is perhaps too sweeping, but was certainly true of central Italy.[89] Only the conquest of Cisalpine Gaul brought the gold of the Pennine Alps within range, while silver, copper and iron were derived from Elba, Sardinia, Calabria and Sicily.[90]

In the East, Rome's clash with Macedonia in the successive wars of 214-167 BC led to the probable closure of the Macedonian mines;[91] Delos was declared a free port in 166, under the tutelage of Athens, and the final revival of the Laurion mines took place *c.* 150 BC, marked by the growth of the 'New Style' tetradrachms after their introduction in 196 BC.[92] Slaves were still clearly used on a large scale, to judge by the two attested revolts of 134 and 104 BC, and we may suppose that the conditions and methods of mining and smelting had not changed materially.

The questions of ownership, administration and the nature of the workforce in Roman mines have been generally discussed on a number of occasions, but mainly in a historical or juristic sense with the aid of the literary evidence, including epigraphy.[93] The juridical position was complex and it is difficult to generalize, but under the Republic mines in newly acquired territory became the property of the Roman people and could be leased to individuals or groups, or handed over to municipalities; in the course of time actual private ownership seems to have developed until, with the Empire, ownership was once more vested with the state. Actual administration was under the control of provincial procurators, who in turn leased mines to individuals or groups.

Of more immediate concern is the composition of the workforce, and again the position is complex. Slaves undoubtedly formed a large element under the Republic with a tendency for this to diminish in the second to first centuries BC.[94] Egypt was a special case and in the Ptolemaic mines the workers were convicts, prisoners or paid workers who were almost entirely free men, either individual entrepreneurs or those who worked under forced labour (liturgy). Under the Empire, mines were clearly worked by a mixture of slaves and free paid workmen, accompanied by the introduction of convicts, as earlier in Egypt, the so called *servi poenae* who were condemned to *metallum, opus metalli* or *ministerium metallicorum*, possibly punishments of different grades.[95] Prisoners of war were also employed and supervised, like convicts, by military units. Among those condemned to labour in mines and quarries in the later Empire were persecuted Christians, while the numbers of chattel-slaves may have diminished with the introduction of *metallarii*, workers attached to mines and sold with them, as *coloni* were sold with landed estates.

In the West the Iberian peninsula was to be an area of conflict between Rome and Carthage, and ultimately became the most important metal-producing area for the late Republic and early Empire. Its early history was one of colonization on the coast by Greeks and Phoenicians, and ultimately of control by the Carthaginians after the First Punic War of 264-241 BC; in the Second Punic War (218-201 BC) Rome ousted the Carthaginians from Spain, and finally destroyed Carthage in 146 at the end of the Third Punic War (149-146 BC). Even so, Spain and its tough native population proved hard to subdue; the main victory was in 133 BC with the fall of Numantia, but north-western Spain with its rich deposits of gold did not succumb until the campaign of 26-19 BC.

Ancient writers made frequent reference to the mineral wealth of the peninsula and Davies adds his personal observations to give a detailed description of the exploitation of gold, silver, copper, lead, tin, iron and so on, particularly in the first centuries BC and AD.[96] From the point of view of the ownership and exploitation of these mines, two passages are of particular importance. The first is from Diodorus (5.36.3-4) who notes that, once the Romans had gained control of most of Spain, many Italians flocked to the mines and in their desire for gain made great fortunes; it has been cited as one of the most striking pieces of evidence for emigration from Italy under the Republic for commercial purposes.[97] The passage continues with the statement that the entrepreneurs purchased a mass of slaves whom they handed over to those working the mines, presumably their bailiffs or overseers. The second passage is from Strabo (3.147-8) in his description of mines in Spain, where he quotes a statement of Polybius about the silver mines of Carthago Nova (Cartagena) in the middle of the second century BC: 40,000 men were at work there, bringing in 257,000 drachmae a day to the Roman people. In their discussion of the bearing of these passages on the legal and financial position of the Spanish mines, some have claimed that the mines were run by the great *societates publicanorum* of the equestrian order at Rome, but another view is that these were small-scale contractors.[98] This theory had been propounded earlier and the Spanish mines compared with those in the Laurion peninsula, operated by numerous lessees with small gangs of slaves.[99] The mechanism was probably that leases were granted to these contractors by the governor's quaestors and that they included a provision for the paying of a levy (*vectigal*) at a fixed rate to the state.[100] The most recent discussion of the question sets out the opposing views and favours the role of *publicani*.[101] By the beginning of the Empire, ownership of the mines was taken into the emperor's hands and they were managed by *procuratores metallorum*, *equites* or freedmen, who exercised direct control over large mining areas; smaller mines were run by *conductores*, best described as entrepreneurs.

Slaves, then, were an important element among the mine-workers of the Republic and continued to be so under the Empire, on the evidence of the Aljustrel tables, considered below. Unfortunately, as in other mining areas, post-Roman exploitation has removed much of the evidence for structures, so that little survives archaeologically of workers' quarters, whether for slave or free. There was clearly a long tradition, to judge by the discovery of simple huts of the eighth to seventh century BC at Riotinto with Near Eastern parallels.[102] In an enumeration of the slight archaeological evidence, we may take in sequence the main mining areas of the peninsula: the south-east, and especially the silver mines in the area of Carthago Nova (Cartagena) and their associated production of lead; the Sierra Morena along the Guadalquivir, with deposits principally of copper and argentiferous lead ores; the north-west with its rich gold deposits and, to a lesser extent, tin; and the south-west, extending from the western end of the Sierra Morena to the southern districts of Portugal, including Riotinto, with rich deposits of copper and iron ores, as well as of gold and argentiferous lead.[103]

As regards the origin of the slave-workers at the Carthago Nova mines, Domergue argues that they were part native Iberian and part from eastern slave-markets such as Delos until its destruction by Mithridates in 88 BC.[104] In any case, the intense exploitation of the deposits in the south-east was diminishing by the time of Augustus, and in the early years of the Empire the emphasis was being switched to the Sierra Morena and the south-west, and above all to the newly conquered north-west with its rich deposits of gold. Normally, the method of mining was by shafts to reach veins, followed by stoping or the cutting of generally horizontal galleries in order to extract the ore, as in the Greek mines of the Laurion peninsula; but where the overburden was friable it could be removed by water power, a process known as hushing, coupled with controlled separation of ore from its parent gravels etc. by hydraulicking, the use of washing tables, processes particularly applicable to the rich deposits of the north-west.[105] One of the hazards of the Iberian mines was the presence of water in the workings, in contrast to the aridity of the Laurion peninsula. Various methods were used to drain this away and these fall within the field of mining practice; but mechanical means – screws, chains of buckets, waterwheels, pumps – were also used and required heavy manual labour. We may suppose that slaves provided the motive power and to that extent the devices will be described here, as will the equipment of the miners themselves.

Domergue argues that the miners, largely slaves, of the Sierra de Cartagena occupied the ridges between the ravines of the mining area and were grouped in small villages around the shafts and furnaces; the evidence of the settlements at San Ramon or Mariana, or of the foundry at La Balsa, has largely been removed by modern mining.[106] Chronologically, the Sierra Morena does not seem to have been fully exploited until the final years of the end of the second century BC, with the final pacification of Hispania Ulterior.[107] The mining settlements seem to have been dispersed in the same fashion as those of the Sierra de Cartagena, small hamlets placed on south-facing slopes of hills near mine shafts, composed of closely packed huts; an exception is Sortijon del Cugna pleasantly set on the river bank. As before, the evidence has still to be studied in detail after excavation has taken place, though two sites, Diogines and Cerro del Plomo, have given good evidence for the unpleasant working environment; at La Loba recent excavation has shown a settlement with long parallel buildings set obliquely on the slope between the mine shafts above and the smelting-foundries below (fig. 50).[108] The graffiti on the pottery from the huts are in Iberian characters, but one cannot be sure whether the inhabitants were slave or free.

Despite the subjugation of the peninsula by the end of the Republic, apart from the northern territory of the Astures and Cantabri, mining activity seems still to have concentrated in the south-east and the Sierra Morena, possibly because of the need for silver to pay the troops in the Sertorian War and the struggles between Caesar and the sons of Pompey.[109] The troubled conditions of the first century BC may have inhibited activity in the south-west, apart from mines at Riotinto and Aljustrel producing copper, silver and possibly iron, but after the Augustan reorganization this area and the north-west (Galicia and Asturia) were intensively exploited in the first two centuries AD to produce gold, silver, tin, lead and iron, followed by a marked slackening of activity in the third and fourth centuries. In the north-west, altitude and climate imposed a pattern of seasonal activity. Domergue cites the case of the mine at Las Rubias, set at a height of 1,700 m (5,500 ft), where the irregular settlement of huts is dominated by a small military post with heated rooms, of mid-first-century date.[110] At the lower level of 1,100 m (3,600 ft) is the mine of La Corona de Quintanilla and a settlement composed of huts with walls built of pebbles and clay and thatched roofs, with hearths sometimes inside and sometimes outside.[111]

The study by Domergue and Hérail of the gold mines in the valley of the river Duerna, west of Léon, reveals mining settlements established *c.* AD 15/20, that is some thirty to forty years after the completion of the conquest

Fig. 50a. Miner's pick from La Loba

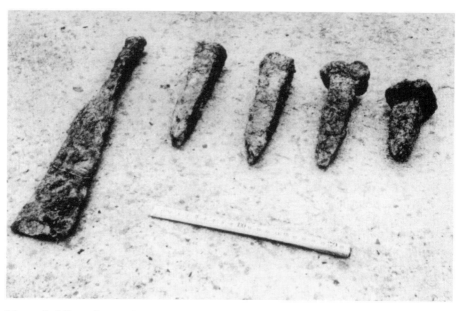

Fig. 50b. Miners' tools from La Loba

of north-west Spain. They were typically set on *coronas*, plateau sites defended by deeply cut ditches intended to carry water for the hydraulicking of the gold deposits as well as for the domestic needs of the inhabitants. The latter may have been the local tribe of the Orniaci, though the one Iron Age *castro* excavated shows oval or circular houses which contrast with the lines of rectangular huts of, say, La Corona de Quintanilla.[112] The huts themselves are simple irregular rectangles of 5 x 5 m maximum, set in conjoined lines, and the slight occupation material indicates a low standard of living.

At Huerña, excavation in 1972-3 revealed huts of native design of the second half of the first century AD, possibly replaced by Roman-type buildings, with rooms heated by hypocausts, a century later, unless these were intended for a military garrison.[113]

The evidence for the status of the mining population in the north-west is by no means clear cut and Domergue suggests two possibilities.[114] In the first, the Astures conquered by Augustus were regarded as enslaved and removed bodily to the mining areas, for instance the tribe of the Orniaci to the middle reaches of the Duerna; in the second, the Romans allowed the Astures to retain their free status (*peregrini* or *deditcii*) but compelled them to work in the mines under the supervision of Roman officials assisted by the army. The latter offered greater economic advantages, but whatever the case, it is clear that by the end of the second century AD paid free workers were being employed.

There was some Republican mining activity at Riotinto in the south-west but by and large the main operations in that area belong to the first and second centuries AD.[115] At Riotinto, an area extending from Dehesa to Corta Lago still retains evidence of cemeteries and buildings in spite of later working.[116] The Dehesa cemetery contained simple cremation burials, possibly of slave-workers, while on the northern edge of the Corta Lago mine extensive traces of house walls were found, extending in date to *c.* AD 170-80, and overlying indications of Republican mining activity.[117] Structural evidence was even more clear at the end of the eighteenth century: wall gates, columns and pilasters, with a cemetery stretching for 2 km along the slag heaps.[118] The cemetery produced inscriptions of which four can be identified as those of slaves.[119] Apart then from small settlements near different mines, there is good evidence for a small mining town with the usual Roman public buildings (forum, shops, baths and so on) and a population of 1,000-2,000 workers, perhaps largely slaves. The contrast between Riotinto and other mining areas of the south-west on the one hand and those of the south-east on the other is to be explained, Domergue argues, by the emergence of imperial control of the industry as compared with the fragmented activity of the Republic.[120]

Farther west, in the south of Portugal, similar urban sites have been recognized at Aljustrel and San Domingos.[121] In the nineteenth century house foundations were noted at San Domingos, as well as fragments of columns, bases and capitals, and a large cemetery; at Aljustrel recent excavation has confirmed the town site to the south-east of the mine, with traces of Roman houses, while the cemetery at Valdoca has produced almost 500 burials, of which nearly two-thirds lacked grave goods, suggesting slave-burials.[122]

The evidence for the composition of the workforce in the south-west is clearer than in the north-west, thanks to the discovery of the two inscribed bronze sheets at Aljustrel, the ancient Vipasca. Both were found in ancient slag heaps, the first (Vipasca I) in 1876 (fig. 51), and the second (Vipasca II) in 1906; they are apparently close in date, I of c. AD 100 or a little later, II dating to the reign of Hadrian, and, though incomplete, are essentially a list of mining regulations, some of general application and others specific to the Vipasca mines. Frequently published, they have been described in detail by Domergue, who has also provided lists of translations of both, sometimes with commentaries, in English, French, German, Portuguese and Spanish.[123]

In both tables slaves receive specific mention: Vipasca I, ch. 2: rate of tax on slave-sales; ch. 3: exemption of freedmen and imperial slaves from charges for the use of public baths; ch. 5: slaves are excluded from payments by the barber to the mine lessee; ch. 7: lists of slaves and paid workmen (*mercenarii*) used by those exploiting the slag heaps and spoil heaps are to be rendered to mine lessees and payment made accordingly, with appropriate penalties, but with exemptions for slaves and freedmen working in foundries for copper and silver. Vipasca II, para. 10: the procurator shall punish a slave who has stolen ore by whipping and sending him for sale, with the further condition that he be constantly fettered and banned from mining areas, while the money from his sale shall be returned to his master (in the case of free workers, their property shall be confiscated and they are banned from mining areas); para. 13: similar punishments are decreed for slaves or free workers who damage the underground workings or surface installations; para. 17: similar punishments are also decreed for breaking the rules about seeking or working ore in the proximity of drainage tunnels.

In general, we learn from these incomplete documents that the Aljustrel mines were under the overall administration of the *procurator metallorum* and were worked by *conductores* (Vipasca I) or *occupatores* or *coloni* (Vipasca II), the two latter terms possibly representing stages of mining work.[124] The workers could be free or slaves, and there is a marked difference of severity of punishment for the two classes; on the other hand, slaves seem to have had a share in the general amenities provided at the mine.

Domergue has attempted a graphic description of daily life at the Aljustrel mine in the second century AD:[125] the mine shafts below the ridge formed by the 'chapeau de fer', the weathered ores converted to ferric oxide (*gossan*) above the copper ores; the smelting furnaces emitting choking

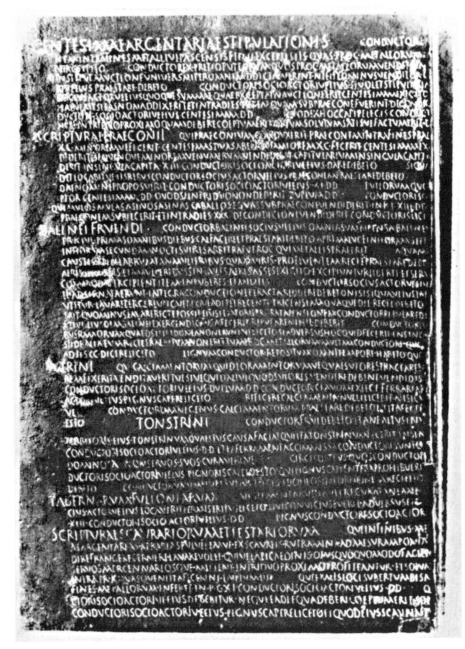

Fig. 51. Inscribed bronze tablet from Vipasca (I)

smoke; lines of mules with panniers of ore passing other lines with panniers of slag being taken to the spoil heaps; the settlement on the opposite side of the ridge along the valley bottom (750 m (2,500 ft) long by 300 m (1,000 ft) across), with other hamlets nearby. Despite the absence of the mine-workers there is a great deal of activity – in the forum an auction of slaves and animals with the town crier in evidence; a discussion on the closing down of a mine; a public whipping of a slave for the theft of ore; the passage of soldiers; a school in session; activity at the mining office; women leaving the baths; a barber's shop; a cobbler's; a laundry and so on. He would argue that the life evoked by the Aljustrel tables is a form of indirect exploitation by a number of lessees with Romanized conditions, whereas in the north-west the direct administration employed large bodies of the local population who retained their indigenous way of life.

It follows that the material evidence for the life of the mine-workers (clothing, equipment and so on) does not indicate whether they were free workers or slaves, while mechanical devices might also have been worked by both. One carved relief found in 1875 (fig. 52), probably at Los Palazuelos near the modern mining centre of Linares in the province of Jaen, has been frequently cited and depicted as an illustration of a group

Fig. 52. Relief from Linares depicting miners on their way to work

of miners on their way to work in the second century AD.[126] Domergue discusses it in detail; although damaged, it depicts two, possibly three, files of workers of whom there are five in the front file.[127] Although the execution is summary, they are shown wearing short tunics and across the abdomen a feature interpreted by some as a protective apron of leather strips, but by Domergue as a haversack slung from one shoulder. With his right hand, the rear figure carries tongs over his shoulder and in his left an object described as a bell or, by Domergue, as a leather purse or bottle; the next man carries a miner's pick on his right shoulder, and the next what appears to be an earthenware lamp; the fourth is holding a possible strap passing over his right shoulder, while the fifth is too damaged by later chiselling to be sure what he is carrying. Earlier interpretations have suggested an underground scene but Domergue argues for the open air, as two or more files would find it impossible to move in the typical narrow mine gallery.

The Los Palazuelos relief is too rudimentary to give any idea of further details of the miners' costume and for that we must turn to archaeology. Over fifty years ago such evidence figured in the publication of finds from the Spanish mines and has been recently reviewed.[128] The mines of the south-east and south-west have produced sandals (espadrilles) of esparto with a thick coiled sole, corded upper and shaped heel, and a possible knee pad.[129] The same mines have produced bonnets of plaited esparto or palm leaf, beret- or cone-shaped, and sometimes with a stiffened lower edge, secured by a cord passing beneath the chin.[130] The need for drinking water below ground was met by amphorae for bulk supply, but the miners evidently carried personal water bottles, flat circular costrels of woven esparto lined with pitch, like the excellent example from the mine at Mazarrón (fig. 53),[131] as well as knapsacks or haversacks of esparto for food. Bottles or gourds of leather or bladders may also have served as water containers or for the oil used to fill the small earthenware (occasion-ally lead) lamps placed in niches in the galleries for lighting, as suggested by Domergue for the object held by the rear figure in the Los Palazuelos relief,[132] and as in the Laurion mines. But as already noted, others have identified this object as a bell and such objects of bronze are recorded, perhaps serving as signals for the start and end of shifts and used by foremen.[133] There is little evidence for fetters worn by slaves despite the specific statement in Vipasca II.10 that a slave convicted of the theft of ore should be flogged, kept *in perpetuis vinculis* and not allowed to stay in any mining area; presumably this last provision explains their sparsity, though Domergue lists four occurrences.[134] He gives no details apart from a reference to the earlier paper by Gossé, who mentions the discovery of human remains in a gallery of the Roman mine of La Fortuna, Murcia, among which was a tibia bearing an iron fetter.[135]

Among the implements used by the miners for cutting the ore (fig. 54), the pick in various forms was the most important and was almost always

Fig. 53. Woven esparto water bottle from Mazarrón

of iron. As noted in the description of the Laurion tools, there was little change over the centuries; they have been described by various authors.[136] Domergue gives a thorough discussion of mining tools and distinguishes a simple pick, pick-hammers (two types), a two-pointed pick and a pickaxe and adds others: wedges, points (gads), hammers, punches, chisels, tongs, adzes, hoes, shovels and forks.[137] He describes various wooden objects, wedges, shovels and trays of uncertain use. The transport of ore from the working face to the bottom of the shaft was effected by means of bags of roughly stitched leather or commonly of woven esparto reinforced with rope and equipped with rope handles, also of esparto.[138] The Mazarrón bag illustrated by Domergue was full of ore when found (fig. 55).[139] He argues that such bags were carried slung from one shoulder or on the back and doubts Gossé's assumption that they were dragged by a strap round the miner's forehead as he crawled along the gallery.

The Spanish mines are notable for the survival of timber structures of various kinds which shed light on Roman methods of winning the ore;

166

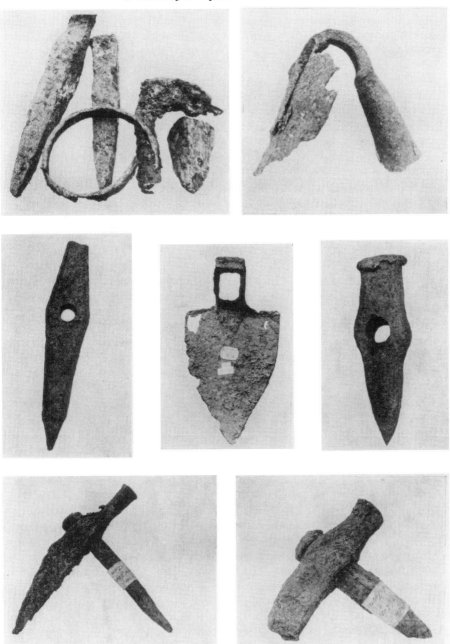

Fig. 54. Roman mining tools found in Baetica

167

among these are certain mechanical devices used at the surface and below ground which involved the application of human effort, no doubt of slave-workers in some cases (the use of animal power cannot be excluded, however). The raising of ore from the foot of a shaft to the surface was a problem dealt with in various ways of increasing complexity; the simplest method was a straight lift by means of ropes of plaited esparto equipped with hooks to hold the handles of the ore bag.[140] The grooving of the shaft edge caused by this method has been noted. A simple windlass with the rope wound on a drum and placed over the mouth of the shaft would represent a step forward, while the insertion of a block and pulley device would make it possible to move the windlass back from the shaft mouth, or to use a windlass at lower levels of a mine. There is slight evidence for the use of a horizontal toothed wheel working by cogs to transfer horizontal to vertical movement. In this last case, men or animals could turn the toothed wheel by walking with it, a method requiring ample space, whereas the simple windlass was operated by levers placed in the ends of the cable-drum.

The Spanish mine shafts as they penetrated deeper into the ground, sometimes as much as 250 m (over 800 ft), encountered water in contrast to the dry conditions of the Laurion peninsula.[141] Two main methods were used to deal with this problem: inclined channels cut at an angle to the mine galleries allowed the water to flow away into a valley by gravity, or the water was lifted to the surface by various means.[142] The raising of ground water to the surface is the method of interest here since whatever the degree of sophistication, human effort, for instance of slaves, was the necessary requirement, unless animals were used. Simple baling by means of scoops and buckets, the latter being passed from hand to hand until the water could be emptied into a drainage channel, was the simplest solution but not particularly effective. The commonest bucket was of esparto (fig. 56), whereas those of bronze were less common.[143] Turning to mechanical methods, we find traces of Archimedean screws of wood in the mines, sometimes mounted in series.[144] From terracotta models and wall-painting it is clear that a treading action was used to turn the screw, though there is archaeological evidence for the use of a cranked iron handle.[145] Less common is the endless chain of buckets which was operated by a treadmill: bronze buckets with collars were attached to the chain and lifted the water in a dredging action. Apparently restricted to the mines in the south-west of Spain was the waterwheel proper (fig. 57). It was presumably easy to adapt the principle of the millwheel, where a flow of water was used to drive a vertically mounted wheel, to its reverse whereby manual power turned the wheel in order to raise water from a lower to a higher level. Vessels were attached to the rim of the wheel or it was equipped with wooden compartments; treading action on the rim raised the water through the diameter of the wheel, and it would appear that the wheels were operated in pairs, and sometimes in series, to lift the water

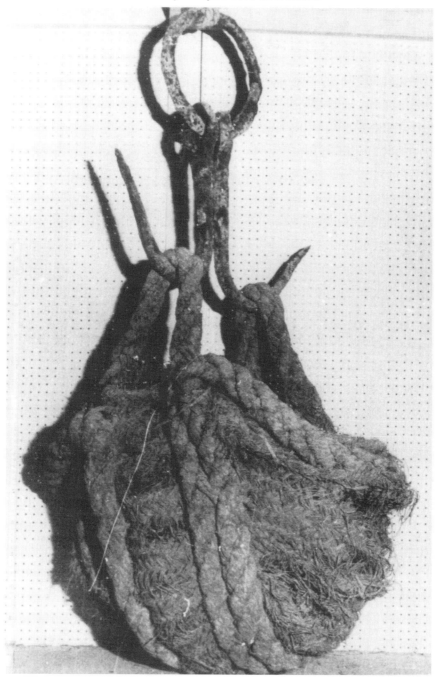

Fig. 55. Woven esparto bag for carrying ore from Mazarrón

Fig. 56. Bucket made of esparto from Mazarrón

through a considerable vertical distance. Finally, two examples of force pumps have survived (fig. 58), one of bronze and one of lead, and are regarded as means of draining water from underground workings, though other uses are possible; they seem to belong to the second and first centuries BC.[146]

Domergue makes the pertinent comment that the cutting of cross-tunnels for the drainage of water from the mine galleries, or the installation of mechanical devices to lift water from below, sometimes in series one above the other, or even the combination of both methods, were tasks beyond the resources of the small mining entrepreneurs (*coloni, conductores*).[147] He would argue that they were the responsibility of the central fisc which would put the work out to specialist contractors on a tendering basis, as indicated by the provisions of Vipasca I.

Finally, there are survivals in the Spanish mines of timbers dressed to meet the problems of working conditions. Access to working faces in Republican mines was gained by the exploitation of outcrops which were gradually pursued into the face of the hill and subsequently drainage channels, with their easy gradient, would have served the same purpose. Vertical shafts were difficult to use, though we may suppose the lowering

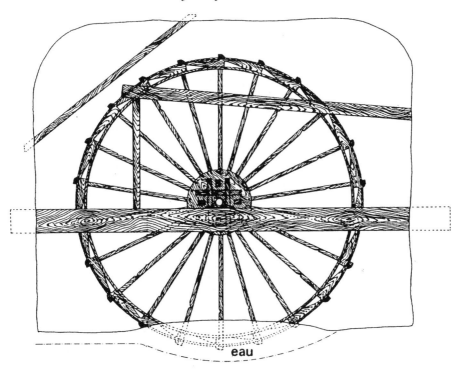

eau

Fig. 57. Reconstruction of Roman waterwheel from the mine at S. Domingos

and raising of workers by the rope and windlass for raising ore might have served. In the south-west twin shafts appear, one of which has footholds cut in the wall which, with the assistance of a fixed rope, would have permitted access to and from galleries. In square-section shafts such footholds appear in opposed faces, but whether for actual climbing with a rope or for the insertion of cross-timbers is uncertain. A simple method of negotiating short vertical rises was to use an oak trunk with notches cut into the face to act as footholds, as in the Mazarrón mine.[148] The narrow galleries of the Spanish mines did not normally need supports and a common safety precaution was to leave pillars of rock, which it was forbidden by the Vipasca tables to tamper with; but clearly a rich ore body would be totally removed and in that case there is evidence at Mazarrón for propping or framing to resist lateral or vertical pressure.[149] Nevertheless, there are instances of roof collapses in the form of workers' skeletons found, for instance, in mines at Potosi and Cala in the Sierra Morena and the south-west.[150]

The mineral wealth of Gaul did not rank as high in Roman eyes as that of the Iberian peninsula, but in Republican times there was a need to secure territory in Transalpine Gaul in order to safeguard communications

Fig. 58. Bronze force pump from Sotiel Coronada

with Spain. The Greek colony of Massilia, long friendly to Rome, had
protected this route but after the Second Punic War was herself threatened
by the surrounding Gaulish tribes who had been friendly to Hannibal.
Roman intervention led to victory in 121 BC and the foundation of the

colony of Narbo. As in Spain, Italian merchants flocked to the area, not so much to exploit mines as to trade wine for slaves. With Caesar's conquest of Gaul between 58 and 50 BC and the reorganization of the provinces in 27 BC, the original pacified area of the south – *Provincia* – became Gallia Narbonensis and the rest the 'Three Gauls' of Gallia Belgica, Gallia Lugdunensis and Aquitania.

Even before the Roman conquest, the Celtic society of Gaul was using gold, silver and bronze coins in fairly large quantities, though it is argued that much of these, especially in the two precious metals, was not so much a means of exchange for goods and services as a form of bullion or treasure for special purposes, kept within the control of the tribal élites. Whether this is so or not, there was a strong demand for gold, silver, copper and tin for such coins, and for iron for tools and weapons. Coins were needed to pay the Roman troops and contact with Rome promoted a monetary economy based on bronze coins until, with the foundation of the Roman mint at Lyons *c.* 10 BC, Roman coins began to replace the local issues.

The mineral wealth of Gaul was mentioned by various Classical authors from Republican times to the late Empire.[151] A number of general surveys in modern times list the mining areas but there is no overall study comparable to that of the Spanish mines.[152] The first useful studies were by the mining engineer, Daubrée (1868 and 1881); these were linked to the 1867 Exposition Universelle in which material from the Spanish mines figured and the 1878 Exposition Internationale in which the Laurion cupellation process was displayed. Later, Davies devoted a chapter to Gaul in which the importance of the fringes of the Massif Central and the southern part of Britanny is evident; the workings, especially of iron, in the area west of the Rhine are also of note.[153] More recently there has been a growth of interest in the subject, marked by regional studies of mines and metallurgical techniques. A two-day conference at Toulouse University in 1980 was followed by a similar two-day colloquium in Paris in 1986.[154] A recent synthesis of this work by King also covers quarries: on the workforce, he states '... most [mines] were probably run on the labour of nominally free citizens in Gaul and Germany, since there is little evidence for slaves.'[155] There may be some truth in this since much of the mining was on a small scale and there is no evidence for a major industry operating under a system of tight regulation, as at Vipasca where the use of both *mercenarii* and *servi* is attested by epigraphy.

The nearest to the Spanish mines, in type and proximity, are the copper mines of the Sironais in the eastern Pyrenees, investigated by Dubois and Guilbaut. Here, eleven mines have been recognized, marked by a complex system of galleries, some still accessible and others defined by extensive areas of subsidence. Exploitation, which, on the evidence of impressions on the walls of shafts and galleries, was undertaken by hammer and gad, on the pottery evidence (including Dressel 1A amphorae) continued from *c.* 100 BC until abandonment by, at latest, some point in the first half of the first century AD. The mines fell within the territory of the Tectosages, where Strabo (4.1.3) mentions the mining of gold. Dubois and Guilbaut suggest exploitation by Italian entrepreneurs who had settled in Gallia Narbonensis,[156] and possibly slaves formed part of the workforce, though no evidence of occupation or cemeteries has been found.

The Massif Central and its fringes were evidently an important mining area and among its inhabitants the Arverni (commemorated in the area known as the Auvergne) were recorded in ancient literature as one of the powerful tribes of Gaul. In his description of them, Strabo (4.2.3) talks of their 'empire' (*archê*) which stretched from the Atlantic to the Rhône, south to the Pyrenees and north to the Rhine and certainly their king, Bituitus, was active in the struggles against the Romans until his surrender in 121 BC, while later Vercingetorix, an Arvernian noble, led the revolt against Caesar based on the *oppida* of Gergovia and Alesia. Strabo also repeats the story, originally recorded by Posidonius and quoted by Athenaeus (4.37), of Luerius, father of Bituitus, riding across a plain in a chariot and scattering gold and silver coins to his followers. Some French historians and numismatists, such as Jullian and Colbert de Beaulieu,[157] have argued for the veracity of the tradition, with an Arvernian 'empire' in the west matched by a Belgic authority in the east, and in particular that the Arverni were the first to strike gold coins *c.* 200 BC, copies of Macedonian gold staters, and retained the right to strike for much of Gaul until the downfall of Bituitus in 121 BC. But this view has been sharply criticized by numismatists on this side of the Channel.[158] The arguments are complex but it can surely be said that the Arverni were a powerful tribe with ready access to gold and silver, and this must have a bearing on the ore deposits of these precious metals and their early exploitation.

In the Limousin, the north-western area of the Massif Central, there is evidence for mining for gold on a large scale, in the territory of the Lemovices.[159] The deposits were worked, first by panning in streams and later by open-cast trenches following the veins, from the late Iron Age into the Roman period, but archaeological evidence is slight and there is no indication of the composition of the workforce. Strabo (4.2.2) mentions silver mines in the territory of the Ruteni and Gabali in the southern part of the Massif and Barruol and Gourdiote[160] have established the presence of mines for argentiferous lead (open cast and underground) in the upper valley of the Orb (Hérault), again of the first century BC into the first half of the first century AD. The main site of Luscours has produced evidence of housing and workshops, with basalt mills for the grinding of ore, but nothing can be said of the status of the workforce. However, the discovery of lead tags and seals with metallurgical iconography and legends incorporating the letter 'S' may indicate *Societas* ..., or a group of lessees acting as entrepreneurs and possibly employing slave-labour. There was certainly imperial control by the time of Tiberius, AD 14-37, on the basis of the inscription found near Rodez (Aveyron) in 1890 (fig. 59); this is a dedication

Fig. 59. Inscription from Rodez in honour of Zmaragdus, mine overseer

to a certain Zmaragdus, overseer (*vilicus*) of a group of imperial slaves in the local mines, who was evidently an imperial freedman of eastern origin.[161] There are similarities to the *collegium* of slave ?*lapicidae* (quarrymen) in the Luna quarries where an inscription has a dedication by the *vilicus* Hilario and is dated to *c.* 16 BC.[162] But what remains uncertain is whether these imperial slaves actually worked in the mines or were employed in an administrative capacity.

In Brittany the fairly considerable deposits of iron, tin, argentiferous lead and so on were exploited over a considerable period.[163] Copper was evidently imported in the Roman period for the manufacture of bronze, to be used eventually in small workshops for the making of bronze articles. Iron mining and smelting were largely on a local basis, and most villas were equipped with their own forge for iron and bronze working. However, it is possible that in north-east Brittany, in the territory of the Namnetes, an absence of villas but a prolific supply of tin and iron may indicate control by the imperial administration, with the use of slave-labour.

Iron mining and smelting were evidently widespread throughout Gaul and, as in Brittany, organized on a local basis, though there is epigraphic evidence which suggests imperial control and leasing of mines and foundries, possibly in connection with supplies to the army.[164] Iron was so widely used that individual villas with access to iron ore seem to have smelted it to produce the metal, which could then be worked to produce

175

tools and agricultural implements. Alternatively, an *oppidum* such as Alesia (Mont-Auxois), with a history running from the Iron Age to Gallo-Roman times, was evidently smelting locally mined iron ores to supply workshops in an industrial quarter, from which the products were sold over a wide area;[165] bronze working was also a notable feature. But of the status of the workers we know nothing.

Little has been published on actual mining equipment and we have to go back to early papers to find illustrations of picks, hammers, lamps, grinding mills, rakes, wedges and so on.[166] A rare instance of the discovery of human remains in underground workings was that made in the ancient mine of Saint-Félix de Pallières (Gard), where they were found in association with Roman lamps (fig. 60).[167] Daubrée concluded that these were Roman burials made in even earlier mine workings, but it seems reasonable to conclude that these were Roman mine-workers trapped by an underground fall, as Davies claimed.[168] As so often, however, nothing can be said about their status.

It is natural to consider Britain after Gaul in any discussion of Roman mineral resources.[169] Ancient writers make specific mention of tin in Cornwall (Diod. 5.22), gold, silver and iron (Strabo 4.5.1-2), while Caesar (*BG* 5.12) and Tacitus (*Agric.* 12) mention tin, iron, gold and silver,

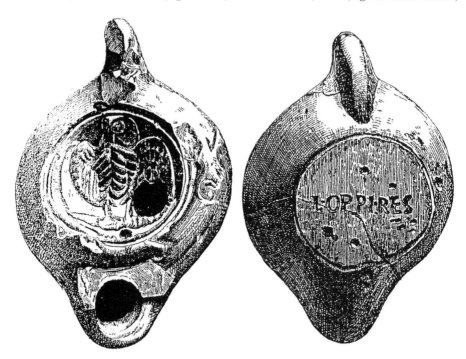

Fig. 60. Roman lamp found in mine at Saint-Félix de Pallières

presumably as factors influencing Rome's attitude to the eventual province. Certainly deposits of argentiferous lead were quickly exploited after the conquest of AD 43 onwards, though the silver content of the ore was found to be disappointingly low. The sources included the Mendips, South Wales, Shropshire and Montgomery, North Wales, Derbyshire and Yorkshire, and the origin can often be determined by tribal or place-names forming part of the stamps on the pigs or ingots of lead, of which 64 instances have been recorded.[170] In the Mendips, work began in the reign of Nero, possibly even earlier in AD 49, under military control, and followed in other areas (North Wales by AD 74, Yorkshire by AD 91) as the conquest moved north. Private lessees (*conductores*) followed the military under the supervision of the imperial authority (*procurator metallorum*). Little can be said about the workforce, but military control may indicate the use of prisoners of war, while the arrival of *conductores* may have led to the introduction of slave-labour. The suggestion by Frere that lessees may have been largely eliminated in the reign of Hadrian and replaced by prisoners seems to argue that the lessees were working the mines themselves;[171] this is perhaps too sweeping and some were no doubt supervising a labour force. Unfortunately, little survives in the way of actual workings.[172]

Britain seems largely to have depended for gold on Ireland in pre-Roman times, and the only known source in the Roman period was Dolaucothi in Carmarthenshire, where open-cast workings exposed by water power were followed by deep mining, on the evidence of galleries and the remains of timbers, including a small fragment of a waterwheel for the drainage of the workings.[173] An auxiliary fort has been located at Pumpsaint and partly excavated; its Flavian / Trajanic date suggests that exploitation of the gold deposits closely followed the Roman conquest and was under military control, with the possibility of the use of prisoners as labour. To the north the Llanio fort was garrisoned by the Second Cohort of Asturians, recruited from the gold-mining area of north-west Spain, and it has been suggested by Nash-Williams that the unit provided the technical expertise required for the exploitation of the deposits, though this theory has been dropped in the second edition.[174] Again, Frere seems to regard slaves and lessees as alternative labour forces, whereas the real contrast is between free paid workmen and slaves, both of whom could be employed by lessees, as at Vipasca.[175]

Of copper and tin little can be said, except that for the former, to judge by stamped ingots, both individual lessees and companies were operating in Shropshire, North Wales and Anglesey, while tin may have been intensively mined in Cornwall in the later Roman period, when Spanish output had declined and there was an increased demand for pewter. The main sources of iron were the Sussex and Kent Weald, the Forest of Dean and the Northamptonshire / Lincolnshire area, but, as in Gaul, production was largely for local use in towns and villas and there is no indication of organized mining on a large scale, though iron working may have been carried on under military control, as at Corbridge. A recent study illustrates how ore could be moved to villa sites for smelting and subsequent smithing, in this case from the Forest of Dean to the alluvial levels of the Severn estuary.[176]

One other province, Dacia, must be mentioned in view of the intense discussion of the role of slaves in the Roman gold mines of the Transylvanian Alps of modern Romania. Trajan's Dacian wars of AD 101-2 and 105-6 led to the defeat of Decebalus and the formation of the new province with its capital at Ulpia Trajana, the former native stronghold of Sarmizegethusa. The salient created by the new province extended north of the Danube to beyond the present town of Cluj (Napoca) to include the lower valley of the Somes (Samus), but excluding the Carpathians. The gold-mining area lay in the west of the province, in valleys which extend into the hills, here rising to nearly 2,000 m (6,500 ft). Important sites were Ampelum, the modern Zlatna, which was the administrative centre of the mining district and higher in the hills Alburnus Maior (Roşia Montana), where much of the mining took place; both were dependent on Apulum (Alba Iulia) on the river Marisus (Mures), where co-existed a legionary fortress (*Legio XIII Gemina*), a *colonia* and eventually a second town, a *municipium*, until all were abandoned in the 270s.

Davies describes the Dacian mines and it is clear that gold was the pre-eminent metal, though silver, tin, copper and iron were also exploited in Roman times.[177] More recently, a general study by Noeske of the administration and inhabitants of the Dacian goldfields in the Roman period has assembled a great deal of information on these aspects, as well as details of mine buildings and military dispositions; it also collects the inscriptions on stone from Ampelum and Alburnus Maior, as well as republishing the well-known group of 25 wax writing-tablets from Alburnus Maior. It is clear that by right of conquest Trajan and his successors took the gold-mining district as an imperial domain, administered by a procurator responsible to the military governor. We have literary authority (Eutrop. 8.6.2) for the depopulation of Dacia and the necessity to impose a Roman system of administration on the new territory. Skilled miners were introduced, notably the Pirustae from Dalmatia, while inscriptions from Ampelum and Alburnus Maior indicate that administrators and lessees came to the territory from Italy and the western provinces and, after the Marcomannic Wars, from the eastern provinces of Asia Minor.[178] Slaves figure so rarely in the stone inscriptions that no positive conclusions can be drawn, while the wax tablets from Alburnus Maior, largely contracts of various kinds of the period before the Marcomannic Wars, mention slaves in four instances; three of these relate to the sale or purchase of slaves, one a girl six years old, without any indication of their role, while the fourth mentions a slave called Secundus, who is described as *actor* contributing 267 denarii to a partnership. In no case is there a clear connection with the mining industry, and Noeske holds that there is no evidence for slave-labour in the Dacian mines (apart, of course, from imperial slaves employed in administration) and that the four mentioned were household slaves.[179] In this he follows Mrozek, who took issue with those who argued for a major role for slaves in the Dacian gold mines.[180] Mrozek argued that there was no tradition of slave-labour in Dacia, and that the need was met by the use of paid workmen and, if this failed, by convicts (*damnati*). The evidence in neither case is satisfactory and there is no proof for the use of *damnati*.[181]

Archaeologically, Davies gives some detail of mine workings, and notes galleries with the use of picks and gads, fire-setting and hushing to remove overburden.[182] In a mine chamber at Roşia Montana, near the gallery producing some of the wax tablets, in 1855 were found the remains of a waterwheel with a compartmented rim, and subsequently it was argued that the gallery depth of 60 m (200 ft) would have required 25 pairs of such wheels, arranged in series.[183] Whatever the size of the original installation, the techniques of mining and drainage are reminiscent of the Spanish mines, and a good case could be made for the use of slaves as well as paid free workmen.

In his study of the Dacian mines Noeske considers the public and private buildings to be found in an imperial mining district, though lack of excavation in Dacia means that evidence from elsewhere and epigraphy have to be brought into play.[184] The residence of the procurator (*praetorium*) no doubt included living-quarters for freedmen, slaves and families, but these would have been administrative and household staff. The housing for mine-workers, slave or free, in the Dacian district is unknown, apart from the contract for the sale of half a house recorded in one of the wax tablets from Alburnus Maior; this was evidently private property of a better class than that for the workers, to judge by the single-roomed huts, 5 x 3 m (16 x 10 ft), recorded from the silver mines of Domavia in former Yugoslavia.[185]

Dalmatia itself, as the Roman province in the larger geographical area of Illyricum, was a rich source of gold, argentiferous lead and iron in pre-Roman and Roman times, and it has already been noted that skilled miners from the tribe of the Pirustae were transferred to the Dacian gold mines in the reign of Trajan. The evidence is scattered. Davies discusses the Illyrian provinces and his map shows a concentration in the Sana district of former Yugoslavia where the rich iron deposits were exploited;[186] inscriptions show that at first they were worked by a leaseholder of the imperial mining administration (*conductor*) but were taken back under the control of the procurator in AD 209 and run by an overseer (*vilicus officinae ferrariae*).[187] There is no evidence for the workforce. A second concentration lies in the Rama and Nasva valleys west of Sarajevo and it is probable that Roman exploitation of alluvial gold began soon after the conquest in AD 9, but the evidence is still slight; both Davies and Wilkes note a slave

179

secretary (*commentariensis*) to the imperial administration of the gold mines based at Salona.[188] The third concentration lies north of Sarajevo where the argentiferous lead deposits were extensively mined in the Drina valley from an uncertain date but possibly as early as pre-Flavian times.[189] The main activity is thought to have begun in the reign of Marcus Aurelius and epigraphic evidence from Domavia indicates that it continued into the first half of the third century, when the official in charge is named as *procurator argentariarum* (or *metallorum*) *Delmaticarum et Pannoniarum*. Excavation at the site a century ago revealed the *curia* and bath building as well as surface traces of at least 120 houses.[190] These were set close together on two level areas in the steep-sided valley of the Saska, and the difficulty of the site may have dictated the smallness of the houses, though it would be tempting to think of them as slave-quarters;[191] there is a similarity to the clustered housing of the Valduerna in north-west Spain but, as there, it may be preferable to think of local inhabitants who were granted citizenship and paid for their work. On the other hand, one find from the area of the bath building, which is described as 'eine halbe Pferdefessel' is clearly part of slave-shackles, with an attached chain, and strengthens the slavery hypothesis.[192] The actual mines are ill-recorded but in the 1950s it was still possible to see surface traces of Roman structures as well as slag heaps.[193] At Skelani, 16 km (10 miles) south of Domavia, was a town site, possibly associated with a customs post;[194] by the third century some wealthy inhabitants had slaves, so the practice was well in evidence.[195]

North of the Adriatic was the Alpine province of Noricum, which extended as far as the Danube. Its early incorporation into the Empire (16 BC) reflected the Roman desire for a buffer province in the north and its function as a trading area between the Celtic world and Italy. A study of the province emphasizes the importance of mining in the economy of the first and second centuries AD.[196] Although deposits of gold, for example at Wiesenau (possibly worked by Dalmatian miners as in Dacia), argentiferous lead, copper and zinc were exploited, the chief interest centred on iron for which the province became famous, particularly the so called *ferrum Noricum* or steel, invented in Noricum and distributed to other parts of the Empire. The ability to smelt iron at a high enough temperature in conjunction with carbon produced a metal of sufficient hardness to be noted by Pliny (*NH* 34.41). The important mines lay in the mountainous areas of northern Carinthia and Styria, while smelting took place in settlements near the mines.[197] The distribution of iron implements and tools centred on the important *oppidum* on the Magdalensberg, north of Klagenfurt; this already existed as a Celtic capital and trading centre in the second century BC and Roman merchants established their own quarter from *c.* 100 BC.[198] When the province was established it naturally became the chief Roman town of Noricum until replaced by nearby Virunum *c.* AD 50. But the Magdalensberg town, before its abandonment, had developed a range of public buildings and houses which clearly indicate the wealth of the settlement.[199] The inhabitants were a mixture of native *peregrini* and Italian merchants, often freedmen from north Italy in the first place and subsequently from farther south; intermarriage produced a mixed but stable population. Metalwork was a principal export, especially iron, and there was a notable link with the great business houses in Aquileia. Comparison has been made with Delos, even to the extent of a suggestion that its growth was linked with the destruction of Delos in 88 BC.[200] If so, it seems fair to suppose that slaves from the Danube lands could also have passed through on their way to the Mediterranean. Certainly, fragments of at least four slave-shackles have been recorded from the site, to be dated to the first half of the first century AD.

Imperial slaves seem to have acted in a supervisory capacity at the mines, which were part of the imperial *patrimonium*. From *c*. AD 100 the mines seem to have been leased to individuals, *conductores ferrariarum Noricarum*, with their own administrative staff, again probably freedmen and slaves. As regards the workforce in the mines, epigraphy attests both free-born natives and slaves working side by side in quarries, and it seems likely that the same was true of the iron mines.[201] As with agriculture, Alföldy argues for a loose and liberal relationship between owners and slaves.[202] The mines were largely unaffected by the Marcomannic Wars of the later second century; but on the other hand slaves seem to decrease until the labour force was largely free-born, as too in agriculture.[203] But of material archaeological evidence for slaves in Norican mines, the evidence is still to seek, apart from some traces of equipment and so on at Hütten-berg.[204]

Salt

Salt was a vital commodity in the ancient world, both as a seasoning and a preservative, though the archaeology of its extraction in the Mediterranean area and details of the workforce involved remain largely unknown, apart from a number of familiar clichés. For the Roman Empire Rostovtzeff described the process of extraction as 'almost a blank', and equally was unable to offer much detail for the Hellenistic East and Republican Italy, apart from emphasizing the tendency to state monopoly and control, particularly for tax purposes, and the importance of the trade.[205] He had dealt earlier with the legal position of the industry and apart from emphasizing the monopoly aspect drew a distinction between those engaged in extraction (*salarii* or *salinatores*) and those in trading (*mancipes*).[206] Frequently, and particularly in the provinces, the working of the salt was farmed out to lessees (*conductores*), as with mines and quarries; they were organized similarly into companies (*societates*), and paid a rent (*vectigal*) to the treasury (*fiscus*).

The sources of salt are usefully summarized in *RE*:[207] sea salt, salt

181

mines, salt springs, salt lakes and desert salt, and again the importance of the salt trade is stressed, for example between the Mediterranean and Thrace. The direct correlation between the interchange of salt for Thracian slaves, reminiscent of the slave-wine correlation in the Celtic West, was recognized by the use of the word *halônêtos* for slave (Poll. 7.14), a point also noted in Daremberg-Saglio (*s.v. sal*), though the term is there given as *halônêton* (Suidas *s.v.*). Daremberg-Saglio, dealing with the workers, *salarii* or *salinatores*, adds the rather dogmatic comment: 'presque tou-jours de condition servile', based on Cicero's reference (*De imp. Pomp.* 6) to *familiae in salinis*. Both articles in fact refer to the importance of Ostia as the main source of salt for Rome and central Italy, with lessees using slave-labour (*gens Salinatoria*), who were frequently given the *nomen gentilicum* of *Salinator* or *Salinatorius* when they were freed. Millar records two instances of labour in salt works as equivalent to convict labour in mines and quarries.[208]

The date of the foundation of Ostia is disputed;[209] tradition, supported by epigraphy, records that it was the work of the fourth king of Rome, Ancus Marcius, in the seventh century BC.[210] Ennius and Florus saw it as a far-sighted act of statesmanship, but Livy saw it as a natural advance to the sea with the need to secure the salt supply as a primary motive. The route by which the salt from Ostia reached Sabine territory before Rome conquered the area and occupied the coast was the Via Salaria, one of the oldest Roman roads.[211] From Rome it probably led to the earliest salt works on the left bank of the Tiber, but with the transference of the *salinae* to the right bank, when Ostia was founded in the fourth century BC, this epony-mous stretch became the Via Ostiensis.[212] The method of extracting the salt was to concentrate the sea water in rectangular basins by the gentle tidal flow; these were then dammed and evaporation by solar heat led to crystallization; the salt was then raked to the side and piled into conical heaps for drying. The process can be seen today in the Guérande peninsula of southern Brittany where the tide runs over salt marshes and is then led along a network of small canals to the *veillets* or shallow reservoirs, where the depth is a mere 50 mm (2 in) and evaporation correspondingly quicker. Production at Ostia was clearly on a large scale, to judge by the nature of the administration.[213]

In northern latitudes salt obtained simply by solar evaporation was not practicable and from the Iron Age onwards small brine boiling sites were established on the salt marshes of favourable coastal situations; it was no doubt a cottage industry, practised mainly in the summer months and probably in association with the pasturage of cattle. Some preliminary evaporation was achieved in good weather conditions, and the concen-trated brine then boiled in coarse earthenware pans supported on props over hearths, producing a mass of discarded debris, as seen in the so-called Red Hills of Essex; the salt was probably transported in crude pottery containers, which with the kiln debris formed the so called 'briquetage' of

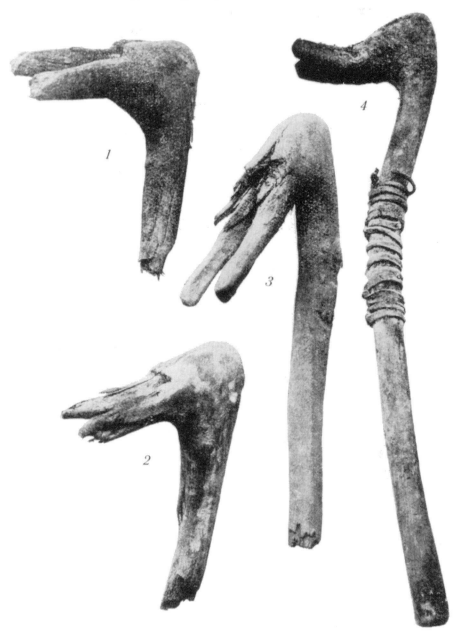

Fig. 61. Pick handles from salt mines at Dürrnberg

the industry.[214] This method of salt making persisted into the Roman period, but it seems unlikely that this small-scale production was subject to imperial control, though the trade in salt may have been taxed. On the other hand, there was now increased exploitation of inland brine springs in the West Midlands, claimed to have begun as early as the sixth to fifth centuries BC. This would have lent itself to production on a larger scale, with official control perhaps through the medium of the army.[215] But unfortunately, nothing can so far be said about the workforce and Roman salt making, at least in the provinces, can only be discussed in terms of processes, with one possible exception.

In certain geological conditions, thick beds of salt exist below ground

Fig. 62. Wooden shovels from salt mines at Dürrnberg

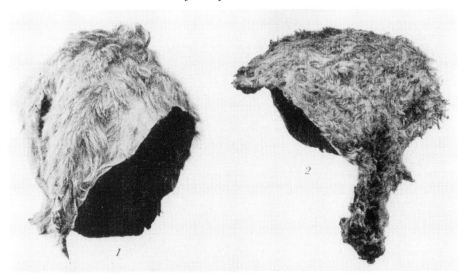

Fig. 63. Hide caps from salt mines at Dürrnberg

and can be exploited by mining with techniques similar to those used for the mining of metal ores. In Noricum, corresponding to the eastern part of Austria, two sites, the Dürrnberg bei Hallein and the better known Hallstatt, have salt mines which were exploited from prehistoric times into the Roman period.[216] At the Dürrnberg the pre-Roman activity has been dated from Hallstatt to mid La Tène times, and material evidence has survived of galleries with shoring and of miners' equipment such as picks (fig. 61) and shovels (fig. 62), both of wood, and of personal effects, such as leather shoes, caps (fig. 63) and leather satchels (fig. 64), probably for food.[217] We may suppose that techniques and equipment persisted unaltered into Roman times, but it is difficult to say whether there was any change in the status of the workforce. The more famous Hallstatt mines have not produced such good evidence of timber props and shoring for the galleries, but again examples of picks, shovels, clothes and other items of personal equipment have survived.[218] The method and chronology of the mining process have been well summarized by Barth, who would date the complex from the Late Bronze Age, *c.* 1,000 BC, until a move in the second century BC to a geologically safer area at Dammwiese. He illustrates graphically systems of horizontal or inclined galleries reached by sloping adits and the equipment of different mine complexes, but again we are dealing with an essentially pre-Roman activity.[219] There is certainly evidence for a Roman settlement (*vicus*) dating from *c.* AD 50 to the end of the fourth century, which was probably linked with the salt deposits, though this is not proved.[220] In fact, the historic method of salt extraction from as early as AD 1311 was by flooding the underground chambers with water; the resultant

Fig. 64. Leather satchel from salt mines at Dürrnberg

brine, free of impurities such as clay, was then led away to boiling sheds for evaporation.[221] It is possible that the Romans may have adopted a similar approach, less dependent on underground working, in which case little can be said about the use of slaves.

Certainly, in Gallia Belgica, as in Britain, the Romans made use of salt springs, such as those of Lorraine or the Jura, but again there is a lack of detailed archaeological evidence.[222] On the Belgian coast, in the territory of the Menapii and Morini, evidence has been recovered for a more industrialized form of salt boiling which succeeded the Iron Age salterns;[223] the two well-known inscriptions dedicated by *salinatores* from this area found at Rimini[224] may suggest forced labour from these peoples working in *salinae* on the Adriatic coast, though Will's study argues that they were salt merchants supplying the Roman army of the Rhine.[225]

Slaves in Corn- and Weaving Mills
and their Use in Lifting Devices

Introduction

Much has been written about the productivity of slave as opposed to free labour, and many modern writers have argued that the use of free workers was economically advantageous. Another theory on which discussion has centred is that the institution of slavery inhibited inventive talents in antiquity since there was no financial benefit to be derived from the introduction of machinery so long as there was an ample and reliable supply of labour in the form of slaves. There is, though, general agreement that, at least in ancient Greece, there was nothing in the way of factories or mass production in the modern sense. In the fifth and fourth centuries BC the different trades and manufactures were performed by small associations or in individual workshops by free citizens, metics and slaves working side by side, and the workshop output was correspondingly modest.[1] An earlier and more detailed discussion argues that Greek society was unfavourable to the formation of large organizations, because of the swift growth and decay of individual enterprises.[2] Even Xenophon's argument (*Poroi* 4.43) that Athens could benefit economically by the employment of large additional numbers of slaves in the silver mines was phrased in terms of state employment and the lease of slaves to individuals.

But this by no means conflicted with specialization, which increasingly became the order of the day.[3] This was particularly true of milling and baking and of all the processes involved in the making of cloth. Originally these had been domestic activities: in his chapter on various forms of servile work Guirand makes the point that the grinding of corn at home for the making of bread was slaves' work, and quotes literature to demonstrate that it was a form of punishment for disobedient slaves, who might be shackled in a manner which made it impossible for them to carry the flour to their mouths.[4] He then argues that the practice whereby the mistress of the house was assisted by slaves in spinning and weaving, as recorded in Homer, never disappeared in Greece and that both bread and cloth making were the province of women slaves in the domestic sphere. However, he cites abundant literary evidence to show an increasing tendency towards semi-industrial production outside the home, although individual workers might well carry out a whole series of operations; this

187

transition resulted in the employment of male slaves.[5] There was now a trend towards specialization in cloth making, which took the form of the production of particular garments by particular individuals, as at Athens, or by different city-states, a trend also apparent in other trades.[6]

The preceding chapter has discussed the use of slaves for labour in a number of primary industrial processes where working conditions were arduous and unpleasant. This was particularly true of underground work in mines and in the secondary smelting process, though it has to be remembered that where skill was a primary consideration, for example in the selection and quarrying of stone, particularly marble, craftsmen with free status might well be employed. The position is complicated for the Roman period by the presence of imperial slaves and freedmen, who served in an administrative capacity in mining districts and are better recorded, epigraphically, than the humbler workers, whatever their status. Finally, and again for the Roman period, we have the use of convict labour in imperial mines and quarries, the victims having in fact the status of slaves (*servi poenae*) though, confusingly, existing slaves could be condemned to the same punishment.[7]

Corn-mills

Work in corn-mills and the associated bakeries was arduous and unpleasant, and provides a good example of a secondary industrial process in which forced labour was used in the Roman world. There is no archaeological evidence known to the writer for a workforce of this kind in Greek and Hellenistic establishments, though commercial bakeries employing slaves existed in, for instance, Athens by the end of the fifth century.[8] In his careful discussion of the development of the grain-mill, Moritz argues for a progression from the saddle-quern in the fifth century BC to the 'hopper-rubber' of the fourth century, as at Olynthus, where grain was fed into a hopper in the form of a slit in the upper stone, which was itself moved laterally in a short to-and-fro action by a lever.[9] He argues that this form became widespread throughout the Greek world, including Magna Graecia, and was the *mola trusatilis* of Republican Italy as late as the second century BC. His discussion of Greek rotary mills dwells on the curious lag in the application of horizontal rotation to the grinding of grain when the principle was already well established in the potter's wheel and the olive-mill, but his argument is conclusive, particularly when the introduction of the rotary quern in Western Europe cannot be dated earlier than the La Tène period, say *c.* 100 BC.[10] This 'beehive' type was in turn superseded by a flatter version, with thin upper and lower stones, in the Roman period, and this was to become the standard household type in provincial Roman archaeology, produced for export from quarries where suitable stone could be obtained, for example lava from Andernach in the Rhineland, as well as from local sources.

Fig. 65. Sarcophagus of P. Nonius Zethus depicting a donkey-mill

From the point of view of this study it is the larger version of the grain-mill, what Moritz calls the 'Pompeian donkey-mill', used in combined milling and baking establishments (*pistrina*), that is of interest because of the involvement of slave-labour.[11] This is without prejudice to the question of whether this type preceded the hand-mill or vice-versa.[12] The principles of the donkey-mill are well known: a solid lower stone (*meta*), conical in shape, is mounted on a solid base and supports an upper stone (*catillus*), hollow and shaped like an hourglass; the many examples from Pompeii are of a dark grey, very hard lava. One certain production source in Italy has now been identified at Orvieto,[13] though Pompeii may have drawn its supply from nearer at hand. On each side of the waist of the *catillus* were sockets designed to receive horizontal beams, which were then apparently connected by a framework of two vertical and an upper horizontal beam, the whole designed for the attachment of the horse or ass which drove the mill. For details of the harnessing and for the types of animal used we are dependent on reliefs (figs 65-66).[14] But it is clear that the latter could be a horse or an ass; in any case, literary evidence suggests that only the poorest quality of animal was used,[15] and there is some evidence that the ass was the common motive power, since the paved track around the mill is only *c*. 450 mm from the wall of the bakery in certain cases at Pompeii, while mill bases are little more than 1 m apart.[16] It was this very narrowness which led some writers to suppose that a pair of slaves might have operated such grain-mills by pushing on the beams in the sockets of the *catillus*; one relief in the Museo Laterano might show such a method but Moritz does not regard it as very convincing and claims that it might represent a kneading machine, as recorded in the *pistrinum* in Insula 14 of Reg. VI at Pompeii.[17]

Moritz discusses the general point of whether slaves and animals could be regarded as interchangeable in the operation of grain-mills, as ancient literature might suggest. He argues that this is a misreading and that the slaves who are mentioned are operating the hand-mills which were an ubiquitous feature of the smaller domestic household. This view is

189

Fig. 66. Relief from the Vigna delle Tre Madonne depicting a donkey-mill

strengthened by references to fettered slaves in mills, where the practice would have severely limited their mobility. So, although slaves are clearly shown to have been present in *pistrina*, it seems probable that their role was to act as drivers for the broken-down nags and donkeys turning the mills, to feed grain into the hoppers, to collect flour as it emerged into the channel surrounding the *meta* and to transfer it to the kneading troughs; here other slaves would have operated the kneading machines (fig. 67), before the dough was moulded into loaves for baking in the ovens. All this would have been menial work, conducted in dark, hot and dusty conditions, and it is no surprise that the *pistrinum* was a place to which slaves could be sent, in fetters, for imprisonment or punishment.[18] Though legal sources suggest that it was not until the fourth century AD that convicts were sent to *pistrina*, the literary sources such as Plautus indicate that fettered slaves were confined in them as early as 200 BC. The most graphic account of conditions in a *pistrinum* occurs in the *Metamorphoses* of Apuleius (9.11-13); written in the early second century AD; the hero Lucius

Fig. 67. Sarcophagus of L. Annius Octavius Valerianus depicting a kneading machine

is turned into an ass and in the course of his adventures is sold to a baker who puts him to work in his mill.[19] This makes it clear that horses and mules were turning the grindstones night and day; they were blinkered and in a poor physical state. Slaves were also there, being used to goad the animals and for various menial tasks; clothed in rags, they bore the marks of the lash, and some were tattooed on their foreheads (not branded, as commonly stated – see below), had their heads half-shaved, and wore fetters. Conditions were bad due to smoke (presumably from the baking ovens), flour dust, heat and darkness lit only by small oil-lamps.

Substantial remains of *pistrina* survive in Italy, at Pompeii, Herculaneum and Ostia, all sites which have been extensively excavated, which suggests that they are likely to have been characteristic features of many other Roman towns. In fact, a few instances of millstones are recorded from elsewhere in Italy.[20] Pompeii and Herculaneum, of course, have a convenient *terminus ante quem* in the eruption of AD 79; for Pompeii alone the number of donkey-mills runs into three figures (fig. 68),[21] and it would appear that *pistrina* there were modest establishments serving small districts.[22] At Herculaneum, the one example so far discovered, in Insula Orientalis Secunda, seems to have been similar and was a conversion of a

Fig. 68. View of oven and mills in Via Vicolo, Pompeii

number of rooms of a better-class house in the period immediately before the eruption.[23] This is identified, by a bread stamp, as the property of the *pistor* S. Patulcus Felix. At Ostia, on the other hand, the two *pistrina* so far found are much bigger;[24] the first, on the Via dei Molini (fig. 69), occupied an area of 950 sq. m and comprised milling areas with nine donkey-mills, a kneading room with four kneading basins, and two ovens;[25] the second, on the Semita dei Cippi, was bigger still and also covered all the processes from grinding of the corn to the baking of loaves.[26] Both, according to Meiggs, are probably Hadrianic in date. It might be argued that at Ostia the bakeries were supplying a number of small shops and even Rome itself; corn was arriving from overseas at the port and being stored in the large granaries in both the port and the town.[27] At Pompeii, and probably Herculaneum too, the bakeries also served as retail outlets and were good examples of vertical integration.

Plans are fairly standardized at Pompeii, but the bakery lying behind the house in Region VI (III.3) shows the complete range of facilities and has been frequently cited.[28] The house itself is of normal *atrium* type with a staircase in the south-east angle serving an upper storey fronted by a gallery supported on piers at the corners of the *impluvium*. The bakery occupied the area normally given over to a peristyle. The main feature is a central room with four mills, around which are ranged a stable with

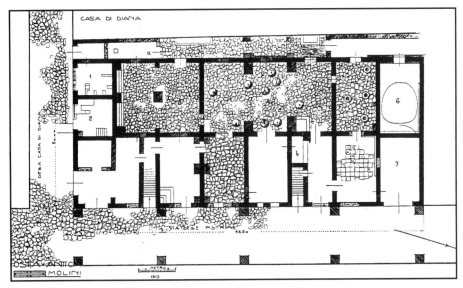

Fig. 69. Plan of *pistrinum* on the Via dei Molini at Ostia

manger for the donkeys used to turn the mills, a kneading room, an oven and a storeroom. Carrington describes the mill-room as an open yard, but it is more likely to have been roofed, and probably the surrounding rooms carried an upper storey to provide a dormitory for the slave workforce. This house is dated to the first century AD, but in other cases bakeries were added to pre-existing houses of the Republican period, for example at the House of Sallust (VI.II.4) and the House of Pansa (VI.VI.7), in both cases adjoining but not communicating with the earlier house.[29] Such bakeries might have been operated independently of the house owner by a lessee or by his dependants, as were the shops which were also a feature of Pompeii in the first century AD, as the city became steadily more commercialized.

The numbers employed in a *pistrinum* such as House VI.III.3 might well have numbered up to twenty: those driving the donkeys turning the mills, those bringing the grain from the granary, those collecting the flour to take to the kneading room, where two to three would have been employed, and the bakers themselves. It was clearly a profitable business, to judge from the elaborate monument dedicated to the *pistor*, M. Vergilius Eurysaces and his wife Atistia, outside the Porta Maggiore (*Porta Praenestina*) at Rome (fig. 70).[30] It belongs to the second half of the first century BC, the period when the Pompeian mills were in full operation, and all the symbolism (corn measures on the side of the monument, the use of the word *panarium* to describe it, and the milling and baking friezes on the north and south sides) gives a vivid impression of an industry in which slaves were an important part of the workforce.

193

Fig. 70. Frieze depicting bread making on the monument of M. Vergilius Eurysaces, *pistor*, outside Porta Maggiore, Rome

194

6. Slaves in Corn- and Weaving Mills and their Use in Lifting Devices

Two factors combined to bring about the decline of the donkey-mill in the later Roman Empire: first, the supply of bread by the state, for example to the population of Rome, and the growth of public bakeries to provide the *panes gradiles*, of which 274 are listed in the *Notitia Dignitatum*, and second, the diminution of the supply of slaves.[31] This shortfall was met by such devices as the recruitment of African workers or the consignment of convicts to serve their sentences in *pistrina*.[32] A third solution introduced in state industries, the tying of children to their parents' trade or of partners to that of their spouse, again did not fully meet the deficiency in that sector.[33] Since the *Codex Theodosianus* makes it clear that donkeys and slaves were operating together in the mills, the decline of one affected the other and animals were gradually replaced by water power.[34] Water-mills are first mentioned in a law of AD 398 and by the sixth century were universal,[35] and the use of slaves must have declined *pari passu*. Elsewhere in the Empire water-mills were in operation at an early date and donkey-mills were correspondingly rare.[36] The best known example is, of course, Barbegal near Arles, which, despite previous errors of structural interpretation and calculations of output, must have supplied the needs of the population of Arelate.[37] Benoit suggested a date of *c.* AD 300, possibly 308-16 when Constantine was in Arles,[38] while Wikander compares the mills on the Janiculum to Barbegal, proposing a date between AD 100 and 400, with a leaning towards the reign of Aurelian.[39] Nevertheless, though water power replaced animal and man power, there must still have been a demand for workers, free or slave, to carry sacks of grain to the grind-stones and flour from them.

Ancillary workers in milling and baking, probably of slave status, were equally prominent at an earlier date, especially in Italy. Mention has already been made of the proximity of *pistrina* to the granaries (*horrea*) at Ostia. The grain is most likely to have been moved from the port to the granaries, and from there to the mills, in sacks (fig. 71). The workers involved were the *saccarii*, equivalent to dockers at the port and porters in the warehouses, and the numbers must have been large in Ostia and Rome, as also in the supplying provinces of Egypt, Africa, Sicily, Gaul and Spain. Rickman has suggested that $10\frac{1}{2}$ million sacks were moved during the year at Ostia.[40] Other imperial slaves served in the granaries in an administrative capacity (*horrearii*) under the control of an overseer (*vilicus*), such as Zmaragdus.[41] The physical allocation of grain to bakers was undertaken by the *mensores* working closely with the *saccarii*.[42] A good depiction of *saccarii* unloading grain appears on a tombstone fragment at Mainz (fig. 72).[43]

Finds of donkey-mills have been made elsewhere in the Empire.[44] Moritz noted a concentration in North Africa, consistent with its importance as a grain-producing area: they are recorded in Algeria, from Saint-Charles near Constantine (fig. 73), Philippeville and Sétif, and from three agricultural sites (?farmsteads) in Tunisia (Henchir el-Mzira,

Fig. 71. Fresco depicting the loading of a corn ship

196

Fig. 72. Fragment of tombstone from Mainz depicting *saccarii*

Fig. 73. Donkey-mill from Saint-Charles, Algeria

Henchir el-Hendba, and Henchir Debdeba). But their discovery may indicate isolated use rather than *pistrina*, and the Sétif example is clearly of the same Pompeian type, presumably operated by hand, as indeed occurs at Pompeii in association with donkey-mills proper.[45] This small type may have been both prevalent and long lasting: examples were noted by the author on a visit to Jordan in 1993, at Umm Qais (Gadara), Petra and Mount Nebo, in the excavation of the Byzantine monastery at Siyagha. In an early paper Lindet records fragments of a *meta* and *catillus* from 'Phoenicia', and in Gaul from Paris, Amiens and Clermont-Ferrand.[46] From Narbo (Narbonne) in Gallia Narbonensis, the earliest settled area of Gaul, there is also the tombstone of the baker, Marcus Careieus Asisa, himself a freedman, with a relief of a donkey-mill, comparable in every respect to those found in Rome (fig. 74).[47] This is strong supporting evidence for the presence of *pistrina* in this Romanized area. For Britain, the evidence is slight: the well-known *catillus* from Princes Street, London, in the Museum of London,[48] to which can now be added the *catillus* fragment from Canterbury.[49]

Weaving, dyeing and fulling mills

The preparation of linen and woollen textiles is another aspect of life in the ancient world where it is possible to detect a change to semi-industrial methods analogous to those described in milling and baking, which in turn affected the nature of the labour supply. At the two extremes stand the approaches to spinning and weaving depicted by Homer and the presence in the late Roman Empire of state factories for the production of linens and woollens, primarily to meet the needs of the army. In the *Odyssey* Penelope is portrayed, despite her high rank, as occupied with spinning and with weaving Laertes' burial robe as part of her scheme for repelling her importunate suitors. The wool which provided the raw material came largely from the domestic flock of sheep and weaving was carried out on an ordinary household loom of the upright type.[50] But some trend towards specialization and concentration in workshops was always likely, not least with the growth of urban settlement, and for Athens Westermann cites from the manumission documents 40 women engaged in wool working (*talasiourgou*).[51] The same development was no doubt true for Republican and later Italy and, in spite of efforts to foster spinning and weaving as domestic virtues, for instance by Augustus himself in his family, it seems likely that as time went on most of the inhabitants of the Empire bought ready-made clothes, or at least cloth from professional weavers.[52] Diocletian's Price Edict of AD 301 lists various woollen and linen garments from different provinces and cities, and other authors confirm that some towns were important cloth-producing centres. The proximity of the raw materials was important: wool towns must have drawn their supplies from good sheep pastures, and the good flax produced in Egypt explains why

Fig. 74. Tombstone of M. Careieus Asisa, baker, from Narbonne

Alexandria was an important centre for linen. But Diocletian's Edict was largely concerned with finer cloths and Jones argues that the cheaper textiles for everyday use were produced locally, and that the industry was very widely dispersed.[53]

By the fourth century there was evidently some state involvement in the production of woollen and linen garments for the army, since the *Notitia Dignitatum* lists *gynaecea* (for woollens) and *liniphya* (for linens), which Jones describes as 'large state factories';[54] this is perhaps misleading with its overtones of the great cotton-mills of the Industrial Revolution, and all that may be implied may be open-plan *fabricae* with a number of hand-looms, probably not more than double figures. But meanwhile the compulsory requisitioning of military garments continued, spread over the villages and towns of the various provinces, and met from small workshops which were run, in the towns, by guilds of wool and linen weavers. The workforce was evidently mixed, part free and part slave.[55] In Egypt, as might be expected, the Alexandrian weavers were free, and Jones suggests that elsewhere the small family workshops might have employed a mixture of labour. On the other hand, the weavers employed in the fourth-century imperial *gynaecea* and *linyphia* were state slaves, according to Jones; Millar argues that most of these state employees were in principle free but, like *coloni* in agriculture, bound to their occupation.[56] What is clear is that consignment to *gynaecea* or *linyphia* was regarded in the fourth century as an appropriate penalty for persecuted Christians or free persons convicted of a misdemeanour, as with mines and bakeries.[57] So it is possible that here is another instance of convict labour used to supplement a declining slave-labour force. The silk industry (and possibly that for finer woollens) was evidently of a different nature: this was a luxury trade with wealthy merchants and skilled weavers of free status which need not be considered here;[58] the same may be said of cotton which, at least in the northern provinces of the Empire, can be classed 'as a rare luxury fabric'.[59]

Archaeologically speaking, the processes of spinning and weaving are marked by certain classes of artefact, but these exhibit nothing specifically relating to the workers' status.[60] Preliminary treatment of the raw material differed according to whether it was wool or flax: wool needed scouring to remove the greasy lanolin and was then apparently dyed in the fleece; with flax it was necessary to separate the fibres from the woody core and bark by various procedures, of which retting, or soaking for long periods, was an essential part.[61] Spinning was the first operation in the weaving process, and here such artefacts as distaffs, spindles and spindle-whorls are the primary evidence. But the process was very individual and apparently confined to women (*quasillariae* in the Roman world) with no necessity for specific premises. It may well have been carried out by slave-girls, on the evidence of the Pompeii graffito from the Via della Fortuna recording the weights of wool (*pensa*) distributed to the thirteen workers and stating whether they were spinning the stronger warp thread or the weaker weft.[62]

Even more difficult to define archaeologically is the subsequent weaving process. There is general agreement that the loom typical of ancient Greece was the warp-weighted vertical loom, well represented on the *lekythos* in the Metropolitan Museum, New York (fig. 75);[63] this continued into the Roman period, at least in the provinces, and was followed by the improved two-beam vertical loom, again depicted in reliefs, wall-painting and manuscript illustration.[64] There is less certainty whether the raised

Fig. 75. *Lekythos* in the Metropolitan Museum, New York, depicting a warp-weighted vertical loom

horizontal loom, a standard medieval type, already existed in the Roman period, though the remains of a small horizontal frame for tapestry weaving have been claimed at Herculaneum.[65] The normal archaeological evidence is of rows of loom-weights found in excavation, but it has rarely been possible to recognize the emplacements for the loom itself. It has, in fact, been claimed that the sparse traces of loom-weights in Gallia Belgica indicate that the two-beam vertical loom, which required no weights, was in general use in the province.[66]

If the primary activities of spinning and weaving have yielded little archaeological evidence, there are on the other hand a number of structural survivals of the dyeing and finishing processes, largely, as one would expect, from Pompeii and Herculaneum, to such an extent that 'it would appear as if wool making was the chief industry of Pompeii'.[67] Maiuri quotes the presence of weavers (*textores*), fullers (*fullones*), dyers (*infectores* and *offectores*), and felters (*coactiliarii*); the *fullones* were clearly the largest group and it was the rich heiress Eumachia who built the elaborate headquarters for their trade association near the south-east corner of the Forum. She was the widow of M. Numistrius Fronto, chief magistrate in AD 2/3, who hailed from Numistro in northern Lucania, the highlands of which, with those of Samnium, carried the flocks of sheep from which the wool came.[68] Maiuri makes the point that the *fullonicae* were not purpose-built but were adaptations of, or insertions into, private houses in Pompeii's later years.[69] It should, however, be noted that the *fullonica* in the Via dell'Abbondanza (I.6.7) was a late structure specifically designed for the purpose,[70] which again serves to emphasize the growing commercialization of the city. Some cleansing of the wool to remove grease and foreign bodies was carried out before spinning and weaving, and Wild also states that dyeing of wool took place in the fleece, and of flax in the shank.[71]

201

However, he also holds that wool cloth was dyed in the piece, and it is this process which has left structural evidence. But much wool cloth and linen were left in their natural state, or at best bleached in order to give an impression of freshness and cleanliness.

We begin then with the *fullonica* or fulling establishment where woollen cloth was received from the loom and trodden in vats containing stale urine or water containing crushed stems of the plant soapwort or fuller's earth; this had the effect of extracting any remaining grease, after which the cloth was rinsed in basins of clean water before being hung out to dry and bleach. The cloth could be brushed or carded while still damp to raise the nap and then cropped with large shears so as to give a smooth, soft finish. If coloured cloth was desired, it could be obtained by its immersion into vats of dyestuff, which were heated by fires beneath. While this was the final process for newly woven cloth, it is clear that such establishments also served as laundries for soiled clothing, and no doubt linen was cleaned there as well as woollen cloth.

Examples of *fullonicae* at Pompeii are well known and have been frequently illustrated: those in the Via Stabiana (VI.14.21-2) and the Via di Mercurio (VI.8.20-1) give a clear picture of the insertion of laundry premises in the rear of earlier houses.[72] The peristyle of the latter also produced wall-paintings, now in Naples Museum, with scenes of fulling and rinsing, carding and drying (?bleaching) of cloth, and finally of the screw-press which finished the cloth.[73] These scenes clearly indicate the fairly unpleasant and arduous nature of the work, and it seems likely that slaves were employed; in fact, Room 36 of the Via di Mercurio *fullonica* is described as a 'Sclavenzimmer'.[74] Other examples are recorded from these early excavations (VII.12.17; VII.12.22-3 and 24-5) but the more recently excavated planned *fullonica* (*fullonica Stephani*) in the Via dell'Abbondanza (I.6.7) is of considerable interest (figs 76-77).[75] It belongs to the final phase of the city, and displays a wide entrance from the street into a

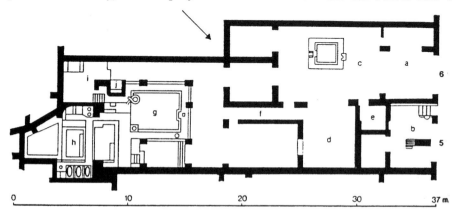

Fig. 76. Plan of the *fullonica Stephani* in the Via d'Abbondanza, Pompeii

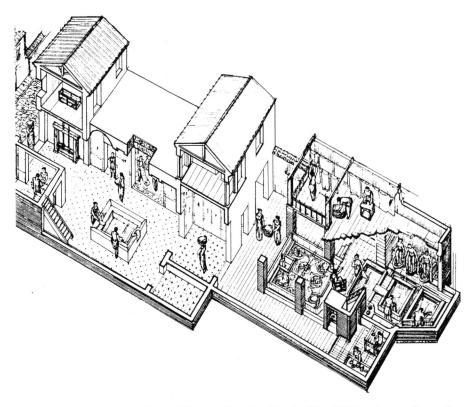

Fig. 77. Reconstruction of the *fullonica Stephani* in the Via d'Abbondanza, Pompeii

customer area with a press, of which the remains survived.[76] At the rear
were the treading and washing basins with a stepped arrangement of vats
to facilitate the flow of water. The laundering process clearly fascinated
the Pompeians, and other depictions of the various stages appear at the
House of the Vettii (VI.15.1).

Another type of fabric, but one in which weaving plays no part, is felt,
in which fibres, usually wool, are compressed so that they adhere to each
other to form a relatively impermeable sheet.[77] This was used not only for
a roof covering as today, but also for caps, shoes and cloaks, where the
ability to shed water was paramount. For evidence of the making of felt
there is a remarkable wall-painting from a cloth manufactory and shop on
the Via dell'Abbondanza in Pompeii (IX.7.7-5); unfortunately, the excavations did not extend beyond the street frontage to reveal the plan, but it
would appear that the shop lay left of the entrance and the works to the
right.[78] The whole enterprise was the property of M. Caecilius Verecundus,
a *vestiarius*, who is shown at the end of the fresco holding a large square
of fabric;[79] it is clear that not only felt but other cloths, for example fine

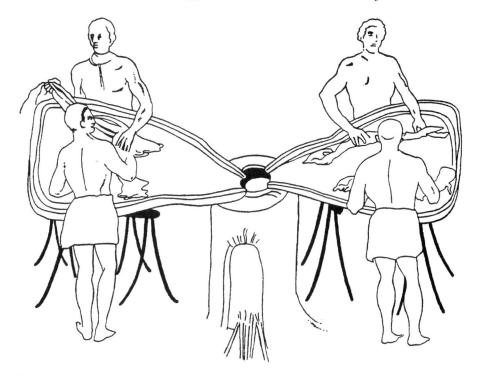

Fig. 78. Felt makers from a wall-painting outside Verecundus' workshop in Pompeii

linens, were on sale. In sequence from left to right, the painting depicts two seated figures engaged in carding the wool, from which it was passed to the four standing felt makers (*lanarii coactiliarii,* or in the Pompeian dialect above their heads, *quactiliarii*); to the right is another seated carder, and finally the standing figure of the *vestiarius,* Verecundus, already mentioned. Interest centres on the four felt makers (fig. 78), naked except for brief trunks and strongly muscled; they stand on either side of two shallow triangular troughs which funnel into a central boiler fired from below. The boiler held the hot liquid for coagulating the felt (vinegar was one such medium, according to Pliny, *NH* 8.192), and the workers are engaged in rolling and immersing the wool fibres in the liquid in the troughs, from which the surplus flowed back into the boiler. No doubt there were further stages of pressing and rolling to produce the sheets of felt, but these are not shown. Spinazzola distinguished the workers: the pair facing he regards as older and more intelligent, and the pair seen from the back as strongly built country lads acting as assistants. It would not be fanciful to conclude that these four workers, operating in an unpleasant environment in the heat of a Pompeian summer, were slaves, just as those treading and rinsing clothes in a *fullonica.*

Dyeing might equally well have been a process where unpleasant conditions would have called for slave-workers. The process might take place at a *fullonica* as at the large establishment in the Via di Mercurio (VI.8.20-1), or at the House of the Ephebe (I.7.19), where four tanks and amphorae with colouring matter were noted,[80] or in separate premises as at Herculaneum (Ins. Orientalis II, 11), where two *dolii* containing colouring matter were heated by furnaces below.[81]

Archaeological evidence for textile manufacture, including finishing processes, in the provinces of the Empire is largely confined to epigraphy and sculpture; these sources have been discussed by Wild and little more need be said.[82] The grave-relief from Sens has two scenes, one of the fulling of cloth (fig. 79) and the other of nap-cropping,[83] while another from Arlon has two scenes possibly representing dyeing (fig. 80).[84] Two inscriptions, from Cologne and Alzey, of a master fuller and fuller respectively, indicate that this operation, and presumably the weaving of cloth, was taking place

Fig. 79. Scene depicting fulling of cloth from tombstone from Sens

Fig. 80. Scene depicting dyeing from funerary monument from Arlon

on a relatively large scale.[85] Cropping shears themselves are recorded from the big hoard of ironwork from Great Chesterford (fig. 81), as are slave-shackles.[86] This is the only association which might point to the use of slaves in the textile industry. Wild argues that the claims for structural evidence for fulling and dyeing in Britain, at Silchester, Chedworth, Titsey and Darenth, have not been substantiated.[87] Trade in textiles, possibly involving the use of slave-labour, is depicted in sculptural reliefs, as on the third-century grave monument of the Secundinii at Igel, near Trier, with scenes showing workers delivering cloth to the landowner's warehouse, or roping up bales of cloth, and barges carrying bales of cloth being towed

Fig. 81. Cropping shears
from Great Chesterford,
Cambs

along a river (fig. 82).[88] Quite possibly some of the workers shown were of
servile status. Other scenes portray the activities which must have formed
the basis of the prosperity of the Secundinii: a clothing workshop, inspec-
tion of cloth, pack animals with bales and a cart.[89] Another illustration of
a barge with bales appears on the stone built into the church of Saint-
Martin at Vieux-Viton, near Arlon, Belgium.[90]

There has been some discussion of the textile industry in Gallia Belgica
and of the role of the Secundinii family in particular.[91] Much of this has
been speculative and must always be so in view of the difficulty of any
attempt to arrive at social and economic conclusions through the interpretation of iconography; the difficulty is compounded by our ignorance of the
family villa, so far unexcavated, and whether woollen cloth was woven
there. One view is that the Secundinii were entrepreneurs and that wool
was woven by their *coloni* on a cottage basis, but the status of the workers
is unknown. Even more speculative suggestions, such as the import of fine
wool from Aquitania and Spain, and the shipment of finished cloth upstream and into the interior of Gaul, must remain unproven. It is certainly
true that the laden boat on the monument is travelling upstream, but Trier
might equally well have been the destination with the cloth going into
store eventually to meet civil and military contracts. Another small piece
of evidence for cloth making in the Trier area (though in the territory of

206

Fig. 82. Relief from the Igel Monument depicting a barge carrying bales of cloth being towed along a river

the Mediomatrici) is the fullery found at the *vicus* excavated at Schwarzenacker in 1966-9.[92]

There has already been some discussion of state woollen mills (*gynaecea*) and dye works (*baphia*) and their role in supplying garments for the fourth-century Roman army; the linen mills (*linyphia*) were less common but should be included. The question of the labour force requires further examination. Charbonnel argues that the shortage of manpower, itself the result of demographic change, a decline in slave numbers as wars of conquest diminished, and a general distaste for manual work, affected state bakeries, armouries and mints, and that the main solutions were the binding of workers to their occupations, as with *coloni* in agriculture, and, less importantly, the use of convict labour.[93] She would place textile workers, whether spinners, weavers, or dyers, at the bottom of the social scale, and would argue that they were slaves or of servile status, since the *Codex Theodosianus* describes them alone as *mancipi* or *ex familia*. This might suggest that the textile industry was less affected by the manpower shortage, though we know that consignment to a *gynaeceum* was accepted as a penalty in the late Empire.[94] Charbonnel suggests that textile workers were women, though the Pompeii and other depictions indicate that men were involved in some of the more arduous operations such as fulling.[95] Wild notes that *gynaeceum* is a Greek loan word for women's quarters but suggests that weavers were probably men.[96] Whatever the case, slaves of some kind or other worked in late Roman textile factories, just as in mines and bakeries; other state enterprises, such as armouries and mints, were not used, for obvious reasons, for the detention of convicts, and it may be that slaves proper were only employed there in isolated and closely supervised instances.[97] But the actual numbers employed in state factories, whatever their status, remain uncertain, as Charbonnel admits;[98] literary and archaeological evidence are equally uninformative.

The structural evidence for *gynaecea*, *linyphia* and *baphia* is similarly scanty and has been discussed by Wild. He suggests a sequence of spinning by women workers in their own quarters and weaving by men in special workshops under supervision. Dyeing of wool took place before combing and spinning, but fulling, presumably of undyed cloth, followed weaving, and it seems likely that the necessary *fullonicae* may have formed part of the *gynaecea*, though Wild thinks they may have been elsewhere, commenting: 'No archaeologist has yet claimed, so far as I know, to have found a *gynaeceum* in any of the places where the *Notitia* records one.'[99] Millar cites the *fabrica* at Sardis in his section on imperial clothing factories,[100] but in the *Notitia* this is an arms factory, *fabrica scutaria et armorum*; on the other hand, Foss suggests the possible presence there of a *gynaeceum*, since excavation has revealed small dye works and fulling establishments.[101] There has been some discussion on the location of the *gynaeceum* listed in the British section of the *Notitia* (*Occ.* 11.68) at Venta. For long taken to have been at Winchester (Venta Belgarum), it has been conjectured to have been at Caistor-by-Norwich (Venta Icenorum), with Caerwent (Venta Silurum) as a third possibility, though less likely;[102] the case for an East Anglian location was in Manning's view strengthened by the incidence of single- and double-ended iron wool combs in the area. Wild, however, sees no link between the two and prefers Winchester;[103] on the other hand Taylor has expressed doubt about a massive switch to pastoralism on the downs of southern England, and his view swings the argument in favour of East Anglia.[104] The point remains unresolved, but East Anglia was a rich wool-producing area in the Middle Ages and no doubt earlier, and the distribution of fetters may argue for slave-labour.

In Gallia Belgica *gynaecea* are listed in the *Notitia* at Trier, Metz and Tournai, and Wightman makes the interesting suggestion that at Trier the so-called *horrea* in the north-west corner of the city, and close to the Mosel, might have been warehouses for the storage of the cloth woven in the *gynaecea*.[105] Again, we can say nothing of the weavers, whether they were piece-workers working on outlying estates as *coloni* or conceivably slaves working in a central factory.

In Spain, the literary evidence points to the use of fine wool for high-quality cloth, while flax was grown in coastal areas and river valleys for the weaving of linen. Esparto grass from the Cartagena area was also used for basketry, ropes, clothing and shoes, as already noted from Roman mines. Cabeyo de Alcalá seems to have been a textile centre in the first century AD on the evidence of loom-weights, while at El Cuatrón (Faras-dués, Zargoza) the remains of rock-cut basins fed by water from the river Agonia and used for the preparation of flax have been located by excavation;[106] the site was abandoned in the second century AD. In neither case can anything be said about the status of the workers, and for this recourse must be had to epigraphy. The Vipasca tablets from Aljustrel, Portugal, have been discussed above in connection with mining and Table I, cap. vi contains rules prescribing the running of fullers' shops *c*. AD 100 in this mining centre. Other regulations have specific mention of slaves and free paid workmen, and quite possibly slaves were employed in these *fulloni-cae*. The second illustration is the Sasamón table of AD 239 in Burgos museum (fig. 83).[107] Found in the ancient Segisano, this tablet records the members of a *collegium* in the town connected with cloth making.[108] Among the later names is a man described as a *pectenarius* or wool-comber, and two described as fullers (*fullones*). One of the latter, Elenus, lacks a *nomen gentilicium* and must be regarded as a slave.

Water- and weight-lifting and other mechanical devices

In Chapter 5, in the section dealing with mines, something has been said about the various mechanical methods of removing ground water from working levels, by waterwheels, endless chains, Archimedean screws or force pumps, all dependent on human or animal power for their motive

Fig. 83. The Sasamón table in Burgos Museum

force. It was argued that where men were employed, they were commonly of servile status. In this chapter, a similar use of slaves and animals to power smaller or larger rotary corn-mills has been discussed, and it was noted that for one reason or another there was eventually a move to the water-mill; this converse of the waterwheel for drainage employed the force of moving water to drive a vertically mounted wheel which in turn, through gearing, transmitted this rotary action to horizontally mounted grindstones. The other concepts, the application of hot air or steam, were known to the Alexandrian inventors,[109] but were used more in a spirit of curiosity than in a practical way. In the early period of the Roman Empire, there was no particular incentive to adopt machines as prime movers, so long as there was an ample supply of slaves to meet this need, and of course slaves were already being used as the motive power in the machinery for mine drainage. The connection then is not so simple as some have argued, that the presence of slaves militated against the adoption of machines, but rather that a shortage of slaves led to a search for other means of driving machinery that were already known. This difference of approach between the earlier and later Empire is emphasized by the story related by Suetonius (*Vesp.*18) about the emperor's treatment of the mechanical engineer (*mechanicus*) who described to Vespasian a device for moving heavy columns to the Capitol; Vespasian rewarded the inventor but declined his offer on the grounds that it would rob the poor of their jobs (*sineret se plebiculam pascere*). A similar but more ruthless conservatism towards innovation is evident in Pliny's story (*NH* 36.195) of the inventor who came to Tiberius with a formula for unbreakable glass but was executed for his pains.

Analogous to the use of various devices for the draining of water from mine galleries was their employment to provide water for the irrigation of land, or for bath buildings, industrial installations, public fountains and even private villas, in both the Greek and Roman periods.[110] In agriculture, the simplest form of irrigation was to raise water from a canal or other source by means of the counter-balanced beam and bucket (*shaduf*) or the animal-driven bucket and pulley.[111] Both seem to have been characteristic of peasant communities of the Near and Middle East and the essential drawback is the failure to provide a continuous flow. It seems probable that where a supply of labour was freely available, as in Egypt, the water-screw was in wide use, operated on a shift basis. Apart from archaeological survivals, as in the Spanish mines, the device appears in terracotta models in the Archaeological Museum in Cairo and the British Museum (fig. 84), and in Pompeian wall-painting.[112]

Double action force pumps in bronze and wood have been recorded from a number of sites.[113] Their presence in the fillings of wells suggests that this was a device for lifting water for use at the surface, but more specialized functions, for example as bilge-pumps in ships, indicate their use for removing water also. Both these functions would have been intermittent and the suggestion that a force pump might have served to supply the pressure-main pipeline at Lincoln would have required the presence of a constant labour force, possibly slaves, operating a twin-handled mechanism like a fire engine in post-medieval England.[114]

The largest installations were, of course, the compartmented water-

Fig. 84. Terracotta model of water-screw

Fig. 85. Relief from the Tomb of the Aterii in the Lateran Museum, depicting a treadmill

wheels and the bucket-chains running round the circumference of a drive-wheel or on an extension of its axle. A geared drive was also possible, with animal power driving a horizontal wheel which meshed with the required vertical wheel. But direct drive was also possible with both, and the man-driven treadwheel, for which slave-labour would have been appropri-

Fig. 86. Relief from Capua depicting a treadmill

ate, gave the required motive power. The so called 'squirrel-cage' mechanism, in which men operated inside the wheel, seems unlikely, if only because of the constant spillage of water on to the operatives, and it seems more probable that they worked the wheel from the outside, either from above or from the side. Their use in mine-drainage is well known, but their presence at urban sites such as Ostia, Cosa and Pompeii indicates their use to fill cisterns to supply public baths and so on.

There is a certain amount of literary and epigraphic evidence for the labour force operating these various devices.[115] Egyptian papyri suggest free labour for irrigation pumps, but elsewhere slaves, convicts and prisoners provided the *homines calcantes*, as Vitruvius called them (*De arch.* 10.4.3, 6.3). Condemnation *ad metalla* may well have taken the form of arduous and unpleasant work on waterwheels in mines, rather than in the mine galleries themselves, since supervision was correspondingly easier.

Vitruvius (*De arch.* 10.4-8) not only describes various devices for raising water but also discusses (10.2) simple cranes in the form of blocks and pulleys, mounted on shearlegs, for the lifting of heavy weights. The particular application he cites (10.2.1) is for temples and public works in general, and one can envisage their use in the lifting of blocks and ornamental features such as cornices to a considerable height. The lifting rope is passed finally to a windlass or, indirectly, round a drum and then to a windlass; in each case the windlass is operated by handspikes (*vectes*) placed in the ends of the windlass. For greater weights a large drum was operated on the 'squirrel-cage' principle by men working inside it (*homines calcantes*) like a treadmill. Another variant is the single mast with compound pulley; the mast was stayed by cables but had the advantage that the load could be deposited to left or right by the appropriate declination of the mast. The motive power, particularly in the case of the treadmill, was especially suitable for slave-labour, since the work was not only physically demanding but also dangerous. Archaeologically, there is little evidence for these various devices, but there are two reliefs, one in the Lateran Museum at Rome (fig. 85) and the other in Capua Museum (fig. 86), which illustrate the use of the treadmill.[116] The Lateran relief, from

214

the tomb monument of the Aterii family, dates from *c.* AD 100, and depicts (probably) a pair of shearlegs with multiple pulleys operated by a tread-mill; Brunn suggests the lifting of an ornamental feature as part of a 'topping-out' ceremony at the conclusion of the building of a temple, also shown in the relief.[117] The Capua relief, mistakenly attributed to Syracuse,[118] was found between 1620 and 1640 among the ruins of the theatre with fragments of columns and statues, and its inscription records the erection of the *proscenium* by the contractor Lucceius Peculiaris as the result of a dream (*ex viso*).[119] The relief depicts in the left-hand portion the erection of a column by means of a pulley at the top of shearlegs; the cables run to a treadmill operated by two ?naked slaves, while another figure carves a Corinthian capital, presumably for the top of the column.[120]

7

Means of Restraint

The taking of prisoners in war and their subsequent employment as slaves necessarily involved physical restraint in order to prevent flight. Later, as the supply of slaves became more dependent on birth or purchase in the market, the danger diminished, but there was always a rebellious or defiant element for which additional security was necessary. The methods varied: the most common was some form of shackling, in different forms according to the physique and temperament of the slave and whether he (or she) was on the move, for example to market, or employed in a more static role, on the farm or in the house. The obvious drawback was the check on mobility imposed by shackling and consequently marking of the person or wearing of identity discs or collars were methods adopted later, to assist in capture in case of flight. Finally, the slave might be removed from his normal place of work in cases of serious misdemeanour and confined in a detention centre (*ergastulum*) or sentenced, as we have seen above, to labour under supervision in mines, bakeries or textile-mills, a penalty also imposed on free individuals as a form of punishment. These, then, are the heads under which restraint is discussed in this chapter, but there is a chronological difference in that Greek practice was virtually confined to shackling, whereas the other forms were practised by the Romans, some at an earlier, some at a later date. As in other aspects of slavery, literary evidence is important and sometimes virtually all that is available. Each section will make some use of the information in an introductory way.

Shackling

Wallon's wide-ranging survey of slavery in antiquity, though outdated in some respects, can still prove useful. Using documentary evidence, he discusses first restraint in Greece and the Orient and as measures against revolt and flight mentions fetters for legs, arms and necks, the tattooing of the forehead after a slave's first offence, the public proclamation of a slave's flight, and the pursuit of fugitives by a specialized class of slave-hunters known as *drapetagôgoi*.[1] For Rome he lists the barriers against flight: foot- and neck-shackles, branding (*stigma*), proclamations and rewards, slave-hunters (*fugitivarii*), and the penalties prescribed for those who sheltered runaway slaves, again with references drawn from Classi-

217

cal texts.[2] Similarly, the two standard encyclopaedias, Daremberg-Saglio and Pauly-Wissowa, base their entries relating to slaves and shackles almost entirely on literary evidence and provide a useful background but one that is necessarily incomplete because of the lack of physical detail.[3]

In greater detail, Daremberg-Saglio discusses the flight of Roman slaves and measures such as branding (the runaway is described as *inscriptus*) and the half-shaving of the head (*semirasus* or *semitonsus*).[4] The Pauly-Wissowa entry is the forerunner of Westermann and is a general historical and geographical survey. More detailed evidence on shackles appears in Daremberg-Saglio under various entries: *collare*, *collaris* (*deraion*, *kloios*), *compes*, *pedicae* (*pedê*), *manica* (*cheires*, *cheir*), as well as under the general heading *servi*. More general terms for shackles appear in Greek and Latin literature, such as *desmos* (pl. *desma*, later *desmoi*) and *catenae*, and hence figuratively as prison, while specific terms such as *krikoi pedôn* and *compedis orbes* occur to describe fetter rings. Other terms also occur, particularly in Latin, such as *catulus*, *numellae*, *nervus*.

It is no part of this work to give an exhaustive list of literary references to shackling and a few illustrative examples will be sufficient. For the Greek world there is a number of historical accounts of the use of fetters, particularly to restrain prisoners in warfare and, since this was a primary source of slaves in both the Greek and Roman periods, these have a particular importance. In three instances we hear of the dedication of fetters after a military coup or victory. The first dates from *c.* 600 BC when the ruling faction in Samos, the landowners known as the *Geomoroi*, were ousted by the citizens with the aid of a Megarian force which had attacked the Samian colony of Perinthos. The Megarians were defeated and ostensibly shackled by their captors, who took them back to Samos where they freed themselves and killed the *Geomoroi*. They were rewarded with Samian citizenship and the fetters were hung in a newly built banqueting hall called *Pedetes* ('fettered') (Plut., *Qu. Graec.* 304-5). The second episode fell within the succeeding half century, when Sparta, encouraged by an ambivalent pronouncement of the Delphic oracle, marched on Tegea in Arcadia with a supply of fetters in the baggage train. The Spartans were defeated, chained in their own shackles and set to work on the Tegean fields where the oracle had said they would 'dance'. Herodotus, who recorded the incident (1.66), saw the fetters in the temple of Athena Alea at Tegea a century later, and even as late as AD 170 Pausanias notes that some were still visible in the temple when he called there on his tour of Arcadia (8.45.3). Thirdly, and again recorded by Herodotus (5.77), the Athenians defeated the Boeotians and Chalcidians in 506 BC in Euboea, and put the captives in fetters. They were eventually ransomed, the usual escape from sale into slavery, and the shackles were hung in the temple of Athena on the Acropolis.

In the fourth century, Alexander's victory at the Granicus led to the capture of Greek mercenaries fighting for the Persians (Arr., *Anab.* 1.16); some 2,000 were put in fetters and sent back to Macedonia to work as slaves, having forfeited their right to be considered as Greeks because they had taken up arms against fellow Greeks. A possible archaeological illustration of this episode is considered below. Towards the end of the century, Diodorus records two instances of the use of fetters in the campaign of Agathocles of Syracuse against the Carthaginians in Africa. His victory in 310 BC was followed by the discovery in the Carthaginian camp of more than 20,000 pairs of manacles in the baggage train (20.13), with which they had expected to shackle their Greek prisoners and throw them into a slave-pen (*sunergesia*). In 307 Agathocles abandoned his army which surrendered to the Carthaginians (20.69.5); the leaders were crucified and the others were fettered and put to work on the land.

When we pass from history to literature the references to shackling are admittedly not based on actual events, but on the other hand reflect practices familiar to people of the time. To the Athenians the plays of Aeschylus portraying the story of Prometheus, especially *Prometheus Vinctus*, gave dramatic effect to one of their well-known folk myths, and the binding of Hephaestus by Zeus to a rock in 'unbreakable shackles' (*Prometheus Vinctus* 6: *arrêktois pedais*) presented no problems of understanding. There is a certain irony in the story related to the role of Hephaestus and Prometheus as master craftsmen, since the introduction of fetters, and even more of locks, represents technical innovation only possible with the introduction of iron and the ability of the smith to work the metal into forms which it was difficult to achieve in bronze.

A fragment from the Old Comedy writer Eupolis' play *hoi Kolakes* preserved in Athenaeus (*Deipn.* 6.237) mentions a slave wearing a collar (*kloios*). A number of references in his contemporary Aristophanes seem to refer less to the shackling of prisoners or slaves than to the penal practice of *apotumpanismos*, a form of crucifixion in which the criminal was stapled naked to a plank (*sanis*) set up on end; the fastenings round ankles, wrists and neck were apparently penannular iron fastenings carried through the plank, to judge from the archaeological evidence of a group of burials at Phaleron discussed below. The excavator refers to passages from Aristophanes' *Thesmophoriazusae* describing the punishment of Mnesilochus who disguised himself as a woman to penetrate the Athenian women's festival, the *Thesmophoria*, in order to find out details of their plot against Euripides, his relative; he is unmasked and fastened to the *sanis* in the charge of a Scythian archer, the slave policeman used in Athens.[5] In his study of this form of punishment, Keramopoullos cites the literary evidence in much greater detail.[6]

Penal practice at Rome in the early days of the Republic involved the shackling of criminals as evidenced by the treatment of debtors in the Laws of the Twelve Tables (Gell. 20.1): 'vincito aut nervo aut compedibus'. These gave the creditor power to take a debtor home if he had failed to pay a debt within thirty days and judgement had been passed against the non-payer in the courts. By placing the offender in shackles, to which heavy weights could also be attached, the creditor became seized of his person and, though this is not stated, could put him to work as a personal slave. This sounds like the origin of slavery as the result of non-payment of a debt: self-sale of this kind occurred in Egypt and Asia Minor, but does not seem to have been acceptable in Greece itself, and appears to have fallen out of practice, at least legally, in Rome by the end of the fourth century BC.[7]

But, in general, shackling was a pre-trial precaution, since imprisonment was not normally a punishment in Republican or Imperial Rome: exile for the upper classes, and flogging or hard labour for the lower, including slaves, were the norm.[8] Historical accounts of chaining, in fact, refer to prisoners rather than captives taken in war. In 399 BC, Rome's war against the Volsci was accompanied by a plague in Rome itself; as part of a general propitiation of the gods, prisoners were loosed from their chains and not subsequently taken back into custody (Livy 5.13). In AD 32, three Roman knights charged with conspiracy against Tiberius were put in chains; the tribune Julius Celsus managed to loosen the chain, passed it over his head and by pulling the two ends sharply committed suicide by breaking his neck (Tac., *Annals* 6.14).

Historical accounts of the taking of prisoners for eventual sale as slaves are common, especially in Caesar's *Gallic War*: 57 BC – the capture and sale of 53,000 of the Aduatuci (2.33); 56 BC – the capture and sale of the Veneti (3.16); 52 BC – the distribution of one prisoner to each soldier as his booty after the capture of Alesia and the defeat of Vercingetorix (7.89). However, they lack the dramatic detail of the Greek incidents, with their use of shackles. Instead, a phrase used both by Caesar (3.16) and Tacitus (*Annals* 13.39: Corbulo's campaign against the Armenians in AD 59) – *sub corona vendere* – indicates the use of, presumably, wreaths of leaves on prisoners' heads to denote that they were for sale. Aulus Gellius (*Noctes Atticae* 6.4) argues that the practice of selling slaves with a cap on their heads, an indication that there was no guarantee of their status on the part of the vendor, had its origin in the sale of captives with a wreath on their heads. Another phrase found in Livy is *sub hasta vendere* to indicate sale by auction, marked by the planting of a spear in the ground which also suggests a military origin: for example in the war against the Volsci in 431 BC when part of the booty was sold in this manner (4.29.4) and in 215 BC during mobilization for the Second Punic War when Quintus Fabius threatened to sell by auction the slaves of any farmers reluctant to make grain deliveries (23.32.15). There is, however, one reference to the use of fetters by the Roman army for securing captives: Josephus, in his description of military equipment in the Flavian period (*BJ* 3.5.5) mentions the *halusis* or chain carried by the legionary for this purpose, which had a manacle or manacles at each end to attach the prisoner to his captor so that, in Seneca's laconic phrase (*De tranquillitate animi* 10), 'the binders were bound' (*alligatique sunt etiam qui alligaverunt*).

Purely literary references to slaves and fettering abound, but details of the fetters themselves are less common. Plautus, particularly in the *Captivi*, is a useful source for the Republican period. One revealing passage is that in which the aged Hegio orders the two prisoners-of-war (*captivi*) bought from the quaestors on the previous day to be released from their heavy shackles (*catenae*) and to carry a lighter set (1.2.107). A slightly later passage from Lucilius (854) mentions the different categories of shackle used to chain a runaway slave:

> Cum manicis, catulo collarique
> ut fugitivum deportem

Though Daremberg-Saglio equate *collare* with the later inscribed collars, this must surely denote a neck-shackle.[9] Later still, in the second century AD, we read in Apuleius' *Golden Ass* (9.2) of the conditions under which slaves were working in a corn-mill (*pistrinum*) as seen through the eyes of Lucius after his transformation into an ass. The passage was quoted above to emphasize that they were not working the rotary mills themselves, which were turned by animal power, but were engaged on other menial tasks in the mill. The important thing is that Apuleius describes them as wearing shackles on their legs, apart from other distinguishing marks, considered below.

The archaeological evidence corresponding to the literary references to the shackling of slaves and prisoners has recently been considered in detail by the writer and will be discussed generally here.[10] One interesting point is the sparsity of actual shackles in Greece and, curiously, even more so in Italy, where one might have thought that the incidence, particularly on rural sites, would have been quite marked. It is possible that these iron objects may have been overlooked on Italian excavations or, more probably, omitted from excavation reports, but this seems unlikely. They are of distinctive appearance and would have excited comment, and the writer's correspondence with and visits to Italian museums have not added to the total.

For Greece, mention has already been made of the fetters from Kamariza (fig. 47) in the Laurion peninsula. Their presence in the silver mines which were so heavily dependent on slave-labour is an indication that shackling did occur, but it is an isolated example which suggests that it was uncommon. The reason, no doubt, was that leg-shackles restricted mobility in the cramped conditions of the mine galleries, and only a violent or rebellious slave would have been subject to this form of restraint. The type of fetters used were essentially iron rings round the ankles with a connecting link or links; in their developed form, a figure-of-eight link attached to each ring was joined to a small circular link, giving a degree of mobility and allowing a chain to be attached to the central link. A good example is known from Phthiotic Thebes, found attached to the ankles of a burial of a slave or prisoner in the Hellenistic / early Christian cemetery there.[11] A variety of fetters was found on the ankles of eight burials in the large cemetery at Ierissos in Chalcidice (the ancient Acanthus), of Hellenistic date and possibly prisoners taken by Alexander at the battle of the Granicus in 334 BC. The best-preserved had rings joined by a link or multiple links, but others were ankle-rings, composed of round-section bars or flat strips with their ends overlapping or simply butt-jointed, and without any evidence for the connecting link or links.[12]

The presence of what appeared to be neck-, hand- and foot-shackles on a group of seventeen burials of Classical date at Phaleron has already been mentioned; these were in fact interpreted as the metal attachments or iron staples with which condemned criminals were fastened to the plank (*sanis*) in the crucifixion type of punishment known as *apotumpanismos* (fig. 87).[13] The same is likely to be the explanation of iron rings found with skeletons in a limestone shaft at Trypi near Sparta, thought to be the execution pit known as Kaiadas.[14]

Further afield in the eastern Mediterranean examples of fetters seem rare. Two iron rings described as slave-fetters were found with a burial dated *c.* 300 BC at the site of Apollonia in Bulgaria.[15] A similar pair is recorded from a possible slave-burial dated *c.* 250-200 BC at the ancient Pelion (modern Selca) in Albania.[16] In southern Italy, fetters were recently recovered from a pit in the sanctuary of Demeter, possibly of the early fourth century BC, at Policoro, in Campania-Basilicata.[17] These were found in 1985, while another set was found earlier in the 1965-7 excavation. They are described in the report as handcuffs, but seem more likely to be fetters; it is also suggested that they were dedicated by their slave wearers after manumission or having gained freedom through asylum.[18] If so, they could be another instance of the dedication of fetters in Greek temples and public buildings mentioned earlier. Finally, similar fetters are recorded from the villa of Castroreale San Biagio, near Messina, in Sicily; the date is uncertain but the villa was a Republican foundation.[19]

The study of the occurrence of slave-shackles in the western provinces of the Roman Republic and later Empire must begin with the evidence for the trade in slaves between the Celtic and Mediterranean worlds, which is also reflected in sculpture. This trade has already been discussed generally in Chapter 1; the archaeological evidence can now be presented in detail. We have noted a switch in emphasis from the eastern Mediterranean, when Greece was the main market and Asia Minor, the northern Balkans and the Black Sea area provided the main supply, either by warfare or the activities of slave-traders, to the western Mediterranean. Italy, and specifically Rome, continued to import slaves from the East and, ironically, from Greece, but gradually Spain, Gaul, Britain and Germany entered the picture from the second century BC onwards. In sculpture and

Fig. 87. Shackled skeletons from Phaleron

epigraphy, the most striking discovery is the tombstone from the Thracian town of Amphipolis near the mouth of the river Strymon (fig. 88); found in 1939, it suffered during the Second World War when the upper part and inscription were lost, but the significant sculpture on the lower part still survives in the museum at Kavala. The inscription below the stylized funeral banquet scene names the dead man as Aulus Capreilius Timotheus, himself a freedman, who is uniquely described as *sômatenporos*, more properly *somatemporos* or 'slave-dealer', and has been published on several occasions.[20] The lower portion of the stone shows a line of eight slaves moving from left to right, and chained at the neck; they are accompanied by two women and two children, unchained, and the file is led by a guard or the slave-dealer himself in a hooded cloak (*paenula*). In the middle register are depicted two men carrying a cauldron by means of a pole which runs through the ring-handles and rests on their shoulders; two other men are preparing to lift and carry a second cauldron, while a fifth carries an amphora on his shoulder and holds an *oenochoe* in his free hand. The whole provides vivid evidence of the two-way trade between the barbarian and Classical worlds, slaves moving inwards and wine and metalwork outwards. The insatiable barbarian demand for wine was noted by Diodorus Siculus, with a rate of exchange of one amphora of wine for one slave (5.26.3-4). Opinions on the date of the stone vary, from around 100 BC to the first century AD.[21]

Fig. 88. Relief from Amphipolis

For actual examples of such neck-shackles and linking chains we need to turn to north-west Europe, where they appear in Celtic contexts. In Britain, complete examples and parts of others are known from the famous Iron Age hoard of Llyn Cerrig Bach in Anglesey (fig. 89), possibly of a date early in the first century AD;[22] from the hillfort of Bigberry, near Canterbury, Kent, possibly *c.* 50 BC;[23] and, the earliest find (1817), from Lord's Bridge, Barton, Cambridgeshire (fig. 90), probably of the same date as the Llyn Cerrig Bach hoard.[24] From the number of neck-rings they were evidently meant to be used for a file of five to seven slaves, numbers comparable to those shown on the Amphipolis stone. No padlock is used to secure the neck-rings. Instead, an ingenious device of an elongated aperture in one arm of the hinged neck-ring takes a pear-shaped loop through which is passed the whole of the connecting chain and other neck-rings; the Bigberry neck-rings are composed of a curved bar for one arm and chain-links for the other, but the locking principle is the same. Essentially, no captive could free himself from his neck-ring unless the whole chain was passed back in the reverse direction.

The foreign examples are on the whole simpler than the British and the neck-rings seem mostly to have been fastened by riveting. They are

Fig. 89. Iron Age neck-shackles and linking chain from Llyn Cerrig Bach

Fig. 90. Iron Age neck-shackles from Lord's Bridge, Barton, Cambs

recorded from Celtic *oppida* / *emporia* at Lacoste in south-west France, Manching in Bavaria, and Sanzeno in north Italy, which presumably served as staging posts where slaves were gathered before their dispatch to Italy. Two neck-rings from Sanzeno, however, suggest that the locking device known in Britain was also in use there. There is less material evidence for the use of such shackles in the Roman period, though a number without chains were recovered from a Roman building of late date at Colchester (Camulodunum) which may have possibly served as a slave-prison (*ergastulum*). There is also the early record of the neck-shackle and chain preserved in the church of San Pietro in Vincoli in Rome and reputedly used to chain St Peter in the Tullianum, the Roman state prison.[25]

In the post-Roman period there is evidence that neck-shackles continued in use. In Ireland, the seventh-century crannog at Lagore in County Meath has produced two neck-rings, one extremely elaborate, with chains and it seems likely that the slave-trade continued across the Irish Sea. In eastern Europe neck-shackles and chains occur in Czechoslovakia and Bulgaria, of dates between AD 900 and 1200, indicating a continuance of a traffic in slaves between this area and the Byzantine world and the Caliphate.

In addition to the Amphipolis relief with its depiction of the slave-trade in operation, there are at least two other sculptural representations of the use of neck-shackles on Roman monuments. The first is relatively well known and occurs on a column base from the *principia* of the legionary fortress at Mainz. It depicts two captives, presumably Germans, naked except for shoulder capes; their hands are apparently bound behind their backs and they are shackled round their necks by collars linked by a short length of chain. The second is on a tomb from Nickenich in the Rhineland where, again, two cloaked barbarian prisoners are shown with neck-collars joined to a chain held by their captor. They do not have the graphic impact of the Amphipolis relief but show that this was a known method of shackling prisoners taken in military operations, perhaps before they were sent back under guard for sale at a market.

So far we have been considering neck-shackles and chains, principally of the Iron Age, as evidence for the movement of slaves or captives from the fringes of the Classical world to Mediterranean slave-markets, and this method of shackling indicates movement along roads. But fetters for the legs were also in use which may indicate movement by water though, equally, they may indicate a static situation, with a need to keep the wearers immobile, possibly in confinement. A distinctive type is known from a number of sites and belongs to the century before Caesar's conquest of Gaul, *c*. 150-50 BC; it can be termed the Chalon type (fig. 91), from the recovery of three examples from the Saône there in association with other late La Tène objects. Others are known from Glanon, again on the Saône, from the promontory site of Fort Harrouard in the valley of the Eure, from the recent excavation of a Gaulish farm at Herblay, above the Seine north-west of Paris, in Britain from Bigberry, and in northern Italy from Sanzeno. The occurrence of the French examples on or near rivers may suggest water transport (though ritual deposits cannot be discounted), while the Bigberry and Sanzeno finds may indicate the role of *oppida* in the slave-trade. The fetters themselves are ingenious in design, though the basic principle of the barb-spring padlock is present, as in nearly all the

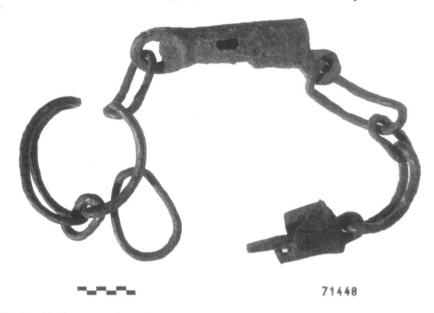

71448

Fig. 91. Chalon-type slave-fetter, Chalon sur Saône

fetters and manacles described below. Each shackle consists of two closed loops curved into a near semicircle and linked to each other by a small oval loop: one shackle is linked at one end by a further loop attached to a swivel bolt at the end of a cylindrical padlock, while a further pear-shaped loop is left free; one loop of the second shackle is attached to a perforation at the other end of the padlock, while the second loop is attached to a perforation at the end of a barb-spring which slides into the padlock for closure, and is released by the insertion of a key into the side of the padlock.

Various explanations, of differing complexity, have been offered of the method of use of the Chalon type, though the problem is that they postulate the presence of a missing element, such as an additional loop. It seems more likely that the extant fetters are complete in themselves, and that the method of attachment was to place the shackle fixed to the swivel-bolt round one ankle and to thread the second shackle and padlock through the free loop, then to place the second shackle round the other ankle and to complete closure by pressing the barb-spring into the open end of the padlock.

Continuing into the Roman period, we find a number of fetters analogous to the Chalon type but with certain significant differences; these are designated the Bengel type on the basis of a well-preserved set from a Roman well at Bengel, near Trier (fig. 92). The main difference is that each shackle is a single penannular piece composed of a concave-section bar with terminal loops from which the bar returns in the hollow of the

228

Fig. 92. Bengel-type fetter

convexity. The terminal loops are attached to rings: on one shackle one ring is attached to a swivel-bolt, while the other ring is free to enable the second shackle and padlock to be passed through it to secure one ankle of the captive; on the other shackle, one loop is attached to the end of a metal bar which slots into the opposite end of the padlock. For closure, this bar is passed through the free ring of the shackle and inserted into the padlock. The end passing into the padlock is perforated to allow a metal pin to be passed through a hole in the top of the padlock and then through the bar. A barb-spring bolt is then inserted into an aperture in the padlock and secures the lower end of this pin (fig. 93). To open the fetters, a key is passed into the side of the padlock in order to compress the barb-spring for withdrawal, after which the pin is removed and the bar of the shackle released.

Two other types of fetter are simpler in design and depend on the attachment of shackles to the bar of a padlock; as a result the shackles have quite often been found in isolation without their padlock (and vice-versa, though a padlock without shackles cannot be regarded as definitive evidence of fetters). In the probably earlier form the penannular shackles are normally concave in section with terminal eyes from which the nor-mally square-section bar is taken back within the concavity and is quite often decoratively treated, for example by twisting. In the eyes are circular or oval loops which slip over the bar of a square- or rectangular-section padlock; access to the bar is gained by a barb-spring which fits through an

Fig. 93. Barb-spring padlock and fetters

aperture in the returned end of the bar and so into the interior of the padlock. The barb-spring is released by the insertion of an L-shaped key into the padlock from the opposite end. This Sombernon type, named after a complete set from the Gallo-Roman site of Mediolanum now in Dijon Museum, is known from both Gaul and Britain, as is the developed form, the Bavay type, so named after a complete set from the Gallo-Roman town of Bavacum (fig. 94). Here, the loops attached to the two eyes of each shackle are treated differently: one is triangular and the other an elongated oval which is bent to form an obtuse, occasionally a right, angle. In use, the shackles were placed round the captive's ankles, the bent loops passed through their triangular counterparts, and the protruding ends of the former then slipped over the padlock bar. It was evidently a device intended to give greater security in that it prevented the forcing apart of the shackle terminals which was possible with the Sombernon type. There are additions and variations to these two related types, such as the use of a 'spacer' between the shackles on the padlock bar, the addition of a swivel-bolt between shackle loops and padlock bar, and the unusual tripartite composition of the shackles on the fetters from Brescia, a rare example from Italy but interesting in that they were still attached to the ankles of an inhumation burial, presumably that of a slave.

In contrast to these fetters, which provided the wearer with a degree of mobility, the Arceau type (fig. 95), found at the eponymous site near Dijon, is rigid and is equivalent for the feet to handcuffs for the wrists: the central box padlock has projecting rings to either side to which are attached one

230

Fig. 94. Bavay-type fetter in Castle Museum, Norwich

end of the two shackles; to the other free ends are attached plates with a perforation which, after insertion into the body of the padlock, are locked by the insertion of a further plate, with barb-springs which pass through the perforations in the shackle-plates. The fetters were opened by the insertion of a key at the opposite end of the padlock case which depressed the barb-springs and allowed the withdrawal of the various elements. The few examples known come from Gaul.

In two other types of fetter, the Villepart and Echzell types, one shackle is attached to a padlock and at the other end is a loop attached to a barbed bolt, which, in the case of the Villepart type, is inserted into the opposite end of the padlock or, in the case of the Echzell type, the other end of the shackle is perforated, slots into an aperture in the upper surface of the padlock, and is secured by a barb-spring bolt inserted into the end of the padlock (fig. 96). The second shackle, where present, is of the Bavay type linked to the first by a chain, or conceivably the wearer was restrained by the single shackle, from which a chain could have run to a staple in the floor or wall. Certainly the Echzell type was in use in the Roman period,

Fig. 95. Arceau-type fetter in Dijon Museum

but both were evidently employed in the post-Roman period also, on the basis of recent research into the slave-trade in eastern Europe in the early Middle Ages.[26]

Although Italy is deficient in fetters of the types just described, there are examples of what may be described as multiple fetters or stocks from Roman farms in the Vesuvius area, which by definition were in use down

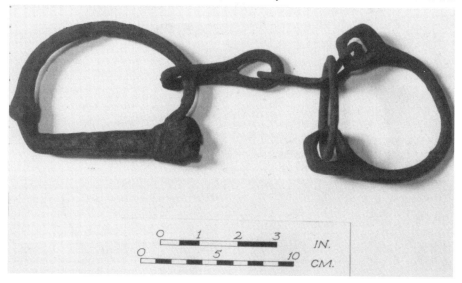

Fig. 96a. Echzell / Bavay-type fetter from Sligo in National Museum of Ireland, Dublin

232

to AD 79. The examples from a known context come from what Rostovtzeff classed as agricultural 'factories', producing wine and olive oil and operated by a workforce of slaves.[27] Others of less certain provenance are preserved in the National Museum in Naples. Two types are present, a linear and a circular (fig. 97); the main features are a round or straight base-plate with vertical pegs at close intervals. Those to be shackled had their ankles placed between the uprights, so were in a prone or sitting position, and were then prevented from escape by a bar passed through loops at the tops of the uprights, which was presumably prevented from disengagement by means of a padlock. But they clearly formed a specialized type which is not yet known from other Republican or Imperial sites.

There remains the other class of shackles intended to restrain the hands, best described by the term manacles. Their purpose was clearly temporary, since the wearer was unable to use his (or her) hands and so could not work on the farm or in the mine, as a fettered slave could. There is, in fact, strong evidence that one particular type was used by the Roman army to secure its captives, and seems to correspond to the chain or *halusis* mentioned by Josephus (*BJ* 3.5.5) as part of a legionary's equipment. There is graphic evidence of it in operation in the reliefs on the Arch of Septimius Severus in Rome depicting Parthian captives (fig. 10).[28] The type which seems to correspond to the literary and sculptural evidence is conveniently termed the Künzing type, after the large number found in a

Fig. 96b. Echzell-type padlock in National Museum of Ireland, Dublin

233

Fig. 97. Pompeii-type shackles

hoard of ironwork buried in the Roman auxiliary fort of Quintana at Künzing on the Danube in lower Bavaria (fig. 98).[29] These handcuffs are, in fact, bipartite but their joint function is attested by the fact that they are linked by chains. One cuff is composed of two curved arms, rectangular in section and hinged by means of interlocking loops. At the open end, the terminal of each arm is an elongated loop turned through nearly a right angle and set in the opposite plane to that of the arm (fig. 99). To close the cuff, it is placed round the wrist so that the two terminal loops meet and an iron ferrule is passed over them; a hook-shaped loop with a chain attached to its terminal eye is passed through the two loops of the cuff and the chain is then carried through the aperture of the hook-shaped loop to form a slip knot. The other cuff is similarly composed of two curved arms, again of rectangular section and hinged by means of interlocking loops, but one arm is attached to a box padlock while the other terminates in a barb-spring arrangement. Closure is simply effected by the insertion of the barbed terminal into the padlock, and opening by the insertion of an L-shaped key into the padlock in order to compress the barbs and permit their withdrawal. Among the complete sets preserved in the Prähistorische Staatssammlung in Munich the linking chains measure around 1.8 m (6 ft), from which it seems clear that one cuff (the first described) was for the captive and the second, with the key, was used by the guard. This

Fig. 98. Künzing-type shackles

Fig. 99. Detail of Künzing-
type shackles

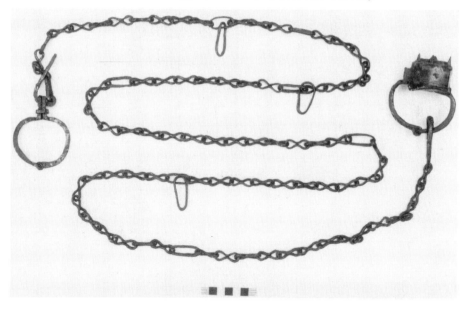

Fig. 100. Extra links on chain of Künzing-type shackles

would equate with the representations on the Arch of Septimius Severus, and probably one guard could control two to three prisoners by means of other chains and cuffs running from intermediate loops on the main chain (fig. 100). The distribution of the Künzing type is essentially military with a predominance on the Rhine and Danube and intervening *limes*, but specimens are also known more widely in Gaul and Britain. The date, where known, appeared at first to be second to third century AD, but the recent discovery of a number during excavation of the Roman fort at Aulnay (Charente-Maritime), dated AD 20-30, makes it clear that they were already in use by the beginning of the Imperial period, and clarifies the reference by Josephus to the use of the *halusis* in the Flavian period.[30]

A few examples survive of handcuffs proper, designed to secure both wrists of the captive. They can be termed the Silchester type as the site has produced a complete set (fig. 101).[31] They are similar to the Arceau type of fetters in that they are of one-piece construction: one cuff has curved arms hinged by interlocking loops which meet at a short straight section before passing into the other cuff, one arm of which terminates in a box padlock and the other in barbed prongs, like the Künzing type. The straight intermediate section has a projecting eye, probably meant for the attachment of a chain passing to the guard.

There are a number of other manacles, normally represented by a single cuff, more massive than those described above and on the whole not susceptible to classification, with one exception. This, named the London

Fig. 101. Silchester-type handcuffs in Reading Museum

Fig. 102. London-type manacles, Museum of London

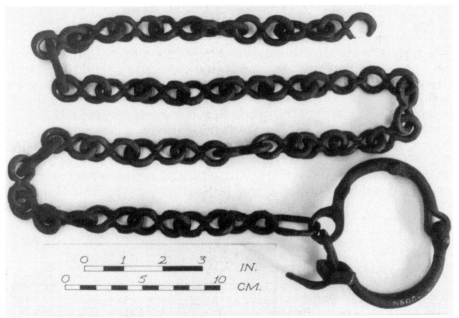

type (fig. 102), may have developed from Roman Republican (as at Numantia) and Iron Age (as at Hod Hill) precursors.[32] It is composed of two curved arms with a riveted hinge (earlier) and interlocking loops (later), with the two terminals treated differently. One is a rectangular loop set at right angles to the plane of the arm, while the other is a small loop in the same

237

plane as the arm, to which are attached an independent elongated loop and a second loop to which is attached a chain. The method of fastening is analogous to that in neck-shackles and chains. The loop at the end of one arm is passed through the rectangular aperture at the end of the other, and the chain is then slipped through the protruding part of the loop and drawn tight.

Neck-shackles are easily distinguishable from manacles and fetters because of their greater diameter, but the latter two can be difficult to separate because the wrist and ankle are not greatly different in diameter. But function is more certain: neck-shackles and linking chains are clearly designed for slaves on the road to market; manacles seem intended for temporary captivity, for instance after a successful military campaign; whereas fetters, though they prevent flight, give sufficient mobility to allow the wearer to work. Fetters, then, can be regarded as the characteristic slave-chains of antiquity, worn in the fields and mines. Their frequency in Gaul and Britain may be relevant to the use of slave-labour in agriculture, but, as noted above, the chaining of *coloni* was also practised, so to cite them for slave-labour, in the absence of other evidence, may be questionable.

Collars and *bullae*

One interesting group of objects designed to deter slaves from flight or to assist in their subsequent recapture is the series of collars, all, apparently, of late Imperial date. They are, in fact, of two types: the first is a narrow strip of metal, usually bronze, carrying an inscription (fig. 103), while the second is an uninscribed metal collar from which is suspended a *bulla*, a small bronze plate, normally round but occasionally rectangular, carrying an inscription.[33] They have been known for a considerable time, especially the *bullae*, which were described by the Italian scholar Lorenzo Pignorio at the beginning of the seventeenth century.[34] They were further studied and published by various scholars in the years before the First World War,

Fig. 103. Roman bronze slave-collar

with a complete listing by Dressel, so far as they were known, in 1899.[35]
The 29 noted by Dressel have gradually increased to 36, with a widening
of the distribution from Italy to North Africa and Sardinia.[36] The inscribed
collar from Sardinia was found in 1935 and its publication after rediscov-
ery in 1973 contains the basic references and conclusions applicable not
only to the Sardinian collar but to the other known examples.[37]

Of the 36, 16 are of the inscribed collar type: where dimensions are
known, the circumference is usually of the order of 400-410 mm ($15\frac{3}{4}$ in),
appropriate for the neck. Two are known of smaller diameter; the circumference of one being just under 380 mm (15 in) has led to a suggestion that
it was for an animal, but the inscription on the other shows it was intended
for a woman, which explains the smaller size.[38] The width of the collars
varies, from as little as 7 mm ($\frac{1}{4}$ in) to as much as 27 mm (*c.* 1 in); the
thickness of the strip is not given, but in the case of the one examined
by the writer in the collections of the Petit Palais in Paris it was 2-2.5 mm
($\frac{1}{8}$ in), corresponding to a width of 8 mm ($\frac{3}{8}$ in).[39] Closure was probably
effected by riveting; this is certainly true of the Petit Palais example and
though the Sardinian example is described as soldered, the illustration
indicates a rivet.[40] The other 20 examples survive as the so-called *bullae*,
small inscribed plates perforated for attachment to plain metal collars (fig.
104). As mentioned above, they are normally round, but two are rectangu-

Fig. 104. Inscribed slave *bulla*

lar; in addition, one is formed from an aureus of Constantine with one face erased to take the inscription, while one is of bone and heart-shaped.[41] Otherwise they are of bronze, or other copper alloy, as are the inscribed collars, with the exception of one of lead from Bulla Regia in Tunisia, considered below. The inscriptions have been incised with a graver or punched with a fine point, with letters approximately 5 mm ($\frac{1}{5}$ in) in height. Where complete (or where restoration is possible), they range from a simple formula, such as that on a collar from Ostia: TENE ME NE FVGIA(M) FVGIO, to quite explicit statements such as that on the *bulla* found near Velletri: ASELLVS SERVVS PRAIECTI OFFICIALIS PRAEFECTI ANNONIS FORAS MVRV(M) EXEVI TENE ME QVIA FVGI REDVC ME AD FLORA(M) AD TO(N)SORES, where the runaway is named as Asellus, slave of Praiectus, an official on the staff of the prefect of the *annona*; Asellus is stated to have crossed the walls of Rome, and his finder is asked to hold him and return him to the temple of Flora, in the same area of the Circus Maximus as the barbers.[42] In a few cases, for example *CIL* XV, 7194, a small reward is also offered (... *accipis solidum*).

The date of the inscribed collars and *bullae* is, as already noted, late and Dressel suggested a period between Constantius and Honorius, which Sotgiu would extend at its maximum to *c.* AD 500.[43] It is further held that their use was a consequence of the law enacted by Constantine, on 31 March 316, prohibiting the marking of slaves on their forehead.[44] Six bear the chi-rho monogram or chrismon (in one case both), suggesting Christian ownership; in particular, the recently published example from Sardinia not only bears the monogram but also the name of the owner, Felix, who is described as an archdeacon (*archidiaconus*). It is quite clear that slavery continued in Christian circles, for example in monasteries where slaves were sold or presented as gifts, though their treatment may have been more humane.[45]

The Italian examples come from Rome and its environs, and much of their interest centres on the information they provide about the topography of Rome. Three are known from North Africa and can from internal evidence confidently be ascribed to that part of the Empire.[46] One is unusual in being a lead collar with the inscription: *Adultera meretrix; tene quia fugivi de Bulla R(e)g(ia)* – 'I am an adulterous whore; keep hold of me because I have fled from Bulla Regia', implying that the wearer is a slave.[47] The second was found at Thelepte in Tunisia; the wearer is described as the slave of a centurion, Emeritus, on the staff of the governor of the province of Valeria Byzacena, and the inscription belongs to the period AD 294-325.[48] It is interesting to note that it was found near the quarries to the south of Thelepte, where the fugitive may possibly have been sent as punishment.[49] The third was found at Lambaesis in Algeria and describes the wearer as *fugitivus*, a runaway slave of Deuterius, *beneficiarius*.[50] The Sardinian collar has no precise find spot and can only be assigned generally to the island.

Marks of identification

The presence of convict slaves in corn-mills (*pistrina*) has already been discussed, with the conclusion that they were not in fact used to turn the mills. Apuleius' well-known description of their miserable conditions of work (*Metamorphoses* 9.12) not only mentions the use of fetters (*pedes annulati*) but also notes that the slaves had their hair half-shaved and their foreheads marked with letters (*frontes litterati et capillum semirasi*). This picture of conditions in the second century AD is foreshadowed by Petronius a century earlier; writing in the time of Nero (*Sat.* 102-6) he tells the story of Encolpius and Giton and their attempt to avoid discovery by their enemies by disguising themselves as slaves. This involved the shaving of their heads and even their eyebrows, and the marking of their foreheads with 'large letters' (*ingentibus litteris*) and the 'usual symbol of runaway slaves' (*notum fugitivorum epigramma*) on their faces.

The practice of the close cropping of the hair of slaves, prisoners and criminals has a long history, even into modern times, and has served the dual purpose of hygiene and identification. A third reference in ancient literature occurs in a letter to Cyprian, Bishop of Carthage, written in AD 258 by a group of Numidian bishops condemned to labour in the mines of their province.[51] They had evidently been beaten and fettered and, in their thanks to Cyprian for his letter of consolation, remark that he had 'smoothed the hair of their half-shorn heads' (*semitonsis capitibus capilla-turam adaequasti*). In his own letter Cyprian refers to the half-shaved heads of the prisoners in the mines (*semitonsi capitis capilli*) and the question remains of their actual appearance: was the whole of the head close cropped or half the head only? The latter would be a more distinctive indication of slave status but the former would make any marking on the forehead clearly visible. Certainty is difficult; in his commentary on the exchange of letters between Cyprian and the Numidian bishops, Clarke opts for the second solution: '... meaning, presumably, with the hair close-cropt on one side', whereas Millar simply raises it as a possibility.[52] The ancient writers do not make it clear: Apuleius simply describes the slaves in the *pistrinum* as *capillum semirasi*, while Petronius seems to suggest the whole of Giton's and Encolpius' heads were shaved in the shipboard episode. The argument for complete shaving is perhaps strengthened by the episode quoted by Jones, when Herodotus (5.35) describes the device used by Histiaeus of Miletus to send a message to his son-in-law, Aristagoras: this involved the shaving of the head of a trusty slave, which was then tattooed and the hair allowed to grow back; on arrival the slave was told to instruct Aristagoras to shave his head when the tattooed message could be read.[53]

The marking of the face, and more specifically the forehead, of slaves as a means of identification was frequently and mistakenly thought to be

241

branding with a red-hot iron, perhaps because this emphasized the general inhumanity of the treatment of slaves in antiquity. In his recent paper, Jones carefully examines the literary and etymological evidence, taking as his starting point the picaresque episode narrated by Petronius.[54] He freely admits that his conclusions had largely been anticipated by other scholars, but the merit of his discussion is that it lays to rest the branding cliché. The main point is that *stigma*, the word used by Petronius and earlier in Alexandrian literature, means a tattooed mark and is derived from the Greek verb *stizein*, to prick. In the Greek world, tattooing of a decorative nature was particularly associated with the Thracians and it would be tempting to suggest that the practice of marking slaves may have originated there, except that the practice was already of some antiquity in the Near and Middle East.

In a discussion of the evidence for actual branding by red-hot irons Jones concludes that this was essentially a Greek and Roman practice for the marking of animals and, in particular, horses.[55] The assumption that *stigma* in the ancient world was this sort of marking applied to humans may have been a misinterpretation which arose from penal branding in medieval and modern times, whereas in fact tattooing was much more likely. But even tattooing, when applied to the forehead or other part of the face, was eventually regarded as inhumane and the law of Constantine of AD 315/316 required that it should be confined to the hands and calves.[56]

The question remains of the nature of the *stigma* tattooed on the forehead of a fugitive slave before the time of Constantine. As noted above, the word used by Petronius is *epigramma*, a well-known indication of runaway slaves (*notum fugitivorum epigramma*). Jones notes an earlier use of this word by the Greek Herodas of Ptolemaic Alexandria, but the evidence for the actual letters or words is meagre.[57] He cites a *scholion* to Aeschines with the words *kateche me. pheugô*, i.e. 'Stop me. I'm a runaway', reminiscent of the words on the late Roman collars and *bullae – tene me ne fugiam* or *tene me quia fugi*.[58] But in fact the tattoo may have been a simple letter, on the analogy of the letter K marked on the foreheads of those guilty of calumny.[59] Quite possibly, Φ, or F (the first letters of *pheugô*, *fugio*) may have been used. But the practice was not confined to slaves, since it was also used, with different legends or symbols, for prisoners-of-war and criminals and even, in late antiquity, for soldiers and workers in military factories (*fabricenses*).[60]

The slave prison (*ergastulum*)

An established view indicates that slaves of a rebellious nature were fettered and confined in special prison buildings (*ergastula*). Thédenat links the introduction of this practice with the growth of large estates after the conquest of Italy, the dispossession of the *coloni* and their replacement by slave-labour recruited from the supply of prisoners of war.[61] As defined by Columella (*De re rustica* 1.6.3), the building is half underground (*subterraneum*) and lit by narrow windows placed high enough above ground level to prevent access by the inmates. According to Columella it was intended for the *servi vincti* as opposed to the *servi soluti*, who were housed in *cellae* or cubicles receiving good natural light. The management of the *servi soluti* was entrusted to the *vilicus* or overseer, and the position of his quarters, as demonstrated in the Pompeian villas, was frequently to one side of the entrance to the *villa rustica*, where he could watch the comings and goings of the labourers. The classic description is that of Varro (*De re rustica* 1.13.2): *vilici proximum januam cellam esse oportet et eum scire, qui introeat aut exeat noctu quidve ferat* ... For those housed in the *ergastulum* something more in the nature of a jailer was required and the word used in fact by Columella is *ergastularius* (1.8.17). The word is attested epigraphically on an inscription from Naples, while Ammianus Marcellinus describes Eunus, the leader of the slave uprising of 136-132 BC in Sicily, as *servus ergastularius*.[62] But, unfortunately, there is no evidence for this individual's quarters, though it seems likely that they could have been in the *ergastulum* itself.

In fact, the archaeological evidence for *ergastula* themselves is conspicuous by its absence. In a recent general study Étienne restates the evidence provided by literary sources and, commenting on the building described by Columella, remarks 'on n'a jamais rencontré un tel ergastulum dans une fouille de villa dans le Latium ou en Campanie', a conclusion also reached by Rossiter in a more recent study of Italian farm-buildings.[63] Some efforts have been made to identify such buildings elsewhere, for example at Chalk, near Gravesend, in Kent (fig. 105) and at Colchester, where the building also produced neck-shackles and human bones.[64] There is also the interesting suggestion that the great *cryptoporticus* beneath the fora in certain Gaulish towns, for example Arles and Amiens, may have served as slave-quarters, but this can be no more than an unsubstantiated hypothesis.[65] It is claimed that *ergastula* also appeared in quarries and corn-mills, but here too archaeological evidence is lacking.[66] As noted above, *pistrina* were workplaces in which fettered slaves were made to work under penal conditions, and they may conceivably have slept there. Another possibility is that the proximity of mills to granaries, as at Ostia, may have led to the use of granaries as *ergastula*. Their features, for example in legionary fortresses and auxiliary forts, have overtones of Columella's description: the long narrow plan, stout walls, the sub-floor ventilated by slit windows, possibly repeated at a high level in the main storage areas, and no doubt the availability of storage compartments in which the slaves could be fettered in Pompeian-type stocks or shackled to beams.[67] But again, the archaeological supporting evidence is lacking.

An epigram of Apuleius (*Apol.* 47) that fifteen free men constitute a nation, fifteen slaves a *familia* or personal staff, and fifteen fettered slaves an *ergastulum*, is used by some writers as support for the view that the

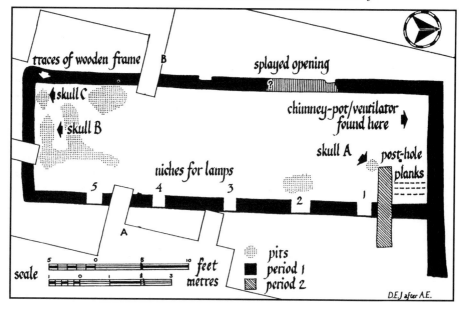

Fig. 105. Plan of possible *ergastulum* at Chalk, near Gravesend, Kent

word *ergastulum* was used by ancient authors to denote a chaingang. The evidence is strong,[68] and if any credence can be given to Apuleius' figure of fifteen, it suggests that this was thought to be a safe number for a chaingang, and consequently that the *ergastulum* as a building was not necessarily very large (or that a portion of some larger building offering secure conditions, for example a granary, could well have served the purpose). Whatever the truth, there is a clear need for the archaeological identification of this enigmatic structure.

8

Flight and Revolt

Introduction

The previous chapter discussed the various ways in which slaves, singly or in groups, could be restrained, and the archaeological evidence for such methods. It scarcely needs to be said that their Greek and Roman owners were acting on the premise that flight or, even more to be feared, organized rebellion were dangers inherent in slavery as a social institution. Naturally, variations in treatment might influence the likelihood of such action, but even a benevolent owner who adopted a humane attitude could not guard against the individual who felt an intense longing to see his native land, or desertion by a group in a period of unrest. Public figures who lost slaves are known to have used their influence with powerful friends and officials in an attempt to recover them: perhaps the best-known instance is the flight of Cicero's librarian, Dionysius, but much later Symmachus put pressure on judicial officials to arrest his runaway slaves.[1]

Much has been written about slave revolts, particularly the First and Second Slave Wars in Sicily in the second century BC, and that led by Spartacus in the first century BC, based on the accounts given in ancient authors. Opinion has varied widely on their significance. At one extreme are those who choose to interpret them in Marxist terms as evidence for the class struggle in ancient times, while at the other are those who see them as short-lived phenomena fostered by social unrest, particularly in its culmination in civil war, or as opportunist movements during hostilities between neighbouring peoples.

Flight or revolt by individuals or small groups can scarcely have left any trace in the archaeological record; even the larger rebellions and the protracted wars in Sicily and on the mainland are as difficult to detect as medieval battlefields, though in Sicily inscribed sling shot have been cited as evidence for the presence of the two sides. Sieges, such as that of Morgantina in Sicily, may offer evidence of urban destruction layers or siege works, but again the material is sparse or non-existent. This chapter will be largely devoted to an historical and geographical account of the topic in Greek and Roman times, and while exceeding the strict terms of this study will serve to round it off.

A number of factors conspired to encourage flight or revolt: opportunity offered the necessary conditions, but harsh treatment by a master obviously provided the impetus. A more subtle but no less potent cause was the nostalgia felt by the individual slave for his native land; a fine example is the graffito on the wall of a slave's room in La Maison du Lac at Delos, mentioned earlier, where the writer expresses his longing for the figs and water of his birthplace at Antioch-on-Maeander. Certainly the Greeks, and later the Romans, were aware of the danger arising from the concentration of slaves of the same nationality in one place or area. Plato (*Laws* 6.777c-d) comments on the frequency of revolts in Messenia where the native population was under Spartan domination; he couples his advice to draw slaves as far as possible from different nationalities with an injunction to treat them properly, statements later repeated by Athenaeus (*Deipn.* 6.264). Aristotle (*Politics* 7.9.9) argues that agricultural slaves should not be drawn from a single tribe, while Ps. Aristotle (*Oecon.* 1.5.6) argues that owners should avoid the practice of purchasing large numbers of slaves of the same nationality 'as men avoid doing in towns'. Finally, Varro (*De re rustica* 1.17.5) gives the same advice and adds that a concentration of slaves of the same nationality is a fertile source of domestic quarrels. It seems quite likely that the principle was based on experience, more particularly the hostility between the ruling class in certain Greek city-states and those whom they had enslaved during an initial invasion and forced into bondage. Prominent among these were the helots of Sparta and especially the Messenians as opposed to the Laconians, whose assistance enabled them to gain independence in 369 BC. The Thessalian *Penestai* were also troublesome, as were no doubt other such groups.[2] By contrast, Athens had no serf class but relied on slaves drawn widely from the ancient world: the Black Sea area, Asia Minor, Egypt, Libya and Sicily; as a result, slave revolts of this ethnic type were not known.[3]

Westermann cites the reported revolt of Argive slaves of *c.* 468 BC, when the slaves took advantage of the absence of menfolk from Argos by taking over the city.[4] From Herodotus' account this was a protracted revolt, since they were only expelled by the sons of the earlier Argives; the slaves then occupied Tiryns and engaged in a long war against Argos under the leadership of the Arcadian, Cleander, until their final defeat. Westermann dismisses this episode as 'unhistorical' and in fact argues that there were no serious uprisings in Greece in the period 500-320 BC. But this is to diminish the significance of three episodes in the later stages of the Peloponnesian War. The first was in 414 BC during the Athenian siege of Syracuse, again described by Westermann as of 'dubious authority' but having a historical value, when a group of slaves in the city rebelled; the revolt was quickly crushed by the Syracusan leader, Hermocrates, using a mixture of trickery and force, but a hard core of 300 slaves took refuge with the Athenians.[5] A year later occurred the frequently cited occupation by the Spartans of Dekeleia, *c.* 25 km (15 miles) north-east of Athens; its loss was a severe blow to the Athenians who were unable to recapture it in the subsequent Dekeleian War which lasted, like the Peloponnesian War itself, until 404 BC.[6] It not only acted as a continual military irritant to Athens but, economically, it interrupted the land route between Athens and the north, especially Euboea, and forced the Athenians to use the longer and more hazardous sea route round Cape Sounion for their corn supply. It was in that context that many of the slave-workers in the Laurion silver mines seized their chance and fled to the Spartans. Their flight did not achieve the freedom they sought and they were regarded as legitimate booty; the Boeotians, allied to Sparta, bought them up cheaply and resold them at a profit.[7] Thucydides speaks of 'more than 20,000 slaves', of whom the greater part were 'artisans' (*cheirotechnai*), and, if the figure is correct, this was a major blow to the Athenian monetary economy. In fact, there has been discussion of whether the figure given by Thucydides refers to one flight in 413 or to a total arising out of the warfare of subsequent years, and doubt has also been expressed about the accuracy of the figure and whether the word *cheirotechnai* refers to labourers in general or to the workers in the mines.[8] But whichever way the truth lies there can be no doubt that the events mark a notable instance of an opportunist flight of slaves, rather than a revolt, engineered by a loss of power by their owners.

The third episode was in 412 BC and it is interesting to observe that it occurred on Chios where tradition asserts that the inhabitants were the first in the Greek-speaking world to use chattel-slaves bought in the market place (Ath., *Deipn.* 6.265b), an innovation linked by others with the sixth-century discovery of iron working on the island (Herod. 1.25) and the growth of craft centres served by a slave workforce.[9] In 412 the Chians defected from the Delian League (Thuc. 8.40.2) and Athens responded by imposing a naval blockade based on Delphinion. These were the very conditions for which the many slaves in the island, badly treated by their owners, were looking and they defected to the Athenians in large numbers. The revolt ended with the occupation of Chios by the Spartans in 406 BC.

In 396 BC the scene shifts to North Africa where, after the success of Dionysius I of Syracuse against the Carthaginians, the latter were faced with a revolt by their allies who were joined by their own slaves. The rebels seized Tynes, but their approach on Carthage faltered and the revolt expired.[10]

Hitherto, warfare on a local or wider scale had evidently served as the catalyst for revolt, but an intriguing story, again preserved by Athenaeus (*Deipn.* 6.265b-266f) from the 'Periplous of Asia' by Nymphodoros of Syracuse written in the third century BC, takes us once again to Chios. Fuks would date this second uprising to the 70s or 60s of the third century BC and would grant it some historical veracity.[11] Building on Thucydides' account of the revolt of 412 and his statement on the large number of slaves in the island and their harsh treatment by their masters, he suggests that unrest was endemic. The runaway slaves gathered in the heavily wooded and mountainous northern part of the island and raided the country estates of the Chians. They were led by a certain Drimakos who successfully resisted the expeditions sent against him by the Chians; ultimately he reached an accommodation with them, by which each side established an independent *modus vivendi*. Finally, in a possibly fictional account, Drimakos was slain and then heroized, though the slave raids continued, eventually to cease through police action or natural causes. Athenaeus also briefly mentions a revolt on the island of Samos (*Deipn.* 6.267a-b): he takes his account from *The Seasons of the Siphnians* by Malakos, who relates how 1,000 slaves took to the mountains and harassed the Samians for six years. A truce was effected, which allowed the rebels to cross to Ephesus (possibly a reminiscence of the role Ephesus played as a place of exile for Samians).

Slave revolts in the eastern Mediterranean did not end after this date, but the area was falling under Roman domination and unrest now seems to reflect an increase in slave numbers farther west. There are recorded instances of conspiracies and risings in the early years of the Roman Republic, as early in fact as the recorded instances in the Greek world. Westermann again, as in the case of the Argos revolt, attaches little importance to them on the grounds that slave numbers were few in both areas and that the episodes are a reflection of later events.[12] But this is to form a conclusion on what can only be a hypothesis about slave-ownership in Greek and Roman society in the fifth century BC, and the numbers employed in the Laurion silver mines argue strongly for a substantial slave presence.

In the period down to the outbreak of the First Slave War in Sicily in 136/135 BC nine outbreaks are recorded in ancient authors of which four belong to the fifth century BC, after which there is a gap until the middle of the third century. Capozza, in a detailed study of these events, distinguishes them from the Sicilian Slave Wars and the Spartacus revolt because of the radical changes in Roman society from the middle of the second century BC;[13] she also groups the small slave risings of the Imperial period with general unrest among the lower classes, a view which perhaps reflects the fashionable view at the time she was writing. Her general conclusions did not command entire agreement at the time of publication: in a review article Dumont displayed complete scepticism, arguing that it was the virtual absence of revolt which was the most striking characteristic of the history of slavery, and that the rare and genuine episodes were the exceptions to this rule;[14] Bosworth, in a more generous review, also expressed doubt about the historicity of the early episodes but in the case of the later revolts accepted that newly enslaved men, particularly of the same nationality, could indeed initiate uprisings.[15]

8. Flight and Revolt

Slave wars to 136 BC

501 BC

A slave conspiracy coincided with an attempt by the Latins, under the leadership of Octavius Mamilius of Tusculum, son-in-law of Tarquinius Superbus, to seize power in Rome to pave the way for the return of Tarquinius and other exiles. The slaves planned to seize strategic points in the city but were betrayed by informers, tortured and crucified.[16]

500 BC

This second conspiracy can be regarded as a further episode in the continuing struggle between the classes in Rome, between Rome and its neighbours, and the attempts by Tarquinius and other Etruscan exiles to restore the monarchy. After abortive efforts to achieve their ends by diplomacy, an attempt was made to foment a revolt in Rome by appealing to the poor and to slaves (including those who, through debt, were in a servile relationship) to rise against the aristocracy. Again, suppression followed the disclosure of the conspiracy by informers. The emphasis differs in the account given by Dionysius (5.53.3-57), who classes the revolt as one by the poor, helped by slaves, and that of Zonaras (7.13.11), who regards it as principally slave-led with assistance from 'others', presumably the free poor. A strong argument against the historicity of the plot of 500 is its curious similarity to the Catiline conspiracy of 63 BC, down to a similarity in the names of the consuls, and the naming of a certain Tarquinius as an informer. As a result, certain scholars have been critical of Dionysius, accusing him of ignorance and invention. Capozza discusses the issue squarely but concludes that the events had a genuinely historical basis.[17]

460 BC

In 462, after a short period of calm, the struggle between patricians and plebs at Rome resumed, again with the additional elements of hostility between Rome and its neighbours, such as the Volsci and Aequi, and plots by the exiles. In 460 BC, a Sabine, Appius Herdonius, led a force of 2,500 exiles and slaves (4,000 according to Dionysius) and seized the Capitol. A relieving force from Tusculum joined the troops in Rome, the Capitol was recaptured and Herdonius killed.

There are variations between the accounts given by Livy (3.15-18; 19.6-12) and Dionysius (10.14-17.1; 10.37.2) summarized by Capozza, of which the most important from the point of view of this study is the origin of the slaves, whether runaways from Rome or in the service of the supporters of Herdonius.[18]

419 BC

In this year, the sources record a plot by a number of slaves to start fires

249

at different points and, in the confusion, to seize the Capitol and then summon the remaining slaves to join in the revolt, kill their masters and seize their wives and possessions. Two slaves gave the plot away, and the conspirators were tortured and crucified.[19]

There has been much discussion of the historicity of all these episodes. Doubters have preferred to see in them a legendary explanation, in the guise of historical narrative, of the internal struggle of the classes in Rome, and of Rome's troubled relations with her neighbours, coupled with the view that slavery was not at this period an important element in the make-up of society. An opposed view accepts that in the primitive agricultural society of the period slaves were limited in number and worked with their owners in a patriarchal system,[20] but suggests that there was already a nucleus of slaves, drawn from prisoners taken in hostilities, who were anxious to regain liberty and return to their homeland. Such groups, however small, could no doubt have been used as a supporting element in the plots hatched by exiles from Rome, such as the Etruscan Tarquins. When the sources speak, for instance, about the exiles from Cameria in 501 BC complaining about the enslavement of their countrymen (Dion. Hal. 5.51.1), or in 500 BC that the rich at Rome were treating their debtors like slaves whom they had purchased (Dion. Hal. 5.53.2) or in 460 BC that *eminebat terror servilis* – fear of their slaves was uppermost (Livy 3.16.3), some weight must be given to such statements. It is true that for Dionysius and Livy, writing at the close of the Republic, and even more for the Byzantine Zonaras, epitomizing in the eleventh / twelfth centuries AD, there may have been an element of *ex post facto* judgement, but nevertheless the presence of slaves, possibly chattel-slaves, and their disaffection in fifth-century BC Rome seem credible.

259 BC

A puzzling gap of nearly a century and a half before the next recorded instance of a conspiracy involving slaves has been much discussed and may be the result of a deficiency in the sources.[21] At all events, five years after the beginning of the First Punic War in 264 BC, a conspiracy of 3,000 slaves and 4,000 *socii navales* plotted the destruction of Rome in its defenceless state, but the plan was foiled by its betrayal (Oros. 4.7.12). Zonaras, the other main source (8.11.8-9), gives more details, in particular that the slaves were prisoners sold to Roman citizens (possibly, as some have suggested, Carthaginians) and that the *socii navales* were Samnites. He also names Erius Potilius, the commander of the allied naval force, as the man who crushed the plot. Much discussion has centred on the identity of the allied force, but the slave element and its restlessness seem credible, even if the conspiracy was abortive.[22]

217 BC

A brief statement by Livy (22.33.1-2), substantially repeated by Zonaras (9.1.1), records the crucifixion of 25 slaves for a conspiracy in the Campus Martius; the same passage relates that a Carthaginian spy who had been active in Rome for two years was caught, had his hands cut off and was expelled from the city (so that, according to Zonaras, he might serve as a warning to the Carthaginians). The two events may have been connected, since the Second Punic War had begun the previous year. The Campus Martius reference is puzzling, and some have suggested a manuscript error and that Livy had recorded that the crucifixion, and not the conspiracy, took place in the Campus Martius.[23]

198 BC

The general view is that this outbreak marked the beginning of the slave revolts and wars of the second and first centuries BC.[24] The conditions were right: the close of the Second Punic (Hannibalic) War in 201 BC had left large concentrations of Carthaginian and other prisoners on Italian territory, so that their servile status and ethnic homogeneity inspired unrest. The events are narrated in some detail by Livy (32.26.9-18) and epitomized by Zonaras (9.16.6).

The revolt was centred on Setia, some 60 km (38 miles) south-east of Rome where the sons of Carthaginian aristocrats were being held as hostages with their retinue of slaves; also there were prisoners from the Punic War (presumably Carthaginians) bought as slaves from the war booty by the inhabitants of Setia. The plot was to seek support from the slaves in the area around Setia, and then from those around nearby Norba and Cercei; when all was ready, there would be a rising in Setia at the moment when the population was absorbed in watching the games to be held there shortly. After the capture of Setia, the plan was to march on Norba and Cercei, free the Carthaginian hostages and prisoners there and recruit the slaves in those towns too. As so often, two slaves revealed the plot to the urban praetor at Rome, L. Cornelius Lentulus (strictly Merula), who marched on Setia with a scratch force of 2,000 men. The potential revolt was quickly quelled, the fleeing slaves were captured and some 2,000 punished. Shortly afterwards news reached Rome that slaves from the earlier conspiracy planned to seize Praeneste; L. Cornelius went there and punished 500 men involved in the plot. Security measures were taken in Rome itself and the praetor instructed the Latin communities to keep the hostages under strict guard and to chain prisoners with fetters of at least ten pounds weight.

196 BC

A brief passage of Livy (33.36.1-3) describes a slave revolt in Etruria which was suppressed by a legion from Rome under the praetor M'. Acilius. Many of the rebels were killed or captured; the leaders were crucified and the others returned to their masters. Granted that Rome had the power to restore order in allied territory, the problem remains of the identity of the slaves in Etruria.[25]

185-184 BC
The final episodes before the Slave Wars in Sicily of the last third of the second century BC, and Spartacus' uprising of 73-71 BC, are briefly narrated by Livy.[26] They were located in Apulia, where in 184 BC the praetor L. Postumius was faced with serious unrest among the slaves who worked as shepherds in that area; they had conspired together and engaged in banditry on the roads and state lands of the area. He sentenced nearly 7,000 men and, though many took to flight, many were punished, presumably executed. In the following year Postumius again quelled a number of serious conspiracies among the shepherds and at the same time repressed traces of the Bacchanalian cult. There has been much discussion of whether the events were connected and possibly they were in view of the appeal of the cult to the poor,[27] but the underlying explanation may lie in the economic conditions of the area: the growth of *latifundia* after the Second Punic War and the distribution of land to the veterans made conditions difficult for the slave-shepherds, while the practice of transhumance made it easy to take refuge in the hills.

Capozza discusses the causation of the five episodes between 259 BC and 185-184 BC and argues that the difficulties for Rome caused by the First and Second Punic Wars provided the essential conditions for revolt: in 259 the Samnite allies, resentful of Rome's domination, made common cause with prisoners forced into slavery; in 217 the plot in the Campus Martius may have been instigated by a Carthaginian agent; the Setia rising of 198 was even more clearly inspired by the Carthaginian hostages and prisoners; the Etruscan revolt of 196 is more difficult to categorize, but she suggests as a hypothesis that Carthaginian or philo-Carthaginian elements were capitalizing on anti-Roman movements; the final unrest of 185-184 may be classed as a complex of economic and cultural factors expressed as an anti-Roman movement.[28]

A large slave population, though economically advantageous, was now seen by Rome to contain the potential danger of a revolt. Rome quickly became aware of the need to control ownership of the *ager publicus* and to rule that landowners should employ free men as overseers. Capozza's final comment, shared by few, is that slaves did not revolt spontaneously but were manipulated by free men, who used them to sap Rome's strength.

Capozza's second study on slave revolts during the period from the middle of the second century BC to the period of the triumvirate of 43 BC has not appeared; instead we have a detailed account and analysis of the Sicilian Slave Wars of 136/135-132 BC and 104-101 BC and the Spartacus revolt of 73 BC.[29] Two other useful sources are Toynbee – a useful chapter on slave insurrections in the post-Hannibalic period – and Finley who covers the Sicilian Wars in a stimulating chapter.[30] Bradley's opening chapter is devoted to slave resistance in the New World in an effort, as he explicitly states, to evoke 'a plurality of contexts'. This tempting course had been followed previously by Barrow and Ingram.[31] But such contrasts between ancient and modern are of dubious value in explaining the past because of marked variations in social and cultural attitudes; they find a curious echo, from an entirely different standpoint, in the attempts by Marxists to interpret slave revolts in the ancient world in terms of modern ideologies of class warfare.

In his discussion of slave unrest before the First Sicilian War, Bradley attaches little importance to the episodes between 501 and 217 BC, except to make the point that it was extremely hazardous to take part in conspiracies.[32] He argues that the episodes in the early second century BC were of a different nature, associated with the aftermath of the Hannibalic War: concentrations of newly enslaved prisoners of one nationality, changes in agricultural conditions and difficulty in supervising a growing slave population were leading to more serious disorder, the precursor of the Sicilian Wars and the Spartacus uprising. The literary sources are discussed in Bradley's first appendix;[33] Diodorus Siculus' account of the Sicilian Wars derives from an immediate predecessor, Posidonius, and its survival depended on the summary excerpts by the Byzantine writers, Photius and the Emperor Constantine Porphyrogenitus, of the ninth and tenth centuries respectively;[34] and the accounts of Spartacus occurring in Plutarch's *Life of Crassus* and in Appian's *Civil Wars* possibly derived from Sallust. Bradley concludes that Roman writers had little interest in the slave population, by which he means their economic position and the morality of the institution. But the slave revolts must surely have excited considerable interest, and indeed alarm, the effect of which must have been as pervasive, if not more so, than any consideration of the ethics of slavery. Practical considerations are likely to have been uppermost in a slave-owner's mind, and particularly the potential for violence in a truculent slave or in a group involved in a plot, giving rise to a feeling of unease: the *terror servilis* attributed by Livy to the citizens of Rome at the time of Herdonius' coup of 460 BC (3.16.3). To some extent for the Greeks and much more so for the Romans manumission was the prize which they could hold before their slaves as a means of securing good conduct, and conversely the savage punishments could be invoked as a deterrent. Finally, Bradley provides a useful bibliography of secondary sources, but unfortunately he does not cite the second edition of the Mainz bibliography on ancient slavery, where the sections on the Sicilian revolts and Spartacus' rising include a number of papers published in the former Communist Eastern Europe and Japan.[35] Studies by Marxist scholars are, of course, of variable value, particularly the curious conclusions advanced by some of them:[36] Spartacus is claimed as 'a precursor of social revolution' or 'the leader of a proletarian unity-front'. Such comments would be ludicrous until one remembers that opposition to such crude conclusions could attract savage penalties which we tend to forget in today's happier atmosphere. Rubinsohn succinctly sums up the Soviet view of Spartacus as 'Marxist glorification of this romantic but minor figure in the history of the late Roman Republic'.

The First Sicilian Slave War, *c.* 136/135-132 BC

The date of the beginning of the war has been a matter for a great deal of discussion, with estimates varying between 141 and 136 BC, the duration of the war being four to five years. The second area of dispute is over the economic condition of the island down to the beginning of the revolt. Sicily had become the first of Rome's provinces after the First Punic War (264-241 BC) and the elimination of Carthaginian power in the island. But Rome's control was not fully confirmed until the Second Punic War (218-201 BC), after which Sicily became the great grain-producer of the Republic, so that Cicero could use Cato's description of it as Rome's storehouse (*cella penaria*).[37] It seems probable that much of the island's economic development may have arisen earlier in the second century as a result of immigration of Roman and Italian entrepreneurs, who were able to acquire areas which had become depopulated after the Punic Wars, rather as they flocked to Spain after Numantia to exploit its mineral wealth.[38] In brief, immigrants are attested at Messana, Tauromenium, Leontini, Agrigentum, Lilybaeum and Panormus, and are classed as *aratores, pecuarii* – large arable farmers and stock-breeders respectively – *negotiatores* and those concerned with the collection of *decumae, scriptura* and *portoria*; some wealthy immigrants had merely chosen to retire there and the origins given for all of them are largely Campania or southern Italy.[39] The Hadrianic writer ascribed the productiveness in grain to the *latifundia*, the large estates formed by the incomers, and the use of fettered slave-gangs, kept in *ergastula* at night (2.7.3). Diodorus, on the other hand, emphasizes the large number of herdsmen employed by the estate-owners, largely out of direct control, armed with makeshift weapons and resorting to brigandage (34.2.27-31). He implies that the initiative for revolt came from this group, who freed the chained slaves in order to swell their numbers. In spite of doubts about the pastoral element in the Sicilian economy, it seems probable that the island had a mixture of stock-raising and crop-growing and its production of grain may have been over-estimated.[40]

If the agricultural economy of Sicily provided the background to the Slave War, the proximate cause, according to Diodorus, was the barbarous treatment of the slaves by their owners, particularly those in the chain-gangs, coupled with the indulgence shown to the semi-nomadic slave-herdsmen. It is also claimed that the owners had reneged on the customary obligation to treat their slaves in accordance with the Greek system to which they were accustomed (maintenance in return for labour), and this had also aroused their resentment.[41] The beginning of the revolt centred on the town of Enna in the heart of Sicily, described by Cicero as the 'navel of Sicily' – *umbilicus Siciliae* – on its high plateau *c.* 1,000 m (3,250 ft) above sea level.[42] It was rich in religious associations; the nearby Lake Pergusa was reputedly where Persephone was snatched away to the Underworld. Diodorus starts his narrative of events in personal terms: the leader was a Syrian house-slave, Eunus, owned by Antigenes of Enna; he was credited with magical powers and chosen by the local slaves to lead an attack on Damophilos, a wealthy and cruel citizen of Enna and his wife, Megallis or Metallis. Under his leadership a band of 400 slaves broke into Enna by night and killed many of the citizens; they finally captured Damophilos and his wife and took them to the theatre, where Damophilos was executed and Eunus declared king. Megallis too was killed, and Eunus declared his mistress, also from Apamea in Syria, to be queen and appointed a Greek, Achaios, to be his adviser. Three days after the initial attack on Enna, Eunus' forces had grown to 6,000 and they began to move into the surrounding countryside. A month later, a parallel rising began in the south of the island, where a Cilician horse-breeder named Cleon assembled a force of 5,000, captured Akragas (Agrigentum) and raided the surrounding countryside. He then joined forces with Eunus, and together they defeated the Roman commander, L. Plautius Hypsaeus, at the head of 8,000 troops. Eunus' forces are stated by Diodorus to have grown to 20,000 and eventually to ten times that number. The subsequent course of the war is largely an account of the presumably annual campaigns, waged by a succession of Roman commanders with varying success, notably L. Calpurnius Piso Frugi, consul in 133 BC. He recovered the city of Morgantina and besieged Enna, where there is a little archaeological evidence in the form of lead sling shot found in the area bearing Piso's name and office.[43] The end of the war came in 132 when the consul P. Rupilius captured the two centres of resistance, Tauromenium (Taormina) and Enna; Cleon was killed and Eunus taken prisoner, eventually to die in captivity. It is difficult to estimate the degree of control exercised by Eunus over the island; Bradley suggests the south-eastern half, from Akragas through Enna to Tauromenium, and argues that control of Enna and Morgantina and the coastal towns of Tauromenium and Catana enabled them to exploit the Leontini plain with its grain resources and so to sustain the rebellion.[44]

It is interesting to note that after the initial attempt by Hypsaeus to quell the slaves, news of his defeat eventually reached Rome and the East, and led to minor disturbances, though these were quickly subdued: a conspiracy of 150 slaves in Rome itself, of 1,000 in Attica (at the Laurion silver mines?), and insurrections in the great slave-market on Delos and elsewhere. These are the parallel episodes noted by Diodorus, but in

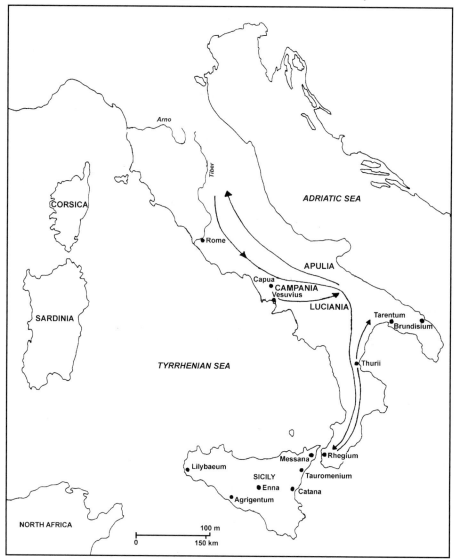

Fig. 106. Map of Sicilian Slave Wars and Spartacus rebellion

addition the fifth-century writer Orosius records outbreaks at Minturnae, on the border of Latium and Campania, where 450 slaves were crucified, and at nearby Sinuessa where 4,000 slaves were suppressed.[45]

In his introductory account of the events leading up to the rising in Sicily, Diodorus makes a passing reference to a rising in Asia Minor which overlapped the final years of the Sicilian War and continued until *c.* 129 BC.[46] The Attalid dynasty at Pergamum came to an end with the early death of Attalus III, who had bequeathed his kingdom to Rome, in 133 BC. His father, Eumenes II, had an illegitimate son, Aristonicus, who on the death of his half-brother seized the kingdom, and, at the head of a mixture of the lower classes, slaves and non-Greeks, defied the Romans until 129, when he was defeated and put to death. According to Strabo, he began his revolt at Leukai, north-west of Smyrna; after an initial defeat he moved inland and assembled a large force of the poor and slaves called the *Heliopolitae*.[47] After his capture, Strabo says he was taken to Rome and died in prison. Opinions vary on the significance of this revolt but the consensus is that this was not a full-blooded slave rising, but rather an attempt at some sort of social revolution, possibly under the influence of Blossius, formerly tutor to the Gracchi. Aristonicus' projected capital of Heliopolis ('City of the Sun') may possibly indicate a Utopian scheme for reform. Dumont discounts the revolutionary aspect and argues that Aristonicus was merely adopting the well-known tactic of enrolling the slaves of one's enemy to increase one's forces.[48] On the other hand, a different view claims that the slave revolt was real and a genuine factor in Aristonicus' attempt to found a kingdom.[49]

Other more shadowy figures are those of Saumacus in the Bosporus and Andriscus in Macedonia.[50] Saumacus is thought to have been a young Scythian at the Bosporan court, possibly a hostage of noble birth, whose revolt coincided with troubled relations between Pelacus of the Scythian kingdom and Mithridates. Of Andriscus little is known, but the Romans began to rework the Macedonian gold and silver mines *c.* 158 BC, and this may have caused resentment and eventually revolt.

Rome evidently took some note of economic conditions in Sicily and a senatorial commission was set up during the governorship of Rupilius, who had ended the war in 132 BC. Its recommendations were embodied in the Lex Rupilia, but this concerned itself with political matters and opinion is divided on whether there was any change in farming policy in the island. In practical terms, slavery on a large scale continued, fed by prisoners from Roman campaigns, largely in the West, during the 120s, and also by the slave-trade in the East, supplied by Cilician piracy and the great slave-market of Delos. So, it seems likely that the agricultural economy continued unchanged, both in Sicily and on the mainland, and Diodorus refers to unrest in Italy in the period immediately before the outbreak of the Second War in Sicily in 104 BC: a conspiracy of 30 slaves at Nuceria and a short-lived revolt of 200 slaves at Capua, south-east and north of Naples respectively.[51] Capua was also the scene in 104 BC of an attempted coup by the Roman *eques* T. Minucius Vettius who, burdened with debt, attempted to establish a local kingdom with an eventual force of 3,500 slaves, a rising quickly suppressed by the Romans.[52] Finally, there is a record by Athenaeus attributed to Posidonius (6.272e-f) of a second slave revolt in the Laurion silver mines in Attica; they killed their overseers, seized the citadel at Sounion, and ravaged Attica before the revolt was quelled. Some have suggested that this was a duplication of the earlier revolt, while others leave the matter unresolved.[53] A study of the Laurion mines accepts that there were revolts in both years, and in fact suggests that active mining in the peninsula ceased *c.* 100 BC.[54] Posidonius' dates (*c.* 135-50 BC) indicate that he would have had first-hand knowledge of the Second Sicilian War and its repercussions. A more specialized study of slavery in the Laurion mines discusses in detail the two reported revolts and their relationship to the Sicilian Wars.[55]

The Second Sicilian Slave War, *c.* 104-101 BC (fig 106)

The immediate cause of the Second War in Sicily was the decision by the governor, P. Licinius Nerva, to put into effect a senatorial decree which stated that no citizen of an allied state could be held in slavery in a Roman province, specifically Bithynians in Sicily; some manumission took place, but pressure from landowners compelled Licinius to refrain from any further hearings. The petitioning slaves, who had assembled at Syracuse, fled to the shrine of the Palici 55 km (35 miles) away to the north-west, a recognized place of asylum for slaves, and there discussed revolt.[56] The first small rising was at Halykiai at the western end of Sicily. An eventual force of 200 slaves attacked local owners but the attempt was quickly subdued by Licinius who used a renegade brigand to betray the rebels.[57] However, news soon came of another rising of 80 slaves, which Licinius countered by moving quickly to Heracleia on the south coast and summoning his subordinate, M. Titinius, to attack the rebels on Mount Caprianus with 600 soldiers drawn from Enna. The slaves' numbers had quickly increased to 2,000 and they were able to defeat Titinius. This gave them a supply of weapons and their numbers quickly rose to 6,000. They chose a slave called Salvius to be their 'king'; possessing similar gifts to Eunus, he rapidly reorganized the army of slaves, which now numbered 20,000 infantry and 2,000 cavalry, and made an attempt to capture Morgantina in the south-east corner of the island. In this he failed but he did defeat Licinius who had arrived at the head of a relieving force. The slave army had now doubled in size and Salvius made a second attack on Morgantina, but again without success. Once more there is some archaeological evidence for the presence of Licinius, in the form of lead sling shot bearing the names of his Sicilian troops.[58]

Meanwhile, as in the First War, another leader emerged, a man called Athenion who, like Cleon, was a Cilician; it is interesting that these two slaves had a common origin and that Cilicians were traditionally a hardy and independent people. Athenion is described by Diodorus as having astrological powers, and again the magical element is reminiscent of Eunus. His rising began in the west of Sicily where he rebelled against his owner; Diodorus describes him as a farm overseer and he used the 200 men in his charge to free those in the *ergastula*, raising his numbers to 1,000.

His numbers then steadily increased to 10,000, when he attempted to capture Lilybaeum, but without success. Salvius himself moved into the Leontini plain with a force now said by Diodorus to number 30,000 (it should be remembered that his army was put at 20,000 foot and 2,000 cavalry at the time of the first siege of Morgantina, and that it then doubled; we have the usual imprecision over numbers which we find in ancient writers). He proclaimed himself king, was retitled Tryphon by his followers after the Seleucid usurper, and summoned Athenion to join him. Athenion duly came with a part of his forces, numbering 3,000, but was not entirely trusted by Salvius, who put him under house arrest. By the end of 104 Salvius had established a stronghold at Triokala, though the extent of his control over the island must remain conjectural.

Our knowledge of the subsequent conduct of the war is sparse. Diodorus' narrative becomes tantalizingly sketchy and little detail can be gathered from other writers such as Florus. In 103 BC L. Licinius Lucullus was sent to Sicily with a force of 16,000 men of mixed nationality, with an experienced soldier, Kleptios, at their head. Lucullus had quelled the revolt at Capua by Vettius the previous year, but this war was on a totally different scale. Salvius (Tryphon) had cemented his relationship with Athenion and the rebels' army met the Roman forces in open country near the town of Skirthaia. Salvius' army was defeated, losing half its estimated strength of 40,000 men, and fled to Triokala, while Athenion was mistakenly thought to have been killed. But Lucullus failed to press home his advantage and the rebels consolidated their position; Florus even noted that Athenion captured Lucullus' camp, but it is not clear where this fits into the chronology.[59] In 102 BC C. Servilius succeeded Lucullus, but was not particularly active. Tryphon died and was succeeded by Athenion, who was energetic in extending the war, possibly even as far as Messana at the north-eastern tip of the island; again there is a little archaeological evidence in the form of sling shot used by the slaves, some bearing the name of Athenion, from the modern centres of Bronte, Troina and Assoro, north-east of Enna.[60] The use of the sling, for war and hunting, increased in Sicily from the fourth to third century BC, and lead sling shot, as opposed to stone or baked clay, were found by the rebels to be vastly superior when they were assailed with them by the Romans. Apart from those used in the First War, two examples are known with inscriptions related to Salvius (Tryphon) in addition to those with the name Athenion.[61]

The war came to an end in 101/100 BC with the appointment of M'. Aquillius, a consul for that year, to conduct the campaign. He fought a pitched battle with the rebels, killed Athenion, and gradually wore them down, reducing their numbers from 10,000 to a hard core of 1,000 under the command of a certain Satyrus. They were all finally captured and sent to Rome, where they were condemned to fight with beasts in the amphitheatre, but chose suicide instead.

An echo of the Aristonicus episode in the First Sicilian War occurs in the shape of a shadowy figure, Saumacus; known from an inscription found in the Thracian Chersonese in 1880, he was the leader of a revolt of Scythian slaves in the Bosporan kingdom of Mithridates VI in the last years of the second century BC. He has been compared with Aristonicus or, by Soviet historians, with Spartacus, but doubt remains over whether this was a genuine slave revolt or an attempt to found a small kingdom.[62]

The Spartacus rebellion, 73-71 BC

The slave rebellion led by Spartacus is one of those events in ancient history which have caught the popular imagination, like the life of Cleopatra or the destruction of Pompeii in AD 79. Not only that, but in the study of ancient history before the collapse of Communist rule in the Soviet Union and Eastern Europe the episode acquired ideological overtones as a paradigm of the class struggle. In the Mainz bibliography over fifty books and papers are listed under the heading 'Spartakus', of which a fair proportion are by East European scholars. In the West, he has been treated most recently with the Sicilian Wars.[63]

The main ancient sources are first, Plutarch's life of Crassus, the final conqueror of Spartacus, in which the Roman leader was paired with the Athenian general, Nicias (*Vitae, Crassus*, 8-11), and secondly Appian, writing a generation later in the middle of the second century AD, whose *Civil Wars* contain five sections in the first book (1.116-20) dealing with the rebellion. Unfortunately, there is no independent evidence from earlier sources to act as a check, since the relevant portions of Sallust and Livy have not survived. Brief sections from other writers are also available as supplementary evidence.

The scene of this uprising was the Italian mainland and, in the first instance, it was centred on Capua, north of Naples (see fig. 106); the town served as a source of supply of gladiators for amphitheatres of the area. The manager (*lanista*) of the training school for gladiators (*ludus*) at Capua, according to Plutarch, kept his slaves destined for the arena under close guard in their barracks. From the evidence of the various sources they were apparently composed of Gauls, Germans and Thracians, and are likely to have been recently enslaved, either through capture in warfare or through trade. The gladiatorial barracks may have resembled those of Neronian date at Pompeii;[64] these had in fact been preceded by barracks of Republican date on the Via di Nola, originally perhaps a private house converted to provide thirteen rooms at ground level with more above, set round a courtyard and identified by a series of gladiatorial graffiti.[65] The early barracks were abandoned, possibly because of insufficient space, *c.* AD 63, and the change made to the much larger barracks installed in the large porticoed courtyard which had originally served as foyer to the large theatre in the complex by the Porta Stabia (fig. 107). First excavated in 1766, it was at first thought to be military barracks or a market, but the

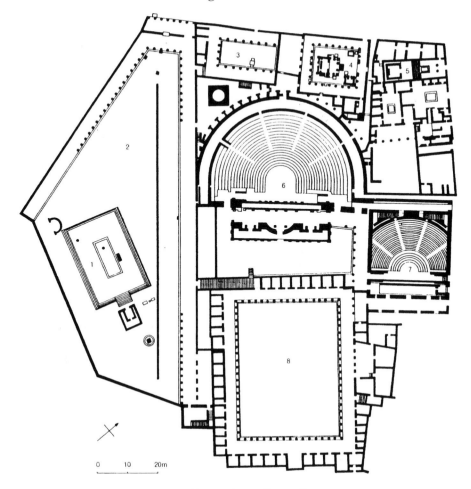

Fig. 107. Plan of the gladiatorial barracks at Pompeii

discovery of a quantity of gladiatorial weapons and armour in ten of the *cellae* or sleeping cubicles put the matter beyond doubt.[66] Ranged round the great courtyard, *c.* 60 m (200 ft) north-south by 50 m (170 ft) east-west, were an estimated 70 *cellae* on two storeys, sufficient to hold, at two per *cella*, 140 gladiators. In addition, there was a communal mess served by a kitchen, quarters for the *lanista* and a small lock-up, still containing one of the multiple type of fetters known from the 'factory farms' round Vesuvius, attached to its wooden base. The *cellae* were small, *c.* 3 x 4 m (10 x 13 ft), with poorly decorated walls, entered by a door from the colonnade or steps leading to an upper veranda for those at the higher level.

At all events, these squalid conditions, coupled with the brutality and violence of the gladiators' lifestyle, impelled them to attempt an escape; of

261

the 200 in the plot, 78 (70 according to Appian) got free with kitchen implements as makeshift weapons. By chance, they intercepted a wagon-train with gladiatorial armour which they seized and so improved their armament. Spartacus emerged as their leader: a Thracian who had served in the Roman army, he was physically strong and intelligent, qualities which made him a natural choice. As his lieutenants he appointed two gladiators named Crixus and Oenomaus, of Gaulish origin according to Orosius.[67] They moved south, repelling their immediate pursuers from Capua and seizing their weapons, and gathered support from slaves in the countryside. They chose the slopes of Vesuvius as a stronghold and were able to defeat the first attack on them by regular Roman troops numbering 3,000; clearly, the rebels had much increased their own numbers, and Plutarch says that they had recruited the slave herdsmen and slave shepherds of the area, with their traditionally independent attitudes. A second Roman force, possibly larger, was sent against Spartacus in 73, but was again ignominiously defeated.

Spartacus now extended his operations southwards into Lucania and Apulia, and his army is said to have reached a figure of 70,000. In 72 BC both consuls were elected to quell the rising and a force of four legions was dispatched against Spartacus. The latter now adopted the plan of moving north in an attempt to cross the Alps and allow his followers to regain their native lands. The Roman forces were again defeated and Spartacus, perhaps because of the problem of maintaining unity among his forces, turned south again and even threatened Rome at one point. Finally, he occupied Thurii on the east coast of the toe of Italy.

By the end of 72, the Romans had appointed Crassus as supreme commander with a force of ten legions; after an initial setback, which Crassus countered by decimation of his own troops, he forced Spartacus into the toe of Italy near Rhegium. Spartacus seems to have toyed with the idea of crossing to Sicily in the hope of raising support there, but instead stayed in the Reggio peninsula where he was besieged by Crassus. In early 71 he made a desperate attempt to break out and make for Brundisium on the heel of Italy. Crassus followed and when Spartacus heard that fresh Roman troops under Lucullus had landed at Brundisium, he turned to face Crassus and after a fierce battle he was killed and his slave army defeated. Pompey too had now arrived from Spain and was able to participate in the final stages of the Roman success, and also to gain the greater part of the credit. Of Spartacus' army many fled to the mountains and were gradually hunted down; 6,000 were taken captive and crucified along the Via Appia.

In a sense, the original plot and escape from Capua began as a dash for freedom, but the sheer success of the gladiators led by Spartacus and the rapid increase in their numbers seem to have caused them serious problems. Their early victories over the Roman forces left them in a state of indecision, best shown in the decision to abandon the march north to the Alps and turn south again. There was evidently no coherent strategy to take the place of the original search for freedom, and this led to improvised tactical responses dictated by the advance of ever larger Roman forces and the slaves' own disunity.

There has been considerable discussion of the objectives in the minds of Eunus and Salvius, the leaders of the Sicilian revolts, and of Spartacus, the leader of the final outbreak on the mainland. There is much evidence that Eunus and Salvius and Athenion, the successor to Salvius, saw themselves as slave kings on the Hellenistic pattern.[68] Thus Eunus took the Syrian title Antiochus and minted his own coins,[69] while Salvius adopted the royal name of Tryphon, a name which appears on sling shot of the Second War. Apart from the fact that many of their followers were first-generation slaves from the eastern Mediterranean, Sicily also had a long tradition of local autocratic rulers.[70] But the power of Rome clearly prevented the establishment of independent kingdoms, and the measures taken by the slave leaders seem at best to have served merely as a means of retaining the loyalty of their followers. Spartacus differed in that he adopted Roman military practice in an effort to achieve freedom for himself and his army, best shown in the early plan to march north and seek their homelands beyond the Alps. In the end, his tactics smacked of desperation and opportunist reaction to the gathering power of his Roman opponents.

Slave revolts after Spartacus

It has already been noted that the supposed revolt of 500 BC may have been an inserted invention of Dionysius of Halicarnassus on the grounds of the curious similarities with the Catiline conspiracy of AD 63. The point is worth making if only to emphasize that ambitious leaders were prone to attempt coups d'état by incorporating rebellious slaves, particularly those of their opponents, in their forces. Before 100 BC there were attempts to seize power locally, as in the case of Vettius at Capua in 104 with his force of 3,500 slaves. The Social War in the early years of the first century BC, and even more the prolonged civil wars which followed, all provided the right conditions for ambitious or embittered men to use the disaffected poor and slaves to support their cause. So Catiline in 63, the violent quarrels of Clodius with Cicero and Pompey in the early 50s and his assassination by Milo in 52 BC, and the riots in Rome in the 40s, all involved the urban plebs and artisans, what in modern terms we might call the proletariat, but also an element of the slave population.[71] But these were not true slave rebellions as in the Slave Wars of Sicily: 'During the age of Caesar and Augustus, slaves played a considerable role in power-politics as organized gangs in the hands of individual party-leaders. Nevertheless, there were no further organized slave-revolts after Spartacus had been overthrown.'[72]

All the same, there were episodes of slave revolt, conspiracy and protest in the earliest years of the Empire and sporadically thereafter,[73] though the presence of troops in the provinces and a developing system of doles, in money or in kind, kept the urban plebs, with whom slaves might naturally ally themselves, in a generally quiescent state. Later, of course, there were the larger protests of impoverished peasantry in Gaul, Spain and North Africa, and again slaves were an element in these; they will be touched upon but cannot be regarded as predominantly inspired by the servile class.

19 BC

A revolt of the Cantabri of northern Spain; they had been taken prisoner by the Romans in the campaigns of 26 BC onwards and sold off as slaves. They slew their masters and fled to their homeland, where they stirred up resistance, but were finally quelled after some difficulty by Agrippa.[74]

AD 14

An abortive attempt by Clemens, slave of Agrippa Postumus, to seize the throne for his master. However, Agrippa was murdered on Planasia, an island south of Elba where he had been exiled, and Clemens changed his tactics; trading on his physical similarity to Agrippa, he impersonated him and gained support in Ostia and Rome itself. His supporters were penetrated by agents of Tiberius, Clemens was captured, and then killed secretly.[75] Štaerman correctly argues that this was not a genuine slave revolt, and compares it with other attempts at usurpation, such as the Telephus conspiracy against Augustus (Suet., *Aug.* 19), the impersonation of Nero by a possible slave after the emperor's death (Tac., *Hist.* 2.8-9), and in the reign of Vitellius the attempt by the slave Geta to impersonate a certain Scribonianus Camerinus (Tac., *Hist.* 2.72).

AD 24

An abortive revolt, dated by Štaerman to AD 21, was instigated in the Brindisi area by Titus Curtisius, a former praetorian guard. He incited the slave herdsmen and slave shepherds, known for their wild nature, to seek their freedom, but the timely presence of the quaestor Catius Lupius, one of whose duties was the supervision of the grazing tracks used by the herdsmen for transhumance (*calles*), nipped the revolt in the bud. Tiberius sent a strong force under the tribune Staius, which took Curtisius and his lieutenants to Rome, where there was already considerable alarm over the growing imbalance between the slave and free population. The episode is reminiscent, both in area and personnel, of the earlier Apulian unrest of 185-184 BC.[76]

AD 64

An attempted gladiatorial revolt at Praeneste, quelled by a local detachment of troops, led to fears of a rising comparable to the Spartacus revolt.[77]

8. Flight and Revolt

AD 68-9

The fall of Nero in AD 68, and the following 'Year of the Four Emperors', led to instances of popular revolt on the side of one claimant to the throne or another. In these episodes, slaves sided with the plebs, while gladiators were used with regular troops. These events cannot be regarded as slave revolts, however, but rather, as Štaerman argues, as opportunist moves reminiscent of the confused days at the end of the Republic.[78]

c. AD 186

There are no further recorded instances of revolt, by slaves on their own or by slaves and plebs combined, until the reign of Commodus, over a century after the 'Year of the Four Emperors'. About AD 186, a certain Maternus deserted from the army and at the head of a large band of brigands, composed of 'runaway slaves, *coloni*, ruined farmers, deserters from the army and so on', ravaged large areas of Gaul and Spain over a period of years.[79] Septimius Severus, during his governorship of Gaul, was unable to suppress this unrest and Rome was compelled to send an army to central and southern Gaul. Maternus' followers split into small groups and worked their way into Italy and finally to Rome. The plan was to assassinate Commodus during a religious festival and declare Maternus emperor, but his ambitions disillusioned a group of his close companions; he was betrayed and executed, but his movement lingered on.[80]

AD 206-7

On a smaller scale and more in the nature of simple brigandage was the movement led by the Italian, Bulla Felix, who as a 'noble robber chief' led a band of 600 peasants and slaves in exploits throughout the area between Rome and Brindisi for two years, until he was betrayed by his mistress and put to death in the arena. His reported remark to a captured centurion, 'Tell your masters to feed their slaves', indicates that there may have been a predominantly slave element in his band and that there was a failure by owners to fulfil their usual obligation towards their slaves, as at the time of the Sicilian Wars of the second century BC, but Thompson suggests that his exploits were simply robbery, whereas the movement led by Maternus was something like revolution.[81]

These last two episodes form the prehistory to the unrest in the late third century led by the so called Bacaudae.[82] The economic disasters of the third century, accentuated by barbarian invasion, caused much distress among the rural population of Gaul and Spain. At the same time there was a blurring of the distinction between slave and *colonus* in the countryside. The major change, eventually given legal recognition, was that some of the small tenant farmers who had formerly been free to move were, by the law of Constantine dated AD 332, tied to the land, even to the extent that any who planned flight should be fettered like slaves.[83] So slaves were no longer chattels to be bought and sold in the market, but were forbidden to be sold apart from the land on which they worked. All this was advantageous to the big landowners but created resentment.

The Bacaudae appear *c.* AD 283-4 and by 286 Diocletian was compelled to appoint Maximian as co-ruler in the West to deal with the problem, apparently with some success. But the unrest continued, especially in the *tractus Armoricanus* between the mouths of the Loire and the Seine, where there were big revolts as late as the first half of the fifth century. They were probably active in other parts of Gaul, and by the middle of the fifth century in Tarraconensis and other parts of Spain. So, it would not be proper to describe the activities of the Bacaudae as a slave revolt, but rather as the grouping of a whole social class, the peasantry, in opposition to the ruling class of landowners, and the movement is linked to the introduction of serfdom in early medieval Europe.

There was also unrest in Africa, and especially Numidia, but in this case associated with the Donatists of the fourth and fifth centuries. Named after a fourth-century bishop, Donatus, they were active *c.* AD 300-600 and are best regarded as a schism rather than a heresy.[84] The so-called *Circumcelliones*, composed of peasants from Upper Numidia and Mauretania, acted as terrorists within the Church and by devoting their lives to martyrdom are reminiscent of the fundamentalists of today. They lived *circum cellas* 'around the shrines' (hence their name) and were active in attacks on villas and Catholic churches in North Africa. A major outbreak occurred *c.* AD 340-8 and their release of slave-labour on the estates no doubt added to their numbers. There may also have been overtones of a nationalist, anti-Roman, feeling, but there is certainly strong evidence that it was a social movement, an uprising of the poor against the rich in the countryside.[85] Landlords, creditors and slave-owners were attacked by the *Circumcelliones* as the militant wing of the Donatist Church, and it is probable that slaves and quasi-servile *coloni* took part in these disturbances.

Epilogue

Ralph Jackson

'*Tene me quia fugio*' was a phrase so familiar in the later Roman Empire that its abbreviated form 'TMQF' inscribed on a bronze *bulla* suspended from a neck-ring[1] was sufficient to alert those who saw it to the fact that the person before them was a slave who might very well have fled his servitude. Such artefacts, tiny pieces of archaeological evidence, are, nonetheless, eloquent testimony both to the embedded nature of slavery in Greek and Roman society and to the ultimate recourse of the disaffected slave. Greece and Rome were slave societies, and if, as has been estimated, one in three people in late Republican Italy, and a similar ratio in Periclean Athens, was a slave,[2] then the fundamental importance of slavery to almost any aspect of those societies cannot be denied. In consequence, ancient slavery is a compelling field of study for historians and has generated a vast literature. Its scope is seemingly endless, and the fascination that it exerts seems to be based in part upon its ubiquity and in part on the very considerable, but unequal and incomplete sources of evidence. For, precisely because slavery was a fact of life, historians must grapple with the problem that many crucial issues for which we would hope to have enlightenment were so much taken for granted that they were seldom written about, and never in sufficient detail.

It is entirely logical that Hugh Thompson's opening chapter should take as its theme the source of slaves since this is a coherent starting point of slavery. But it is also particularly appropriate to the whole field of study of ancient slavery, for there is still no consensus as to the relative importance of the various means of procurement of slaves and it continues to be a burning issue. It is symptomatic of the subject as a whole that even the evidence for something as basic as the supply of slaves is so incomplete that very different hypotheses can be advanced convincingly.[3] Another rich vein for slavery historians is Greek and Roman literature, which can be seemingly endlessly quarried for insights into ancient attitudes to slavery.[4] The gaps can be filled in many ways, and much ingenuity and eloquent argument has been employed, providing a fertile field for stimulating debate. The danger, of course, with such an emotive issue as slavery is that it is particularly susceptible to being shoe-horned into invalid theoretical frameworks. But perhaps this is the nature of the subject, for, in order to try to achieve an understanding of the whole rather than relying on individual aspects or comparatively well-represented but probably atypical slave groups, it is necessary to model the evidence in a variety of ways. Given its centrality, the continued high level of research into slavery is certainly essential.

If in the ancient historical sources the great majority of slaves as individuals is generally silent, then in the archaeological record slaves are almost invariably invisible. At best the information is shadowy, tenuous and often equivocal. For this reason and because the historical accounts are fuller and more accessible, the archaeology of slavery, excepting the epigraphic material, has been largely neglected. Individual sites or aspects have received attention, but the great strength of the present book is that it is the first attempt to draw together all the archaeological material and integrate it with the results of epigraphic, historical and literary studies. As a pioneering work it is in the same vein as, and very much the counterpart to, the late Thomas Wiedemann's *Greek and Roman Slavery*. It is a magisterial survey, packed with data, but more than that it is a fascinating journey through time and place as we are led around the ancient world, from Homeric Greece to the late Roman Empire in a thoughtful, cogent examination and assessment of the archaeology of Greek and Roman slavery. Inevitably, the result is often frustrating or unsatisfying because of the limitations of the evidence. But in other respects it is a most illuminating study, because of the very elegant way that the archaeological material is woven into the geographical and historical backgrounds.

Hugh Thompson's primary aim was to locate and elucidate slave-run establishments. By examining the archaeological contexts of those settings in which particular slave workforces were known to operate, he attempted to distinguish the 'fingerprints' of slavery, in short, to find the slaves on the *latifundia*, and in the mines, state weaving mills and so on. Sometimes, it seems, the evidence takes us closer to 'probably' than 'possibly', but rarely do we get beyond that, and there is frequent recourse to the qualified past conditional. This is hardly surprising, and it is as it should be, since it is notoriously difficult to ascertain the function of a room or building from its ground plan alone. For example, while there is sometimes an understandable tendency to conjecture contiguous units or ranges of small unpretentious rooms as slave *cellae,* rather than, for example, storerooms, there is usually no inherent reason why these should not have been occupied by forced free labour, free paid workmen or others at the lower end of society. And can we necessarily assume that slave accommodation was invariably purpose-made? If not, how might we hope to recognize, archaeologically, slave-quarters contrived in an existing structure? Perhaps, too, both types of building might be present on one site. Only at sites like Pompeii, Boscotrecase and Gragnano, where sets of iron stocks were found in rooms associated with *cellae*, do we appear to be on safer ground.

A similar problem arises when attempts are made to discern the slave-hospitals apparently provided at some *latifundia*. There are references or allusions to such *valetudinaria* in the works of Cornelius Celsus, Columella, Tacitus and Suetonius, and they are further attested on inscriptions. However, these sources give no description of the appearance, arrangement or detailed organization of the buildings, and none has yet been recognized in the archaeological record. A distinctive type of building in Roman legionary fortresses, and a less distinctive type in auxiliary forts, has for long been identified as the military *valetudinarium*, but even if such an identification is correct – and it is by no means assured – there is no reason to anticipate the same architectural model on *latifundia*.[5] Perhaps even more so than the *cellae*, slave hospitals might be expected to take the form of rooms or suites of rooms attached to or incorporated in other buildings, and, as such, they are likely to remain elusive in the absence of discoveries of distinctively medical artefacts found *in situ*. Nevertheless, Hugh Thompson, by the detailed analysis of the published data from excavations, sometimes combined with his own knowledge of the sites and their topography, succeeds in creating a picture, albeit an impressionist one, of the settings in which slaves were required to work, whilst still preserving the integrity of the evidence. His cautiously drawn conclusions are judicious, whether they entail a positive or negative identification. For, while it is true that if we are to find the material remains of slavery they have to be actively sought and the evidence robustly interrogated, it is essential not to push that evidence too far, since the avoidance of false certainties is especially critical in this field.

An important component of Hugh Thompson's book, perhaps the most important, is his research on the artefacts of slavery, principally the devices for restraint. If the inscribed neck-rings and *bullae* personalize slavery (though they de-personalized slaves) and offer a vivid glimpse of the reality of slavery for individuals, then a reminder of the sheer scale of things is provided by certain of the historical writers. One of the most graphic references is the celebrated passage in Diodorus Siculus, where it is recorded that the Carthaginian army in 310 BC had with it 20,000 pairs of manacles in the expectation of enslaving that number of the enemy. Whether or not we accept the number at face value, it conjures up a powerful image. The various restraints – manacles, handcuffs, shackles, stocks and fetters – for the hands, feet or neck of individuals or chain-gangs, though not all exclusive to slavery, are, perhaps, the most direct and emotive physical evidence of slavery. As the initial stimulus for his research on slavery Hugh Thompson devoted to them a full and detailed study,[6] in which he defined with great clarity and authority the occasions and modes of use of the different types, from the Late Iron Age neck-shackles of north-west Europe, evocative of the slave-trade, to the fetters worn by unreliable slaves in the fields and mines, and the stocks used to secure recalcitrant slaves in the *ergastula*. One of the several difficulties in identifying iron shackles is their close similarity to the hobbles or spans, which were sometimes fastened to the ankles of ponies and draught animals for the purpose of control. Such a conflation of form may have been determined purely by their common function, but in view of the virtual equation of slaves with animals, as part of the farm livestock, by writers from Aristotle to Varro,[7] function may not have been the sole determinant.

In a Roman province like Britain, virtually devoid of written sources, and where inscriptions are few and far between outside military circles, archaeological remains, by default, are a valuable potential source for evidence of slavery and slave-trading, albeit a source rarely providing unequivocal evidence. The wooden ink writing-tablets found at the fort of Vindolanda are a case in point. To the handful of Romano-British inscriptions mentioning *servi* or *familiae* can now be added personal correspondence between slaves in the province at a time shortly before the construction of Hadrian's Wall.[8] They are a striking reminder that archaeology can very materially add to the corpus of information compiled from other sources, a conclusion surely reached by all those who have read this thought-provoking book.

270

Notes

Preface

1. Thompson 1983.
2. Thompson 1994.
3. Finley 1968a, 229.
4. Vogt 1965; 1974, 211-17.
5. Finley 1968a, 229-36.
6. Wiedemann 1981.
7. Finley 1980; Wiedemann 1987; Garlan 1988.
8. Vogt and Bellen 1971; Herrmann and Brockmeyer 1983.
9. Garlan 1988, 18-19.

1. Sources of Slaves and the Trade in Slaves

1. *Digest* 1.3.4.
2. Wallon 1879, I, 66 – Greek slavery; II, ch. 2 – Roman slavery; Buckland 1908, 1; Lewis and Short 1966, *s.v. servus*; Stuart Jones and McKenzie 1968, *s.v. dmôs*; Wiedemann 1981.
3. Finley 1977, 56; Lencman 1966, 256, 258-9.
4. Wallon 1879, I, 63-4 and ch. 5; Barrow 1928, 1-2 (origins), 3-15 (sources); Westermann 1955, 2ff.
5. Finley 1980, 86.
6. Wiedemann 1987, 8.
7. Finley 1980, 67, 88; Fustel de Coulanges 1885, 3.
8. Garlan 1988, 201-8.
9. Wiedemann 1987, 3-4.
10. Older works: Wallon 1879; Barrow 1928; Westermann 1955.
11. Finley 1968a, 231.
12. Wallon 1879, I, ch. 5; Westermann 1955, 2, 5-6, 28-30.
13. Wallon 1879, II, ch. 2; Barrow 1928, ch. l; Westermann 1955, ch. 9.
14. Buckland 1908, ch. 17.
15. Willetts 1967, 14-17, 70.
16. Finley 1968a, 231.
17. Black Sea and Danube: Finley 1962; Amphipolis tombstone: Finley 1968b.
18. Westermann 1955, 11, 12, 28-34, 37, 57-66, 84-7, 96-8, 123-4, 134-5, 137, 138.
19. Wiedemann 1981, 106-21, nos 101-25.
20. Garlan 1988, 45-53 (sources), 53-5 (trade).
21. Harris 1980.
22. Minns 1913; Glotz 1926; Toutain 1930; Frank 1933-40; Rostovtzeff 1953, 1957.
23. Lencman 1966.

24. *Politics* 1.2.4
25. Westermann 1955, 3-5.
26. Thuc. 7.27.5.
27. Westermann 1955, 6.
28. Westermann 1955, 28.
29. Westermann 1955, 29.
30. Westermann 1955, 60-1.
31. Black Sea: Strabo 7.3.12; 11.2.3; Illyria: Strabo 4.6.7.
32. Barrow 1928, 14.
33. Westermann 1955, 11.
34. Harris 1980, 129.
35. cf. Kirk 1975, 821.
36. Westermann 1955, 3; Starr 1982, 437-8.
37. Bergk 1882, 37 – fr. 4, 11.23ff.
38. Bergk 1882, 37 – fr. 36, 11.8-10.
39. Diehl 1949, 34-5, fr. 79a.
40. Diehl 1949, 93, fr. 43.
41. Finley 1962, 52-3.
42. Willetts 1967, 8-9, 17, 70.
43. Ducrey 1968, 54-5, 111.
44. Finley 1968a, 168.
45. Lauffer 1979, 165.
46. For the sequence of events: Ducrey 1968, 155-9.
47. For the mines, cf. Lauffer 1979, 54 n. 3.
48. For the mining suggestion see Ducrey 1968, 82.
49. Ducrey 1968, 149-70.
50. Ducrey 1968, 171-93.
51. Finley 1962, 57-8.
52. For Plato references see Ducrey 1968, 176 n. 3.
53. Dittenberger 1915-24, vol. 3, 263.
54. Westermann 1955, 10; Finley 1962, 52.
55. Lauffer 1979, 140ff., tab. 80.
56. Finley 1962, 52-3.
57. Finley 1962, 53, n. 2.
58. Westermann 1955, 7.
59. Finley 1962, 57-9; Garlan 1988, 53-5.
60. Westermann 1955, 11-12.
61. Finley 1968a, 173.
62. See Ziebarth 1929, 18.
63. Garlan 1988, 19.
64. The evidence is conveniently assembled in a number of studies: Wielowiejski 1956; Himmelmann 1971; Ziomecki 1975; Raeck 1981.
65. Volkmann 1961, 154.
66. Volkmann 1961, 102.
67. Volkmann 1961, 166.
68. Ducrey 1968, 187-9.
69. Ormerod 1924, 190ff.; Ziebarth 1929, 31-43.
70. Ziebarth 1929, 22-3.
71. Minns 1913, 438; Rostovtzeff 1922, 69, 71, 145; Diod. 20.25.
72. Ormerod 1924, 260-70.
73. Ziebarth 1929, 107-8.

74. Ormerod 1924, 131.
75. Phlegon: Müller *FHG* 606, 12; Jacoby *FGH* 257, F12, 13.
76. Calderini 1908, 408-10.
77. Westermann 1955, 31ff.
78. Finley 1962, 55 n. l.
79. Fraser and Rönne 1957, 96-7.
80. Westermann 1955, 37.
81. Rostovtzeff 1941, ii, 675, 1262-3.
82. Bang 1910 and 1912, of which the first is relevant for this period.
83. Johnson 1953.
84. Johnson 1953, 112.
85. Westermann 1955, 61.
86. For example, Plautus, *Captivi* 7, 971ff.; *Menaechmi* 29ff.; *Curculio* 645ff.; *Poenulus* 84ff.; *Rudens* 39ff.; Terence, *Eunuchus* 115.
87. Glotz 1926, 193; Westermann 1955, 37; Garlan 1988, 54.
88. Blavatsky 1974.
89. Every month: Garlan 1988, 54; Westermann 1955, 12, is doubtful. Agora: *kuklos* (Hesychius), *kukloi* (Pollux 7.11), *pratêrion* (Diod. Sic. 15.7), *pratêros lithos* (Pollux 3.78).
90. Lapalus 1939; Cocco 1970; Bruneau 1975; Coarelli 1982.
91. Le Roy 1993, 204ff.
92. Le Roy 1993, 208; Rauh 1992.
93. Coarelli 1982, 134ff.
94. Musti 1980, 197ff.
95. Lucilius in Warmington 1938, vol. 3, 38.
96. Volkmann 1961, 166.
97. Ziebarth 1929, 42-3.
98. Ormerod 1924, 248-60.
99. Starr 1960, 172-3.
100. Ormerod 1924, 90-1, 259; Starr 1960, 194-6.
101. Starr 1960, 197-8.
102. Ormerod 1924, 257-9.
103. Finley 1962, 56.
104. Bang 1910; 1912.
105. Bang 1912, 220; Barrow 1928, 15-16.
106. Gordon 1924, 109-11.
107. Frank 1916; Barrow 1928, 211-12.
108. Westermann 1955, 96-7.
109. Mainz: Büsing 1982, Taf. 21, 39.3. Nickenich: Andrikopolou-Strack 1986, 179.
110. Cichorius 1896-1900, Taf. XXXI and XXXIII.
111. Brilliant 1967, pls 54A and 55A.
112. Finley 1968a, 231; Harris 1980.
113. Thyateira: a dedication of imperial date by workers and agents in the slave-market to their benefactor, a slave-dealer, *sômatemporos* (*OGIS* 524). Ephesus: an inscription of AD 42-3 was set up by the slave-traders there, *qui in statario negotiantur*, to a Roman patron (Keil 1923, nos 25-6). Magnesia-on-Meander: Kern 1900, no. 240. Acmonia: *MAMA* vi, 260. Sardis: *REG* 90, 1977, no. 422.
114. Bang 1910, 232-3.
115. Harris 1980, 128.
116. *OGIS* 262.
117. Oates 1969.

118. Roger 1945; Finley 1968b; Kolendo 1978; Duchêne 1986.
119. Harris 1980, 126.
120. Puteoli: for the imperial period Harris 1980, 138 n. 92. Pompeii: Harris 1980, 126 and 138, n. 93.
121. Naples Museum – Inv. 9067.
122. Étienne 1966, 223.
123. *Pitture e Mosaici* 1991, iii, 255 and pl. 121.
124. Meiggs 1973.
125. Lapalus 1939, 95.
126. Harris 1980, 129-32.
127. Wallon 1879, 46-66; Westermann 1955, 98-100.
128. Wallon 1879, 57.
129. Westermann 1955, 12.
130. Harris 1980, 126, 131.

2. Slaves in Greek Agriculture

1. White 1970, ch. 1.
2. *RE s.v.* Landwirtschaft, 639-43.
3. French 1964, ch. 1.
4. Piggott 1965, 121 and fig. 64.
5. Heitland 1921, 22-4; Hasebroek 1931, 33-9.
6. Hasebroek 1931, 141.
7. *RE* s.v. Landwirtschaft, 634.
8. Hasebroek 1931, 58-72.
9. Cambitoglou *et al.* 1971, 1988.
10. Cambitoglou 1981.
11. Cambitoglou 1981, 34-5 and figs 4, 5, 8-10.
12. Boardman 1967.
13. Boardman 1967, 34-40.
14. Boardman 1967, 252-3.
15. Boardman 1967, 253; Finley 1973b, 131.
16. Heitland 1921, 25; Hasebroek 1931, 230ff., 272, 284ff.; Westermann 1955, 3.
17. Hopper 1979, 149-50.
18. Isager and Hausen 1975, 19.
19. Isager and Hausen 1975, 20-9; Hopper 1979, 71-92.
20. Hopper 1979, 151.
21. Jameson 1977-8.
22. Pečírka 1973; Hopper 1979, 152.
23. Hopper 1979, 154-5.
24. Heitland 1921, 28-112.
25. Jones, A.H.M., 1968, 3.
26. Wycherley 1962, ch. VII; Robertson 1964, ch. XVII; Lawrence 1984, ch. 21.
27. Robinson and Graham 1938; Robinson 1946.
28. Robertson 1964, 297; Lawrence 1984, 240.
29. A point made in Jameson 1991, 191-2.
30. Wycherley 1962, 221 n. 12.
31. Robinson and Graham 1938, 217.
32. Pečírka 1973; Jones, J.E., 1975.
33. Jones, J.E., 1973.
34. Young 1956.

35. Young 1956, 143.

36. Young 1956, 134, 144-6.

37. Young 1956, 138.

38. Pečírka 1973, 121.

39. Pečírka and Dufková 1970.

40. Pečírka 1973, 123.

41. Pečírka 1973, 142.

42. Pečírka 1973, 145-6.

43. Boeotia: Bintliff 1985; Megalopolis: Lloyd 1985; Argolid: van Andel 1986 and 1987 – the second paper notes considerable expansion in the Classical period (317-18 and figs 9, 10).

44. Keller and Rupp 1983.

45. Lambrinoudakis 1984.

46. Heitland 1921, 59-60, quoting Xen., *Mem.* 2.8.

47. Heitland 1921, 118.

48. Heitland 1921, 119-22.

49. Heitland 1921, 122-30.

50. Heitland 1921, 123; Westermann 1955, 31-6.

51. Westermann 1955, 37.

52. Wiegand and Schrader 1904, ch. X.

53. For example, Robertson 1964, 298-9.

54. Wiegand and Schrader 1904, 285-97, Abb. 298-316.

55. Robertson 1964, figs 124-5.

56. Kent 1948.

57. Kent 1948, 280.

58. Pečírka 1973, 140.

59. Kent 1948, 291-2, 299-300.

60. Kent 1948, 295-300.

61. Pečírka 1973, 139 n. 2; Robinson 1946, 453-71.

62. Kent 1948, 251, fig. 4.

63. Kent 1948, 252.

64. Bruneau and Ducat 1983, 249-50 (date), plan VI opp. 247 (Theatre Quarter), and plan II opp. 161 (Lake Quarter).

65. Chamonard 1922, 127-34 and pls III-IV (La Maison du Dionysos), 417-23 and pls XIX-XXII (La Maison du Lac).

66. *BCH* 19 (1895), 474; 51 (1927), 234-8; the Carian Antioch is said to have been founded by Antiochus II in 281-260 BC, which provides a useful *terminus post quem* for the Delian graffito.

67. Chamonard 1922, 432-5 and pl. XXVIII.

68. Chamonard 1922, 136-9 and pls XIV-XVIII.

69. Chamonard 1922, 139-52 and pls III-IV.

70. Bruneau and Ducat 1983, 52.

3. Slaves in Roman Agriculture: the Republic

1. Dunbabin 1948, 212.

2. Dunbabin 1948, 212.

3. Finley 1979, 4-5; Dunbabin 1948, ch. VII.

4. Barker 1981, 23-30.

5. Martin 1973, 99.

6. Schmiedt and Chevallier 1959; Adamesteanu 1965.

7. Adamesteanu 1973.

8. *Kokalos* 3 (1957), 18-30; 14/15 (1968-7), 397-420.

9. Vallet 1984-5.

10. *Kokalos, NotScav, Atti* of successive Congressi Internazionali di Studi sulla Sicilia Antica and of Convegni di Studi sulla Magna Grecia.

11. Vallet *et al.* 1976.

12. Vallet *et al.* 1976, 301-3, 401-28.

13. Adriani *et al.* 1970; Allegro *et al.* 1976.

14. Belvedere in Allegro *et al.* 1976.

15. De Miro 1980.

16. Martin and Vallet 1980.

17. Reports in *AJA* 61 (1957) to 92 (1988).

18. Pelagatti 1980-1, pls CLXIII, CLXVII.

19. Gsell 1929, 2-3.

20. Gsell 1929, 3-8; White 1970, 17-18.

21. *RE, s.v.* Landwirtschaft, col. 643.

22. Gsell 1929, ch. III.

23. Fantar 1970, 397-8.

24. White 1970, 17.

25. Gsell 1929, 46-7.

26. cf. Gsell 1929, ii, 226-7, 299-300; iv, 134-6, 173-4.

27. Westermann 1955, 58, nn. 11-13.

28. Crawford 1986, 388-9, map 8.

29. Westermann 1955, 58 the background is discussed in Frankfort 1959.

30. McKay 1975, ch. I; Graham 1966, 6-9; Boethius and Ward-Perkins 1970, 64-75.

31. Mansuelli 1963, figs 1-6, 8.

32. Mansuelli 1963, 56-61; Graham 1966, 8.

33. Boëthius and Ward-Perkins 1970, 64.

34. Ward-Perkins 1964, 14.

35. Scullard 1967, ch. VII.

36. Scullard 1967, ch. VI.

37. Scullard 1967, chs IV and V.

38. Boëthius 1962, 299; Boëthius and Ward-Perkins 1970, 65.

39. Heitland 1921, 135-8.

40. Heitland 1921, 135-42.

41. Jones, G.D.B., 1962; 1963, 127ff.

42. Potter 1979, 94ff.

43. Potter 1979, 16, tab. 1.

44. *Ager Cosanus*: Dyson 1978; Biferno valley: Barker *et al.* 1978; San Vicenzo, San Giovanni, Metaponto / Croton: Macready and Thompson 1985a; Venosa / Gravina: Vinson 1972.

45. Frederiksen 1984.

46. White 1967, 63.

47. *CAH* VIII (1989), 236.

48. Sicily: Finley 1979; southern Etruria: Potter 1979, 125.

49. For example, Jones, A.H.M., 1968, 8.

50. For the capture and sale of prisoners in the third century and later see Westermann 1955, 60ff.

51. Westermann 1955, 64-5; Heitland 1921, 162.

52. Gummerus 1906, 54-5.

53. Heitland 1921, 178-87; White 1970, 24 – 'a strangely neglected master'; Spurr 1986, xi n. 6.

54. Barker *et al.* 1978.

55. Greenidge and Clay 1986, 3.

56. Rossiter 1978, ch. IV.

57. Rostovtzeff 1957, ii, 564 n. 23; Crova 1942, ch. 5.

58. Ruggiero 1881.

59. Rostovtzeff 1941, 496-7 n. 26; Rostovtzeff 1957, ii, 551-3 n. 26 and 564-5 n. 23.

60. *CTP*, nos 37-64; Kockel 1985, 534 and Abb. 23.

61. Kockel 1985, 570-1.

62. Kockel 1985, 542-3, Abb. 23, no. 96, and 28-9; de Caro 1987.

63. Carrington 1931; Day 1932; White 1970, 434-9.

64. cf. Carrington 1931, 125-9; White 1970, 442-5.

65. Rossiter 1978, 2, 66, map 1.

66. Graham 1966, 10.

67. Carandini 1988, 370, fig. 2.

68. Normal complement: Shatzman 1975, 481-2.

69. *NotScav* 19 (1922), 459-78.

70. Rostovtzeff 1957, 580 n. 23: 'probably many more'.

71. Webster 1985, 197-9.

72. Rossiter 1978, 48 n. 8.

73. For a detailed description of the stocks, see Chapter 7.

74. *NotScav* 20 (1923), 275-80.

75. Rostovtzeff 1957, 580; Crova 1942.

76. cf. Rostovtzeff 1957, 580, n. 23.

77. White 1970, 437-8: he suggests a workforce of 30 slaves.

78. *NotScav* 18 (1921), 442-60 and plan, fig. 12; Carrington 1931, 119.

79. Villas 2 and 5 at Castellammare di Stabia: Ruggiero 1881; Day 1932, 200, tab. A; Villa 27 at Boscoreale: *NotScav* 18 (1921), 426-35.

80. Villa 27, Courtyard B: *NotScav* 18 (1921), 427-8 and plan, fig. 7.

81. Boëthius *et al.* 1962, 313-20.

82. Boëthius *et al.* 1962, figs 285-9.

83. Cotton 1979, 67.

84. Cotton and Metraux 1985, 81-2.

85. Widrig 1980, 122 and fig. 4.

86. Potter 1980.

87. Lugli 1926; Giuliani 1966, 74, no. 70, fig. 73.

88. Lugli 1926, 513-14, fig. 20.

89. As does Rossiter 1978, 45.

90. Horace himself employed eight slaves on the home farm: *Satires* 2.7.118.

91. cf. Heitland 1921, 215-17.

4. Slaves in Roman Agriculture: the Empire

1. cf. Heitland 1921, 213-50.

2. Gummerus 1906, 92; Heitland 1921, 250-69; White 1970, 401-5 and ch. XIII; Spurr 1986, particularly the number of citations of the three agronomists in his Index of Sources, 158-9.

3. Their numbering (1-12) follows that given in Rostovtzeff 1957, ii, 551 n. 26, extended in Day 1932, 202-3, tab. C.

4. Carrington 1931, 111 n. l.

5. Day 1932, 200, tab. A; Ruggiero 1881.

6. Villa 2: Ruggiero 1881, xix-xx, 326, and tav. X,10: '… che potrebbero chiamarsi ergastola'; Villa 5: Ruggiero 1881, xxi, 333-9 and tav. XII.

7. Kockel 1985, 529-31, and Abb. 11, 18 (statue of shepherd) and 23, no. 100.

8. Ruggiero 1881, tavv. III, VII – the scale is in Neapolitan palms, one palm being equivalent to 26.4 cm (10 $\frac{3}{8}$ in).

9. Ruggiero 1881, xxi.

10. Kockel 1985, 542-3 and Abb. 28, 29; de Caro 1987.

11. Kockel 1985, 343.

12. *MA* 7 (1897), 398ff., esp. 489-96 and tav. XIVR; *MP* 5 (1899), 12-13, plan.

13. Carrington 1931, 119, 127; White 1970, 434-5.

14. *MP* 5 (1899), 30.

15. Carrington 1931, 122.

16. Excavation: *NotScav* 1921, 423-6; *cellae* described, 423; plan, 424, fig. 5. Rossiter 1978, 45.

17. *NotScav* 1910, 139ff.; 1922, 480ff.; Maiuri 1947.

18. Maiuri 1933, 186ff. and figs 87-98.

19. Day 1932, 197; Rostovtzeff 1957, 648 n. 94. Graffito: *NotScav* 1927, 98; Della Corte 1924.

20. Widrig 1980, 124 and fig. 6.

21. Potter 1979, figs 32, 35 and 38.

22. Rossiter 1978, 48 nn. 19 and 20; Manacorda 1982, 57, 65, 68.

23. Carandini 1985.

24. Carandini 1985, vol. i, 48-57 and figs 37, 39, 42.

25. Carandini 1985, vol. i, fig. 139.

26. Carandini 1985, vol. i, fig. 157.

27. Carandini 1985, vol. i, fig. 158.

28. Carandini 1985, vol. i, fig. 166.

29. Carandini 1985, vol. i, figs 167-8.

30. Carandini 1985, vol. i, fig. 246 – Lambaesis.

31. Dyson 1978, fig. 6.

32. Bruno and Scott 1993, 183-4.

33. Mansuelli 1957 and 1971.

34. Mansuelli 1962.

35. cf. Heitland 1921, 210-12, 296-300, 361-85.

36. Wilson 1983, 69-72.

37. Rostovtzeff 1957; Frank 1933-40; *CAH* in the latest revised volumes.

38. Percival 1988.

39. Britain: Rivet 1969a; Pannonia: Thomas 1964; Spain; Fernandez Castro 1982.

40. Percival 1988, 52.

41. Rostovtzeff 1957, 312 and pl. LVIII, 1.

42. Wilson 1966, 24-6, 40.

43. Rostovtzeff 1957, 93.

44. Percival 1988, 60-1.

45. Rostovtzeff 1957, 213; his suggestion that the personification of Spain on a first-century Ostia mosaic (533 n. 27) shows her as a corn-producing province with Sicily, Africa and Egypt is not supported by Meiggs (1973, 448) who states that the female head is bound with a wreath of olive.

46. Menéndez Pidal 1982, 319-28 (Republic); 382-94 (Upper Empire), and 566-9 (Lower Empire); 549-64 (villas of the later Empire).

47. Menéndez Pidal 1982, 34-9.

48. Keay 1988, 76.

49. Gorges 1979, 11-17.

50. Gorges 1979, study: 23-57; period maps: figs 4-8.

51. Gorges 1979, 147-8.

52. Gorges 1979, 323-4.

53. Gorges 1979, pl. L.

54. Gorges 1979, pl. LI, 6.

55. Gorges 1979, 150.

56. Frias 1954-5, 192 and fig. 65 – not mentioned by Gorges.

57. Gorges 1979, 322 and pl. LXV, 2.

58. de Alarcão 1988, 62-72.

59. Milren: de Alarcão 1988, 67 and fig. 32; Torre de Palma: de Alarcão 1988, 67 and fig. 136.

60. de Alarcão 1988, 68.

61. de Alarcão 1988, 71-2.

62. Gorges 1979, 147-8 (Liedena villa), 472 (Monte de Meio, Beja).

63. Gorges 1979, 479; *ergastulum* – pl. LXId.

64. Gorges 1979, 453-4.

65. Gorges 1979, 148, 407-8, pl. LVI; *ergastulum*: pl. LVI, A, room 4.

66. *Informacion Arqueologica* no. 3, Sept.-Dec. 1970, 84.

67. Keay 1988, 68.

68. Wilson, A.J.N., 1966, 42-54.

69. Rostovtzeff 1957, 331-2.

70. Kehoe 1988, 7-12

71. Picard 1990, 62-75.

72. Rostovtzeff 1957, 313, pl. LIX, 329, pl. LXIII, l; Dunbabin, K., 1978.

73. Rostovtzeff 1957, 315; Westermann 1955, 58.

74. Rostovtzeff 1957, pl. LXIII, 1.

75. Picard 1990, 131-6, 150-1; Kehoe 1988, 24-7, 77-8; Gsell 1932, 414-21.

76. Duncan-Jones 1963, 88.

77. Inscriptions from the Bagradas valley: Kehoe 1988, 17; archaeological evidence from the *fundus Aufidianus*: Peyras 1975, 190-6.

78. Leveau 1975, 860.

79. Ponsich 1964, 242, fig. 3.

80. Oates, D., 1953, 97-8, fig. 7.

81. Picard 1990, 25-39, 49-53.

82. cf. Peyras 1983 and Foucher 1964, 120-3 and fig. 15 for centuriation in the territory of Hadrumetum (Sousse).

83. Leveau 1984, 200-1.

84. Gauckler 1896, 197.

85. Picard 1990, 162; Aurigemma 1926, figs 10, 11.

86. Picard 1990, 163.

87. Berthier 1967.

88. Lézine 1968, 150; Picard 1990, 164-5.

89. Picard 1990, 164.

90. Picard 1990, 164, 185.

91. Thouvenot 1958, 21.

92. Étienne 1960, 156-60.

93. Lancel and Bouchenaki 1971, 31-4 and plan, 32.
94. Ballu 1903.
95. Ballu 1903, 81-9, pl. XXI.
96. Lézine 1968.
97. Boëthius and Ward-Perkins 1970, 462-9.
98. Beschaouch *et al.* 1977, 34-6.
99. Blanchard-Lemée 1975, 208.
100. Finley 1973b, 191 n. 18.
101. Finley 1985, 179, under a heading 'Further thoughts (1984)'.
102. Drinkwater 1983, ch. 8.
103. Wightman 1970, 157; 1975, 592f.; 1985, 129 – '... unlikely that slaves formed a major part of the work force'.
104. King 1990, 95, 97.
105. MacMullen 1987, especially conclusion 375-7; Samson 1989, especially 100.
106. Samson 1989, 102-5.
107. Samson 1989, 110.
108. West 1935, 158.
109. Wightman 1975, 645-53.
110. Samson 1989, 101.
111. Belova 1987, 105-15.
112. Belova 1987, 115.
113. cf. Grenier 1934, 935-7.
114. Heitland 1921, 480.
115. Percival 1988, 68.
116. Rivet 1988; Ferdière 1988, 184-5; King 1990, 92 n. 20.
117. Joulin 1901; Grenier 1934, 832-7 (main villa), 850-8 (ancillary buildings).
118. Grenier 1934, 857-8; Joulin 1901, 186-8, preferred to think of the villa as one of the residences of successive governors of Narbonensis.
119. Joulin 1901, 143.
120. Joulin 1901, 45, 145; Grenier 1934, 853.
121. Joulin 1901, 157.
122. Joulin 1901, 162-89.
123. Fouet 1969.
124. Fouet 1969, ch. XI.
125. Percival 1988, 67-87.
126. Percival 1988, fig. 17.
127. Grenier 1934, ch. XX.
128. Grenier 1934, ch. XXI.
129. Wightman 1970, 1975, 1985; Drinkwater 1983; Percival 1988.
130. Grenier 1906, 72 (Sorbey; *ergastulum*); 125, plan 6 and 133-4 (Rouhling, '... salles communes pour le travail de nombreux esclaves'); 151(St Ulrich).
131. Wightman 1985, 129.
132. Wightman 1985, 105-14.
133. Wightman 1985, 254-5.
134. Grenier 1934, 869.
135. Agache 1975, 1978.
136. Agache 1978, chs V and VI.
137. Agache 1978, 346-66.
138. Agache 1978, 361 n. 53.
139. del Marmol 1877, 1881; Grenier 1934, 843-9 and fig. 311.

140. Hosté: Grenier 1934, fig. 295; Haccourt: *Arch. Belgica* 132 (1971), 15-32; Athies, Warfusée-sud and Estrées-sur-Noye: Agache 1978, *passim*.

141. Wightman 1985, 114.

142. Holmgren and Leday 1981, 111 and fig. 6.

143. Belova 1987, 105-15.

144. Wightman 1985, 129.

145. Samson 1989, 102-5.

146. Audin and Armand-Calliat 1962.

147. Halbout 1987.

148. Thompson, F.H., 1994.

149. Greek colonization: Rivet 1988, 9-17 and fig. 3; Agatha (Agde): Rivet 1988, 150 and n. 11.

150. Rivet 1988, 79-80.

151. Grenier 1934, 690-1.

152. Wightman 1985, 104.

153. Percival 1988, fig. 26; Rivet 1969b, fig. 5.6; Jones and Mattingly 1990, 240 and map 7.6.

154. Piggott 1958.

155. Frere 1987, ch. 13.

156. Percival 1988, ch. 6.

157. Richmond 1969; Collingwood and Richmond 1969, ch. VII.

158. Neal 1989.

159. Stevens 1966; Rivet 1969b; Percival 1988, ch. 6.

160. Park Street: Rivet 1964, 44; Frere 1987, 259; Hambleden: Frere 1987, 259; Llantwit Major: Frere 1987, 259, 273 n. 3.

161. Frere 1987, 262.

162. Štaerman 1987.

163. Collingwood and Wright 1965, nos 902 and 1436.

164. Goodburn and Waugh 1983, 93.

165. Collingwood and Wright 1965, no. 179; Noeske 1977, 288-9.

166. Frere 1987, 262; Rivet 1964, 159.

167. Frere 1987, 257.

168. Stead 1967; Stead 1976; Fitzpatrick 1985.

169. Wightman 1985, 243-50.

170. Oelmann 1928; Grenier 1934, 784-95.

171. Medieval hall: Oelmann 1928, 121-2; kinship group: Percival 1988, 134-6; King 1990, 153-4.

172. Fremersdorf 1933; Grenier 1934, 814-19.

173. Percival 1988, 84-6.

174. Reinecke 1916; Wagner 1928, 72-3 and Abb. 15.

175. Drack and Fellmann 1988, 133-7, Abb. 91.

176. Oberentfelden: Drack and Fellmann 1988, 457-9 and Abb. 418; Winkel: Drack and Fellmann 1988, 550-5 and Abb. 92, 511-15.

177. Rostovtzeff 1957, 233.

178. Alföldy 1974, 130, fig. 18.

179. Alföldy 1974, 120-1.

180. Alföldy 1974, 173-5.

181. Alföldy 1974, figs 14-16 and 30.

182. Alföldy 1974, 117ff.

183. Alföldy 1974, 43.

184. Thompson, F.H., 1994.

185. Kolosovskaja 1987; Alföldy 1974, 127-32, though the two differ on the role of slaves in agriculture.

186. Alföldy 1974, 129.

187. Alföldy 1974, fig. 18.

188. Wilkes 1969, 399-405.

189. Wilkes 1969, figs 23, 24, but on 403 slave-owning is suggested.

190. Wilkes 1969, figs 8 and 22: Dracevica; 399 and fig. 22: simple villas.

191. Thomas, E.B., 1964, 336.

192. Percival 1988, 89; Smarje: Thomas, E.B., 1964, 349.

193. Mócsy 1974, 169.

194. Thomas, E.B., 1964, Abb. 29, 40.

195. Mócsy 1974, 73, 77.

196. Mócsy 1974, 241.

197. Örvényes: Thomas, E.B., 1964, 108; Winden am See: Thomas, E.B., 1964, 209, 364, Abb. 108.

198. Thomas, E.B., 1964, 383-6.

199. Percival 1988, 90.

200. Mócsy 1974, 169ff.

201. Mócsy 1974, 300ff., fig. 50.

202. Mócsy 1974, 305.

203. Rostovtzeff 1957, 251ff.

204. Prisovo: Hoddinott 1975, 153-4 and fig. 28; Chatalka: Hoddinott 1975, 209-12, figs 46, 47.

205. Hoddinott 1975, 217-20 and fig. 51.

206. Poulter 1983, 86.

207. Poulter 1983, 89, fig. 3.

5. Slavery in Quarries and Mines

1. Dworakowska 1975, 94.

2. Wycherley 1974 and 1978; Osborne 1985, 93-110; 1987, 81-7.

3. Osborne 1987, 88.

4. Osborne 1987, 84.

5. cf. Osborne 1985, 102-3.

6. Osborne 1985.

7. Skill and specialization: Burford 1969, 168; stone brought from distance: Burford 1965, 24.

8. Osborne 1985, 108-10

9. Burford 1960, 18 n. 2.

10. Burford 1965, 30.

11. Dworakowska 1975, 96; Osborne 1985, 186.

12. *CAH* iv (1988, 2nd edn), 776-7 and pl. 266.

13. As has been pointed out to me by Dr Roger Wilson, cf. Bell 1980, who suggests Ionic inspiration for the figures and argues for Pythagorean influence rather than victory at Himera.

14. Osborne 1985, 109 and n. 58, citing the case of the *metic* Manes (*IG* II^2, 1673.37) from the Eleusis accounts.

15. Westermann 1955, 12-13; Randall 1953.

16. Randall 1953, 203, 206.

17. Osborne 1985, 105 and n. 41.

18. Behn 1926, 23.

19. Conner 1985, pl. XXVII.

20. Fitzler 1910, 67-73.

21. *RE* iii (1929), 2275-7, *s.v.* Steinbruch.

22. cf. Boëthius and Ward-Perkins 1970, 115-16.

23. Dworakowska 1975, 23.

24. Ward-Perkins 1971, 144-5; 1980, 25.

25. Dworakowska 1975, 69-70.

26. Dworakowska 1975, 10-26.

27. Chester: Thompson, F.H., 1965, 52-3; Hadrian's Wall: Daniels 1978, 42-3.

28. Daniels 1978, 39.

29. cf. *RE s.v.* Steinbruch, 2278-85.

30. *RE s.v.* Steinbruch, 2287-8, and for Egypt: Fitzler 1910, 135-8 and 148-9.

31. *RE s.v.* Steinbruch, 2281-3.

32. *TIR* N.G. 36, *Coptos*, 1958.

33. Meredith 1952, 1953a, 1953b, 1954, 1955.

34. Kraus and Röder 1962; Kraus, Röder and Müller-Wiener 1967.

35. Bingen 1987; Bülow-Jacobsen 1992.

36. Kraus, Röder and Müller-Wiener 1967, 118-19.

37. Peacock 1994, 229.

38. Kraus, Röder and Müller-Wiener 1967, 155-6.

39. Klein 1988, 40-55.

40. Horn 1980, 173-80 and Abb. 115.

41. Bedon 1984, 147-93, esp. 153.

42. Bedon 1984, 152 n. 31; Sapène 1946, 301, inscr. 15.

43. Behn 1926, 33-64.

44. Dworakowska 1983, 174 for bibliography of Röder's publications.

45. Röder 1957, 254.

46. Saint-Leu-d'Esserent: Bedon 1984, 153; Duroin 1971, 6-8; Boulouris: Bedon 1984, 157, citing Léger 1875, 705.

47. Dubois 1908, xxxiv-vii.

48. *CIL* XI, 1356.

49. Johnson 1953, 106ff.

50. Wattenbach 1870, 321; de Rossi 1879, 45ff.; Dubois 1908, xxxvi; Delehaye 1910, 748-65.

51. Delehaye 1910, 748.

52. Mons Porphyrites: Delbrueck 1932, 2; Pannonia: Simonyi 1960; Mócsy 1974, 326.

53. Kraus, Röder and Müller-Wiener 1967, 193-6 and Abb. 23.

54. Delbrueck 1932, 2.

55. Millar 1984.

56. Ardaillon 1897 and Conophagos 1980 represent the two extremes chronologically.

57. Lauffer 1979, 123ff.

58. Lauffer 1979, 140ff. and tab. 8.

59. Conophagos 1980, 341-9.

60. Lauffer 1979, 160ff. and tab. 10, 11.

61. Lauffer 1979, 61-2.

62. Mussche 1986, 38-40; Jones, J.E., 1975.

63. Conophagos 1980, 375-89.

64. Jones, J.E., 1985.

65. Wilsdorf 1952, 139, Taf. 4 and Abb. 37, 38.

66. Lauffer 1979, 52-6 and 269-70.
67. Mussche 1986.
68. *RE s.v.* Bergbau, 127-32; Cordella 1869, 87-115; Ardaillon 1897, 21ff.; Wilsdorf 1952, 198-220, with ills; Lauffer 1979, 20ff.; Conophagos 1980, 168ff. and ills 9.8-11.
69. Lauffer 1979, 61.
70. Survey: des Courtils *et al.* 1982; implements: Wilsdorf 1952, 211ff. and Abb. 39-41.
71. Savvopoulou 1984; Faklaris 1991.
72. Cary 1932, 139.
73. *RE s.v.* Bergbau, 116-17.
74. Cary 1932, 139-42.
75. Casson 1926, 57-71 and map III on 61; Davies 1935, 232-7.
76. Conophagos 1980, 85-6.
77. Conophagos 1980, 84.
78. Lauffer 1979, 123-40 and tab. 6.
79. Young 1956.
80. Rostovtzeff 1941, 1172; Davies 1935, 240-3.
81. Cary 1932, 35-6
82. *RE s.v.* Bergbau, 113; Rostovtzeff 1941, 1173-6.
83. Cary 1932, 141-2.
84. Hanfmann and Mierse 1983, 34-41, plan 1, figs 45-7, 55ff., 139.
85. Hanfmann and Mierse 1983, 84-6.
86. Rostovtzeff 1941, 806 and 1521 n. 76.
87. Fitzler 1910, 86; Rostovtzeff 1941, 317.
88. Rostovtzeff 1941, 382; Meredith 1958, 13 for the difficulty of distinguishing periods of activity.
89. Orth in *RE s.v.* Bergbau, 119; central Italy: Davies 1935, 72.
90. Davies 1935, ch. 11.
91. Cary 1932, 141-2.
92. Conophagos 1980, 122-3.
93. *RE s.v.* Bergbau, 141-55; Täckholm 1937, 89-156; Wilsdorf 1952, 179-89; regional studies: Fitzler 1910, 67-73, 135-8; Domergue 1990, 225-386.
94. Täckholm 1937, 122-3.
95. Millar 1984, 139.
96. *RE s.v.* Bergbau, 120-2; Davies 1935, ch. IV and maps IIIa-c.
97. Wilson 1966, 24-6, 40.
98. Richardson 1976.
99. Wilsdorf 1952, 183-4.
100. Richardson 1976, 144-7.
101. Domergue 1990.
102. Blanco and Luzon 1969.
103. Domergue 1990, 39ff.
104. Domergue 1990, 336.
105. Healy 1978, ch. IV.
106. Domergue 1990, 358-9.
107. Domergue 1990, 185.
108. Diogines and Cerro del Plomo: Domergue 1967 and 1971; La Loba: Domergue 1990, 360 and pl. IIIb.
109. Domergue 1990, 187.
110. Domergue 1990, 361, pl. XIIa.

111. Domergue and Hérail 1978, 251.
112. Domergue and Sillieres 1977, 88 and figs 6, opp. 32, and 19.
113. Domergue and Martin 1977, 12 and 19.
114. Domergue 1990, 346-8.
115. Domergue 1990, 206-7; Jones, G.D.B., 1980, 156-7.
116. Domergue 1990, fig. 17a; Jones, G.D.B., 1980, fig. 2.
117. Dehesa: Jones, G.D.B., 1980, 154 and fig. 5; Corta Lago: Jones, G.D.B., 1980, 156-8 and fig. 4.
118. Domergue 1990, 361.
119. Domergue 1990, 338-9 and tab. XVI.
120. Domergue 1990, 362.
121. Domergue 1990, 361-3.
122. da Veija Ferreira and de Andrada 1960, 4.
123. Domergue 1983, especially 187-8.
124. Domergue 1983, 128-31.
125. Domergue 1990, 364-5.
126. Sandars 1905.
127. Domergue 1990, 351-3 and pl. XXXII.
128. Gossé 1942; Domergue 1990, 408-11.
129. Gossé 1942, pl. V. 4, 5.
130. Gossé 1942, pl. V, 3; Domergue 1990, pl. XVIIIa.
131. Domergue 1990, pl. XVIIIc.
132. Domergue 1990, 461.
133. Domergue 1990, 410-11; Healy 1978, pl. 31.
134. Domergue 1990, 410.
135. Gossé 1942, 54
136. Treptow 1918, 155-91; Davies 1935, 32-3; Wilsdorf 1952, 213, Abb. 43; Healey 1978, 100ff., pls 29 a, b and 30.
137. Domergue 1990, 401-8.
138. Gossé 1942, pl. IV, 3; Domergue 1990, pl. XX.
139. Domergue 1990, 409-10.
140. Domergue 1990, 414-17, pl. XXa.
141. Domergue 1990, 429-32.
142. Domergue 1990, 433-60.
143. Domergue 1990, pl. XVIIa (esparto), pl. XVIIb (bronze).
144. Bienkowski 1987, Taf. 29; Domergue 1990, pl. XXI and figs 38-40, 42, 1-4.
145. Terracotta models: Healy 1978, pl. 25; Oleson 1984, figs 71, 86; wall-painting: Oleson 1984, fig. 101.
146. Domergue 1990, 459, pl. XXIIa, b.
147. Domergue 1990, 460.
148. Gossé 1942, pl. V, 6; Domergue 1990, pl. XVIIId.
149. Gossé 1942, pls I, II 1-3; Domergue 1990, fig. 34, B.
150. Domergue 1990, 354.
151. Davies 1935, 76f.
152. Domergue 1990.
153. Davies 1935, 76-93 and map II; 165-9 (area west of Rhine).
154. Toulouse: *Mines et fonderies antiques de la Gaule* (1982); Paris: *Les mines et la métallurgie en Gaule et dans les provinces voisines* (1987).
155. King 1990, 119-25.
156. Dubois and Guilbaut 1982, 116.

157. Jullian 1909 (vol. 2), 546; 1909 (vol. 3), 1; Colbert de Beaulieu and Richard 1969.

158. Nash 1975; Allen 1980, 18-19.

159. Tamain and Ratz 1982.

160. Barruol and Gourdiote 1982.

161. *CIL* XIII, 1550; Chantraine 1977.

162. *CIL* XI, 1356.

163. Galliou 1982.

164. Local basis: King 1990, 121-2; epigraphic evidence: 'conductor ferreari-arum' at Nimes, *CIL* XII, 4398; 'procurator ferrariarum' at Lyons, *CIL* XIII, 1797.

165. Mangin 1982.

166. Daubrée 1868 and 1881.

167. Daubrée 1881, 210.

168. Davies 1935, 81-2.

169. Davies 1935, 140-64; Jones and Mattingly 1990, 179-96.

170. Collingwood and Wright (2nd edn) 1995, 38-66 (no. 2404); Rivet and Smith 1979, 279, 331, 403-4, 487.

171. Frere 1987, 278.

172. Haverfield 1905, 227-33; Davies 1935, 148-50, 158-9, 161.

173. Lewis and Jones 1966; Boon and Williams 1966.

174. Nash-Williams 1954, 40 and 108; Jarrett 1969.

175. Frere 1987, 276.

176. Fulford and Allen 1992.

177. Davies 1935, 198-208.

178. Pirustae: Noeske 1977, Abb. 2; eastern provinces of Asia Minor: Abb. 3.

179. Noeske 1977, 345.

180. Mrozek 1964; contrast Tudor 1957.

181. Millar 1984, 141-2.

182. Davies 1935, chs I and VIII *passim*.

183. Oleson 1984, 276-9 and figs 154-7.

184. Noeske 1977, 286-95.

185. Wilkes 1969, 377-8 and fig. 19.

186. Davies 1935, 182-97, and map VI.

187. Wilkes 1969, 267-8.

188. Davies 1935, 186-9; Wilkes 1969, 272; slave secretary: *CIL* III, 1997.

189. Davies 1935, 189-95, Wilkes 1969, 277ff. and fig. 11.

190. Radimský 1893.

191. Wilkes 1969, 377f. and fig. 19.

192. Radimský 1893, 248-9 and fig. 64.

193. Pašalić 1954.

194. Wilkes 1969, 280.

195. Patsch 1909, 157-9.

196. Alföldy 1974, 113-17.

197. Alföldy 1974, fig. 11.

198. Alföldy 1974, 44ff.

199. Alföldy 1974, 70ff. and fig. 2.

200. Alföldy 1974, 45 and 297 n. 37.

201. Alföldy 1974, 109 and 316 n. 22; 127 and 129.

202. Alföldy 1974, 131.

203. Mines: Alföldy 1974, 175; agriculture: Alföldy 1974, 190ff.

204. Davies 1935, 173-4.

205. Rostovtzeff 1957, 340.
206. Rostovtzeff 1902, 411-15.
207. *RE s.v.* Salz, 2075-99.
208. Millar 1984, 140.
209. Meiggs 1973, 16-20.
210. *CIL* XIV, 4338.
211. Ashby 1927, 59ff.
212. Meiggs 1973, left bank of Tiber: pl. I, F; right bank: pl. I, E; Via Ostiensis: 479ff.
213. Meiggs 1973, 268.
214. Cunliffe 1991, 465-8; de Brisay and Evans 1975; Fawn *et al.* 1990.
215. West Midlands: Cunliffe 1991, 468; army (for Britain): Jones and Mattingly 1990, 224 ff.
216. Alföldy 1974, 113.
217. Kyrle 1913, figs 14-18 (galleries with shoring), figs 21, 22 (picks), fig. 24 (caps), fig. 26 (satchels), fig. 27 (shoes) and fig. 28 (shovels).
218. Hofman and Morton 1928.
219. Barth 1982, figs 1, 2 (sloping adits), fig. 5 (equipment).
220. Noll 1958, 40.
221. Barth 1982, 31-2.
222. Wightman 1985, 141.
223. Thoen 1975.
224. *CIL* XI, 390, 391.
225. Will 1962.

6. Slaves in Corn- and Weaving Mills and their Use in Lifting Devices

1. Will 1972, 648-60.
2. Guiraud 1900, 86ff.
3. Guiraud 1900, 52ff.
4. Guiraud 1900, 122-35.
5. Guiraud 1900, 54-6 (semi-industrial production), 61 (series of operations).
6. Guiraud 1900, 56-8.
7. Millar 1984, 137-43.
8. Moritz 1958, 34; Singer *et al.* 1956, 107-11 is compressed and not totally reliable.
9. Moritz 1958, chs VI-IX and figs 3-4.
10. Guiraud 1990, ch. VIII; Curwen 1937 and 1941; Childe 1943; Cunliffe 1991, 465 has only a brief paragraph on this key artefact.
11. Moritz 1958, ch. XI.
12. Moritz 1958, ch. XIV.
13. Peacock 1986.
14. Moritz 1958, pls 5b, 7a.
15. Moritz 1958, 100.
16. Moritz 1958, 82-3, 98.
17. Museo Laterano: Moritz 1958, pl. 8; kneading machine: Moritz 1958, 82; Mau and Kelsey 1899, 384 and fig. 214.
18. Millar 1984, 143-4.
19. In general, Millar 1981; in detail, Millar 1984, 129-30.
20. Moritz 1958, 94.

21. Moritz 1958, 74.
22. Meiggs 1973, 274.
23. Maiuri 1977, 55 and pl. XXX, fig. 52; 1958b, 456-61 and figs 409-15.
24. Meiggs 1973, 274.
25. Not 9950 sq. m, as Meiggs unfortunately states; Calza 1915.
26. Calza *et al.* 1954, 125.
27. Meiggs 1973, 280ff. and figs 22-4; fig. 24 in particular shows the key position of the large granary on Via dei Molini.
28. Mau 1908, 407, fig. 236; Carrington 1936, 107 and fig. 13.
29. Carrington 1936, figs 11b and 12.
30. Nash, E., 1962, 329-32 and figs 1096-102, with bibliography.
31. Population of Rome: van Berchem 1939, 104f.; Rickman 1980, 206f.; growth of public bakeries: Jones, A.H.M., 1964, 699.
32. Recruitment of African workers: *CTh* 14.3.17; convicts: *CTh* 9.40.3; Millar 1984, 144.
33. Charbonnel 1964.
34. *CTh* 14.3.7, 364.
35. Jones, A.H.M., 1964, 699.
36. Moritz 1958, ch. XVI.
37. Benoit 1940; Roos 1986.
38. Benoit 1940, 63-71.
39. Wikander 1979, 20, 23-4.
40. Rickman 1971, 11.
41. *CIL* VI, 30855; Rickman 1971, 178.
42. Rickman 1980, 204.
43. Behn 1911, 420; Ledroit 1930, 20.
44. Moritz 1958, ch. XII.
45. Moritz 1958, pl. 5a, in background.
46. Lindet 1899, 1900, 26 and fig. 14: *meta* and *catillus* from 'Phoenicia'; Lindet 1900, 29 and fig. 5: Paris, Amiens and Clermont-Ferrand.
47. *Comptes Rendus* 1908, 496-8; Espérandieu 1925, 190, no. 6903, correcting the inscription.
48. *AntiqJ* 9 (1939), 220.
49. Frere and Stow 1983, 183, no. 1 and fig. 72, 1.
50. Blümner 1912, 98-205.
51. Westermann 1955, 13; *IG* II^2, 1553-78; but Tod 1950, 20 points out that they were not necessarily only engaged in spinning.
52. Jones, A.H.M., 1974c, 352.
53. Jones, A.H.M., 1974c, 355.
54. Jones, A.H.M., 1974c, 356.
55. Jones, A.H.M., 1974c, 358-60.
56. Millar 1984, 144.
57. Millar 1984, 145.
58. Jones, A.H.M., 1974c, 361-3.
59. Wild 1970, 18-19.
60. Blümner 1912; Patterson 1956; Wild 1970.
61. Wild 1970, ch. III.
62. *CIL* IV, 1507.
63. Crowfoot 1936-7, pl. 6.
64. Wild 1970, 69-70, pl. XIa, b and figs 59-60.
65. Maiuri 1958a, 463, fig. 420.

66. Wightman 1985, 95, 150.

67. Maiuri 1960, 119-20.

68. Ward-Perkins and Claridge 1976, 52.

69. Maiuri 1960, 123-4.

70. Spinazzola 1953, 763.

71. Wild 1970, 23, 80.

72. Overbeck and Mau 1884, fig. 193; Mau 1908, fig. 230.

73. Overbeck and Mau 1884, figs 194-6.

74. Overbeck and Mau 1884, 395.

75. Spinazzola 1953, 763-85.

76. Spinazzola 1953, figs 744, 764, 766.

77. Wild 1970, 60.

78. Spinazzola 1953, 189-95, fig. 1 and tavv. II, LV, LXI.

79. Spinazzola 1953, tav. d'agg. 2.

80. Maiuri 1958b, 76.

81. Maiuri 1958a, 464, fig. 422.

82. Wild 1970, 81-4.

83. Espérandieu 1913, 2768.

84. Espérandieu 1913, 4125, 4136.

85. *CIL* XIII, 8345 and 6264.

86. *VCH Essex* iii, pl. IXA.

87. Wild 1970, 80-1, 85-6.

88. Dragendorff and Kruger 1924, Taf. 10, 1; 56, Abb. 33; Taf. 16, 3 and 17, 5.

89. Dragendorff and Kruger 1924, Abb. 31; Taf. 10, 1 and Abb. 47; Abb. 46; Abb. 32.

90. Espérandieu 1913, 4120.

91. Zahn 1976; Drinkwater 1977-8.

92. Kolling 1972.

93. Charbonnel 1964.

94. Millar 1984, 144-5.

95. Charbonnel 1964, 66.

96. Wild 1976, 51, 52.

97. Charbonnel 1964, 78.

98. Charbonnel 1964, 65.

99. Wild 1976, 51, 52.

100. Millar 1984, 144.

101. Foss 1976, 7-8, 15.

102. Manning 1966, 60-2.

103. Wild 1967, 648ff.; 1970, 9; 1982, 117, 119.

104. Taylor 1967, 304-6.

105. Wightman 1970, 117-19 and figs 11 and 12.

106. Giner 1984, 56-7, fig. 25 and pl. II, 2.

107. *CIL* II, Supp. 5812.

108. Giner 1984, pl. LXXVII.

109. Gille 1956.

110. Oleson 1984, chs 2-5.

111. Oleson 1984, figs 1-2.

112. Oleson 1984, figs 86, 101.

113. Oleson 1984, 178-9.

114. Oleson 1984, 221-3.

115. Oleson 1984, 396-7.

116. Singer *et al.* 1956, figs 578 and 603.
117. Brunn 1898, 84-7 and fig. 27.
118. Singer *et al.* 1956, fig. 578.
119. *CIL* X, 1, 1883, 3821.
120. Jahn 1861, Taf. IX, 2.

7. Means of Restraint

1. Wallon 1879, i, 314ff.
2. Wallon 1879, ii, 281ff.
3. *DS* IV, ii, 1260-80, s.v. *Servi. RE* Supplementband VI, 1935, *s.v. Sklaverei.*
4. *DS* IV, ii, 1278.
5. Pelekides 1916, 930ff.
6. Keramopoullos 1923.
7. Buckland 1908, 402; Barrow 1928, 2; Westermann 1955, 30, 59.
8. Crook 1967, 271ff.; Millar 1984.
9. *DS* I, ii, 1290.
10. Thompson, F.H., 1994; publication references appear in the catalogue there unless otherwise stated.
11. *ADelt* 29 (1973-4), *Chronika* B^2, 548-9; Savvopoulou 1984, fig. 7.
12. Savvopoulou 1984, figs 2-7; Faklaris 1991, fig. 1.
13. Pelekides 1916, 25 and 49-64; Keramopoullos 1923, 11ff.
14. Themelis 1982.
15. Venedikov 1963, 320, no. 1104 – a reference kindly brought to the writer's notice by Miss Joyce Reynolds.
16. Tirana NHM 1302; Eggebrecht 1988, 374, no. 286.
17. Pianu 1989, 98, tav. XIII, 2.
18. Curti 1989, 28.
19. Wilson, R.J.A., 1990, 220 and fig. 177.
20. Roger 1945; Finley 1968a; Kolendo 1978.
21. Finley 1962, 57; Kolendo 1978, 29.
22. Fox 1946, 37-9, figs 20-1; 64-5; 84-5; and pls X, XI, XXXVII.
23. Thompson, F.H., 1983, 274, figs 16, 18, pl. XXXVII.
24. Clarke 1821, 61 and pl. IV, 13.
25. Cancellieri 1855, 98-111 and tav. IV.
26. Henning 1992.
27. Thompson, F.H., 1994, 128-9.
28. Brilliant 1967, pls 52-9.
29. Herrmann and Brockmeyer 1969, 129, 139-41, and Abb. 9, 10.
30. Feugère 1992, 50, 53, nos 98-100.
31. Thompson, F.H., 1994, 107-8.
32. Thompson, F.H., 1994, 89-91.
33. One inscribed collar is known of iron – *CIL* XV, 7194; the word *bulla* appears in the inscription on one of the collars – *CIL* XV, 7173.
34. Pignorio 1613, 21.
35. *CIL* XV, 877-902, nos 7171-99.
36. Bellen 1971, 27-9.
37. Sotgiu 1973/4.
38. *CIL* XV, 7176 and 7194; Sotgiu 1973/4, 692 and nn. 9 and 17.
39. Inv. DUT 121; *CIL* XV, 7182.
40. Sotgiu 1973/4, 689, tav. CXII.

41. Aureus: *CIL* XV, 7191; bone and heart-shaped plate: *CIL* XV, 7197.

42. Ostia: *NotScav* 1916, 418f. and fig. 7; Velletri: *CIL* XV, 7172.

43. Dressel: *CIL* XV, 897; Sotgiu 1973/4, 694, n. 18.

44. Law of Constantine: *CTh* 9.40.2.

45. Sotgiu 1973/4, 695.

46. Sotgiu 1973/4, 691, nos 31, 33, 35.

47. Sotgiu 1973/4, 691, no. 31.

48. Sotgiu 1973/4, 691, no. 35.

49. *Revue Africaine* 87 (1943), 149-65.

50. Sotgiu 1973/4, 691, no. 33.

51. Cyprian, *Ep.* 77.3.

52. Clarke, G.W., 1989, 283 n. 10; Millar 1984, 128.

53. Jones, C.P., 1987, 146.

54. Jones, C.P., 1987.

55. Jones, C.P., 1987, 151-5.

56. *CTh* 9.40.2.

57. Jones, C.P., 1987, 140.

58. Jones, C.P., 1987, 148.

59. *DS* IV, ii, 1510, *s.v. stigma.*

60. Jones, C.P., 1987, 148-50.

61. The basic facts are summarized both by Thédenat in *DS* II, i (1892), 810-11, *s.v. ergastulum*, and also in *RE* VI.1 (1907), 431, again *s.v. ergastulum.*

62. Naples inscription: *CIL* X, 8173; *servus ergastularius*: Ammianus Marcellinus 14.11.33.

63. Étienne 1974, 264; Rossiter 1978, ch. IV.

64. Chalk: Johnston 1972, 123-4; Colchester: Hull 1958, 107-13, 118, pls XXIA and XXIB.

65. King 1990, 77-8.

66. *DS* II, i (1892), 810-11.

67. The upper parts of granaries rarely survive, cf. Rickman 1980, 50.

68. Étienne 1974, 250-2, for a discussion of the relationship between *ergastêrion, ergasterium* and *ergastulum.*

8. Flight and Revolt

1. Cicero, *Ad fam.* 13.77; Symmachus, *Letters* 9.140.

2. Aristotle, *Pol.* 2.9.1269a, 36-7; Xenophon, *HG* 2.3.36; de Sainte-Croix 1981, 147-62.

3. de Sainte-Croix 1981, 146.

4. Westermann 1955, 18; Herod. 6.83.

5. Polyaenus, *Strat.* 1.43.

6. Thucycides 7.27-8; Xenophon, *Hell.* 1.1.35.

7. *Hell. Oxyrh* 12.4-5.

8. Figure given by Thucydides: Lauffer 1979, 214ff.; accuracy of figure etc.: Lauffer 1979, 140ff.; cf. de Sainte-Croix 1981, 506, who thinks the word implies skilled workers in general.

9. Westermann 1955, 4, who also cites vine-growing as a Chian industry requiring slaves.

10. For a discussion of the episode, see Kotula 1966.

11. Fuks 1968.

12. Westermann 1955, 59.

13. Capozza 1966, 13.

14. Dumont 1977.

15. Bosworth 1968.

16. Dionysius Halicarnassensis 5.51.3; briefly, Zonaras 7.13.11.

17. Capozza 1966, 30-3.

18. Capozza 1966, 51-2.

19. Livy 4.45.1-2; Dionysius Halicarnassensis 12, fr. 6, 6.

20. Capozza 1966, 71-2 and 161-2.

21. cf. Capozza 1966, 75-7.

22. Capozza 1966, 79-86.

23. Capozza 1966, 95-100.

24. Westermann 1955, 63; Wiedemann 1981, 198.

25. Rome's power: Capozza 1966, 124; slaves in Etruria: Capozza 1966, 136-7.

26. Livy 39.29.8-9, 41.6-7.

27. Capozza 1966, 158.

28. Capozza 1966, 162-4.

29. Bradley 1989.

30. Toynbee 1965, 313-31; Finley 1979, 137-47.

31. Barrow 1928, ch. IX, with appendix ii on slavery in the West Indies; Ingram 1895, 281-5, and appendix vii on slavery as an industrial system, contrasting the conditions in the southern states of the USA with those in the north.

32. Bradley 1989, 41-4.

33. Bradley 1989, 133-9.

34. Wiedemann 1981, 199-200.

35. Bradley 1989, 170-83; second edition of the Mainz bibliography: Herrmann and Brockmeyer 1983, 149-53.

36. Rubinsohn 1987.

37. Cicero, *Verrine* 2.2.5.

38. Wilson, A.J.N., 1966, 56.

39. Wilson, A.J.N., 1966, 55-6, 59, 61.

40. Bradley 1989, 47-50; Wilson, R.J.A., 1990, 21.

41. Westermann 1945.

42. Cicero, *Verrine* 2.4.106.

43. Degrassi 1963-5, 1088.

44. Bradley 1989, 60-4.

45. Orosius 5.9.4.

46. Diodorus 34.2.26; rising not mentioned by Bradley.

47. Strabo 14.1.38.

48. Dumont 1966

49. Vavřínek 1975.

50. Rostovtzeff 1941, ii, 757 and n. 24, 807-11 and nn. 78-80 (Aristonicus); ii, 767-9 and n. 35 (Saumacus); ii, 757-8 (Andriscus).

51. Diodorus 36.2.1.

52. Diodorus 36.2.2-6.

53. Toynbee 1965, ii, 317 and n. 2.

54. Conophagos 1980, 122-3.

55. Lauffer 1979, 227ff.

56. Diodorus 11.89.6-8.

57. Diodorus 36.3.1-6.

58. *IG* XIV, 2407.

59. Florus 2.7.11.

60. *IG* XIV, 2407.

61. Manganaro 1982, tavv. 6-8.

62. Rubinsohn 1980.

63. Bradley 1989, ch. V; sources in appendix 1, 136-9; Herrmann and Brock-meyer 1983.

64. Mau 1908, 164-70.

65. Ville 1981, 297 and n. 165.

66. Ville 1981, 298-9; Mau 1908, 167-70.

67. Orosius 5.24.1.

68. Bradley 1989, 116ff.

69. Manganaro 1982, 237-40 and tav. 6, 1-3.

70. Finley 1979.

71. cf. Brunt 1974a, sec. vff.

72. Vogt 1975, 92.

73. Štaerman 1981.

74. Dio Cass. 54.11.2-5.

75. Tacitus, *Annals* 2.39-40; Dio Cass. 57.16.3-4.

76. Tacitus, *Ann.* 4.37.

77. Tacitus, *Ann.* 15.46.

78. Tacitus, *Hist.* 1.4; 1.32f.; 2.34f.; 3.64; 3.76; 3.77-9; 4.3.

79. Thompson, E.A., 1974, 306-11.

80. Thompson, E.A., 1974, 308-9; Herodian 1.10.

81. Thompson, E.A., 1974, 310; Dio Cass. 77.10.

82. Thompson, E.A., 1974, 310.

83. Jones, A.H.M., 1974b, 300: 'While tied *coloni* were thus reduced to a quasi-servile status, agricultural slaves were converted into serfs.'

84. Frend 1952, ch. I.

85. Jones, A.H.M., 1974a, 324ff.

Epilogue

1. *ILS* 9454; Wiedemann 1981, no. 221.

2. Cartledge and Bradley, 'slavery', in *OCD*.

3. Scheidel 1997; Harris 1999.

4. e.g. Fitzgerald 2000, but see Bradley 2001.

5. Harig 1971; Jackson 1993, 88-9.

6. Thompson 1994.

7. Bradley 2000.

8. Bowman and Thomas 1994.

Abbreviations and Bibliography

Abbreviations

AA = *Acta Antiqua* (Budapest)
AAA = *Archaiologika Analekta ex Athenon* (Athens)
AAn = *Archäologischer Anzeiger* (Berlin)
AAWM = *Abhandlungen der Akademie der Wissenschaft und der Literatur* (Wiesbaden)
ADelt = *Archaiologikon Deltion* (Athens)
AHR = *American Historical Review* (New York)
AJA = *American Journal of Archaeology* (New York)
Amp = *Ampurias* (Barcelona)
Ant = *Antiquity* (Cambridge)
AntAf = *Antiquités Africaines* (Paris)
ANRW = *Aufstieg und Niedergang der römischen Welt* (Berlin)
AntiqJ = *Antiquaries Journal* (London)
Arch = *Archaeologia* (London)
ArchBelg = *Archaeologia Belgica* (Brussels)
ArchC = *Archaeologia Classica* (Rome)
Arche = *Archeologia* (Warsaw)
ArchJ = *Archaeological Journal* (London)
ASAN = *Annales de la Société Archéologique de Namur* (Namur)
Ath = *Athenaeum. Studi Periodici di Letteratura e Storia dell'Antichità* (Pavia)
BAA = *Bulletin d'Archéologie Algérienne* (Paris)
BAC = *Bollettino di Archeologia Cristiana* (Rome)
BAM = *Bulletin d'Archéologie Marocaine* (Casablanca)
BAR = *British Archaeological Reports* (Oxford)
BEFAR = *Bibliothèque de l'École Française d'Athènes et Rome* (Rome)
BCH = *Bulletin de Correspondance Hellénique* (Paris)
BGTI = *Beiträgen zur Geschichte der Technik und Industrie* (Berlin)
BICS = *Bulletin of the Institute of Classical Studies* (London)
BIFAO = *Bulletin de l'Institut Français d'Archéologie Orientale* (Cairo)
BJ = *Bonner Jahrbücher* (Kevelaer)
BM = British Museum (London)
Brit = *Britannia* (London)
BSA = *Annual of the British School at Athens* (London)
BSGW = *Bericht der König.-Sächsischen Gesellschaft der Wissenschaften* (Leipzig)
CAH² = *Cambridge Ancient History*, 2nd edn (Cambridge)
CAN = *Cahier des Annales de Normandie* (Caen)
CBA = Council for British Archaeology
CE = *Chronique d'Égypte* (Brussels)
CEFR = *Collections de l'École Française de Rome* (Rome)
CIL = *Corpus Inscriptionum Latinarum* (Berlin)

CJ = *Classical Journal* (Menasha / Ohio)
CL = *Collection Latomus* (Brussels)
Con = *Conimbriga* (Coimbra)
CP = *Classical Philology* (Chicago)
CTP = *Corpus Topographicum Pompeianum* (Rome)
DAI = Deutsches Archäologisches Institut (Berlin)
DS = Daremberg, C. and Saglio, E., *Dictionnaire des Antiquités Grecques et Romaines* (Paris, 1875-)
EAAC = *Enciclopedia d'Arte Antica Classica* (Rome)
EAE = *Excavaciones Arqueologicas en España* (Madrid)
EAD = *Exploration Archéologique à Delos* (Paris)
EcHR = *Economic History Review* (London)
Eir = *Eirene* (Prague)
Epig = *Epigraphica* (Milan)
FGH = *Fragmente der griechischen Historiker* (Berlin / Leiden)
FHG = *Fragmenta Historicorum Graecorum* (Paris)
Gal = *Gallia* (Paris)
Germ = *Germania* (Frankfurt, Mainz)
GR = *Greece and Rome* (Oxford)
GZMS = *Glasnik Zemalijskog muzeja a Sarajevu* (Sarajevo)
Hesp = *Hesperia* (Athens / Baltimore)
Hist = *Historia* (Wiesbaden)
IA = *Informacíon Arqueológica* (Madrid)
IG = *Inscriptiones Graecae* (Leiden)
ILS = *Inscriptiones Latinae Selectae* (ed. H. Dessau) (Berlin, 1892-1916)
JA = *Jahrbuch für Altertumskunde* (Vienna)
JEA = *Journal of Egyptian Archaeology* (London)
JFA = *Journal of Field Archaeology* (Boston)
JRA = *Journal of Roman Archaeology* (Ann Arbor)
JRS = *Journal of Roman Studies* (London)
JW = *Jahrbuch für Wirtschaftsgeschichte* (Berlin)
Kok = *Kokalos. Studi pubblicati dall'Istituto di storia antica dell'Università di Palermo* (Palermo)
KWRGZ = *Kulturgeschichtlicher Wegweiser durch das Römisch-Germanische Zentralmuseum* (Mainz)
Lat = *Latomus* (Brussels)
MA = *Monumenti antichi* (Rome)
MAAR = *Memoirs of the American Academy in Rome* (Rome)
MAMA = *Monumenta Asiae Minoris Antiqua* (Manchester)
MCV = *Mélanges de la Casa de Velázquez* (Madrid)
MDAI (K) (R) = *Mitteilungen des Deutschen Archäologischen Instituts (Kairo) (Rom)* (various)
MEFRA = *Mélanges d'archéologie et d'histoire de l'École Française de Rome et d'Athènes* (Paris)
Mines et fonderies = *Mines et fonderies antiques de la Gaule 1982*, Conference proceedings (Paris)
MP = *Monuments et mémoires. Fondation Piot* (Paris)
NAH = *Noticiario arquelógico hispanico. Arqueología* (Madrid)
NC = *Numismatic Chronicle* (London)
NotScav = *Notizie degli scavi di antichità* (Rome)

OCD = *The Oxford Classical Dictionary*, 3rd edn (eds S. Hornblower and A. Spawforth) (Oxford, 1996)
OGIS = *Orientis Graeci Inscriptiones Selectae* (Leipzig)
OIRF = *Opuscula Instituti Romani Finlandiae* (Rome)
OR = *Opuscula Romana* (Stockholm)
PBA = *Proceedings of the British Academy* (London)
PBSR = *Papers of the British School at Rome* (London)
PCPS = *Proceedings of the Cambridge Philological Society* (Cambridge)
PP = *La parola del passato* (Naples)
P&P = *Past and Present* (Kendal)
RA = *Revue archéologique* (Paris)
RACE =*Revue archéologique de l'Est et du Centre-Est* (Dijon)
RC = *Revue de Comminges* (Saint-Gaudens)
RE = Pauly-Wissowa, *Real-Encyclopädie der klassischen Altertumswissenschaften* (Stuttgart)
REG = *Revue des études grecques* (Paris)
REL = *Revue des études latines* (Paris)
RGF = *Römisch-Germanische Forschungen* (Mainz)
RGK = *Römisch-Germanisches Korrespondenzblatt* (Trier)
RIB = *Roman Inscriptions of Britain* (Oxford)
RIGI = *Rivista Indo-Greca Italica* (Naples)
RINASA = *Rivista dell'Istituto Nazionale d'Archeologia e Storia dell'Arte* (Rome)
RLO = *Der römische Limes in Österreich* (Vienna)
SAL = *Society of Antiquaries of London* (London)
TIR = *Tabula Imperii Romani*
TZ = Trierer Zeitschrift (Trier)
VCH = *Victoria County History* (London)
WMBH = *Wissenschaftliche Mitteilungen aus Bosnien und der Hercegovina* (Vienna)
WPZ = *Wiener Prähistorische Zeitschrift* (Vienna)
YCS = *Yale Classical Studies* (New Haven)

Bibliography

Adamesteanu, D. 1965. 'Metaponto (Matera): Appunti fotointerpretativi', *NotScav* 19, Suppl., 179-84
———— 1973. 'Le suddivisioni di terra nel Metapontino', in Finley (ed.) 1973a, 49-61
Adriani, A. 1970. *Himera* i: *campagne di scavo 1963-1965* (Rome)
Agache, R. 1975. 'La campagne à l'époque romaine dans les grandes plaines du nord de la France d'après les photographies aériennes', *ANRW* II.4, 658-713
———— 1978. *La Somme pré-romaine et romaine* (Mémoires de la Société des Antiquaires de Picardie 24, Amiens)
Alföldy, G. 1974. *Noricum* (London / Boston)
Allegro, N. 1976. *Himera* ii: *campagne di scavo 1966-1973* (Rome)
Allen, D.F. 1980. *Coins of the Ancient Celts* (ed. by D. Nash; Edinburgh)
Andrikopolou-Strack, J.-N. 1986. *Grabbauten des 1. Jahrhunderts n. Chr. im Rheingebiet BJ* Beiheft 43 (Cologne)
Ardaillon, E. 1897. *Les mines de Laurion dans l'antiquité* (Paris)
Ashby, T. 1927. *The Roman Campagna in Classical Times* (London)
Audin, A. and Armand-Calliat, L. 1962. 'Entraves antiques trouvées en Bourgogne et dans le Lyonnais', *RACE* 13, 7-38

Aurigemma, S. 1926. *I mosaici de Zliten* (Rome)

Ballu, A. 1897, 1903, 1911. *Les ruines de Timgad, antique Thamugadi* (2nd edn 1903; 3rd edn 1911; Paris)

Bang, M. 1910. 'Die Herkunft der römischen Sklaven', *MDAI (R)* 25, 223-51

——— 1912. 'Die Herkunft der römischen Sklaven', *MDAI (R)* 27, 189-221

Barker, G. 1981. *Landscape and Society: Prehistoric Central Italy* (London)

———, Lloyd, J. and Webley, D. 1978. 'A classical landscape in Molise', *PBSR* 46, 35-51

Barrow, R.H. 1928. *Slavery in the Roman Empire* (London)

Barruol, G. and Gourdiote, R. 1982. 'Les mines antiques de la haute vallée de l'Orb (Herault)', *Mines et fonderies*, 79-91

Barth, F.E. 1982. 'Prehistoric saltmining at Hallstatt', *Bulletin of the Institute of Archaeology, London* 19, 31-43

Bedon, R. 1984. *Les carrières et les carriers de la Gaule romaine* (Paris)

Behn, F. 1911. 'Römische Schiffe in Deutschland', in *Alterthümer in unserer heidnischen Vorzeit* 5, 416-21 (Mainz)

——— 1926. *Steinindustrie des Altertums* (Mainz)

Bell, M. 1980. 'Stylobate and roof in the Olympieion at Akragas', *AJA* 84, 359-72

Bellen, H. 1971. *Studien zur Sklavenflucht im römischen Kaiserreich* (Forschungen zur antiken Sklaverei 4, Wiesbaden)

Belova, N.V. 1987. 'Die Sklaverei im römischen Gallien', in Štaerman (ed.) 1987, 103-46

Benoit, F. 1940. 'L'usine de meunerie hydraulique de Barbegal (Arles)', *RA*, 19-80

Bergk, T. 1882. *Poetae Lyrici Graeci* (4th edn; Leipzig)

Berthier, A. 1967. 'Établissements agricoles antiques à Oued Athmenia', *BAA* 1, 7-20

Beschaouch, A., Hanoune, R. and Thébert, Y. 1977. 'Les ruines de Bulla Regia', *CEFR* 28

Bienkowski 1987. 'The Sotiel Coronada Archimedes screw in Liverpool re-examined', *MDAI Madrid* 28, 135-40

Bingen, J. 1987. 'Première campagne de fouille au Mons Claudianus: rapport préliminaire', *BIFAO* 87, 45-52

——— 1990. 'Quatrième campagne de fouille au Mons Claudianus: rapport préliminaire', *BIFAO* 90, 65-81

Bintliff, J. 1985. 'The Boeotia survey', in Macready and Thompson (eds) 1985a, 196-216

Blanchard-Lemée, M. 1975. *Maisons à mosaiques du quartier central de Djemila (Cuicul), AntAf* Études 1

Blanco, A. and Luzón, J.M. 1969. 'Pre-Roman silver mines at Riotinto', *Ant* 43, 124-31

Blavatsky, T. 1974. 'Über den Sklavenmarkt am Aktion', *Klio* 56, 497-500

Blümner, H. 1912. *Technologie und Terminologie der Gewerbe und Künste bei Griechen und Römern* (2nd edn; Leipzig)

Boardman, J. 1967. *Excavations in Chios 1952-1955: Greek Emporio, BSA* Suppl. vol. 6

——— and Vaphopoulou-Richardson, C.E. (eds) 1984. *Chios: a Conference at the Homereion in Chios* (Oxford)

———, Griffin, J. and Murray, O. (eds) 1986. *Oxford History of the Classical World* (London)

Boëthius, A. (ed.) 1962. *Etruscan Culture, Land and People: archeological research* and studies conducted in San Giovenale and its environs by members of the Swedish Institute in Rome (Columbia)

—— 1978. *Etruscan and Early Roman Architecture* (2nd edn [rev. R. Ling and T. Rasmussen]; Harmondsworth)

—— and Ward-Perkins, J.B. 1970. *Etruscan and Roman Architecture* (Harmondsworth)

Boon, G.C. and Williams, C. 1966. 'The Dolaucothi drainage wheel', *JRS* 56, 122-7

Bosworth, A.B. 1968. 'Review of Capozza 1966', *JRS* 58, 272-4

Bowman, A.K. and Thomas, J.D. 1994. *The Vindolanda Writing-tablets* (Tabulae Vindolandenses II) (London)

Bradford, J. 1956. 'Ancient field systems on Mt. Hymettos, near Athens', *AntiqJ* 36, 172-80

Bradley, K.R. 1989. *Slavery and Rebellion in the Roman World 140 BC-70 BC* (London)

—— 2000. 'Animalizing the slave: the truth of fiction', *JRS* 90, 110-25

—— 2001. 'Imagining slavery: the limits of the plausible', *JRA* 14, 473-7

Brilliant, R. 1967. *The Arch of Septimius Severus in the Roman Forum*, MAAR 29

Bruneau, P. 1975. 'L'Agora des Italiens, servait-elle de marché aux esclaves?', *BCH* 99, 273-5

—— and Ducat, J. 1983. *Guide de Délos* (3rd edn; Paris)

Brunn, H. 1898. 'I monumenti degli Aterii', *Kleine Schriften* 1, 72-102 (Berlin / Leipzig)

Bruno, V.J. and Scott, R.T. 1993. *Cosa IV: the Houses* (Pennsylvania)

Brunt, P.A. 1974a. 'The Roman mob', in Finley (ed.) 1973a, 74-102

—— (ed.) 1974b. A.H.M. Jones, *The Roman Economy* (Oxford)

Buckland, W.W. 1908. *The Roman Law of Slavery* (Cambridge)

Büdinger, M. (ed.) 1870. *Untersuchungen zur römischen Kaisergeschichte* III (Leipzig)

Bülow-Jacobsen, A. 1992. 'The excavations and ostraca of Mons Claudianus', *Proc. XIXth Congress of Papyrology, Cairo, 2-9 September 1989*, 49-63

Burdeau, F. (ed.) 1964. *Aspects de l'empire romain* (Paris)

Burford, A. 1960. 'Heavy transport in classical antiquity', *EcHR* 2nd ser. 13, 1-18

—— 1965. 'The economics of Greek temple building', *PCPS* new ser. 11, 21-34

—— 1969. *The Greek Temple Builders of Epidauros* (Liverpool)

Busing, H. 1982. *Römische Militärarchitektur in Mainz*, RGF 40

Calderini, A. 1908. *La manomissione e la condizione dei liberti in Graecia* (Milan)

Calza, G. 1915. 'VI. Ostia. Sterri nell'edificio delle Pistrine', *NotScav* 12, 242-58

——, Becatti, G., Gismondi, I., De Angelis d'Ossat, G. and Bloch, H. 1954. *Scavi di Ostia* i: *Topografia Generale* (Rome)

Cambitoglou, A. 1981. *Archaeological Museum of Andros: Guide* (Athens)

—— 1988. *Zagora* II (Athens)

——, Coulton, J.J., Birmingham, J. and Green, J.R. 1971. *Zagora* I (Sydney)

Cancellieri, F. 1855. *Notizie del Carcere Tulliano* (Rome)

Capozza, M. 1966. *Movimenti servili nel mondo romano in età repubblicana* (Rome)

Carandini, A. (ed.) 1985. *Settefinestre: una villa schiavistica nell'Etruria romana* (Modena)

—— 1988. *Schiavi in Italia* (Rome)

Carrington, R. C. 1931. 'Studies in the Campanian *villae rusticae*', *JRS* 21, 110-30

—— 1936. *Pompeii* (Oxford)

Carter, J. C. and D'Annibale, C. 1985. 'Metaponto and Croton', in Macready and Thompson (eds) 1985a, 146-57

Cary, M. 1932. 'The sources of silver for the Greek world', *Mélanges Glotz*, i, 133-42 (Paris)

Casson, S. 1926. *Macedonia, Thrace and Illyria* (Oxford)

Chamonard, J. 1922. *Exploration archéologique en Délos,* viii: *Le Quartier du Théâtre* (Paris)

Chantraine, P. 1977. *Dictionnaire étymologique de la langue grecque: histoire des mots*, IV, 1 (P-Y) (Paris)

Charbonnel, N. 1964. 'La condition des ouvriers dans les ateliers impériaux aux IVe et Ve siècles', in Burdeau (ed.) 1964, 61-93

Childe, V. G. 1943. 'Rotary querns on the Continent and in the Mediterranean basin', *Ant* 17, 19-26

Cichorius, C. 1896-1900. *Die Reliefs der Traianssäule* (Berlin)

Clarke, E.D. 1821. 'An account of some antiquities found at Fulbourn in Cambs.', *Arch* 19, 56-61

Clarke, G.W. 1989. *The Letters of St Cyprian of Carthage* 4 (Letters 67-82) (New York / Mahwah, NJ)

Coarelli, F. 1982. ' "L'Agora des Italiens" a Delo: il mercato degli schiavi', *OIRF* 2, 119-45

Cocco, M. 1970. 'Sulla funzione dell'Agora degli Italiani', *PP* 25, 446-9

Colbert de Beaulieu, J.B. and Richard, J.C. 1969. 'La numismatique de la Gaule et la numismatique de Narbonnaise', *Rivista de Studi Liguri* 35, 90-100

Collingwood, R.G. and Richmond, I.A. 1969. *The Archaeology of Roman Britain* (London)

Collingwood, R.G. and Wright, R.P. 1965, 1995. *The Roman Inscriptions of Britain I* (1st edn 1965, Oxford; 2nd edn 1995, with addenda and corrigenda by R.S.O. Tomlin, Stroud)

Collingwood Bruce, J. 1978. *Handbook to the Roman Wall* (13th edn [ed. C.M. Daniels]; Newcastle upon Tyne)

Conner, P. 1985. ' "Wedding archaeology to art": Poynter's Israel in Egypt', in Macready and Thompson (eds) 1985a, 112-20

Conophagos, C.E. 1980. *Le Laurium antique et la technique grecque de la production de l'argent* (Athens)

Cordella, A. 1869. *Le Laurium* (Marseilles)

Cotton, M. A. 1979. *The Late Republican Villa at Posto, Francolise* (London)

———— and Métraux, G.P.R. 1985. *The San Rocco Villa at Francolise* (London)

Crawford, M. 1986. 'Early Rome and Italy', in Boardman *et al.* 1986, 387-416

Crook, J.A. 1967. *Law and Life of Rome* (London)

Crova, B. 1942. *Edilizia e tecnica rurale di Roma antica* (Milan)

Crowfoot, G.M. 1936-7. 'Of the warp-weighted loom', *BSA* 37, 36-47

Cunliffe, B. 1991. *Iron Age Communities in Britain* (3rd edn; London / New York)

Curti, E. 1989. 'Il culto d'Artemis Bendis a Eraclea', *Studi su Siris-Eraclea, Archaeologia Perusina* 8, 23-30

Curwen, E.C. 1937. 'Querns', *Ant* 11, 133-51

———— 1941. 'More about querns', *Ant* 15, 15-32

Daubrée, A. 1868. 'Aperçu historique sur l'exploitation des métaux dans la Gaule', *RA* 17, 298-313

———— 1881. 'Aperçu historique sur l'exploitation des mines métalliques dans la Gaule', *RA* 41, 201-21, 261-84, 327-53

da Veija Ferreira, O. and de Andrada, R.F. 1960. 'A necrópole de Valduca (Aljustrel)', *Con* 5

Daniels, C.M. 1978. *See* Collingwood Bruce, J. 1978

Davies, O. 1935. *Roman Mines in Europe* (Oxford)

Day, J. 1932. 'Agriculture in the life of Pompeii', *YCS* 3, 165-208

de Alarcão, J. 1988. *Roman Portugal* (Warminster)

de Brisay, K.W. and Evans, K.A. (eds) 1975. *Salt: the Study of an Ancient Industry* (Colchester)

de Caro, S. 1987. 'Villa rustica in località Petrario (Stabiae)', *RINASA* 3rd ser. 10, 5-89

Degrassi, A. 1963-5. *Inscriptiones Latinae Liberae Rei Publicae* (Florence)

Delbrueck, R. 1932. *Antike Porphyrwerke* (Berlin / Leipzig)

Delehaye, H. (ed.) 1910. *Acta Sanctorum 64: Novembris III* (Brussels)

Della Corte, M. 1922. 'Boscotrecase', *NotScav* 19, 459-78

——— 1924. 'Case e abitanti a Pompei', *RIGI* 8, 109-31

del Marmol, E. 1877. 'La villa d'Anthée', *ASAN* 14, 165-94

——— 1881. 'La villa d'Anthée', *ASAN* 15, 1-40

De Miro, E. 1980. 'La casa greca in Sicilia, *philias charin*', *Miscellanea di studi classici in onore di Eugenio Manni* 2, 707-37

de Rossi, G.B. 1879. 'I santi quattro coronati', *BAC*, 45-96

de Sainte-Croix, G.E.M. 1981. *The Class Struggle in the Ancient Greek World* (Ithaca)

des Courtils, J. 1982. 'Des mines d'or à Thasos', *BCH* 106, 409-17

Diehl, E. 1949. *Anthologia Lyrica Graeca* (3rd edn; Leipzig)

Dittenberger, W. 1915-24. *Sylloge Inscriptionum Graecarum* (3rd edn; Leipzig)

Domergue, C. 1967. 'La mine antique de Diogines (province de Ciudad Real)', *MCV* 3, 31-5

——— 1971. 'Cerro del Plomo, mina El Centenillo (Jaén)', *NAH* 16, 346-55

——— 1983. 'La mine antique de Aljustrel (Portugal) et les tables de bronze de Vipasca', *Con* 22, 5-193

——— 1990. *Les mines de la Péninsule Ibérique dans l'antiquité romaine* (Paris)

——— and Hérail, G. 1978. *Mines d'or romaines d'Espagne: le district de la Valduerna (León). Étude géomorphologique et archéologique* (Toulouse)

——— and Martin, Th. 1977. 'Minas d'oro romanas de la provincia de Leon, II: excavaciones de 1972-1973', *EAE* 94

——— and Sillieres, P. 1977. 'La Corona de Quintanilla: excavaciones 1971-1973: exploraciones 1973', *EAE* 93 (Minas de Oro Romanas de la Provincia de Léon, I)

Drack, W. and Fellmann, R. 1988. *Die Römer in der Schweiz* (Stuttgart)

Dragendorff, H. and Kruger, E. 1924. *Das Grabmal von Igel* (Trier)

Drinkwater, J.F. 1977-8. 'Die Sekundinier von Igel und die Woll- und Textilindustrie in Gallia Belgica: Fragen und Hypothesen', *TZ* 40/41, 107-25

——— 1983. *Roman Gaul* (London)

Dubois, C. 1908. *Étude sur l'administration et l'exploitation des carrières marbres porphyre, granit etc dans le monde romain* (Paris)

Dubois, C. and Guilbaut, J.E. 1982. 'Antiques mines de cuivre du Sironais (Pyrénées Ariégoises)', *Mines et fonderies*, 95-123

Duchêne, H. 1986. 'Sur la stèle d'Aulus Caprilius Timotheos Somatemporos', *BCH* 110, 513-30

Ducrey, P. 1968. *Le traitement des prisonniers de guerre dans la Grèce antique* (Paris)

Dumont, J.C. 1966. 'A propos d'Aristonicos', *Eir* 5, 189-96

——— 1977. 'La signification de la révolte', *REL* 45, 89-98

Dunbabin, K. 1978. *The Mosaics of Roman North Africa* (Oxford)

Dunbabin, T.J. 1948. *The Western Greeks* (Oxford)

Duncan-Jones, R.P. 1963. 'City population in Roman Africa', *JRS* 53, 85-90

Duroin, P. 1971. *Les ateliers des tailleurs de pierre de Saint-Leu-d'Esserent* (Amiens)

Dworakowska, A. 1975. *Quarries in Ancient Greece* (Warsaw)

—— 1983. *Quarries in Roman Provinces*, Bibliotheca Antiqua 16 (Warsaw)

Dyson, S.L. 1978. 'Settlement patterns in the Ager Cosanus: the Wesleyan University Survey 1974-1976', *JFA* 5, 251-68

Eggebrecht, A. (ed.) 1988. *Albanien: Schätze aus dem Land der Skipetaren* (Mainz)

Espérandieu, E. 1925. *Receuil général des bas reliefs statues et bustes de la Gaule romaine* (Paris)

Étienne, R. 1960. *Le quartier nord-est de Volubilis* (Paris)

—— 1966. *La vie quotidienne à Pompéi* (Paris)

—— 1974. 'Recherches sur l'ergastule', *Actes du Colloque 1972 sur L'Esclavage*, 249-66 (Paris)

Faklaris, P. V. 1991. 'The fettered men of Acanthus', *AAA* (for 1986), 178-84

Fantar, M.H. 1970. 'Kerkouane', *EAAC* Suppl., 397-8

Fawn, A.J. *et al.* 1990. *The Red Hills of Essex* (Colchester)

Ferdière, A. 1988. *Les campagnes en Gaule romaine* (Paris)

Fernandez Castro, M.C. 1982. *Villas romanas en España* (Madrid)

Feugère, M. (ed.) 1985. *Les objets en fer dans les collections du Musée Archéologique de Saintes (Ier-XVe siècle)* (Saintes)

Finley, M.I. 1962. 'The Black Sea and Danubian regions and the slave trade in antiquity', *Klio* 40, 51-9

—— (ed.) 1968a. *Slavery in Classical Antiquity* (2nd edn; Cambridge)

—— 1968b. 'Aulus Kapreilius Timotheus, slave trader', *Aspects of Antiquity*, 162-76 (London)

—— (ed.) 1973a. *Problèmes de la terre en Grèce ancienne* (Paris)

—— 1973b. *The Ancient Economy* (London)

—— (ed.) 1974. *Studies in Ancient Society* (London / Boston)

—— 1975. *The Ancient Economy* (2nd edn; London)

—— 1977. *The World of Odysseus* (2nd edn; London)

—— 1979. *Ancient Sicily* (2nd edn; London)

—— 1980. *Ancient Slavery and Modern Ideology* (London)

—— 1985. *The Ancient Economy* (3rd edn; London)

Fitzgerald, W. 2000. *Slavery and the Roman Literary Imagination* (Cambridge)

Fitzler, K. 1910. *Steinbrüche und Bergwerke in ptolemäischen und römischen Ägypten* (Leipzig)

Fitzpatrick, A.P. 1985. 'The distribution of Dressel 1 amphorae in North-west Europe', *Oxford Journal of Archaeology* 4 (3), 305-40

Foss, C. 1976. *Byzantine and Turkish Sardis* (Cambridge, Mass. / London)

Foucher, L. 1964. *Hadrumetum* (Paris)

Fouet, G. 1969. *La villa gallo-romaine de Montmaurin*, XXe Supplément à *Gallia*

Fox, C. 1946. *A Find of the Early Iron Age from Llyn Cerrig Bach, Anglesey* (Cardiff)

Frank, T. 1916. 'Race mixture in the Roman Empire', *AHR* 21, 689-708

—— 1933-40. *Economic Survey of Ancient Rome* (Baltimore)

Frankfort, T. 1959. 'Les classes serviles en Étrurie', *Lat* 18, 3-22

Fraser, P.M. and Rönne, T. 1957. *Boeotian and West Greek Tombstones* (Lund)

Frederiksen, M. 1984. *Campania* (ed. by N. Purcell; London)

Fremersdorf, F. 1933. *Der römische Gutshof Köln-Müngersdorf*, *RGF* 6

French A. 1964. *The Growth of the Athenian Economy* (London)

Frend, W.H.C. 1952. *The Donatist Church* (Oxford)

Frere, S.S. 1987. *Britannia* (3rd edn; London)

—— and Stow, S. 1983. *Excavation in the St George's Street and Burgate Street Areas, Archaeology of Canterbury* 7 (Maidstone)

Frias, T.O. 1954-5. 'Excavaciones en la villa romana de Santerva del Burgo (Soria)', *NAH* 3-4, 169-94

Fuks, A. 1968. 'Slave war and slave troubles in Chios in the third century BC.', *Ath* 46, 102-11

Fulford, M.G. and Allen, J.R.L. 1992. 'Iron-making at the Chesters villa, Woolaston, Gloucestershire: survey and excavation 1987-91', *Brit* 23, 159-215

Fustel de Coulanges, N.M. 1885. 'Le colonat romain', *Recherches sur quelques problemes d'histoire*, 1-186 (Paris)

Gabba, E. and Vallet, G. (eds) 1980. *La Sicilia antica* (Naples)

Galliou, P. 1982. 'Mines et métaux de l'ouest de la Gaule', *Mines et fonderies*, 21-32

Garlan, Y. 1982. *Les esclaves en Grèce ancienne* (Paris)

—— 1988. *Slavery in Ancient Greece* (trans. J. Lloyd; Ithaca / London)

Gauckler, P. 1896. 'Le domaine des Laberii à Uthina', *MP* 3, 177-229

Gille, B. 1956. 'Machines', ch. 18 in Singer *et al.* 1956

Giner, C.A. 1984. *Tejido y cesteriá en la Península Ibérica* (Madrid)

Giuliani, C.F. 1966. 'Tibur: part II', *Forma Italiae Reg.* I.3 (Rome)

Glotz, G. 1926. *Ancient Greece at Work* (London / New York)

Goodburn, R. and Bartholomew, P. (eds) 1976. *Aspects of the Notitia Dignitatum*, *BAR* Suppl. Ser. 15 (Oxford)

Goodburn, R. and Waugh, H. (eds) 1983. *RIB* i: *Epigraphic Indexes* (Oxford)

Gordon, M.L. 1924. 'The nationality of slaves under the early Roman Empire', *JRS* 14, 93-111

Gorges, J.G. 1979. *Les villas hispano-romaines* (Paris)

Gossé, G. 1942. 'Las minas y el arte minero de España', *Amp* 4, 43-68

Graham, J. W. 1966. 'Origins and interrelations of the Greek house and the Roman house', *The Phoenix* 20, 3-31 (Toronto)

Greenidge, A.J.H. and Clay, A.M. 1986. *Sources for Roman History 133-70 BC* (3rd edn; Oxford)

Grenier, A. 1906. 'Habitations gauloises et villas latines dans la cité des Mediomatrices: étude sur la développement de la civilisation gallo-romaine dans une province gauloise', *Bibliothèque de l'École des Hautes Études: section de sciences historiques et philologiques*, 157e fasc. (Paris)

—— 1934. *Manuel d'archéologie* vi.2: *archéologie gallo-romaine* (Paris)

Gsell, S. 1929. *Histoire ancienne de l'Afrique du nord* (2nd edn; Paris)

—— 1932. 'Esclaves ruraux dans l'Afrique romaine', *Mélanges Glotz*, i, 397-415 (Paris)

Guiraud, P. 1900. *La main-d'oeuvre industrielle dans l'ancienne Grèce*, Bibliothèque de la Faculté des Lettres, 12 (Paris)

Gummerus, H. 1906. *Der römische Gutsbetrieb als wirtschaftlichen Organismus nach den Werken des Cato, Varro und Columella*, *Klio* 5 (Beiheft)

Halbout, P. (ed.) 1987. *Corpus des objets domestiques et des armes en fer de Normandie du Ier au Xve siècle*, *CAN* 20 (Caen)

Hanfmann, G.M.A. and Mierse, W.E. (eds) 1983. *Sardis from Prehistoric to Roman Times* (Cambridge, Mass. / London)

Harig, G. 1971. 'Zum Problem "Krankenhaus" in der Antike', *Klio* 53, 179-95

Harris, W.V. 1980. 'Towards a study of the Roman slave trade', *MAAR* 36, 117-40

——— 1999. 'Demography, geography and the sources of Roman slaves', *JRS* 89, 62-75

Hasebroek J. 1931. *Griechische Wirtschafts- und Gesellschaftsgeschichte bis zur Perserzeit* (Tübingen)

Haverfield, F. 1905. 'Romano-British Derbyshire', *VCH Derbyshire* i, 191-263 (London)

Hayes, P. 1985. 'The San Vincenzo survey, Molise', in Macready and Thompson (eds) 1985a, 129-35

Healy, J.F. 1978. *Mining and Metallurgy in the Greek and Roman World* (London)

Heitland, W.E. 1921. *Agricola* (Cambridge)

Henning, J. 1992. 'Gefangenenfesseln in slawischen Siedlungsraum und der europäische Sklavenhandel im 6. bis 12. Jahrhundert', *Germ* 70, 403-26

Herrmann, E. and Brockmeyer, N. 1983. *Bibliographie zur antiken Sklaverei* (Bochum)

Himmelmann, N. 1971. *Archäologisches zum Problem der griechischen Sklaverei*, *AAWM* 13

Hoddinott, R.F. 1975. *Bulgaria in Antiquity* (London / Tonbridge)

Hofman, E. and Morton, F. 1928. 'Der prähistorische Salzbergbau auf dem Halstätter Salzberg', *WPZ* 15, 82-101

Holmgren, J. and Leday, A. 1981. 'Esquisse d'une typologie des villas gallo-romaines du Berry d'après les prospections aériennes', *Gal* 39, 103-22

Hopper, R.J. 1979. *Trade and Industry in Classical Greece* (London)

Horn, H.G. 1980. 'Die antiken Steinbrüche von Chemtou / Simmithus', in Horn and Rüger (eds) 1980, 173-80

——— and Rüger, C.B. (eds) 1980. *Die Numider* (Cologne)

Hull, M.R. 1958. *Roman Colchester*, *SAL* Research Report 20 (London)

Ingram, J.K. 1895. *A History of Slavery and Serfdom* (London)

Isager, S. and Hansen, M.H. 1975. *Aspects of Athenian Society in the Fourth Century BC* (Odense)

Jackson, R.P.J. 1993. 'Roman medicine: the practitioners and their practices', *ANRW* II, 37.1, 79-101

Jahn, O. 1861. 'Über Darstellungen antiker Reliefs welche sich auf Handwerk und Handelsverkehr beziehen', *BSGW* (Phil.-Hist. Klasse), 291-374

Jameson, M.H. 1977-8. 'Agriculture and slavery in Classical Athens', *CJ* 73, 122-45

——— 1991. 'Private space and the Greek city', in Murray and Price (eds) 1991, 191-2

Jarrett, M.G. 1969. *The Roman Frontier in Wales* (2nd edn; Cardiff)

Johnson, J.O. 1953. *Excavations at Minturnae* 2 (i): *Republican Magistri* (Rome)

Johnston, D.E. 1972. 'A Roman building at Chalk, near Gravesend', in Kent, *Brit* 3, 112-48

Jones, A.H.M. 1964. *The Later Roman Empire 284-602* (Oxford)

——— 1968. 'Slavery in the ancient world', in Finley (ed.) 1968a, 1-15

——— 1974a. 'Were ancient heresies national or social movements in disguise?', in Jones 1974d, 308-29

——— 1974b. 'The Roman colonate', in Jones 1974d, 293-307

——— 1974c. 'The cloth industry under the Roman Empire', in Jones 1974d, 350-64

——— 1974d. *The Roman Economy* (ed. P.A. Brunt; Oxford)

Jones, C.P. 1987. 'Tattooing and branding in Greco-Roman antiquity', *JRS* 77, 139-55

Jones, G.D.B. 1962. 'Capena and the Ager Capenas', *PBSR* 30, 116-207

——— 1963. 'Capena and the Ager Capenas, Part II', *PBSR* 31, 100-58

——— 1980. 'The Roman mines at Riotinto', *JRS* 70, 146-65

——— and Mattingly, D. 1990. *An Atlas of Roman Britain* (Oxford / Cambridge, Mass.)

Jones, J.E. 1973. 'An Attic country house below the Cave of Pan at Vari', *BSA* 68, 355-452

——— 1975. 'Town and country houses of Attica in Classical times', in Mussche (ed.) 1975, 63-140

——— 1985. 'Laurion: Agrileza, 1977-83: Excavations at a silver-mine site', in *Archaeological Reports for 1984-5*, 106-23, Society for the Promotion of Hellenic Studies and the British School at Athens (London)

Joulin, L. 1901. *Les établissements gallo-romains de la plaine de Martres-Tolosanes* (Paris)

Jullian, C. 1908-26. *Histoire de la Gaule* (8 vols; Paris)

Keay, S. 1988. *Roman Spain* (London)

Kehoe, D.P. 1988. *The Economics of Agriculture on Roman Imperial Estates in North Africa*, Hypomnemata 89 (Göttingen)

Keil, J. 1923. *Inschriften, Forschungen in Ephesos* 3, 91-168 (Vienna)

Keller, D.R. and Rupp, D.W. 1983 (eds) *Archaeological Survey in the Mediterranean Area*, BAR Int. Ser. 155, 207-32 (Oxford)

Kent, J.H. 1948. 'The temple estates of Delos, Rheneia and Mykonos', *Hesp* 17, 243-338

Keramopoullos, A.D. 1923. *O Apotympanismos* (Athens)

Kern, O. 1900. *Die Inschriften von Magnesia am Maeander* (Berlin)

King, A. 1990. *Roman Gaul and Germany* (London)

Kirk, G.S. 1975. 'The Homeric poems as history', *Cambridge Ancient History II, Part 2* (3rd edn; Cambridge)

Klein, M.J. 1988. *Untersuchungen zu den kaiserlichen Steinbrüchen an Mons Porphyrites und Mons Claudius in der östlichen Wüste Ägyptens* (Bonn)

Kockel, V. 1985. 'Archäologische Funde und Forschungen in den Vesuvstädten I', *AAn* 1985, 495-571

Kolendo, J. 1978. 'Les esclaves dans l'art antique: la stèle funéraire d'un marchand d'esclaves thraces découverte à Amphipolis', *Arche* 29, 24-34

Kolling, A. 1972. 'Schwarzenacker an der Blies', *BJ* 172, 238-57

Kolosovskaja, J.K. 1987. 'Die Sklaverei in Dakien', in Štaerman (ed.) 1987, 211-40

Kotula, T. 1966. 'A little-known revolt of Africans and slaves against Carthage (Diod. Sic. XIV, 77)', *Meander* 21, 362-71

Kraus, T. and Röder, J. 1962. 'Mons Claudianus', *MDAI (K)* 18, 80-120

———, Röder, J. and Müller-Wiener, W. 1967. 'Mons Claudianus – Mons Porphyrites', *MDAI (K)* 22, 108-205

Kyrle, G. 1913. 'Der prähistorische Salzbergbau am Dürrnberg bei Hallein', *JA* 7, 1-58

Lambrinoudakis, V. 1984. 'Ancient farmhouses on Mount Aipos', in Boardman and Vaphopoulou-Richardson (eds) 1984, 295-304

Lancel, S. and Bouchenaki, M. 1971. *Tipasa de Maurétanie* (Algiers)

Lapalus, E. 1939. 'L'Agora des Italiens', *EAD* 19

Lauffer, S. 1979. *Die Bergwerkssklaven von Laurion* (2nd edn; Wiesbaden)

Lawrence, A.W. 1984. *Handbook of Greek and Roman Architecture* (4th edn [rev. R.A. Tomlinson]; Harmondsworth)

Ledroit, J. 1930. 'Die römische Schiffahrt im Stromgebiet des Rheins', *KWRGZ* 12

Léger, A. 1875. *Les travaux publics, les mines et la métallurgie au temps des Romains* (Paris)

Lencman, J. A. 1966. *Die Sklaverei im mykenischen und homerischen Griechenland* (Wiesbaden)

Le Roy, C. 1993. 'Encore l'*agora* des Italiens à Délos', in Mactoux and Geny (eds) 1993, 183-208

[no authors] 1987. *Les mines et la métallurgie en Gaule et dans les provinces voisines* (Paris)

Leveau, P. 1975. 'Paysans maures et villes romaines en Maurétanie césarienne central', *MEFRA* 87, 857-71

——— 1984. *Caesarea de Maurétanie: une ville romaine et ses campagnes*, *CEFR* 70

Lewis, C.T. and Short, C. 1966. *A Latin Dictionary* (Oxford)

Lewis, P.R. and Jones, G.D.B. 1966. 'The Dolaucothi gold mines, I: the surface evidence', *AntiqJ* 49, 244-72

Lézine, A. 1968. *Carthage-Utique: études d'architecture et d'urbanisme* (Paris)

Lindet, L. 1899. 'Les origines du moulin à grains', *RA* 3rd ser. 35, 413-27

——— 1900. 'Les origines du moulin à grains', *RA* 3rd ser. 36, 17-44

Lloyd, J.A. 1985. 'The Megalopolis survey in Arcadia: problems of strategy and tactics', in Macready and Thompson (eds) 1985a, 217-24

Lugli, G. 1926. 'La Villa Sabina di Orazio', *MA* 31, 456-598

McKay, A.G. 1975. *Houses, Villas and Palaces in the Roman World* (London)

MacMullen, R. 1987. 'Late Roman slavery', *Hist* 36, 359-82

Macready, S. and Thompson, F.H. (eds) 1985a. *Archaeological Field Survey in Britain and Abroad*, SAL Occasional Paper, new ser. 6 (London)

——— (eds) 1985b. *Influences in Victorian Art and Architecture*, SAL Occasional Paper, new ser. 7 (London)

Mactoux, M.-M. and Geny, A. (eds) 1993. *Mélanges Pierre Leveque* (Paris)

Maiuri, A. 1933. *La casa del Menandro e il suo tesoro* (Rome)

——— 1947. *La Villa dei Misteri* (Rome)

——— 1958a. *Ercolano: i nuovi scavi (1927-1958)* (Rome)

——— 1958b. *Pompeii* (8th edn; Rome)

——— 1960. *Pompeii* (Guide Book 3; Rome)

——— 1977. *Herculaneum* (Guide Book 53; Rome)

Manacorda, D. 1982. *Il frantoio della villa di Lucus Feroniae, I Volusi Saturnini: una famiglia romana della prima età imperiale* (Bari)

Manganaro, G. 1982. 'Monete e ghiande inscritte degli schiavi ribelli in Sicilia', *Chiron* 12, 237-44

Mangin, M. 1982. 'Caractères et fonctions de la métallurgie du fer à Alésia', *Mines et fonderies*, 237-58

Manning, W.H. 1966. 'Caistor-by-Norwich and the *Notitia Dignitatum*', *Ant* 40, 60-2

Mansuelli, G.A. 1957. 'La villa romana nell'Italia settentrionale', *PP* 12, 444-58

——— 1962. *La villa romana di Russi* (Rome)

——— 1963. *La casa etrusca di Marzabotto*, *MDAI (R)* 70, 44-62

——— 1971. 'Urbanistica e architettura della Cisalpina romana fino al III sec. e.n.', *CL* 111

Martin, R. 1973. 'Rapport entre les structures urbaines et les modes de division et d'exploitation du territoire', in Finley (ed.) 1973a, 97-112

——— and Vallet, G. 1980. 'L'architettura domestica', in Gabba and Vallet (eds) 1980, i, 2, 321-52

Mau, A. 1908. *Pompeji in Leben und Kunst* (2nd edn; Leipzig)
—— and Kelsey, F.W. 1899. *Pompeii, its Life and Art* (New York)
Meiggs, R. 1973. *Roman Ostia* (2nd edn; Oxford)
Menéndez Pidal, R. (ed.) 1982. *Historia de Espana* II, i (Madrid)
Meredith, D. 1952. 'The Roman remains in the Eastern Desert of Egypt', *JEA* 38, 94-111
—— 1953a. 'The Roman remains in the Eastern Desert of Egypt (cont.)', *JEA* 39, 95-106
—— 1953b. 'The Eastern Desert of Egypt: notes on inscriptions', *CE* 28, 126-41
—— 1954. 'The Eastern Desert of Egypt: notes on inscriptions', *CE* 29, 103-23
—— 1955. 'The Eastern Desert of Egypt: notes on inscriptions (corrigenda)', *CE* 30, 127-9
—— 1958. *Tabula Imperii Romani: Map of the Roman Empire based on the International 1:1,000,000 Map of the World. Sheet NG36. Coptos* (Oxford)
Miles, D. (ed.) 1982. *The Romano-British Countryside. Studies in Rural Settlement and Economy*, *BAR* Ser. 103 (Oxford)
Millar, F. 1981. 'The world of the *Golden Ass*', *JRS* 71, 63-75
—— 1984. 'Condemnation to hard labour in the Roman Empire from the Julio-Claudians to Constantine', *PBSR* 52, 124-47
Minns, E.H. 1913. *Scythians and Greeks* (Cambridge)
Mócsy, A. 1974. *Pannonia and Upper Moesia* (London)
Mommsen, T. (ed.) 1892-8. *Chronica Minora* ii (Berlin)
Moritz, L. A. 1958. *Grain-mills and Flour in Classical Antiquity* (Oxford)
Mrozek, S. 1964. 'Les esclaves dans les mines d'or romaines en Dacie', *Arche* 15, 119-28
Murray, S. and Price, S. (eds) 1991. *The Greek City from Homer to Alexander* (Oxford)
Mussche, H.F. (ed.) 1975. *Thorikos and the Laurion in Archaic and Classical Times* (Ghent)
—— 1986. *Thorikos: la vie dans une ville minière de la Grèce antique* (Brussels)
Musti, D. 1980. 'Il commercio degli schiavi del grano: il caso di Puteoli – sui rapporti tra l'economia italiana della tarda reppublica e le economie ellenistiche', *MAAR* 36, 197-215
Nash, D. 1975. 'The chronology of Celtic coinage in Gaul: the Arvernian "hegemony" reconsidered', *NC* 135, 204-18
Nash, E. 1962. *Pictorial Dictionary of Ancient Rome* ii (London)
Nash-Williams, V.E. 1954. *The Roman Frontier in Wales* (Cardiff)
Neal, D.S. 1989. 'The Stanwick villa, Northamptonshire: an interim report on the excavations of 1984-88', *Brit* 20, 149-68
Noeske, H.C. 1977. 'Studien zur Verwaltung und Bevölkerung der dakischen Goldbergwerke in römischer Zeit', *BJ* 177, 277-416
Noll, R. 1958. 'Römische Siedlungen und Strassen im Limesgebiet zwischen Inn und Enns (Oberösterreich)', *RLO* 21
Oates, D. 1953. 'The Tripolitanian Gebel: settlement of the Roman period around Gasr Ed-Danun', *PBSR* 21, 81-117
Oates, J.F. 1969. 'A Rhodian auction of a slave-girl', *JEA* 55, 191, 210
Oelmann, F. 1921. 'Die Villa rustica bei Stahl und Verwandtes', *Germ* 5, 64-73
—— 1928. 'Ein gallorömischer Bauernhof bei Mayen', *BJ* 133, 51-152
Oleson, J.P. 1984. *Greek and Roman Mechanical Water-lifting Devices: the History of a Technology* (Dordrecht)
Ormerod, H.A. 1924. *Piracy in the Ancient World* (Liverpool)

Osborne, R. 1985. *Demos: the Discovery of Classical Attika* (Cambridge)
——— 1987. *Classical Landscape with Figures* (London)
Overbeck, J. and Mau, A. 1884. *Pompeji in seinen Gebäuden, Alterthümen und Kunstwerken* (Leipzig)
Painter, K. (ed.) 1980. *Roman Villas in Italy*, BM Occasional Paper No. 24 (London)
Pašalić, E 1954. 'L'exploitation des mines dans l'antiquité en Bosnie-Herzegovine', *GZMS* 9, 47-74
Patsch, C. 1909. *WMBH* 11
Patterson, R. 1956. 'Spinning and weaving', in Singer *et al.* 1956, 191-220
Peacock, D. 1986. 'The production of Roman millstones near Orvieto, Umbria, Italy', *AntiqJ* 66, 45-51
——— 1994. 'Mons Claudianus and the problem of the "granito del foro": a geological and geochemical approach', *Ant* 68, 209-30
Pečírka, J. 1973. 'Homestead farms in Classical and Hellenistic Hellas', in Finley (ed.) 1973a, 113-47
——— and Dufková, M. 1970. 'Excavations of farms and farmhouses in the Chora of Chersonesos in the Crimea', *Eir* 8, 123-74
Pelagatti, P. 1980-1. 'L'attività della Soprintendenza alle Antichità della Sicilia Orientale', *Kok* 26/27, Atti del V Congresso Internazionale sulla Sicilia antica, 694-73
Pelekides, S. 1916. 'Phaleron excavation', *ADelt* 7, 49-64
Percival, J. 1988. *The Roman Villa* (London)
Peyras, J. 1975. 'Fundus Aufidianus', *AntAf* 9, 181-222
——— 1983. 'Paysages agraires et centuriations dans le bassin de l'Oued Tine', *AntAf* 19, 209-53
Pianu, G. 1989. 'Scavi al santuario di Demetra a Policoro', *Studi su Siris-Eraclea* (*Archaeologia Perusina* 8), 95-112 (Rome)
Picard, G.-C. 1990. *La civilisation de l'Afrique romaine* (2nd edn; Paris)
Piggott, S. 1958. 'Native economies and the Roman occupation of North Britain', in Richmond (ed.) 1958, 1-27
——— 1965. *Ancient Europe* (Edinburgh)
Pignorio, L. 1613. *De Servis* (Augsburg)
Ponsich, M. 1964. 'Exploitations agricoles romaines de le région de Tanger', *BAM* 5, 235-52
Potter, T.W. 1979. *The Changing Landscape of South Etruria* (London)
——— 1980. 'Villas in south Etruria: some comments and contexts', in Painter (ed.) 1980, 73-81
Poulter, A.G. 1983a. 'Town and country in Moesia Inferior', in Poulter (ed.) 1983b, 74-118
——— (ed.) 1983b. *Ancient Bulgaria* (Nottingham)
Radimský, W. 1893. 'Generalbericht über die bisherigen Ausgrabungen der römischen Stadt Domavia in Gradina bei Srebenica', *WMBH* 1, 218-53
Raeck, W. 1981. *Zum Barbarenbild in der Kunst Athens im 6. und 5. Jahrhundert v. Chr.* (Bonn)
Randall, R.H. 1953. 'The Erechtheum workmen', *AJA* 57, 199-210
Rauh, N.K. 1992. 'Was the Agora of the Italians an *Établissement de Sport?*', *BCH* 116, 293-333
Reinecke, S. 1916. 'Burgweinting unweit Regensburg. Villa rustica', *RGK* 9, 54-7
Richardson, J.S. 1976. 'The Spanish mines and the development of provincial taxation in the second century BC', *JRS* 66, 139-52
Richmond, I.A. (ed.) 1958. *Roman and Native in North Britain* (Edinburgh)

———— 1969. 'The plans of Roman villas in Britain', in Rivet (ed.) 1969a, 49-70

Rickman, G. 1971. *Roman Granaries and Store Buildings* (Cambridge)

———— 1980. *The Corn Supply of Ancient Rome* (Oxford)

Rivet, A. L. F. 1964. *Town and Country in Roman Britain* (2nd rev. edn; London)

———— (ed.) 1969a. *The Roman Villa in Britain* (London)

———— 1969b. 'Social and economic aspects', in Rivet (ed.) 1969a, 173-216

———— 1988. *Gallia Narbonensis* (London)

———— and Smith, C. 1979. *The Place-names of Roman Britain* (London)

Roberts, C. 1985. 'The chronology of the sites of the Roman period around San Giovanni: methods of analysis and conclusions', in Macready and Thompson (eds) 1985a, 136-45

Robertson, D.S. 1964. *A Handbook of Greek and Roman Architecture* (2nd edn; Cambridge)

Robinson, D.M. 1946. *Excavations at Olynthus, pt. XII: Domestic and Public Architecture* (Baltimore)

———— and Graham, J.W. 1938. *Excavations at Olynthus, pt. VIII: the Hellenic House* (Baltimore)

Röder, J. 1957. 'Die antiken Tuffsteinbrüche der Pellenz', *BJ* 157, 213-71

Roger, J. 1945. 'Inscriptions de la région du Strymon', *RA* 2, 49-51

Roos, R. 1986. 'For the fiftieth anniversary of the excavation of the water-mill at Barbegal: a correction of a long-lived mistake', *RA* 47, 327-33

Rossiter, J.J. 1978. *Roman Farm Building in Italy*, *BAR* Int. Ser. 52 (Oxford)

Rostovtzeff, M. 1902. *Geschichte der Staatspacht in der römischen Kaiserzeit bis Diokletian* (Berlin)

———— 1922. *Iranians and Greeks in South Russia* (Oxford)

———— 1941. *Social and Economic History of the Roman Empire* (Oxford)

———— 1953. *Social and Economic History of the Hellenistic World* (Oxford)

———— 1957. *Social and Economic History of the Roman Empire* (rev. edn P. M. Fraser; Oxford)

Rubinsohn, Z.W. 1980. 'Saumakos: ancient history, modern politics', *Hist* 29, 50-70

———— 1987. *Spartacus' Uprising and Soviet Historical Writing* (trans. by J.G. Griffith from German edn of 1983; Oxford)

Ruggiero, M. 1881. *Degli scavi di Stabia dal 1749 al 1782* (Naples)

Samson, R. 1989. 'Rural slavery, inscriptions, archaeology and Marx', *Hist* 38, 99-110

Sandars, H.W. 1905. 'The Linares bas relief and Roman mining operations in Baetica', *Arch* 59, 311-32

Sapène, B. 1946. 'Autels votifs, atelier des marbriers et sanctuaire gallo-romains découverts a Saint-Béat (Haute Garonne) en 1946', *RC* 4e trimestre, 283-325

Savvopoulou, T. 1984. ' "Slaves" in the Ierissos cemetery. A social distinction', *Acts of the First Panhellenic Symposium on the History and Archaeology of the Chalkidiki*, 97-111 (Thessaloniki)

Scheidel, W. 1997. 'Quantifying the sources of slaves in the early Roman empire', *JRS* 87, 156-69

Schmiedt, G. and Chevallier, R. 1959. *Caulonia e Metaponto: applicazioni della fotografia aerea in ricerche di topografia antica nella Magna Graecia* (Florence)

Schneider, H. (ed.) 1981. *Sozial- und Wirtschaftsgeschichte der römischen Kaiserzeit*, *JW* 1971

Scullard, H.H. 1967. *The Etruscan Cities and Rome* (London)

Shatzman, I. 1975. *Senatorial Wealth and Roman Politics* (Brussels)

309

Sieveking, G. de G., Longworth, I.H. and Wilson, K.E. (eds) 1976. *Problems in Economic and Social Archaeology* (London)

Simonyi, D. 1960. 'Sull'origino del toponimo "Quinque Ecclesiae" di Pecs', *Acta Antiqua* 8, 165-84

Singer, C., Holmyard, E.J. and Williams, T.I. (eds) 1956. *A History of Technology, ii: The Mediterranean Civilizations and the Middle Ages, c. 700 BC to AD 1500* (Oxford)

Sotgiu, G. 1973/4. 'Un collare di schiavo rinvenuto in Sardegna', *ArchC* 25/6, 688-97

Spinazzola, V. 1953. *Pompeii alla luce degli scavi nuovi di Via dell'Abbondanza (anni 1910-1923)*, i-iii (Rome)

Spurr, M.S. 1986. *Roman Arable Cultivation in Italy*, *JRS* Monograph no. 3

Štaerman, E.M. 1981. 'Der Klassenkampf der Sklaven zur Zeit des römischen Kaiserreiches', in Schneider (ed.) 1981, 307-35

—— (ed.) 1987. *Die Sklaverei in den westlichen Provinzen des römischen Reiches im 1-3. Jahrhundert* (Stuttgart)

Starr, C.G. 1960. *The Roman Imperial Navy, 31 BC-AD 324* (2nd edn; Cambridge)

—— 1982. 'Economic and social conditions in the Greek world', *CAH*[2] III.3, 417-41

Stead, I.M. 1967. 'A La Tène III burial at Welwyn Garden City', *Arch* 101, 1-62

—— 1976. 'The earliest burials of the Aylesford culture', in Sieveking *et al.* 1976, 401-16

Stevens, C.E. 1966. 'The social and economic aspects of rural settlement', in Thomas (ed.) 1966, 108-28

Stuart Jones, H. and McKenzie, R. 1968. Liddell and Scott, *Greek-English Lexicon* (rev. edn; Oxford)

Täckholm, U. 1937. *Studien über den Bergbau der römischen Kaiserzeit* (Uppsala)

Tamain, A.L.G. and Ratz, D. 1982. 'Les aurières de l'ouest du Massif Central (France) dans leur contexte géologique et archéologique', *Mines et fonderies*, 33-78

Taylor, C.C. 1967. 'Late Roman pastoral farming in Wessex', *Ant* 41, 304-6

Themelis, P. 1982. 'Kaiadas', *AAA* 15, 183-201

Thoen, H. 1975. 'Iron Age and Roman salt-making sites on the Belgian coast', in de Brisay and Evans (eds) 1975, 56-60

Thomas, C. (ed.) 1966. *Rural Settlement in Roman Britain*, CBA Research Report 7 (London)

Thomas, E.B. 1964. *Römische Villen in Pannonien* (Budapest)

Thompson, E.A. 1974. 'Peasant revolt in late Roman Gaul and Spain', in Finley (ed.) 1974, 304-20

Thompson, F.H. 1965. *Roman Cheshire* (Chester)

—— 1983. 'Excavations at Bigberry, near Canterbury, 1978-80', *AntiqJ* 63, 237-78

—— 1994. 'Iron Age and Roman slave-shackles', *ArchJ* 150, 57-168

Thouvenot, R. 1958. *Maisons de Volubilis: le palais dit de Gordien et la maison à la mosaïque de Venus* (Rabat)

Tod, M.N. 1950. 'Epigraphical notes on freedmen's professions', *Epig* 12, 3-26

Toutain, J. 1930. *The Economic Life of the Ancient World* (London / New York)

Toynbee, A.J. 1965. *Hannibal's Legacy* (London)

Treptow, E. 1918. 'Der älteste Bergbau und seine Hilfsmittel', *BGTI* 8, 155-91

Tudor, D. 1957. *Istoria sclavajului in Dacia romana* (Bucharest)

Vallet, G. 1984-5. 'L'apporto dell'urbanistica. Le fait urbain en Grèce et en Sicile à l'époque archaïque', *Kok*, Atti del VI Congresso Internazionale di Studi sulla Sicilia Antica, 30-1, 133-63

———, Villard, F. and Auberson, P. 1976. 'Mégara Hyblaea i: Le quartier de l'agora archaïque', *MAHEFR*, Suppl. 1

van Andel, T.H. 1986. 'Five thousand years of land use and abuse in the Southern Argolid, Greece', *Hesp* 55, 103-28

——— 1987. 'The evolution of settlement in the Southern Argolid, Greece: an economic explanation', *Hesp* 56, 303-34

van Berchem, D. 1939. *Les distributions de blé et d'argent à la plèbe romaine sous l'empire* (Geneva)

Vavřínek, V. 1975. 'Aristonicus of Pergamum: pretender to the throne or leader of a slave revolt?', *Eir* 13, 109-29

Venedikov, L. (ed.) 1963. *Apollonia: les fouilles dans la nécropole d'Apoloneia en 1947-1949* (Sofia)

Ville, G. 1981. *La gladiature en Occident des origines à la mort de Domitien*, *BEFAR* 245

Vinson, P. 1972. 'Ancient roads between Vinosa and Gravina', *PBSR* 40, 58-90

Vogt, J. 1965. *Sklaverei und humanität. Studien zur antiken Sklaverei und ihrer Erforschung* (2nd edn 1972; rev. 1983)

——— 1975. *Ancient Slavery and the Ideal of Man* (trans. T. Wiedemann; Oxford)

——— and Bellen, H. 1971. *Bibliographie zur antiken Sklaverei* (Mainz)

Volkmann, H. 1961. *Die Massenversklavungen der Einwohner eroberte Städte in der hellenistisch-römischen Zeit* (Wiesbaden)

Wagner, F. 1928. *Die Römer in Bayern* (Munich)

Wallon, H. 1847, 1879. *Histoire de l'esclavage dans l'antiquité* (2nd edn 1879; Paris)

Ward-Perkins, J.B. 1964. *Landscape and History in Southern Italy* (Second J.L. Myres Memorial Lecture; Oxford)

——— 1971. 'Quarrying in antiquity: technology, tradition and social change', *PBA* 57, 137-58

——— 1978. *Roman Imperial Architecture* (2nd edn; Harmondsworth)

——— and Claridge, A. 1976. *Pompeii AD 79* (London)

Warmington, E.H. 1938. *Remains of Old Latin* (= Paulus, ex Fest. 88.4) (London)

Wattenbach, W. (ed.) 1870. 'Passio Sanctorum Quattuor Coronatorum', in Büdinger (ed.) 1870, 321-56

Webster, G. 1985. *The Roman Imperial Army* (3rd edn; London)

West, L.C. 1935. *Roman Gaul: the Objects of Trade* (Oxford)

Westermann, W.L. 1945. 'Slave maintenance and slave revolts', *CP* 40, 1-10

——— 1955. *The Slave Systems of Greek and Roman Antiquity* (Philadelphia)

White, K.D. 1967. 'Latifundia', *BICS* 14, 62-79

——— 1970. *Roman Farming* (London)

Widrig, W.M. 1980. 'Two sites on the ancient via Gabina', in Painter (ed.) 1980, 119-40

Wiedemann, T.E.J. 1981. *Greek and Roman Slavery* (London)

——— 1987. *Slavery*, Greece and Rome, New Surveys in the Classics 19 (Oxford)

Wiegand, T. and Schrader, H. 1904. *Priene* (Berlin)

Wielowiejski, J. 1956. 'Le problème de l'identification des esclaves dans l'art grec', *Arche* 8, 266-72

Wightman, E.M. 1970. *Roman Trier and the Treveri* (London)

——— 1975. 'Rural settlement in early Roman Gaul', *ANRW* II.4, 584-647

——— 1985. *Gallia Belgica* (London)

Wikander, O. 1979. 'Water-mills in ancient Rome', *OR* 12, 13-36

Wild, J. P. 1967. 'The gynaeceum at Venta and its context', *Lat* 26, 648-76

—— 1970. *Textile Manufacture in the Northern Roman Provinces* (Cambridge)

—— 1976. 'The gynaecea', in Goodburn and Bartholomew (eds) 1976, 51-8

—— 1982. 'Wool production in Roman Britain', in Miles (ed.) 1982, 109-22

Wilkes, J.J. 1969. *Dalmatia* (London)

Will, E. 1962. 'Le sel des Morins et des Ménapiens', *Lat* 58, Hommages à Albert Grenier, 1649-57

—— 1972. 'L'artisanat. Technologie et travail servile, Id', *Le monde grec et l'Orient*. 1: *Le Ve siècle (510-43)*, 648-60 (Paris)

Willetts, R.F. 1967. *The Law Code of Gortyn* (Berlin)

Wilsdorf, H. 1952. *Bergleute und Hüttenmänner im Altertum bis zum Ausgang der römischen Republik* (Berlin)

Wilson, A.J.N. 1966. *Emigration from Italy in the Republican Age of Rome* (Manchester)

Wilson, R.J.A. 1983. *Piazza Armerina* (London)

—— 1990. *Sicily under the Roman Empire* (Warminster)

Wycherley, R.E. 1962. *How the Greeks Built Cities* (2nd edn; London)

—— 1974. 'The stones of Athens', *GR* 21, 54-67

—— 1978. *The Stones of Athens* (Princeton)

Young, J.H. 1956. 'Studies in south Attica: country estates at Sounion', *Hesp* 25, 122-46

Zahn, E. 1976. *Die Igeler Säule bei Trier* (5th edn; Cologne)

Ziebarth, E. 1929. *Beiträge zur Geschichte des Seeraubs und Seehandels in alten Griechenland* (Hamburg)

Ziomecki, J. 1975. *Les représentations d'artisans sur les vases attiques* (Warsaw)

Index

Page numbers in *italics* refer to illustrations.

Gaul
  agriculture, 68, 78, 111-21
  cloth production, 201, 205-8, 209
  ergastula, 243
  gladiators, 260, 262
  pistrina, 198
  quarries and mines, 142, 171-6
  revolts, 265, 266
  salt production, 186
  shackles, 226, 227, *228*, 229-31,
    232-3, 236
  slaves, as source of, 4, 6, 20, 24, 25,
    34, 36
  see also Aquitania; Gallia Belgica;
    Gallia Lugdunensis; Gallia
    Narbonensis
Gaza, 16, 35, 42
Geiseric, 36
Gela (Sicily), 68, 69, 71, 72
Gelon of Syracuse, 14, 69, 71, 134
Gerasa (Palestine), 35
Gergovia (France), 174
Germania
  agriculture, 123-5
  shackles, 226, 233-6
  slaves, as source of, 4, 35, 260
Geta, 264
Giton, 241
gladiators, 7, 84, 260-2, 264, 265
Glanon (France), 227
Glanum (France), 121
Gloucester (Britain), 122
Gomphoi (Thessaly), 25
Gophna (Judaea), 26
Gortyn (Crete), 3, 5, 13, 28
Goths, 34, 36, 37
Gracchi
  Gaius, 23, 81, 107
  Tiberius, 79, 81
  tutor to, 257
Gragnano (Italy), villa, 84, *85*, 268-9
granaries (*horrea*), 192, 195, 243, 244
Granicus, battle of, 16, 218, 222
Great Chesterford (Britain), shears,
    205, *206*
Gryneion (Asia Minor), 16
Guiry-Gadancourt villa (France), 119
gynaecea, 199, 200, 208-9

Haccourt (Belgium), 119
Hadrian's Wall (Britain), 122, 137

Hadrumetum (Tunisia), 111
Haliartos (Boeotia), 23
Halieis (Argolis), 59
Hallstatt (Austria), 185
Halton Castle (Britain), 122
Halykiai (Sicily), 258
Hambleden (Britain), 122
Hamilcar, 14, 134
handcuffs, 236, *237*
Hannibal, 21, 22, 78
Hebron (Judaea), 35
Heliopolis (Asia Minor), 257
Helvius, 26
Hemeroskopeion (Spain), 106
Henchir Debdeba (Tunisia), 198
Henchir el-Hendba (Tunisia), 198
Henchir el-Mzira (Tunisia), 195
Henseir Sidi Hamdan (Tripolitania),
    108
Heraclea Minoa (Sicily), 71, 258
Heracleia (Asia Minor), 24
Heraia (Elis), 30
Herblay (France), 227
Herculaneum (Italy), 20, 191-2, 201,
    205
Hermae, 18
Hermion (Argolis), 59
Hermocrates, 246
Hermotimus, 13, 19
Herodas, 242
Herodotus, 9, 19, 153, 218, 241, 246
Hesiod, 1, 11, 48, 49-50
Hieron, 6, 71
Hilario, 175
Himera (Sicily), 14, 69, 70, 72, 134
Himeros, 24
Hippo Regius (Algeria), 111
Hippocrates, 71
Hippodamus, 69
Hipponax, 12
Hispalis (Spain), 25, 36
Histiaeus of Miletus, 241
Hod Hill (Britain), 237
Homer
  on agriculture, 48, 49-50, 68
  on cloth production, 187, 198
  on slaves, 1-2, 4-5, 9-11, 12
hospitals, 93, 269
Hosté (Belgium), 119
Huerña (Spain), 161
Huns, 34, 36, 37